American Furniture

AMERICAN FURNITURE 2008

Edited by Luke Beckerdite

THE CHIPSTONE FOUNDATION

Milwaukee

CHIPSTONE FOUNDATION BOARD OF DIRECTORS
Edward S. Cooke Jr.
Charles Hummel
Ted Kellner
Peter M. Kenny
W. David Knox II   *Chairman and* CEO
John S. McGregor
Jonathan Prown   *Executive Director*
Alison Stone
Stanley Stone III
Allen M. Taylor   *Vice President*

EDITOR
Luke Beckerdite

BOOK AND EXHIBITION REVIEW EDITOR
Gerald W. R. Ward

EDITORIAL ADVISORY BOARD
Glenn Adamson, *Director of Graduate Studies, Victoria & Albert Museum*
David Barquist, *Curator of American Decorative Arts, Philadelphia Museum of Art*
Wendy Cooper, *Curator of Furniture, Winterthur Museum*
Leroy Graves, *Upholstery Conservator, Colonial Williamsburg Foundation*
Robert A. Leath, *Vice President, Collections & Research, Old Salem Museums & Gardens*
Alan Miller, *Conservator and Independent Furniture Consultant, Quakertown, Pennsylvania*
Sumpter Priddy III, *Decorative Arts Scholar and Dealer, Alexandria, Virginia*
Robert F. Trent, *Independent Furniture Consultant, Wilmington, Delaware*
Gerald W. R. Ward, *Katharine Lane Weems Senior Curator of Decorative Arts and Sculpture, Art of the Americas, Museum of Fine Arts, Boston*
Philip Zea, *Executive Director, Historic Deerfield*

Cover Illustration: Detail of the pier table illustrated on page 121, Philadelphia or Pittsburgh, Pennsylvania, 1830–1835. Mahogany with tulip poplar and white pine; marble, glass. H. 37", W. 40", D. 19". (Private collection; photo, Gavin Ashworth.)

Design: Wynne Patterson, Pittsfield, VT
Copyediting: Fronia Simpson, Bennington, VT
Typesetting: Aardvark Type, Hartford, CT
Printing: Meridian Printing, East Greenwich, RI

Published by the Chipstone Foundation, 7820 North Club Circle, Milwaukee, WI 53217
Distributed by Antique Collectors' Club, Ltd., Easthampton, MA, and Woodbridge, Suffolk, UK
Distributed to the Trade by National Book Network, Inc.

© 2008 by the Chipstone Foundation
All rights reserved
Printed in the United States of America   5 4 3 2 1
ISSN 1069-4188
ISBN 0-9767344-3-5

Contents

Editorial Statement *Luke Beckerdite*	VII
The Documentary and Artistic Legacy of Nathaniel Gould *Kemble Widmer II and Joyce King*	1
Early American Shaved Post-and-Rung Chairs *Jennie Alexander, Peter Follansbee, and Robert F. Trent*	26
Furnishing the Craftsman: Slaves and Sailors in the Mahogany Trade *Daniel Finamore*	61
Philadelphia Pier Tables and Their Role in Cultures of Sociability and Competition *Nicholas C. Vincent*	88
The Written Evidence of Furniture Repairs and Alterations: How Original Is "All Original"?, Part II *Nancy Goyne Evans*	131
Book Reviews	209
Recent Writing on American Furniture: A Bibliography *Gerald W. R. Ward*	239
Index	248

Editorial Statement

American Furniture is an interdisciplinary journal dedicated to advancing knowledge of furniture made or used in the Americas from the seventeenth century to the present. Authors are encouraged to submit articles on any aspect of furniture history, essays on conservation and historic technology, reproductions or transcripts of documents, annotated photographs of new furniture discoveries, and book and exhibition reviews. References for compiling an annual bibliography also are welcome.

Manuscripts must be typed, double-spaced, illustrated with black-and-white prints or transparencies, and prepared in accordance with the *Chicago Manual of Style*. Computer disk copy is requested but not required. The Chipstone Foundation will offer significant honoraria for manuscripts accepted for publication and reimburse authors for all photography approved in writing by the editor. Low resolution digital images are not acceptable.

Luke Beckerdite

American Furniture

Kemble Widmer II and Joyce King

The Documentary and Artistic Legacy of Nathaniel Gould

Figure 1 Title page of Nathaniel Gould's account book covering the years 1763 to 1781. (Courtesy, Massachusetts Historical Society; photo, Gavin Ashworth.) The account book has a few entries from the late 1750s that may have been transferred from an earlier book and a few entries that post-date Gould's death in 1781. The later entries may have been recorded by Gould's attorney Nathan Dane.

▼ ON MAY 1, 1758, A YOUNG tradesman named Nathaniel Gould (1734–1781) made the first entry in his daybook, recording the sale of a walnut table to Salem, Massachusetts, tailor Samuel Archer Jr. Before the discovery of Gould's account book and daybooks (fig. 1) in the Nathan Dane Papers in the Massachusetts Historical Society, he was regarded as one of many furniture makers active in Salem during the third quarter of the eighteenth century. When correlated with existing furniture and documentary references to Gould in other sources, the entries in these journals demonstrate that Gould parlayed the patronage of Salem's merchant elite into considerable financial success.[1]

The earliest daybook covers the years 1758 to 1763. A five-year gap between the last entry in that journal and the first entry in the later one indicates that Gould originally had three daybooks. The other surviving daybook has entries from 1767 to Gould's death in 1781 and continues to 1784. Together with his account book, these documents shed light on the furniture, trade practices, marketing strategies, and business transactions of one of Salem's finest cabinetmakers.[2]

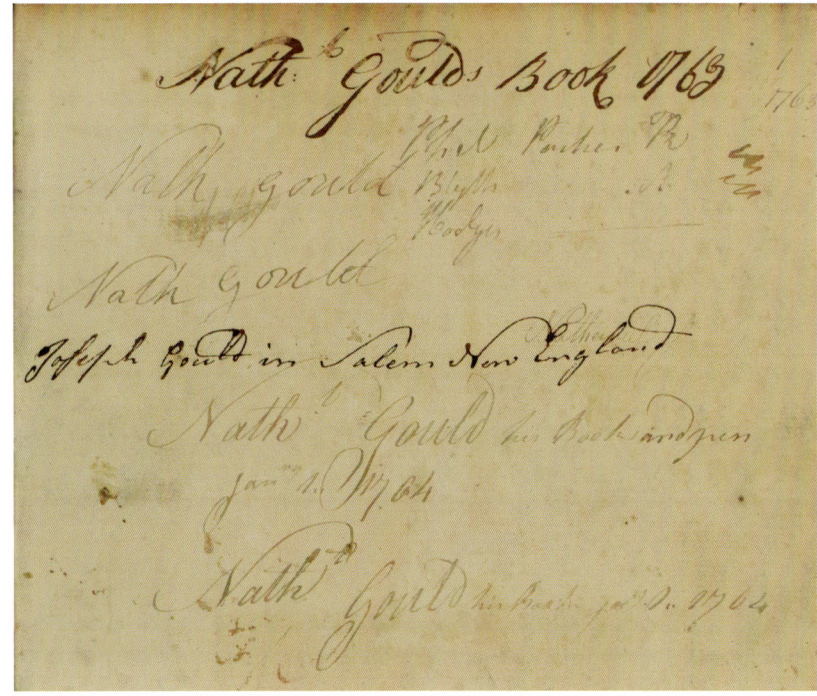

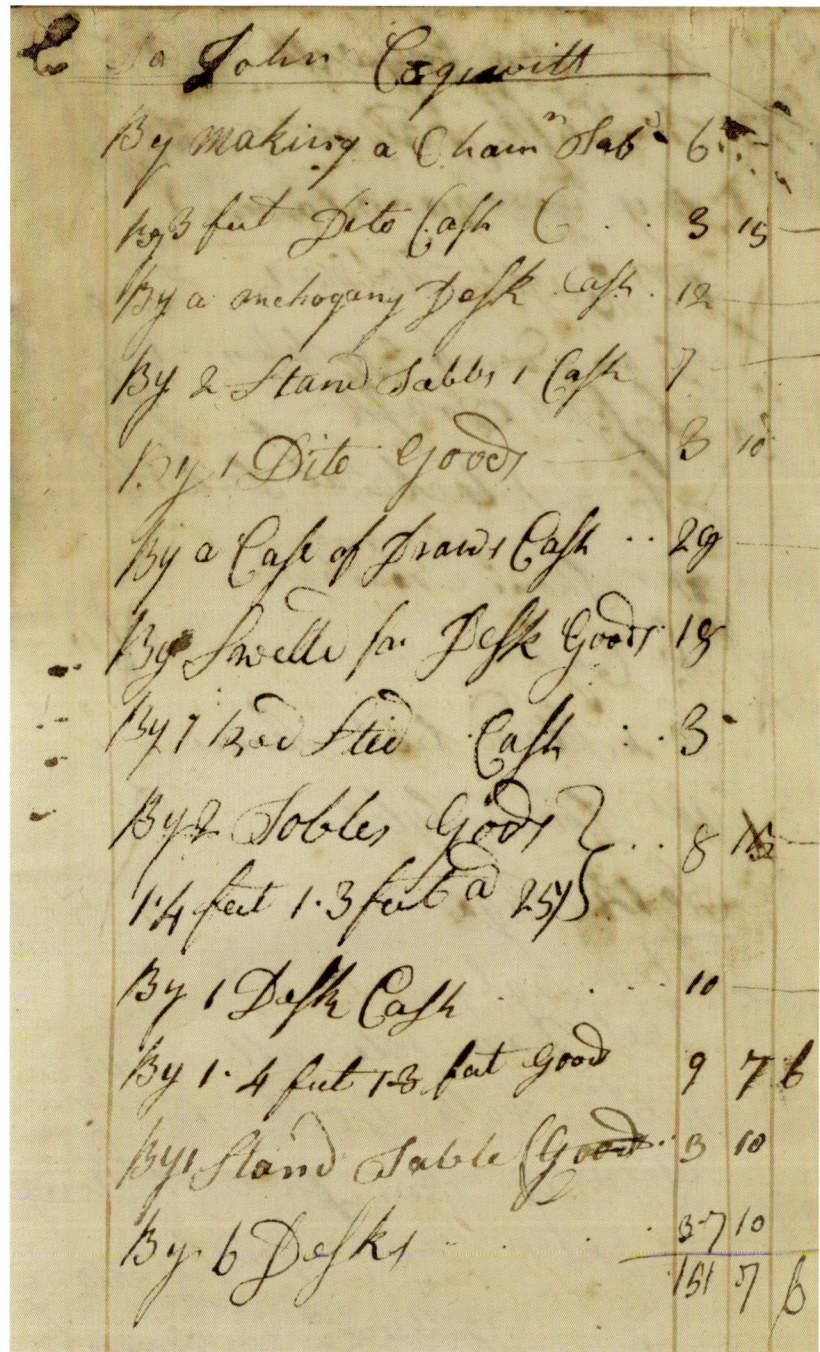

Figure 2 Ca. 1759 credit entry for John Cogswell in Nathaniel Gould's daybook covering the years 1758 to 1763. (Courtesy, Massachusetts Historical Society; photo, Gavin Ashworth.) At the end of each line Gould wrote "cash" or "goods" to designate the form of payment. The word "goods" could refer to furniture or other commodities sold by Gould, including wood, sugar, fishing line, and wine.

Born on November 17, 1734, Gould was the son of Nathaniel (1697–1746) and Elizabeth (French) Gould (1698–1746). Both parents died when Nathaniel Jr. was only twelve, too young to have begun serving an apprenticeship with his father. Guardianship passed to his uncle James Gould (1696–1771), a wheelwright, on January 3, 1747.[3]

Although no indenture documents for Nathaniel are known, it is possible that he trained with Charlestown, Massachusetts, cabinetmaker Thomas Wood (1708–1800). Gould probably completed his term by December 1756, when he was described as a cabinetmaker residing in Charlestown in a transaction involving his sale of inherited property. Four years later he married Wood's daughter Rebecca (1739–1807) and shortly thereafter began doing business with his father-in-law. Gould's earliest daybook records the sale of mahogany, walnut, and furniture hardware to Wood in 1761. Over the next fourteen years, Gould continued to provide hardware while purchasing two beds and forty desks from his father-in-law. Most of the desks were made of cedar and probably intended for export.[4]

The theory that Gould came of age as a cabinetmaker in Charlestown is further supported by his relationship with John Cogswell (1738–1819), who may have trained there in the shop of cabinetmaker Timothy Gooding Jr. When Gould became overwhelmed with orders for furniture in June 1759, he subcontracted the production of nine desks, a case of drawers, six tables, four stands, and a bed to Cogswell (fig. 2). The latter artisan was only twenty-one years old at that date and had only recently set up shop in Boston. Gould and Cogswell probably became acquainted while serving their apprenticeships in Charlestown.[5]

Gould arrived in Salem shortly after completing his apprenticeship. On March 14, 1757, he contributed £3.12 to a fund for soldiers from that town who volunteered to defend Fort William Henry during the French and Indian War. Among the donors, Gould was one of the youngest and the only cabinetmaker. His decision to support the fund, which provided £10 for each volunteer, may have been motivated by his cousin James Gould's participation in the expedition. More than half of the contributors, including members of the Cabot, Derby, Pickman, and Dodge families, purchased furniture from Nathaniel over the next few years.[6]

Gould's Daybooks and Account Book
Nathaniel Gould recorded his work and financial transactions chronologically in daybooks. Most of his entries involve the sale of furniture and other goods, including wood, hardware, sugar, fishing line, cloth, and spirits. Gould made many entries daily, but in some instances he grouped transactions, leaving gaps of as much as three weeks. After a customer had settled his or her account, Gould either drew a line through the entry or designated it paid with the abbreviation "pd" (fig. 3) or two angled lines in the left-hand margin. For credits and debits he used the abbreviations "Cr" and "Dr" respectively (fig. 4).

Gould was as meticulous in recording his transactions as he was in making his furniture. He and his workmen listed each item purchased by a

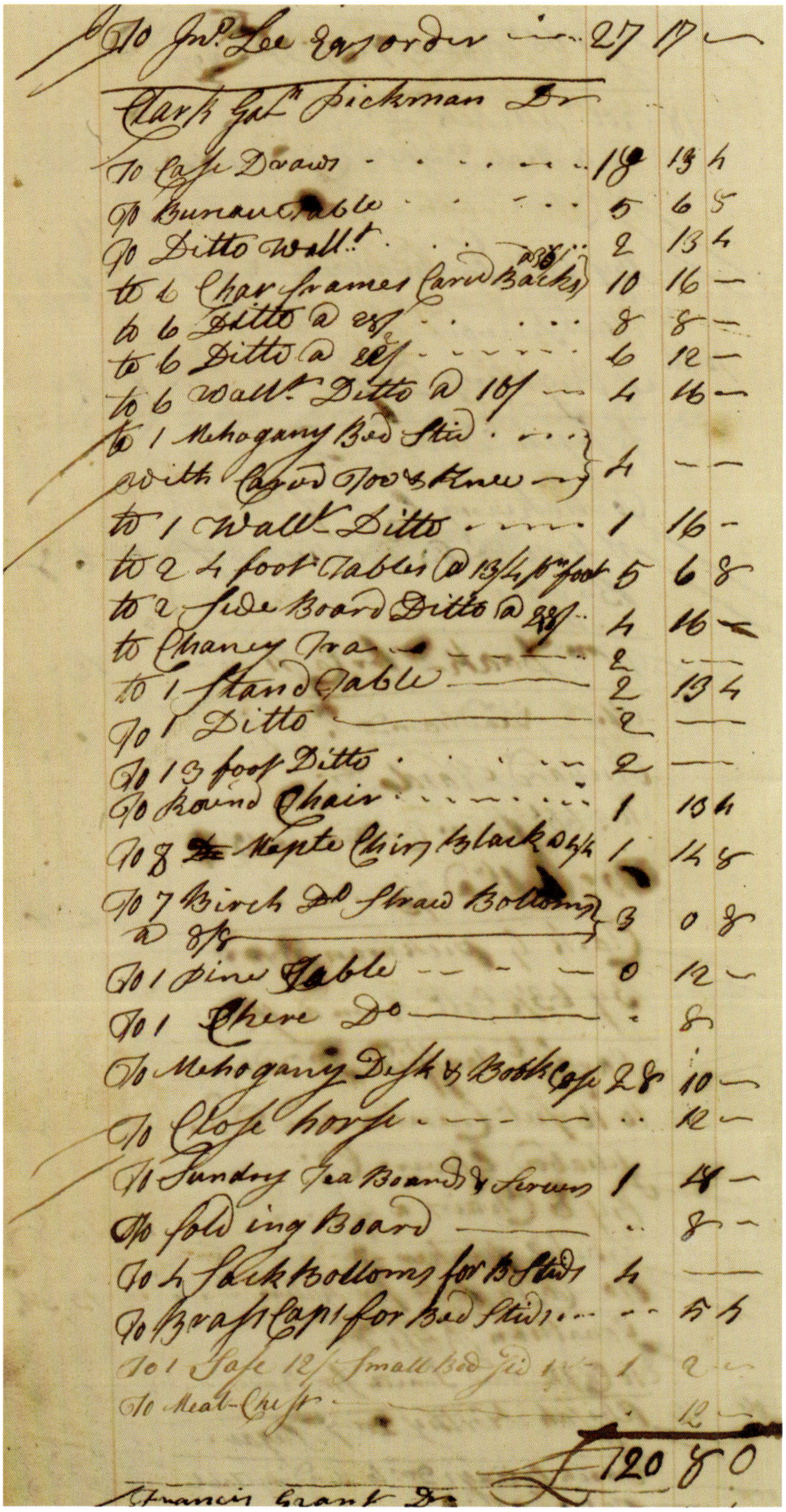

Figure 3 August 24, 1770, debit entry for Clark Gayton Pickman in Nathaniel Gould's daybook covering the years 1767 to 1784. (Courtesy, Massachusetts Historical Society; photo, Gavin Ashworth.)

patron separately, even in commissions involving multiple objects. Gould's pricing for generic furniture forms is often discernible, as in the August 25, 1770, entry for Salem merchant Clark Gayton Pickman (fig. 3). Each of the latter's tables cost 13s. 4d. per linear foot. Like most of his contemporaries,

Figure 4 Detail of page for November 20–26, 1768, in Nathaniel Gould's daybook covering the years 1767 to 1784. (Courtesy, Massachusetts Historical Society; photo, Gavin Ashworth.) Most daybook entries are debits. The credit entry for Philemon Parker dated November 20, 1768, indicates that he performed three days' work for Gould in addition to making a four-foot table and a candlestand. Parker maintained his own shop and was not an employee of Gould.

Figure 5 November 30, 1768, debit entry for Jonathon Very in Nathaniel Gould's daybook covering the years 1767 to 1784. (Courtesy, Massachusetts Historical Society; photo, Gavin Ashworth.)

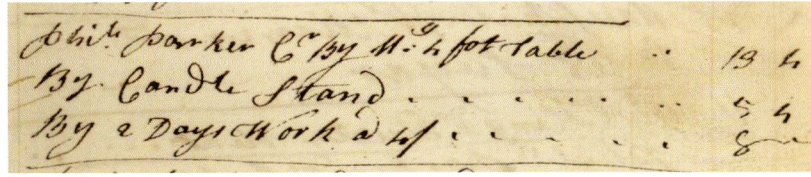

Gould offered standardized furniture forms with options like "carved feet" (fig. 5) and "carved backs" (chairs) available at extra cost. Because Gould's prices changed little from the late 1750s to the Revolution, one can draw conclusions from entries that are not particularly descriptive. If a four-foot table and "mahogany four foot table" have equivalent prices, it is reasonable to assume that both were made of the same wood. The sheer volume of work produced in Gould's shop makes such speculation even more plausible. His workforce appears to have grouped orders for certain forms to expedite production and avoid repetitive setups for cutting stock and joints, turning, finish work, and other tasks.[7]

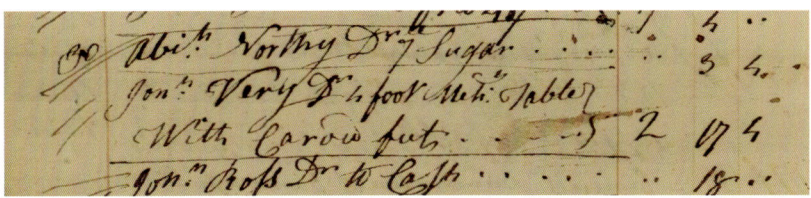

Understanding Gould's business would be difficult without his account book. With entries from February 1763 to 1781, it covers the period of the missing daybook (April 1763 to December 1767). The account book only lists items sold on credit, whereas the surviving daybooks document all sales but have few credit entries. By correlating the information in these records, one can identify the sources of sugar and other goods Gould sold, the ship captains who provided him with mahogany, the merchants who furnished his furniture hardware, and the cabinetmakers to whom he subcontracted work.

Gould specialized in the production of several different forms. During the years covered by his surviving daybooks and account book, he sold 1,144 chairs, 321 conventional table forms, 441 desks, 196 bedsteads, 76 "cases of drawers," 52 "bureau tables," 17 "chamber tables," and 19 desk-and-bookcases (total includes an entry for "½ desk-and-bookcase"). Side chairs, usually offered in sets of six, accounted for most of the seating produced in his shop; however, Gould also made round, close-stool, and easy chairs. His production of seating is surprising, since chairmaking tended to be a specialized trade in New England. Salem chairmakers who were contemporaries of Gould included William Lander, William Gray, and Benjamin Symonds.[8]

The tables listed in Gould's daybooks were described as "round," "square," "card," "silver," "sideboard," "twilight" (toilet), "breakfast," "tea," "chaney" (china), "riting" (writing), and "side." The term "chamber table" probably referred to a cabriole-leg case form, whereas the term

Figure 6 Chest of drawers attributed to the shop of Nathaniel Gould, Salem, Massachusetts, 1781. Mahogany with white pine. H. 36 1/8", W. 39 1/16", D. 21 9/16". (Courtesy, Historic New England; photo, Gavin Ashworth.) This chest descended in the family of Charles Chauncey Foster (1785–1875). In 1816 he married Catherine Cabot (1789–1862), the seventh surviving child of Andrew Cabot (1750–1791) and his wife, Lydia (Dodge) (1748–1807). The chest is probably the "bureau table" that Andrew Cabot purchased from Nathaniel Gould on February 24, 1781 (fig. 7). As the relatively unfigured wood in this chest suggests, the mahogany available to Gould during the Revolution was of lesser quality than that available before the war. The third drawer from the top has plane tears on the surface. Gould might have discarded that drawer front if wood had been more available.

Figure 7 February 24, 1784, debit entry for Andrew Cabot in Nathaniel Gould's daybook covering the years 1767 to 1784. (Courtesy, Massachusetts Historical Society; photo, Gavin Ashworth.) Cabot's inventory listed two mahogany bureaus (Essex County Probate no. 4431, bk. 360, pp. 499–506), and his will directed that his property be divided equally between his children after his wife's death (Suffolk County Probate no. 22925, bk. 105, p. 41).

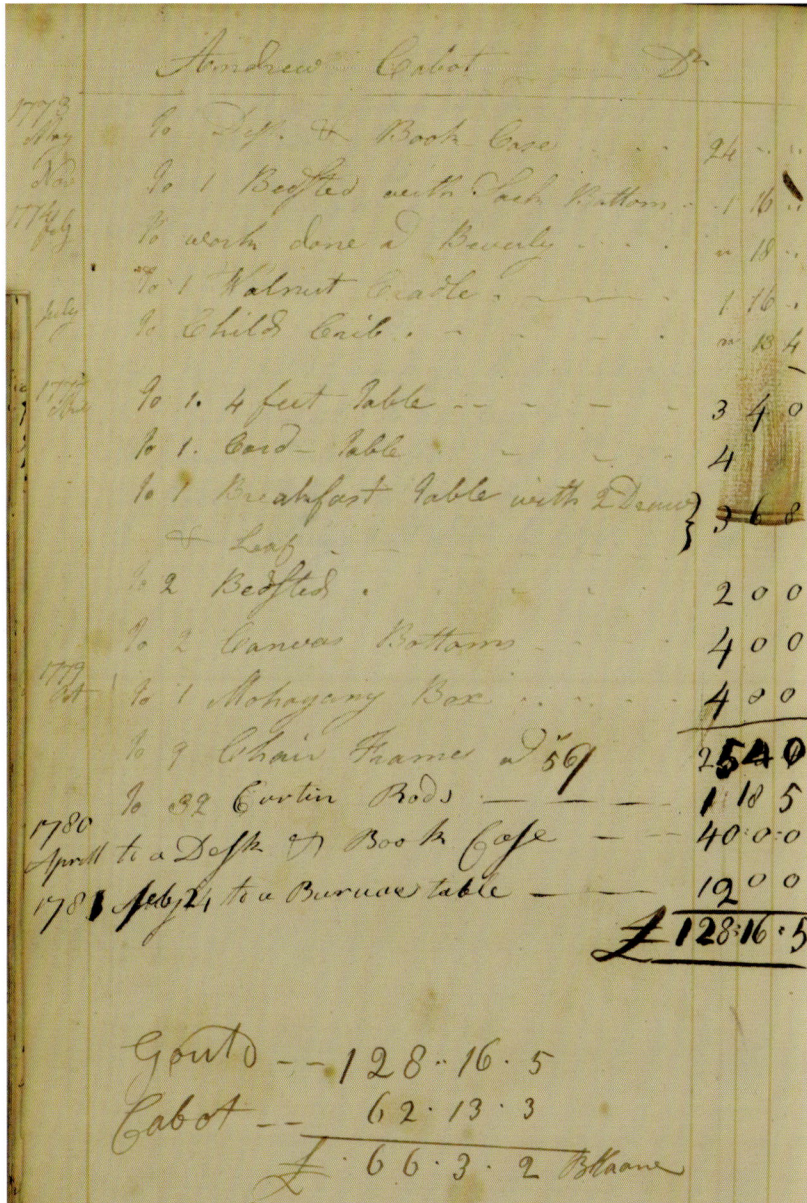

"bureau table" almost certainly denoted a four-drawer chest (figs. 6, 7). The average price Gould charged for a "case of drawers" was too high for a four-drawer chest, suggesting that he reserved that term for a high chest or double chest. On April 15, 1765, Salem tanner Joseph Southwick paid Gould £4.4 for a "case of draws with steps" (fig. 8). Presumably this entry referred to a flat-top high chest with a platform for displaying china or other valuable objects.[9]

One of the most expensive objects made in Gould's shop was a "case of draws swelled ends" commissioned by Salem merchant John Appleton and completed by July 1767 (fig. 9). New England cabinetmakers used the term "swelled" to refer to bombé, blocked, commode (serpentine), and bowed forms, but only bombé shaping was appropriate for the sides of a case. Valued at £17.6.8, Appleton's chest probably resembled the example illustrated

Figure 8   April 15, 1765, debit entry for Joseph Southwick in Nathaniel Gould's account book covering the years 1763 to 1781. (Courtesy, Massachusetts Historical Society; photo, Gavin Ashworth.)

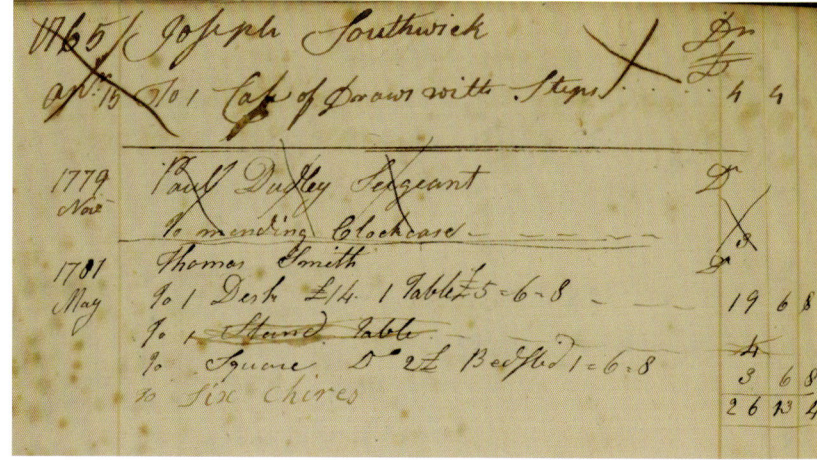

Figure 9   July 1767 debit entry for John Appleton in Nathaniel Gould's account book covering the years 1763 to 1781. (Courtesy, Massachusetts Historical Society; photo, Gavin Ashworth.)

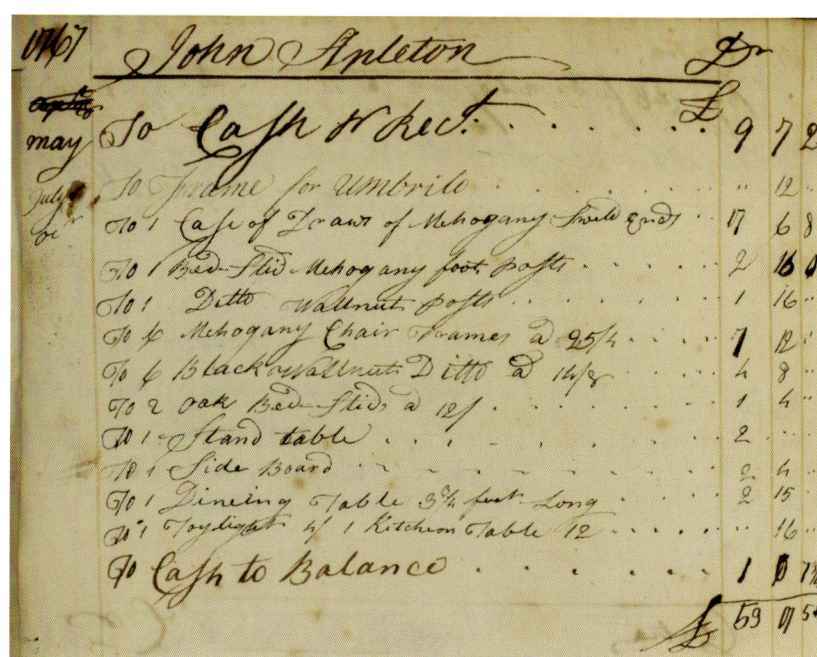

in figure 10. Gould charged the same amount for cases of drawers sold to Mark Hunking Wentworth of Portsmouth, New Hampshire, on November 22, 1764, and Rebecca Orne of Salem, on August 1, 1768, before her marriage to merchant and shipowner Captain Joseph Cabot. This suggests that those examples were also of bombé form.[10]

Equally demanding from the perspective of construction were desk-and-bookcases. Of the nineteen examples listed in Gould's daybooks, six were shipped elsewhere: two to Salem shipmaster Joseph Grafton; one to Marblehead, Massachusetts, merchant Jeremiah Lee; one to Marblehead shipmaster Nicholas Bartlet; one to Beverly shipmaster Josiah Batchelder; and one to Philadelphia minister and merchant Peletiah Webster. The prices charged for five of these desk-and-bookcases were significantly less than those of other examples made in Gould's shop. Lee's desk-and-bookcase is the exception. An April 9, 1775, entry in the cabinetmaker's daybook (fig. 11)

Figure 10 Chest-on-chest attributed to the shop of Nathaniel Gould, Salem, Massachusetts, 1764–1768. Mahogany with white pine. H. 91", W. 44½", D. 22⅞". (Courtesy, Nelson-Atkins Museum of Art, Kansas City, Missouri, William Rockhill Nelson Trust; photo, Jamison Miller.) Gould used the term "case of drawers" to identify both cabriole-leg high chests and chest-on-chests.

indicates that Lee purchased seven pieces of furniture including the desk-and-bookcase and was assessed additional charges for crating each. The corresponding entry in Gould's account book (fig. 12) reveals that Lee purchased the furniture for his daughter Mary (1753–1819) and her husband, Newburyport merchant Nathaniel Tracy (1751–1796). The couple had mar-

Figure 11 April 9, 1775, debit entry for Jeremiah Lee in Nathaniel Gould's daybook covering the years 1767 to 1784. (Courtesy, Massachusetts Historical Society; photo, Gavin Ashworth.)

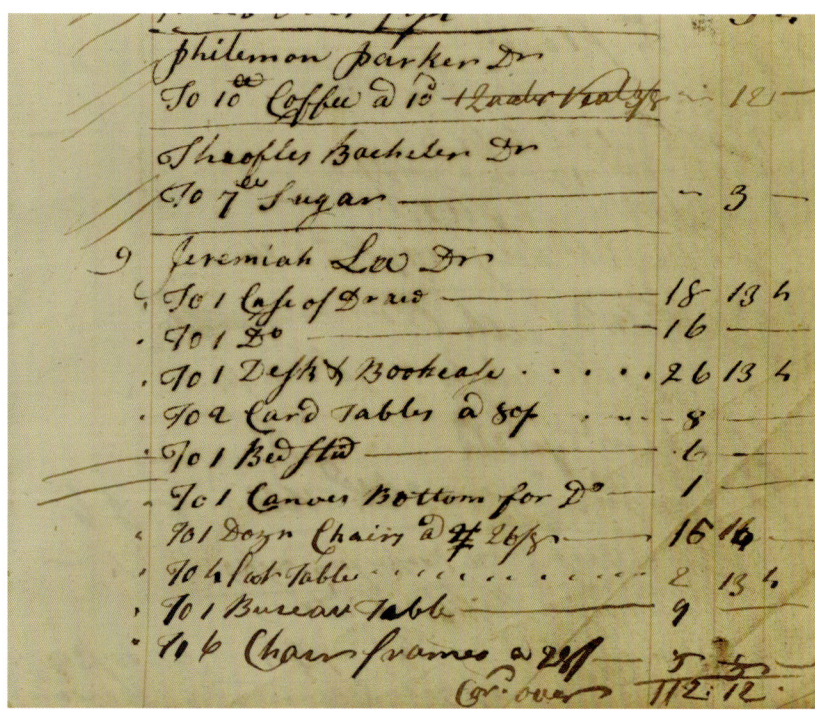

Figure 12 Debit entries for Jeremiah Lee in Nathaniel Gould's account book covering the years 1763 to 1781. (Courtesy, Massachusetts Historical Society; photo, Gavin Ashworth.) The August 20, 1772, entry pertains to furniture for Lee's son Joseph. The April 6, 1775, entry pertains to furniture for Lee's daughter Mary.

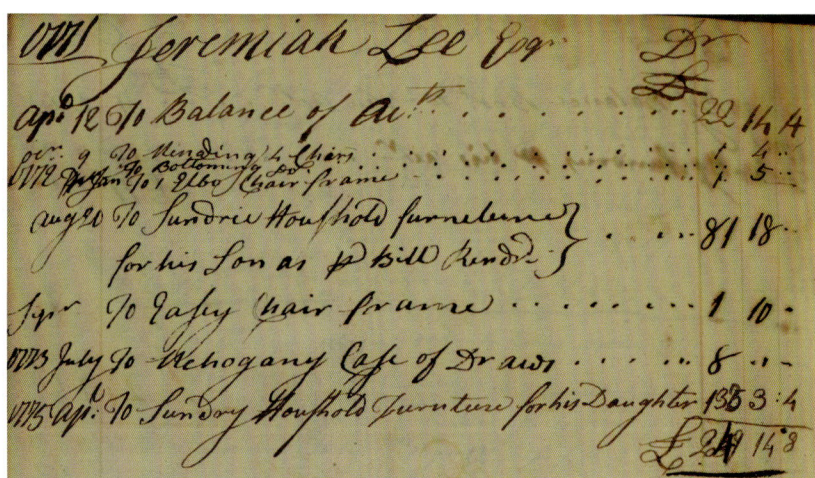

ried one month earlier, which suggests that the furniture commissioned by Lee was part of his daughter's wedding dowry (fig. 13). Most of the individuals who purchased desk-and-bookcases from Gould were members of Salem's merchant elite, including Edward Allen, Joseph and George Cabot, George Deblois, Francis Gardner, Benjamin Goodhue, Thomas Mason, and Richard Routh.[11]

Of all the furniture forms listed in Gould's daybooks, desks appear to have contributed the most to his financial success. Notations regarding charges for "casing" (crating), sales to ship captains, and the use of cedar as a primary wood suggest that at least three-quarters of the desks he sold were intended for export. Gould purchased most of these examples from local cabinetmakers. On June 23, 1768, Philemon Parker charged him £1.4 for a desk that Gould sold for £4 the same day (fig. 14).

Figure 13 Nathaniel Tracy House, Newburyport, Massachusetts, ca. 1771. (Courtesy, Phillips Library Photograph Collection, Peabody Essex Museum.) The desk-and-bookcase that Jeremiah Lee purchased for his daughter was among the original furnishings of this house.

Figure 14 June 23, 1768, debit entry for Nathaniel Leach in Nathaniel Gould's daybook covering the years 1767 to 1784. (Courtesy, Massachusetts Historical Society; photo, Gavin Ashworth.) Gould purchased two desks from Philemon Parker and sold one to Leach. The cedar primary wood of Leach's desk, crating charges recorded by Gould, and his patron's profession as a ship captain suggest that this desk was intended for export. Gould charged £4 for standard cedar and cherry desks and £4.13.4 for slightly more elaborate cedar examples.

Figure 15 Desk-and-bookcase attributed to the shop of Nathaniel Gould, Salem, Massachusetts, ca. 1775. Mahogany and white pine. H. 105", W. 42", D. 22". (Courtesy, Metropolitan Museum of Art, gift of Mrs. J. Russell Sage; photo, Gavin Ashworth, Image © Metropolitan Museum of Art.) The door panels are book-matched and have prominent stripe figure like the plank used for the fallboard.

Gould's shop produced a variety of stands, one hundred of which were described as "standtables." That term probably referred to the square or round tilt-top tea tables with baluster or urn-shaped pillars and simple cyma-shaped legs. Many examples of this form survive from the North Shore of Massachusetts. More specialized variants from Gould's shop included reading, glass, bottle, and candlestands.

Identifying the Work of Nathaniel Gould's Shop
For nearly twenty years scholars have debated the authorship of an imposing desk-and-bookcase bearing the inscription "Nath Gould not his work" (figs. 15, 16) and other case pieces with similar structural and stylistic details.

Figure 16 Detail of the inscription "Nath Gould not his work" on the desk-and-bookcase illustrated in fig. 15. (Photo, Gavin Ashworth.)

Figure 17 Desk attributed to the shop of Nathaniel Gould, Salem, Massachusetts, 1758–1780. (Courtesy, Bernard & S. Dean Levy.) Although this desk is marked "H ˣ RUST," its stylistic and structural features suggest that it originated in Nathaniel Gould's shop. The construction differs from that of the Rust desk illustrated in fig. 19.

In *American Furniture in The Metropolitan Museum of Art II, Late Colonial Period: The Queen Anne and Chippendale Styles* (1985), furniture historian Morrison Heckscher speculated that the desk-and-bookcase was from Gould's shop and that its unusual inscription may represent the sentiments of a disaffected workman who made the object and did not want his master to receive undue credit. Heckscher also referred to an additional eighteenth-century inscription—"Jos— — Gould 177_"—and noted that the design of a block-front desk marked "H ˣ RUST" (figs. 17, 18) was similar to that of the desk-and-bookcase. Since the early 1970s that desk had become a cornerstone for attributing other case pieces to Salem and some examples to the shop of Henry Rust. Indeed, decorative arts scholar Charles Venable argued that the desk-and-bookcase illustrated in figure 15 was made by Rust after comparing its construction to that of the desk marked "H ˣ RUST" and another example inscribed "This desk Made By Henry Rust of Salem / Salem New England / One Thousand seven Hundred and Seventy" (figs. 19–21).[12]

Figure 18 Detail of the mark on the desk illustrated in fig. 17.

Figure 19 Henry Rust, desk, Boston, Massachusetts, 1770. Mahogany with white pine. H. 42", W. 37", D. 18½". (Courtesy, Metropolitan Museum of Art, gift of the family of Edward and Kaye Scheider [2007.158 a-e]; photo, Gavin Ashworth, Image © Metropolitan Museum of Art.) Rust was a competent cabinetmaker, but his work falls short of that performed in Nathaniel Gould's shop.

Venable's attribution of the desk-and-bookcase (fig. 15) to Rust can be refuted on several points. Although the desk marked "H ˣ RUST" is attributed to the same shop that produced the desk-and-bookcase, evidence suggests that the chiseled inscription on the former is not a maker's mark. The construction of the other desk (fig. 19), which has an authentic inscription, differs significantly from that of the desk-and-bookcase. This is most appar-

Figure 20 Detail of the inscription on the desk illustrated in fig. 19. (Photo, Gavin Ashworth.)

ent in the dovetailing of their drawer sides and backs, since the pins and tails on the desk are the reverse of the more conventional ones on the desk-and-bookcase (figs. 22, 23). Similarly, the desk-and-bookcase has lap-joined backboards, whereas those on the desk are butt-joined. Other structural features cited by Venable as evidence that these pieces originated in the same shop are generic. The glue blocks supporting the feet and drops on the desk-and-bookcase and desks are essentially the same as those used by Salem cabinetmakers Abraham Watson and John Chipman, and double-beaded

Figure 21 Detail showing additional writing and drawing on the desk illustrated in fig. 19. (Photo, Gavin Ashworth.)

Figure 22 Detail showing the dovetailing at the back of a large drawer from the desk illustrated in fig. 19. (Photo, Gavin Ashworth.)

Figure 23 Detail showing the dovetailing at the back of a large drawer from the desk-and-bookcase illustrated in fig. 15. (Photo, Gavin Ashworth.)

drawer edges are common in furniture from Salem and Marblehead, Massachusetts, as well as other areas of New England. Venable also erred in concluding that the writing on the desk-and-bookcase and desk illustrated in figures 15 and 19 was "by the same hand." The inscription "Nath Gould not his work" is actually by two different individuals (fig. 16), and the "Nath Gould" section matches the cabinetmaker's signature on the title page of his account book (fig. 1) and an invoice to Salem merchant Richard Derby (fig. 24). The fact that the phrase "not his work" is by a different hand supports Heckscher's theory that it was written by one of Gould's workmen. The cursive style of both inscriptions (fig. 16) differs from that on the desk illustrated in figures 19–21.[13]

Figure 24 Invoice from Nathaniel Gould to Richard Derby, Salem, Massachusetts, November 21, 1763. (Courtesy, Peabody Essex Museum.) The invoice is in the Derby Papers, Miscellaneous Receipts, MSS 37, box 15, folder 5.

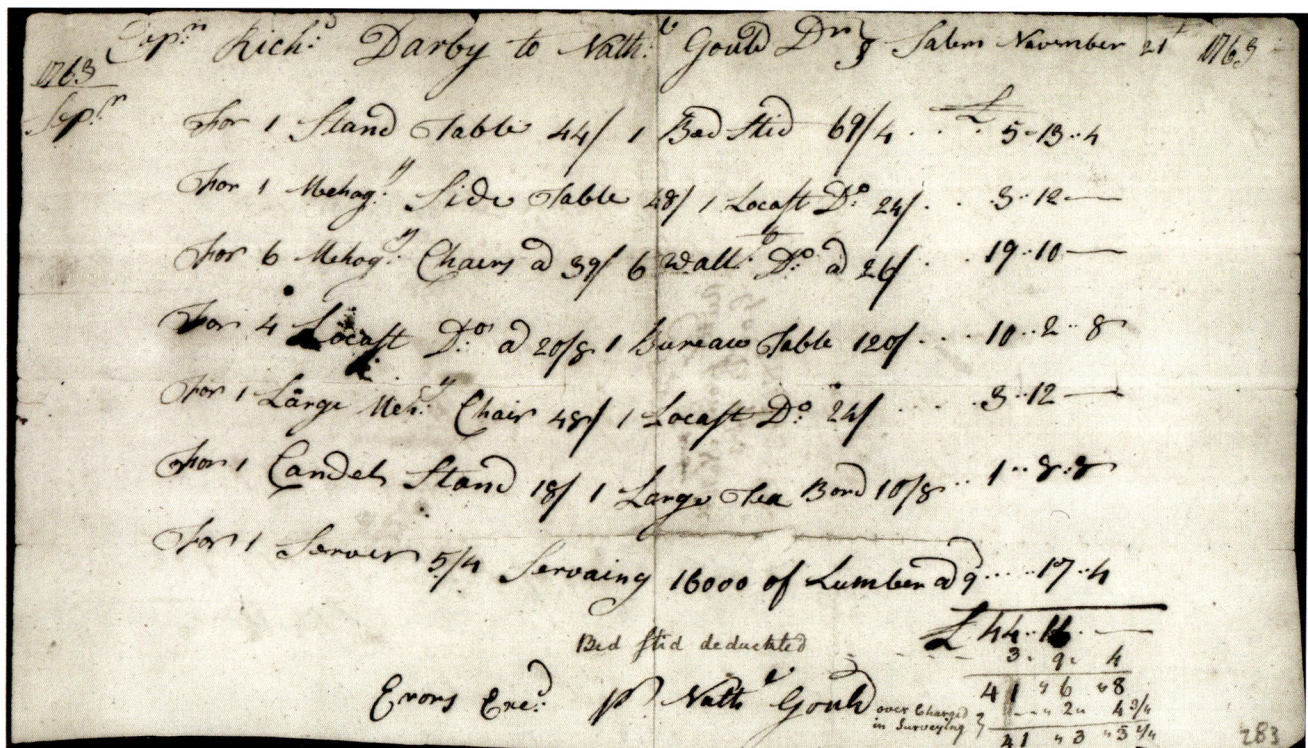

Figure 25   Detail of the right front foot of the chest of drawers illustrated in fig. 6. (Photo, Gavin Ashworth.)

Figure 26   Detail showing the dovetailing and beading of a drawer from the chest-on-chest illustrated in fig. 10. (Photo, Kemble Widmer.)

The construction of case furniture attributed to Gould and other Salem cabinetmakers differs from that of their Boston counterparts. All but two of the case pieces attributed to Gould have claw-and-ball feet with side talons that are vertical rather than being raked back in Boston fashion (fig. 25). His feet are further distinguished by having toes that are almost square in cross section and talons that are undercut slightly on the sides. Gould's secondary woods are generally knot-free and scraped smooth, whereas those in many Boston case pieces display saw kerfs or rough plane marks. His drawer sides and backs are typically 3/8–1/2 inch thick, which provided ample surface for a widely spaced double bead at the top (fig. 26). Most Boston and Salem cabinetmakers limited their beading to the tops of drawer sides. Gould and his workmen constructed their large drawers with the bottom boards set parallel to the front. This practice, which had become common in Salem by the middle of the eighteenth century, differed from the perpendicular arrangement favored by most Boston cabinetmakers. Only in the precision of dovetail joints does Boston casework surpass that associated with Gould's shop. The angles of his pins and tails are often asymmetrical, and his dovetails occasionally have gaps between the joints.[14]

Gould's work can be separated from that of other Salem cabinetmakers, although not by any single diagnostic detail. Like all large urban furniture-making shops, he had a sizable workforce composed of apprentices and journeymen with slightly different work habits. Variations can be observed from piece to piece, but Gould's casework is structurally consistent when evaluated as a group. The prospect doors of his desk-and-bookcases are cut from a solid block of wood; he used square blocking on the lids and top drawers of blocked case furniture; the hinges of his prospect doors and lock faces of his desk lids are surface mounted (fig. 27); his pigeonhole valences have exceptionally vigorous cyma curves (fig. 28); his drawer dividers and fallboard supports are made of mahogany rather than having mahogany

Figure 27 Detail of the lock on the lid of the desk-and-bookcase illustrated in fig. 30. (Photo, Gavin Ashworth.)

Figure 28 Detail of the writing compartment of the desk-and-bookcase illustrated in fig. 15. (Photo, Gavin Ashworth.) Gould typically used clock hinges for prospect doors.

Figure 29 Detail of the number "7" on the back of the third drawer from the chest of drawers illustrated in fig. 6. (Photo, Gavin Ashworth.) The numbers denoted drawer height.

faces glued to white pine boards; and the numbering system he usually employed on large exterior drawers is distinctive (fig. 29).

An exceptional bombé desk-and-bookcase (fig. 30) can be attributed to Gould based on its provenance and stylistic and structural parallels with other furniture from his shop. Oral tradition maintained that the desk-and-bookcase descended in the family of Robert Treat Paine II (1861–1943) and his wife, Ruth (Cabot) Paine (1865–1949). Ruth and her husband shared a common ancestor, Joseph Cabot (1719–1767) of Salem. Ruth descended in the line of Joseph's youngest son, Samuel (1758–1819), whereas Robert descended in the line of Joseph's eldest son, John (1745–1821).[15]

The Cabots were one of Salem's leading families during the mid-eighteenth century. Their patriarch was John Cabot (1680–1742), who emigrated from the Channel Island of Jersey to Massachusetts in 1700 and married Anna Orne (1678–1767) in Salem two years later. Four of their seven children married members of the prosperous Higginson family. John's sons Joseph

Figure 30 Desk-and-bookcase attributed to the shop of Nathaniel Gould, Salem, Massachusetts, 1765–1781. Mahogany with white pine. H. 96⅛", W. 44⅛", D. 22¾". (Courtesy, C. L. Prickett Antiques; photo, Gavin Ashworth.)

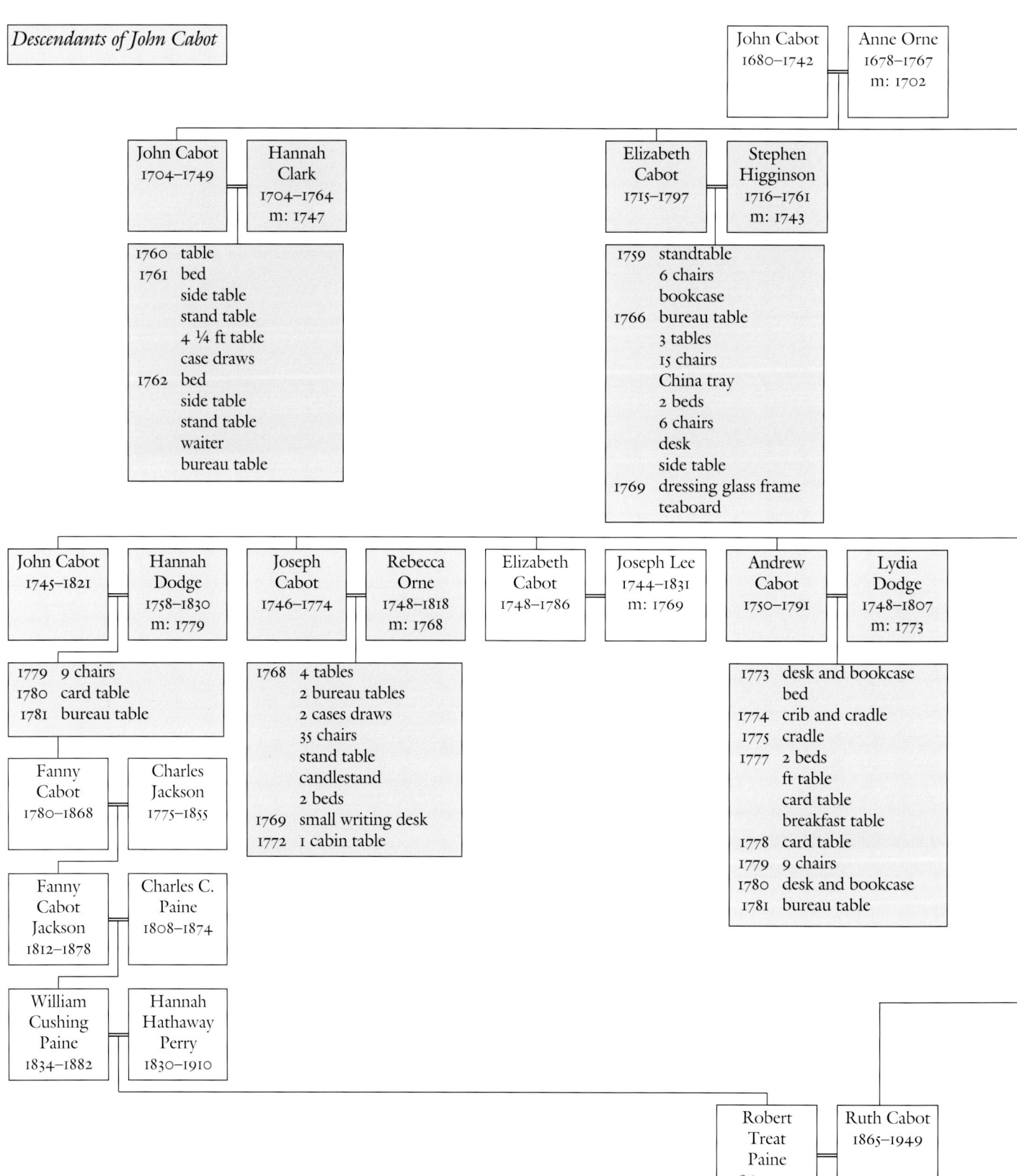

20 KEMBLE WIDMER II AND JOYCE KING

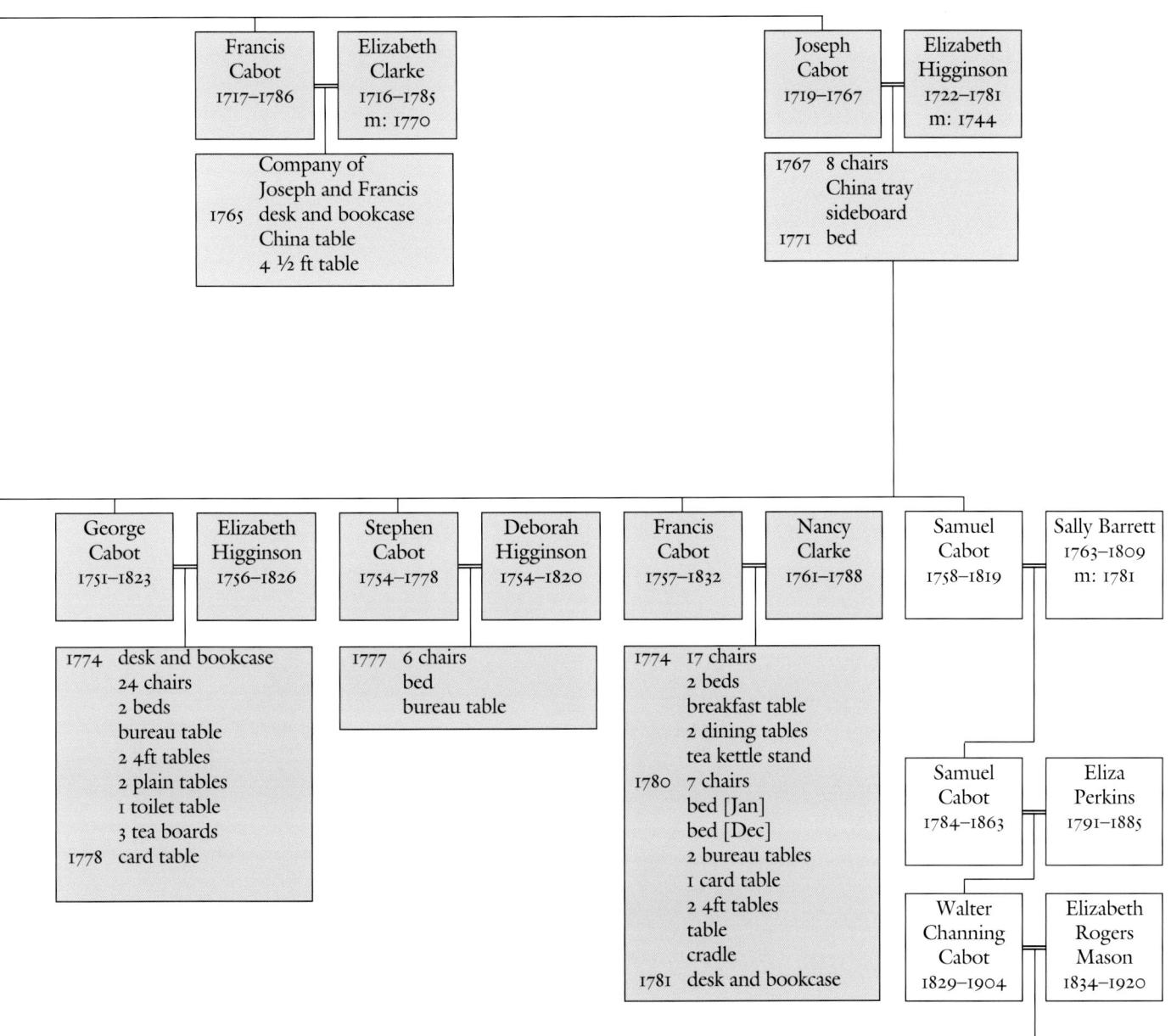

Figure 31 Cabot family tree showing purchases of desk-and-bookcases and lines of descent. (Genealogy by Joyce King; artwork, Wynne Patterson.)

(1719–1767) and Francis (1717–1786) followed him in the shipping business, which, supplemented by other mercantile activities, was the source of the Cabots' great wealth.[16]

Members of the Cabot family commissioned five of the nineteen desk-and-bookcases listed in Gould's daybooks (fig. 31). Joseph and Francis purchased the first example for their business in March 1765. That desk-and-bookcase may have been used in the brothers' office and warehouse on Essex Street in Salem and probably remained there until Francis's death in 1786. His inventory lists two examples. Three of Joseph's children

21 LEGACY OF NATHANIEL GOULD

Figure 32 Composite detail showing the fall-boards of the desk-and-bookcases illustrated in figs. 15 (top) and 30 (bottom). (Photo, Gavin Ashworth.)

Figure 33 Detail showing the door arches and pediment of the desk-and-bookcase illustrated in fig. 30. (Photo, Gavin Ashworth.)

also purchased desk-and-bookcases from Gould. His son Andrew commissioned two, the first for £24 on May 18, 1773, and the second for £40 on April 6, 1780. Andrew's brother George paid Gould £20 for a desk-and-bookcase on March 26, 1774, shortly after marrying Elizabeth Higginson (1756–1826). Seven years later, Gould charged Francis Cabot Jr. £45 for a desk-and-bookcase. At that date, the cabinetmaker's patron was only twenty-four years old. While it is impossible to determine which Cabot commissioned the desk-and-bookcase illustrated in figure 30, Andrew clearly had a taste for bombé furniture. He paid Gould £12 for a "bureau table" on February 24, 1781 (figs. 6, 7), three months before purchasing his second desk-and-bookcase.[17]

Like the desk-and-bookcase illustrated in figure 15, the Cabot example is

Figure 34 Details of the drop on the chest of drawers illustrated in fig. 6. (Photo, Gavin Ashworth.) Compass points on drops associated with Gould's shop and variations in the size and shape of standard components indicate that he and his workmen rarely used patterns.

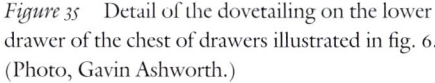

Figure 35 Detail of the dovetailing on the lower drawer of the chest of drawers illustrated in fig. 6. (Photo, Gavin Ashworth.)

made of dense, highly figured mahogany. Although Gould sold large quantities of wood to other Salem cabinetmakers, he reserved some of the best material for his own use. The fallboards on all of his surviving desk-and-bookcases appear to have been cut from the same board (fig. 32), which is remarkable when one considers that the production of these case pieces probably spanned six to ten years. Gould or his workmen oriented each fallboard so the stripe figure drops from one upper corner and rises to the other. Furniture from his shop is distinguished both by the quality of the materials used and the attention given to grain pattern. On the Cabot desk-and-bookcase (fig. 30), the grain of the tympanum board echoes the shape of the upper door rails and panel arches beneath (fig. 33).

The construction of the desk-and-bookcases is nearly identical save for the dimensions of some parts, including foot brackets and drops, and the dovetailing of their lower exterior drawers. Surprisingly, Gould does not appear to have used patterns for transferring the design of such components from piece to piece (fig. 34). As these desk-and-bookcases suggest, most of the major case pieces attributed to him appear to have been commissioned rather than purchased from Gould's stock-in-trade. Concerns for strength apparently led Gould to reverse the pins and tails on the backs of drawers with sides curved to accommodate bombé shaping (fig. 35). The joints of drawers with curved sides and a conventional pin-and-tail arrangement were more likely to separate if the drawers were heavily loaded.[18]

The fastidious construction, superb materials, and exceptionally refined design of Nathaniel Gould's furniture set it apart from that produced by many of his Massachusetts contemporaries. Other Salem cabinetmakers copied some of his shop's details, including the scallop shell drops and pinwheel rosettes seen on furniture illustrated here, but few possessed comparable skill and business acumen. Although he died at the relatively young age of forty-seven, Gould's furniture and the daybooks and account book he left behind illuminate the career of one of Salem's finest and most successful craftsmen.

ACKNOWLEDGMENTS For assistance with this article the authors thank Judy Anderson, Elizabeth Barker, Sidney E. Berger, Allan Breed, Darren J. Brown, John D. Childs, Wendy A. Cooper, Peter Drummey, Sean Farrell, Katherine Flynn, Catherine Futter, Nonnie Gadsden, Kathrine Griffin, Elaine Grublin, Stephen P. Hall, Morrison H. Heckscher, Brock Jobe, Frank Levy, Robert Lionetti, Christine Michelini, Robert D. Mussey Jr., Richard Nylander, Clark Pearce, Clarence, Craig, and Todd Prickett, and Gerald W. R. Ward.

1. Debit entry for Samuel Archer Jr., May 1, 1758, Nathaniel Gould Daybook, 1758–1763 (hereafter cited as NGDB 1), Nathan Dane Papers, Massachusetts Historical Society, Boston. A book listing the complete furniture transactions of Gould and his relationships with other cabinetmakers is planned for future publication.

2. NGDB 1; and Nathaniel Gould Daybook, 1767–1784 (hereafter cited as NGDB 2), Nathan Dane Papers, Massachusetts Historical Society, Boston. Nathaniel Gould Account Book, 1763–1781 (hereafter cited as NGAB), Nathan Dane Papers, Massachusetts Historical Society, Boston.

3. Nathaniel Gould Sr. was described as a "joyner" in several land transactions. See Ebenezer and Deliverance Marsh to Nathaniel Gould, June 17, 1727, Essex County Deeds (hereafter cited as ECD), vol. 46, p. 202. Also see Daniel Cariel and wife Mary to Nathaniel Gould, November 6, 1729, ECD, vol. 53, p. 184; and Probate Records of Essex County, Massachusetts (hereafter cited as PREC), January 1, 1746/47, docket no. 11415.

4. Nathaniel Gould of Charlestown, cabinetmaker, to John Clammons, December 25, 1756, ECD, vol. 104, p. 61. Robert Mussey and Anne Rogers Haley, "John Cogswell and Boston Bombé Furniture: Thirty-five Years of Revolution in Politics and Design," in *American Furniture*, edited by Luke Beckerdite (Hanover, N.H.: University of New England Press for the Chipstone Foundation, 1994), p. 100. Debit entries for Thomas Wood, January (no date given), June 1, and November 6, 1761, NGDB 1. Other sales are interspersed throughout Gould's daybooks and account book. For an example of Gould's purchases from Wood, see the credit entry in NGAB for March 23, 1766, for the purchase of 200 ft. cedar timber, 150 ft. cedar boards, and 16 cedar desks.

5. For more on Cogswell, see Mussey and Haley, "John Cogswell," pp. 73–107. Credit entry for John Cogswell, June 1759, NGDB 1.

6. James Duncan Phillips, *Salem in the Eighteenth Century* (Salem, Mass.: Essex Institute, 1969), pp. 204–10. The amount Gould donated was equal to more than three weeks' wages for a journeyman cabinetmaker. Gould paid Thomas West 22s. 6d. for seven days' work. Credit entry for Thomas West, March 1759, NGDB 1.

7. For furniture with carved feet, see debit entry for Jonathan Very, November 30, 1768, NGDB 1. For "chair frames carved backs," see debit entry for Clark Gayton Pickman, August 25, 1770, NGDB 2 and fig. 3. For the tables, see debit entries for Caleb Foster, May 27, 1774, NGDB 2, and Peter Frye, December 24, 1774, NGDB 2.

8. For more on Salem chairmakers, see Benno M. Forman, "Salem Tradesmen and Craftsmen Circa 1762," *Essex Institute Historical Collection,* no. 107 (January 1971): 65.

9. Inventories provide additional evidence that the term "bureau table" in the Gould daybooks and account book referred to four-drawer chests. In August 20, 1772, Gould sold Marblehead, Massachusetts, merchant Jeremiah Lee one mahogany "bureau table," one walnut "bureau table," one mahogany "case of drawers," one walnut "case of drawers," one "silver table," and thirty-six chairs. Debit entry for Jeremiah Lee, August 20, 1772, NGDB 2. The account book indicates that this order was for his son (fig. 12). The 1785 inventory of Lee's son Joseph listed "one mahogany bureau and one mahogany chest-on-chest in the first floor bedchamber and one walnut bureau and one walnut chest-on-chest in the second floor bedchamber." Inventory of Joseph Lee, October 4, 1785, ECPR, docket no. 16625, transcript book 358, p. 45. Debit entry for Joseph Southwick, April 15, 1765, NGAB.

10. Debit entry for Mark Hunking Wentworth, November 22, 1764, NGAB. Debit entry for Rebecca Orne, August 1, 1768, NGDB 2. For evidence that the term "case of drawers" in the Gould daybooks and account book referred to chest-on-chests and cabriole-leg high chests, see the references to Jeremiah and Joseph Lee in n. 9 above. Four-drawer bombé chests attributed

to Gould's shop are in the collections of the Marblehead Historical Society, Historic New England, Winterthur Museum, Bayou Bend, and a private collector. For a "bureau table swelled," see debit entry for Bartholomew Putnam, May 1781, NGAB.

11. Debit entry for Joseph Grafton, March 13, 1761, NGDB 1. Debit entry for Jeremiah Lee, April 9, 1775, NGDB 2. Debit entry for Nicholas Bartlet, September 24, 1765, NGAB. Debit entry for Josiah Batchelder, May 2, 1765, NGAB. Debit entry for Peletiah Webster, July 1774, NGAB. John L. Currier, *Old Newbury Historical and Biographical Sketches* (Boston: Damrell and Upham, 1896), pp. 551–64.

12. Morrison H. Heckscher, *American Furniture in The Metropolitan Museum of Art II, Late Colonial Period: The Queen Anne and Chippendale Styles* (New York: Random House, 1985), pp. 121–24, 192–95. Margaretta Markle Lovell, "Boston Blockfront Furniture," in *Boston Furniture of the Eighteenth Century,* edited by Walter Muir Whitehill (Charlottesville: University Press of Virginia for the Colonial Society of Massachusetts, 1974), pp. 121–30. Charles L. Venable, *American Furniture in the Bybee Collection* (Austin: University of Texas Press, 1989), pp. 58–68. Israel Sack, Inc., *Antiques from Israel Sack Collection,* 10 vols. (Alexandria, Va.: Highland House, 1981), 4: 898–99.

13. The "H ^{X} RUST" mark on the desk illustrated in fig. 17 may have denoted ownership rather than authorship; however, no individual by that name is listed as a patron in Gould's account book or daybooks. On February 7, 1775, Gould recorded a debit entry for Henry Rust for work performed by Ipswich joiner Stephan Lowater. Gould had paid Lowater twenty-four days' wages (at 3s. 4d. per day) for sawing cedar boards. NGDB 2. Invoice from Nathaniel Gould to Richard Derby, Salem, Massachusetts, November 21, 1763. Derby Papers, Miscellaneous Receipts, MSS 37, box 15, folder 5, Peabody Essex Museum. For more on Chipman's blocking, see Peter A. Louis and Donald R. Sack, "John Chipman: Cabinetmaker of Salem, Massachusetts," *Antiques* 132, no. 6 (December 1987): 1320.

14. Some of Gould's construction details are similar to those of his Boston counterparts. The lower drawers of Gould's case pieces ride on strips of wood glued to the case bottom, and the tops of his chests are attached to the sides with sliding dovetail joints.

15. For more on the Cabot family, see L. Vernon Briggs, *History and Genealogy of the Cabot Family, 1475–1927* (Boston: Charles E. Godspeed & Co., 1927), pp. 44–55.

16. Ibid., pp. 99–107, 167–69, 185–86, 194–96.

17. Debit entry for Joseph and Francis Cabot, March 1765, NGAB. Debit entry for Andrew Cabot, May 18, 1773, NGDB 2; and debit entry for Andrew Cabot, April 6, 1780, NGDB 2. Andrew bought the first desk-and-bookcase three weeks after marrying Lydia Dodge (1748–1807). He commissioned the second shortly after moving to Beverly, Massachusetts. Andrew's 1791 inventory lists one "desk & bookcase" valued at £7.10 and another valued at £4.10. ECPR, no. 4431, bk. 360, pp. 499–506. His wife, who was pregnant with their ninth child when he died, moved to Boston in March 1792. Auctioneer William Lang sold one of the two desk-and-bookcases, a mahogany stand table, and thirteen chairs from Andrew's Beverly house later that year. *Salem Gazette,* June 12, 1792; and Nathan Dane, *Minute Book of Settling Estate of Andrew Cabot* (Boston: Massachusetts Historical Society, 1935), p. 19. The other desk-and-bookcase was still in Lydia's house when she died in July 1807. The estate was divided equally between the couple's children. Suffolk County Probate Records (hereafter cited as SCPR), bk. 105, docket no. 22925, p. 411. Debit entry for George Cabot, March 25, 1774, NGDB 2. The disposition of George Cabot's desk-and bookcase remains a mystery. He gave cash to his son and daughter and established trust funds for his wife, Elizabeth. She received the balance of his estate and later bequeathed everything to her son Henry (1783–1864). SCPR, bk. 121, docket no. 26951, p. 336; and SCPR, bk. 123, docket no. 28045, p. 79. Debit entry for Francis Cabot Jr., August 1781, NGDB 2. Two years after the death of his wife, Nancy (1761–1788), Francis Cabot Jr. left his three children in the care of relatives and moved to Philadelphia. He subsequently relocated to Louisiana, enlisted as a private in the battle of New Orleans, and died in Natchez, Mississippi. His desk-and-bookcase may have been among the "Genteel and Valuable House Furniture and Shop Goods" Francis sold in September 1790. Debit entry for Andrew Cabot, February 24, 1781, NGDB 2.

18. The dovetailing on the chest in the Winterthur Museum and the desk-and-bookcase illustrated in fig. 30 differ from that of other bombé furniture attributed to Gould's shop. On these examples, the pins and tails at the rear of all the drawers are reversed.

Figure 1 Interpreter at Plimoth Plantation, Plymouth, Massachusetts, 2008. (Photo, Gavin Ashworth.) Visible in this interior of a reproduction earthfast dwelling with a tamped earth floor are a shaved chair, a slab bench, baskets, turned bowls, and other wooden artifacts. All these artifacts must continually be repaired and renewed. This provides an opportunity to observe how the objects react to daily use. European paintings and prints help in the reconstruction of such assemblages, which represent interiors dating six years before the earliest extant Plymouth probate inventories.

Jennie Alexander, Peter Follansbee, and Robert F. Trent

Early American Shaved Post-and-Rung Chairs

▼ INTERPRETERS AT the re-created 1627 village at Plimoth Plantation in Plymouth, Masssachusetts, use reproduction furniture, woodenwares, and houses made with numerous woodworking techniques (fig. 1). Over the last fifty-five years, Plimoth Plantation has continually re-formed and replaced the buildings and furnishings, with the explicit goal of becoming more accurate. Some of the furnishings are based on surviving artifacts. However, Continental paintings, prints, and drawings have been an equally important source, not because of the Pilgrims' experience in Leiden, but because seventeenth-century Continental graphics are particularly abundant and varied, whereas English pictorial sources are rare.[1]

The reproduction objects shown in figure 1 pose important interpretative quandaries. Numerous prejudices stand in the way of modern analysis of early New England woodworking, involving confusion about techniques versus historic trades versus modern classifications. The woodworker of the late medieval period inherited any number of furniture-making traditions. Objects produced by these artisans could include shaved and turned post-and-rung seating; chairs with slab or plank seats; trestles with stake or shaved feet; boarded and joined case furniture, tables, and seating; excavated or dug-out case pieces and seating; and structures made of staves or wood rods and vegetable fibers like straw, reeds, willow osiers, and inner bark. All these items were made of wood or other vegetable materials worked in a partially green state and required the use of tools with sharp steel cutting edges.[2]

In exploring early seating, too much has been made of the differences between shaved and turned post-and-rung chairs. The construction of both types of seating involved riving stock; rough shaping with hatchets, drawknives, and shaves; boring mortises with a spoon bit; assembly wherein moisture from wetter posts migrated to and swelled dry tenons; minimal pinning or back-wedging of joints; and no gluing. Some shaved or turned chairs were partially or entirely infilled with panels or with lattice held in grooves plowed in the inner edges of the frames. These chairs blur the distinction between turned and joined seating and, in the case of lattice, between furniture and architectural fixtures. For example, the settle depicted in Joseph's workshop in the Merode Altarpiece combines lattice-work, joinery, turning, and shaving in one object (fig. 2).[3]

Equally confusing are chairs and benches made with shaved posts secured in slab or plank seats (post-and-slab or stake-and-slab, as opposed to post-and-rung). These range from the complex, Germanic *Brettstuhl* (figs. 3, 4)

Figure 2 Right panel from *The Annunciation Triptych,* attributed to Robert Campin (1375–1444), Brussels, 1425–1430. Oil on panel. 25 3/8" x 10 3/4". (Courtesy, Metropolitan Museum of Art, The Cloisters Collection, 1956 [56.70 a-c], Image © Metropolitan Museum of Art). Joseph's settle encompasses various woodworking traditions in one object. The back has rectangular members united by draw-bored, rectangular mortise-and-tenon joints. The finials on the rear posts are sawn. The turned front posts, rails, arms, and side stretchers are shown assembled with cylindrical mortises and tenons. The interstices are filled with riven boards. Although it is not visible, the seat is probably constructed of multiple boards running front to rear and captured in grooves plowed in the front and rear seat rails. On Joseph's workbench is one of the earliest depictions of a brace fitted with a spoon bit, the standard bit used to bore the joints of post-and-rung chairs. The workbench is of post-and-slab construction. The diagonal lattice in the upper panel of the settle's back admits light to the work surface. It resembles similar lattice used in casement frames, sometimes to form ventilators, sometimes used to back oiled paper or thin cheesecloth.

Figure 3   Board backstool, or *Brettstuhl*, southeastern Pennsylvania, 1750–1775. Oak and pine. H. 32 1/8", W. 18 1/8", D. 14 5/8". (Courtesy, Winterthur Museum, gift of Henry Francis du Pont; photo, Laszlo Bodo). The *Brettstuhl* was a Germanic retooling of the Italian board *sgabello*, a mannerist scrolled and carved seat first used in grottoes and hallways. Eventually the *Brettstuhl* descended the social scale and became a type of Germanic folk seating, but even those chairs, like this Pennsylvania example, retain the elaborate construction techniques of the carved courtly versions.

Figure 4   Detail of the *Brettsthul* illustrated in fig. 3. This view shows the two external pins in the through-tenons of the back board and the dovetailed battens of the seat. The octagonal, tapered, shaved legs penetrate through both the dovetailed battens and the seat board and are back-wedged. Something like this construction is seen in prints and paintings of German or Dutch benches with slab or board seats, although their battens tend to be thicker and their stake feet often do not penetrate through the seat.

Figure 5 Slaughterer's bench, probably New England, 1800–1875. Maple. H. 14½", W. 55", D. 16". (Courtesy, Museum of Fine Arts, Boston, gift of Robert F. Trent in memory of Loren Jesse Pollock (1899-1973), 1983.302, photograph © 2008 Museum of Fine Arts, Boston.) This heavy workhorse is now almost colorless from being scrubbed with lye to neutralize blood. The rough top is made of approximately one-third of a maple trunk. The shaved feet are leveled in chopped and gouged housings and penetrate through the top, where they are back-wedged. Such benches were used principally for butchering swine and had to be heavy and level, for stability. Despite its superficial roughness, the bench is designed and assembled with precision.

to utilitarian workhorses (fig. 5). The *Brettstuhl,* derived from the elevated Italian renaissance board *sgabello,* featured through-tenons with exposed, peglike wedges uniting the seat and back, as well as stake feet passing through dovetailed battens in the seat board, as well as the seat itself (fig. 4). It is impossible to force the *Brettstuhl* into any one technological category. It unites technologies from joinery, cabinetmaking, and post-and-slab chairmaking in one object.[4]

These assorted seating categories were not, therefore, mutually exclusive, even when guilds or other regulatory agencies sought to enforce the differences between them. Another important point is that rough surfaces or roughly worked components do not necessarily imply poor workmanship. The slickest veneered case piece can be shoddily constructed, and the roughest-looking post-and-slab bench can be a precision device with accurate, tight joints. The mentality that seeks to sort them into ideal types assumes that each technology belonged to a strict historical discipline. Period illustrations suggest that no such hierarchy existed, unless a guild system intervened. Even then, considerable litigation between London guilds suggests that the guilds themselves could not maintain strict separation between joinery and carpentry or between joinery and turning.[5]

Presumably distinctions between trades were greatest in urban settings. Even there, though, notable exceptions existed. Royal intervention and protection, which overruled guild regulations, were often extended to "strangers," the term for skilled artisans from outside the municipality in question. This protection, often used to attract specialists from other nations, dispensed with protectionism and trade divisions, for the purposes of stylistic or technical innovation and fluid interchange between media.[6]

Also, urban centers were surrounded by rural enclaves, which supplied foodstuffs and fodder to the town or city. In such settings, other ambiguous forms of woodworking flourished, now generically referred to by the English as "field crafts." Such diverse products included rail fencing and wattling; hurdles; rakes, scythes, and flails; basketry, winnowing fans, brooms, trays, bowls, buckets, shovels, and treenware; and yokes, carts, wagons, plows, tackling, and myriad other fixtures. One might extend this category to include larger features like houses, barns, mills, and outbuildings. Much the same could be said for commercial and military shipbuilding. Such things were and are not merely of regional, craft, agricultural, or military interest, and they often violated historical or modern trade boundaries, in terms of the technologies employed to fashion them. Furthermore, rural products were sold in urban enclaves, sometimes over the objections of guilds. Early-twentieth-century English studies of such products, based in an arts-and-crafts nostalgia for preindustrial country life, represented the first detailed recognition of green woodworking techniques and traditional woodworking.[7]

In essence, analysis of early woodworking cannot rely on artificial distinctions between technologies or on urban/rural contrasts or polarities. This is manifest in the case of simpler, turned or shaved, post-and-rung seating. In American decorative arts literature, such chairs are sometimes deemed to be evidence for isolated or deprived circumstances. The so-called "settin' chair," with two or more slats and either shaved or turned posts, was found in all regions of the Canadian Maritimes, Québec province, and the American South and survived into the modern era, when small factories produced such chairs for traditional households. Another incidental idea that accrues to shaved seating, in particular, is that it was so crude (in unspecified ways) that it must have been the work of amateurs, perhaps self-reliant pioneers who made such forms for temporary use until something better could be obtained. European paintings and prints suggest, rather, that shaved chairs coexisted with turned chairs and other seating in both elevated and humble interiors. Such depictions also show furniture forms made with various techniques coexisting in one room, in a manner that seems self-evident, but is not, even allowing all due compensation for artistic license.[8]

Another problem in interpreting shaved post-and-rung chairs is their poor survival rate, by comparison with the many early turned chairs that still exist. One cannot, therefore, assert that shaved chairs per se were common, although they were made throughout Europe and most European colonies. The eight known New England and New York shaved chairs that date from before 1800 are diverse in form, but some general observations about their design and workmanship illuminate the tradition as a whole and point to new directions for future study. Indefatigable furniture scholar Irving P. Lyon first published four of the early New England chairs illustrated here in a 1931 article entitled "Square-Post Slat-Back Chairs." Lyon noted that these chairs did not belong to any of the recognized seventeenth-century seating categories and refuted the idea that they were amateur productions by illustrating numerous European paintings and prints that included such chairs. The writers are indebted to Lyon, but we augment the discussion with discoveries made over the last seven decades. Another key contribution of this article is the explication of modern study chairs that explore the technology and design of shaved chair variants that do not survive. This is particularly true of side chairs, which are abundant in period illustrations but now are rare. A third contribution is the broadening of chronological, geographic, and ethnic representation of the tradition. Shaved post-and-rung chairs are not an obscure tradition from the distant past, but a widespread, continuous tradition that presents many opportunities for interpretation.[9]

Early European Shaved Chairs and New England Cognates

European paintings, prints, and drawings often depict shaved chairs (figs. 6–10) with posts that taper on the sides (fig. 7). Less commonly represented are chairs with posts tapered on three or four sides. When multiple tapers are shown, they usually occur on the rear posts above the seat. It is unclear if the long tapers of these representational chairs were hewn with a joiner's hatchet or sawn lengthwise and then shaved and planed smooth, although hewing was a more common practice.

Figure 6 Jan van der Straat, *Preparing the Eggs of Silkworms,* Florence, Italy, 1550–1575. Ink on paper. Dimensions not recorded. (By gracious permission of Her Majesty the Queen, Royal Library, Windsor Castle.) This drawing shows a set of at least three shaved chairs. They are the most elevated model found in Italian art. The chairs have rounded crests with molded edges and applied roundels, a row of spindles in the back, and conspicuous bridle joints at the tops of the posts. These chairs do not exhibit hewn layback or through-tapering of the sides of the posts. Despite the hobby with which the aristocratic women are occupied, the chairs are not low-seated and do not appear to be utilitarian in intent.

While some Italian renaissance shaved chairs are quite plain, others are embellished in the back with classicizing applied roundels or rows of turned spindles between the slats (fig. 6). A few have posts shaved into square balusters. The Italian interiors in which shaved chairs appear are, surprisingly, quite elevated. The scene is often the Birth of the Virgin. Concern for the status of Mary as spiritual royalty led to depicting the scene in a bedchamber of the Italian aristocracy. Women attending the birth use low-seated shaved chairs to tend fires, cook, wash linens, and swaddle the infant Mary (fig. 9). This suggests that low-seated shaved chairs were gender specific, at least in an Italian context. The Italian chairs usually have both through- tenons and blind tenons. That is, the posts tend to be somewhat broader than they are deep, and therefore the front-to-rear tenons are often through-bored, while the side-to-side tenons are blind.[10]

Figure 7   Hans Holbein the Elder (ca. 1465–1524), detail from *The Martyrdom of Saint Paul*, Augsburg, Bavaria, ca. 1504. Oil on panel. Dimensions not recorded. (Courtesy, Bayerischen Stadtsgemaldsammlungen, Munich.) This view shows a woman seated in a one-slat shaved chair with through-tenons and through-tapered posts. This painting was illustrated in Irving P. Lyon, "Square-Post Slat-Back Chairs," *Antiques* 20, no. 4 (October 1931): 210–16, at p. 211, and was used in the formulation of the chairs shown in figs. 16–18.

Figure 8 Paul Velner, *The Cobbler*, in *Das Hausbuch der Mendelschen Zwölfbrüderstiftung zu Nürnberg*, fol. 93 verso, Nuremberg, Bavaria, 1474. Watercolor on paper. Dimensions not recorded. (Courtesy, Stadtbibliothek Nuernberg.) This cobbler is seated in a shaved armchair with stick arms and one slat. The posture of the cobbler suggests that the seat of this chair is normal in height. The posts appear to be slightly through-tapered on the sides. The artist incorrectly included a through-tenon on the side elevation of the top of the front post.

Figure 9 Hans von Kulmbach (ca. 1485–1522), detail from *Birth of the Virgin Mary*, Nuremberg, 1510–1520. Oil on panel. Dimensions and present location unknown. (Otto von Falke, *Deutsche Möbel des Mittelalters und Renaissance* [Stuttgart: Juluis Hoffman, 1924], p. 51.) The low-seated shaved chair in which the nurse swaddling the Virgin Mary is seated has one tier of rungs and two slats. The posts have long chamfers between the joints and what appear to be bent tops. Elsewhere in the room are a cradle with board sides tenoned into posts, a trestle table, a board bench with hinged back, and a stand with a spindle gallery to hold a bowl under a wall font.

Figure 10   Michael Sweerts, *The Academy*, Brussels, 1656–1658. Oil on canvas. Dimensions not recorded. (Courtesy, Frans Halsmuseum, Haarlem, the Netherlands.) This depiction of art students shows them seated on three-slat shaved chairs. The slats are roughly riven and have arc-shaped cuts on the ends on both top and bottom edges, save for the top slats, which have a straight bottom edge. The chairs are through-tenoned fore and aft but have blind tenons side to side. They appear to have seats about 14–15" high. Another important aspect of this view is that the chairs are part of a set of at least twelve chairs.

Many of the features seen in Italian and northern European art are found in early New England shaved chairs, as Lyon pointed out in "Square-Post Slat-Back Chairs." The armchair illustrated in figure 11 has a history of ownership in the Choate House on Hog Island in Ipswich Harbor. The chair has resided for the last eighty-five years or so in the Pembroke Room at Beauport, where it is drawn up to a table in a dark corner. Despite this obscure modern context, the Choate armchair represents the most compelling evidence that early American shaved chairs reflected the better European cognates and could be elevated in concept and execution. The chair exhibits extremely fine workmanship. The posts are exquisite, through-tapered forms, and they have deep, oblique chamfers on their outer corners to eliminate sharp edges. The rear posts are also relieved on their forward faces above the seat, to provide slight layback. The unusual slanted arms are also tapered and extend beyond the front posts. The rungs and seat rails are

Figure 11 Armchair, Ipswich, Massachusetts, 1650–1700. Maple and ash. H. 37½", W. 25", D. 18". (Courtesy, Historic New England, gift of Constance McCann Betts, Helena Woolworth Guest, and Frasier W. McCann, 1942.3110.) Irving P. Lyon stated that this armchair was acquired by interior designer Henry Davis Sleeper (1878–1934) from the Choate House on Hog Island in Ipswich Harbor in 1919 (Irving P. Lyon, "Square-Post Slat-Back Chairs," *Antiques* 20, no. 4 [October 1931]: 211–12.)

centered on the inner sides of the posts. Originally all the joints were blind, although some have broken through the outer surfaces of the posts later on. The original distribution of pinned joints is lost, because it appears that collector Henry Davis Sleeper (1878–1934), designer and owner of Beauport, instructed a cabinetmaker to glue and pin all the joints of the chair soon after he acquired it.[11]

By comparison, a Rochester, Massachusetts, armchair has much rougher components (fig. 12). The posts are square in section below the seat. Above that point, the sides of the posts taper slightly, and the rear posts are relieved on their front faces, as well. However, the layback of the rear posts is more complex than it seems. The rear posts above the seat taper on all four sides, a feature rarely seen. As in many of the shaved chairs, the slats are located on the exact centers of the inside faces of the rear posts. Curiously, this orientation of the slats slightly decreases the angle of their layback relative to the front faces of the relieved rear posts.

Figure 12 Armchair, Plymouth County, Massachusetts, 1650–1720. Maple, oak, and ash. H. 36¾", W. 20¾", D. 18". (Courtesy, Museum of Fine Arts, Boston, H. E. Bolles Fund, 1971.190, photograph © 2008 Museum of Fine Arts, Boston.) This chair displays the roughest workmanship of the surviving early New England shaved armchairs. Both arms and one side stretcher are either altered or replaced. Traces of red paint remain on the frame.

The Rochester chair has undergone some repairs that make it appear cruder than it was when first made. One or both of the arms may have been altered. The arm mortises are now exposed on the rear surfaces of the rear posts, although it is obvious that all the mortises were originally blind. It is possible that one or both arms were replaced or shortened in length, and one side stretcher may have been altered in length as well. One rear post has warped inward, probably soon after assembly. The overall result is that the chair is wrenched out of square, giving it an odd appearance.[12]

Armchairs Based on European Art and New England Armchairs
In the 1990s John D. Alexander Jr. and Robert Trent collaborated in making a shaved armchair based on the dimensions of the Rochester chair, as recorded by Peter Follansbee (fig. 13). We consciously altered the design to make the modern chair more like comparable examples depicted in European paintings: we reduced the cross-sectional dimensions of the posts and tapered them on the sides, relieved the front faces of the rear posts above the seat to provide layback, and introduced blade or riven arms. The latter detail occurs on some New England and New York turned chairs, but not

Figure 13 John D. Alexander Jr. and Robert F. Trent, armchair, Baltimore, Maryland, 1998. Oak. H. 38⅛", W. 22", D. 17". (Private collection; photo, Gavin Ashworth.)

on the Rochester shaved example. All of the mortises on the Choate and Rochester chairs were originally blind and those for the slats are centered on the back posts. To make our chair more like those represented in European art and to experiment with alternative construction techniques, we through-tenoned the rails and stretchers, set the slats ¼ inch in from the front faces of the rear posts, and cut precise facets on the edges of the posts with a spoke shave. The Rochester example differs in having more deeply chamfered edges.

Because the front posts of our armchair taper to an extremely small rectangle at the top (1¾ inch deep by 1½ inch wide) and the tenons of the seat rails and stretchers are a hefty 1 inch, we cut the mortises for the side seat rails and arms in locations different from those on the Rochester chair. In a post-and-rung chair, the frame is planned around a seat pattern established by the length of the rungs and the cross-sectional diameter of the posts (depending on whether the chair is turned or shaved). In this system, the front rungs are usually somewhat longer than the side and rear rungs, and the side and rear rungs are usually the same length. As the length of the front rungs increases relative to those of the side and rear rungs, the angle between the front and side rungs becomes more acute. Ordinarily chairmakers aim for the center of mass when locating the mortises for the side horizontal members (fig. 14). This is mandatory in turned chairs with round posts, but in shaved chairs with posts that are rectangular in cross section, several options for locating the mortises are available. To avoid having the through-tenoned arms and side seat rails and stretchers emerge too close to the outer corners of the front posts, one plots the mortises slightly inside of the absolute centerlines of the rear surfaces of the front posts. The result of these adjustments is relatively minor, but it seems that most period chairmakers avoided this problem by making their seat plans more squarish, by making the tops of their front posts wider, or by making their horizontal members smaller in diameter. In the case of the modern armchair (fig. 13), concern for where the arm mortises might emerge led us to reduce the diameter of the arm tenons from 1 inch to ¾ inch.

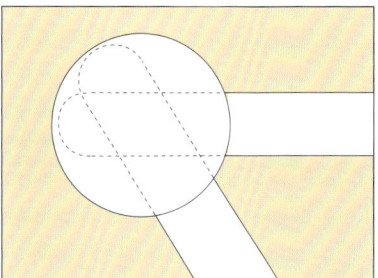 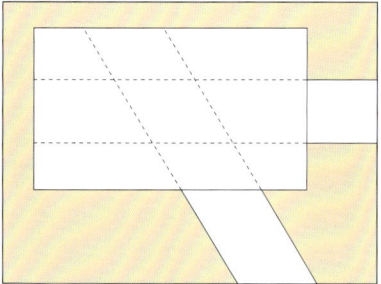

Figure 14 Layout diagrams of side stretchers entering posts. The left diagram shows stretcher tenons entering a turned post, where aiming the mortises for the center of mass is obligatory. The right diagram shows a similar approach in a chair with rectangular shaved posts, wherein the side joints are located at the center of mass, rather than the mathematical center of the rear face of the post. This practice ensures that the through-tenons on the front faces of the posts do not exit too near the front corners.

Figure 15 John D. Alexander Jr., armchair, Baltimore, Maryland, 1998. Oak. H. 38", W. 24¾", D. 18½". (Private collection; photo, Gavin Ashworth.) Many early European prints and paintings depict shaved slat-back chairs as slender as this example. Second or upper rear stretchers are rare in Anglo-American chairs but common in Continental examples.

Shortly after completing the armchair, Alexander began work on another example to explore other techniques that period makers may have used in the construction of shaved chairs (fig. 15). Many of the innovations on the second armchair derive from a classic post-and-rung chair Alexander has made for forty years (see fig. 36). The posts are narrower; the frame is 3 inches wider inside the posts; the frame has two rows of stretchers; the rear posts have severely tapering "heels" or relief cuts on the front faces below the seat; the slats have two pins in each joint; the seat height is 17¾ inches; and the rungs are ⅝ inch in diameter.

This second armchair utilized the same placement of the side tenons as the first armchair. A refinement in the second armchair is tilting the blade arms slightly upward on their outer edges, so that they meet the sitter's elbows exactly. An important aspect of this frame reflects the side elevation of the Thompson armchair illustrated in figure 20. The pronounced, tapering relief on the front faces of the rear posts below the seat automatically enhances the layback created by the relief on the front faces of the rear posts above the seat. That is, tapering the bottoms of the rear posts draws them farther in when the chair is assembled, and the back above the seat is thereby pitched back at a greater angle relative to the seat. One could not have anticipated many of these refinements if one had not made these two armchairs.

Study Side Chairs Based on European Precedents
After constructing the two study armchairs, Alexander made four side chairs that are variations on the small, one-slat shaved chair seen in late medieval and renaissance European art. The one-slat design, most familiar to Americans from Shaker turned sewing and dining chairs, is cheaper than a two- or three-slat format and makes for a more portable chair. While the seat was not exclusive to women, it certainly seems to have been associated with women's work. The one-slat design also has strong ergonomic advantages. Unlike two- or three-slat designs that require hewn layback for comfort, one-slat chairs support the lumbar region but leave the thoracic and cervical regions free to relax slightly back. They seem to have been ubiquitous in early modern Europe, but the authors have not located an extant early example in any European museum. The four study chairs presented here are an important means to assess how such chairs were made and how they functioned.

The first study chair (fig. 16) has through-tenons both fore and aft and side to side. The front and rear posts have through-tapered sides. The posts had a high moisture content at the time of assembly. All the tenons now protrude far beyond the outsides of the posts. Some observers of European prints and paintings have assumed that chairs with protruding tenons are purely the result of joint failure and wracking. However, if chairs with through-tenons are assembled with wet posts, the posts will shrink far down the tenons. If the posts are oriented with the growth rings running from side to side, the shrinkage down the side-to-side tenons will be more extreme. However, wracking, or gradual loosening of the joints with use, can aggravate tenon protrusion. It seems that attempts to tighten the joints of some period chairs later on by driving the posts down the rungs were also

Figure 16   John D. Alexander Jr., side chair, Baltimore, Maryland, 2000. Red oak and white oak. H. 27⁷⁄₈", W. 18½", D. 14⁷⁄₈". (Private collection; photo, Gavin Ashworth.) Aspects of this chair's design were derived from the Holbein painting illustrated in fig. 7.

Figure 17 John D. Alexander Jr., side chair, Baltimore, Maryland, 2000. Red oak and white oak. H. 27⅝", W. 18⅜", D. 14½". (Private collection; photo, Gavin Ashworth.) All of the study side chairs made by Alexander have through-tapered rear posts. The slats and tenons do not protrude as much as those on the chair illustrated in fig. 16, and the slats are parallel to the front faces of the rear posts. On many period chairs, the slats are centered on the inner faces of the rear posts.

Figure 18 John D. Alexander Jr., side chair, Baltimore, Maryland, 2000. Red oak and white oak. H. 27", W. 19¼", D. 15". (Private collection; photo, Gavin Ashworth.) The design of this example was influenced by chairs with shaved rear posts and turned front posts in Lyon's article (Irving P. Lyon, "Square-Post Slat-Back Chairs," *Antiques* 20, no. 4 [October 1931]: 213, fig. 8; 216, fig. 20).

common. The tenons of this first study chair are still secured in their mortises, save for the slat, which is somewhat loose but cannot escape. By contrast, the second study side chair (fig. 17) was made with through-tenons fore and aft but blind tenons side to side. The front posts are straight-sided, but the rear posts are through-tapered on the sides. The chair was assembled with posts that were drier at the time of assembly than those of the first chair. Almost all the through-tenons now protrude only slightly beyond the outsides of the posts. The tenons of this second chair are secure in their mortises. The third study side chair (fig. 18) combines a shaved back with turned front posts. This combination appears in some period sources and is challenging to understand. However, given the subtle levels of prestige attributed to different kinds of workmanship, it is probable that turned front posts slightly elevated the market value of such chairs. Another possibility is that round front posts were thought to be less likely to snag clothing.

Alexander and woodworking student Nathaniel Krause constructed a fourth chair to explore yet another detail seen in European art, a top slat set in open bridle joints (fig. 19). This construction seems counterintuitive, in that one would expect the slat to wrench out of the open joints during use. The open mortises obviously require that the slat be pinned. This chair has a slat secured with two pins in each joint. The locations of the pins were staggered to avoid splitting the posts, and the pins were driven at an angle, to force the slat down into the joints. This chair has not been subjected to use, and the joint has not been "tested," but the many period depictions of such slats suggest that it was not regarded as precarious.

These four study chairs provide some important provisional ideas about the one-slat side chair. First, if the horizontal components are dry or below ambient moisture content at the time of assembly, such chairs could be made with posts that had relatively high moisture content. Second, projection of through-tenons caused by wet posts receding down the horizontal

Figure 19 John D. Alexander Jr. and Nathaniel Krause, side chair, Baltimore, Maryland, 1998. Red oak; cotton canvas tape, and paint. H. 25¾", W. 15½", D. 13". (Private collection; photo, Gavin Ashworth.)

members as they dry is greater when the tenons are driven through the growth ring plane of the posts. Third, the low seat height of 14½ inches is advantageous for using the chair for multiple types of work. A modern seat height of 16½ or 17½ inches is too high. The pre-1700 average seat height of about 21 inches would have made the contrast between work-height seats and regular seats all the more apparent. Fourth, the distance between the rear seat rung and the slat seems less critical to the ergonomic success of the design than seat height. Most one-slat side chairs in period illustrations seem to have slats about 8 inches above the rear seat rung. Narrower or broader slats may have helped in adjusting where the slat hit the lumbar region of shorter or taller people. Fifth, the heavier weight of chairs with posts that tapered from broad bases to narrow tops is offset by the greater stability of such frames. The heavier bottoms do not seem to have reflected a belief that they would wear longer or would be less susceptible to rot or insect infestation.

Shaved Chairs with Parts and Construction Evoking Joined Chairs
A chair with a history of ownership by Rev. William Thompson of Braintree, Massachusetts, is one of two New England examples reminiscent of joined or wainscot chairs (fig. 20). The Thompson chair displays an extraordinary side elevation on the rear posts, which are hewn away above and below the level of the seat; the hewing below the seat constitutes the "heels" alluded to above in connection with the second study armchair (fig. 15). The back posts taper from 2¼ inches deep at the seat to 1⅛ inch deep at the top. Some loss at the bottom of the rear posts, associated with a later conversion of the chair to a rocker, makes it difficult to determine if the same amount of taper once existed below the seat. Currently the bottoms of the posts are 1⅜ inch deep. If the bottoms extended two more inches, the posts would have achieved the same 1⅛ inch depth seen at the tops of the posts. This dramatic tapering on the side elevations of the posts resembles that on the posts

Figure 20 Armchair, probably Braintree, Massachusetts, 1650–1700. Oak and ash. H. 34 3/8" (without rockers), W. 23 5/8", D. 18". (Courtesy, Concord Museum, Concord, Mass.) This chair displays severe tapering of the front and back faces of the rear posts above and below the seat but no taper on the sides. The slats are remarkably shallow in height and have discrete, arc-shaped cuts at the ends.

of some joined chairs. The flat scroll arms of the Thompson chair certainly have a distant relationship to those of French *caqueteuse* joined armchairs, which were influential in England. The arms of the Thompson chair are through-tenoned at the rear, and vertical tenons worked on the front posts emerge through the tops of the arms. These arm tenons are all pinned, as are the top and bottom slats.[13]

The so-called Wayland armchair, whose present location is unknown, is unquestionably the most joiner-like of the early New England shaved chairs (fig. 21). Remarkably, the Wayland chair has a back frame with three cross rails with rectangular mortise-and-tenon joints, combined with a shaved seat rail and two lower stretchers. The three back rails and the upper portions of the back posts are run with scratch-stock moldings of the sort associated with joined furniture. The arms have a vertical scroll profile with a rear scallop underneath, like those of joined chairs. As in many joined armchairs, the front posts are dramatically shaved away on the insides above the seat so that they are as narrow as the vertical scroll arms at the tops.

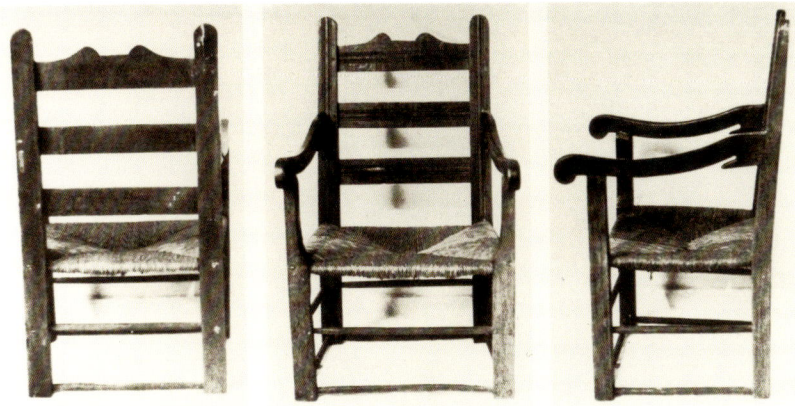

Figure 21 Armchair, eastern Massachusetts, 1675–1725, illustrated in Irving P. Lyon, "Square-Post Slat-Back Chairs," *Antiques* 20, no. 4 (October 1931): 211, fig. 3. This chair has no provenance, but it seems early in date and is in the English tradition. Its posts are tapered in a manner similar to those of the Thompson chair (fig. 20). The three back rails are parallel to the front faces of the rear posts and are pinned, but they are not flush with the front faces of the posts. A central lobe may have broken off the center of the upper back rail.

Figure 22 Armchair, probably Kingston, New York, 1650–1725. Oak. H. 37 3/8", W. 26", D. 18". (Courtesy, Senate House State Historic Site, Kingston, New York, New York State Department of Parks, Recreation and Historic Preservation; photo, Gavin Ashworth.) Although this chair has no history, it may have been collected in the Kingston area early in the twentieth century, when the Senate House functioned as a local historical society. The protruding tenons are the most pronounced seen in any early American shaved chair.

The rest of the Wayland chair's frame conforms to the practices associated with shaved chairs. The rear posts were hewn to profile. All the fore-and-aft round seat rails and stretchers have through-tenoned joints, while all the side-to-side seat rails and stretchers have blind mortises. Ultimately one has to wonder why the maker of this chair did not simply make a full-blown joined armchair. Nothing more about this chair is found in Lyon's papers, and the three photographs published in 1931 are the only record of it.[14]

Lyon published four of the New England armchairs illustrated here in 1931, but four additional examples have emerged in the last two decades. The shaved armchair illustrated in figure 22 is the only example that might

Figure 23 Detail of the right arm on the armchair illustrated in fig. 22. (Photo, Gavin Ashworth.) The maker used a drawshave to shape the rounded ends. The arms are pinned to prevent the arms from rotating in their mortises.

Figure 24 Armchair, Sandwich, Massachusetts, 1719. Maple and ash. H. 36¾". (Brian Cullity, *"A cubberd, four joyne stools & other smalle things": The Material Culture of Plymouth Colony and Silversmiths of Plymouth, Cape Cod and Nantucket* [Sandwich, Mass.: Heritage Plantation of Sandwich, 1994], p. 121.)

have been made by an artisan working in the Dutch tradition. It is made entirely of oak, whereas most other shaved chairs have posts made of diffuse porous hardwoods and horizontal members made of ring porous hardwoods. The rear posts are relieved on their front faces above the seat, but the front posts are not tapered. All the joints are through-tenoned, and the protrusion of the tenons is extreme. This feature, which appears on chairs depicted in many northern European prints and paintings, suggests that the posts of the armchair had high moisture content at the time of assembly. The blade arms with rounded ends are another detail associated with northern European seating. Several New York turned slat-back armchairs in the Dutch tradition also share that detail (fig. 23). The usual blade arm seen in New England slat-backs has arc-shaped or concave cuts on the ends executed with the drawknife, like those on the study armchairs (figs. 13, 15); however, some of the Dutch-looking New York slat-back armchairs have arms with concave end cuts as well.[15]

Two shaved armchairs first published by decorative arts scholar Brian Cullity have histories of ownership in Sandwich, Massachusetts (figs. 24, 25). Both are probably late eighteenth century in date, if the slats and the finials are any indication. The chairs feature curved arms and bent and hewn front posts with cutbacks on the inner faces above the seat to more easily accommodate the sitter. The chair illustrated in figure 24 is virtually complete and has two rows of stretchers. To judge by the present seat height, it may have lost three inches at the bottom. The other chair (fig. 25) has prob-

Figure 25 Armchair, Sandwich, Massachusetts, 1775–1800. Maple and oak. H. 39⅞", W. 23", D. 23". (Benjamin Nye Homestead and Museum, Nye Family of America Association, East Sandwich, Massachusetts; photo, Gavin Ashworth.) The Nye armchair has lost about 6 inches at the bottom and probably has lost a tier of side stretchers and a rear stretcher. The arms are of a form associated with the third quarter of the eighteenth century, making this an extremely late shaved chair.

ably lost a tier of stretchers at the bottom. This example, although modeled with shaving, is strikingly reminiscent of simple, rush-seated joined chairs made in many New England regions during the late eighteenth century. It is unclear if both these chairs were made in the same shop tradition.[16]

A more recent discovery is a large armchair that belonged to Jacobus Nearpass (1715–1805), a Prussian immigrant who settled in Montague, New Jersey, in the mountainous Delaware Water Gap, in the 1740s (fig. 26).

Figure 26 Armchair, Montague, New Jersey, 1740–1780. Maple and ash. H. 51¼", W. 23½", D. 21½". (Chipstone Foundation; photo, Gavin Ashworth.) High-backed chairs of this size almost certainly date after 1725. The frame appears never to have had paint or a resin coating, and the inner bark seat may be the original one.

While later generations of the family thought that Nearpass made the chair himself, nothing about the object suggests Germanic workmanship. The chair is extremely large and displays early baroque proportions. The arms are flat scrolls, much like those of the Thompson chair (fig. 20). All the joints are through-tenoned, and the rear posts are accentuated by slight hewing of the front faces above the seat, and the chair never had a coat of paint or finish. A noteworthy aspect of the frame is the extraordinary 14-inch distance between the seat and the arms. This suggests that such chairs were used with cushions; otherwise the sitter's arms would have been forced up into an uncomfortable position.[17]

Plimoth Plantation Replica Chairs

Unlike the study chairs made by Alexander, shaved chairs made by Robert Tarule, Ted Curtin, Peter Follansbee, and others for use in the re-created 1627 village at Plimoth Plantation have received rigorous use and abuse by interpreters, both inside and outside the houses. The floors of the houses are tamped earth, and rot or insect infestation at the bottoms of the posts have required that some chairs be cut down in height. It seems that chair posts made of ring porous hardwoods (other than white oak) rot more quickly than those with posts made of diffuse porous hardwoods like maple. This may account for the preference for posts made of woods like maple or birch, rather than red oak, ash, or hickory.

Another problem is that the chairs rest on uneven floors. When chairs are sat on under those circumstances, the frames experience uneven stress on the joints because one or two posts are not in contact with the ground. Joints that are stressed in this manner often fail in specific ways, notably shearing of rungs, seat rails, or slats immediately adjacent to the posts. This

Figure 27 Photo showing the replacement of the broken front rung of a reproduction chair made by Robert Tarule for Plimoth Plantation. (Courtesy, Plimoth Plantation; photo, Peter Follansbee.) The broken front rung was removed by boring the tenons. The new rung is being driven through the front post toward the opposite mortise. The replacement rung must be pinned or back-wedged to remain in position.

kind of breakage requires replacement of broken parts. Through-tenoned rungs or seat rails are easily replaced. The broken rung is driven out, and a new one is inserted from the outside (fig. 27). Something like this procedure may have been followed in the old repairs to the Rochester chair arms and side stretcher (fig. 12).

Other damage involves scorching or charring (fig. 28). Period artworks reveal that low-seated chairs were used during cooking, as might be expected when women were moving and lifting heavy kettles off cranes, pushing skillets across the floor of the hearth, frying on griddles, or stirring pots. One chair at Plimoth Plantation was left too close to the fire and experienced severe burns. The burns were not enough to retire the object, but in the past, extreme charring might have led to replacement of parts or to

Figure 28 Peter Follansbee, side chair, Plymouth, Massachusetts, 1998. Maple and oak. H. 32 1/4", W. 19", D. 15 1/2". (Courtesy, Plimoth Plantation; photo, Gavin Ashworth.) This chair was charred while in use near a hearth. It has been cleaned but has not required any replacements. Undoubtedly many period chairs continued to be used after experiencing far more extensive damage than this.

discarding chairs altogether. Certainly this kind of damage helps to explain why low side chairs have not survived in great numbers.

The swiftness with which damage accrues on such chairs is remarkable. Most of these chairs have been in use only five to ten years, during the eight months a year that Plimoth Plantation is open to the public. They have almost all sustained damage, especially to the woven seats. At the same time, it is important to remember that even a damaged chair, or one whose joints have failed and begun to wrack, can be held together for an extraordinarily long time by the vegetable fiber seat alone. Whether these seats were made of twisted rush (usually called "flags" in New England) or of strips of flat or twisted inner bark (possibly called "bast" or "bass" in the seventeenth century), they were incredibly strong and could withstand considerable torsion as a failed chair swiveled around in its joints.

The Broader Tradition of Shaved Chairs in North America
Shaved chairs from other regions of colonial North America display structural variations comparable in variety to those seen in New England and New York examples. Many shaved post-and-rung chairs with round through-tenons from French-settled areas of Canada survive. Also relatively common are Spanish colonial shaved chairs with rectangular through-tenons and to a lesser degree round through-tenons. Four chairs from the

Canadian Maritimes, Delaware, and Virginia give some indication of the range of technical and stylistic diversity seen in these later traditions and suggest the potential for future research.[18]

In 1986 furniture scholar Walter Peddle found the shaved armchair illustrated in figure 29 in the small fishing village of Keels, in the Bonavista Bay area of Newfoundland, about one hundred miles northwest of St. John's. At first glance the Keels chair appears remarkably similar to the Rochester armchair (fig. 12) in having two slats and shaved arms. The Keels chair has a number of features not widely seen in earlier New England examples, however, and it probably dates 1800 to 1825. The slats have scalloped upper edges with a pronounced center cusp. This contour seems to reflect the scalloped crests of early baroque banister backs or the slats of earlier turned slat-backs. The scribed hearts and incised rickrack carving on the slats, while

Figure 29 Armchair, Keels, Newfoundland, 1800–1825. Birch and pine. H. 34", W. 26½", D. 14½". (Courtesy, The Rooms—Provincial Museum, St. John's, Newfoundland, Canada, Walter and Sally Peddle Outport Furniture Collection.) The joints are secured with small wooden pins, supplemented with nails in the seat rails. The rear posts taper above and below the seat in imitation of neoclassical joined seating. Chairs with board seats nailed or pegged to the seat rails commonly appear in vernacular seating from the British Isles, Ireland, and Canada.

Figure 30 Armchair, Topsfield, Massachusetts, 1725–1800. Maple and pine. H. 40", W. 26¼", D. 18¾". (Courtesy, Parson Capen House, Topsfield Historical Society, Topsfield, Massachusetts; photo, Gavin Ashworth.) The chair is stamped "D. LAKE." Its frame combines joined, turned, and shaved work. The seat rails run side to side and the stretchers have rectangular mortise-and-tenon joints. All other joints have round mortises and tenons.

attributed by Peddle to Irish influence, also convey something of the complexity of fancy painting or carving seen on contemporaneous urban seating. The stretchers, seat rails, and arms oversailing the front posts are square in cross section, even though the through-tenons on their ends are round. They may have been intended to evoke early neoclassical joined seating, an impression that would have been stronger when the original reddish wash and brown varnish were new. The maker probably used birch as the primary wood because it resembles mahogany when stained.[19]

An armchair that descended in the Lake family of Topsfield, Massachusetts, is coeval with the Keels example and displays many similar traits (fig. 30). Like most close stools, the Lake chair probably had a stopper in the seat and an accompanying cushion. The seat board and the shelf for a chamber pot rest on the rails, requiring the maker to shave the top surfaces of the round side stretchers to accommodate the boards. Perhaps the most archaic aspect of the frame is the tapering on three sides of the rear posts above the seat. Undoubtedly this was what made Lyon think that the chair was seventeenth century in date. The turned arms may have been inspired by those on early-nineteenth-century Windsors.[20]

Figure 31 Side chair, probably Nova Scotia, Canada, 1820–1870. Birch and ash. H. 29⅞", W. 14¾", D. 17¾". (Courtesy, Plimoth Plantation; photo, Gavin Ashworth.) The maker used billets, or blanks, approximately 3½ inch square for the posts. He probably began by striking lines first to establish the bottom part of the posts, then to establish the skews above the seat. The diameters of the stretchers are much greater than those of the tenons worked on their ends. The maker used a drawknife to shave the ends of the stretchers to conform to the diameter of the mortises. Because the posts were relatively wet at the time of assembly, they shrank around the irregular tenons, binding them securely.

The Canadian chair illustrated in figure 31 has severely hewn rear posts and displays very rough workmanship. The rear posts taper on all four sides above the seat and splay to the side and to the rear. French-Canadian shaved chairs appear to survive in greater numbers than those attributed to other ethnic groups in Canada; however, some scholars believe that some traits of Canadian seating formerly regarded as French may reflect Irish influence.[21]

A chair that may be Swedish in derivation descended in the Robinson family of Wilmington, Delaware (fig. 32). Its design combines early baroque, high-backed proportions with late baroque Germanic detailing, including a scalloped crest, two vasiform banisters, and rectangular stretchers. The stretchers resemble the sawn balusters found on staircases and closet ventilators in the Delaware Valley.

The Robinson chair is idiosyncratic within the Germanic-American traditions of the mid-Atlantic region but remains squarely within the shaved chair tradition. The only major difference is the use of extensive sawing for the baluster forms and perhaps the use of rectangular tenons. However, the frame definitely was made with extensive hewing and shaving. By contrast, the frames of most contemporaneous joined seating in the region were sawn from planks.

Another permutation in the shaved chair tradition is represented by the so-called Moses Hall examples from Virgilina, Virginia, which probably represent the work of an African American artisan (fig. 33). These chairs

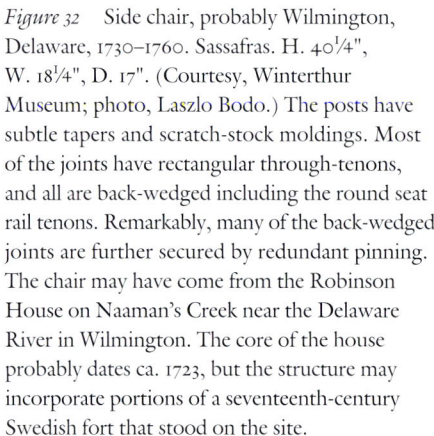

Figure 32 Side chair, probably Wilmington, Delaware, 1730–1760. Sassafras. H. 40¼", W. 18¼", D. 17". (Courtesy, Winterthur Museum; photo, Laszlo Bodo.) The posts have subtle tapers and scratch-stock moldings. Most of the joints have rectangular through-tenons, and all are back-wedged including the round seat rail tenons. Remarkably, many of the back-wedged joints are further secured by redundant pinning. The chair may have come from the Robinson House on Naaman's Creek near the Delaware River in Wilmington. The core of the house probably dates ca. 1723, but the structure may incorporate portions of a seventeenth-century Swedish fort that stood on the site.

Figure 33 Side chair, Virgilina, Virginia, ca. 1903. Maple. H. 37", W. 17", D. 17¼". (Courtesy, Winterthur Museum, gift of Robert F. Trent.) The Moses Hall chairs were discovered by Halifax, Virginia, dealer Robert Pottage, who began acquiring them from local families in the 1960s. The chairs have flat riven slats and were never painted.

were made circa 1903 to furnish a meetinghall built by a chapter of the Grand United Order of Moses, an African American fraternal society. Despite the progressive social aspirations of the organization, the chairs are conservative, vernacular objects. The maker shaved and burnished the posts and stretchers to make the chairs resemble turned seating. The ears at the tops of the posts may have been influenced by the fully relieved, dramatically bent backs on classic Southern post-and-rung chairs or the ears occasionally found on early-nineteenth-century Windsors.[22]

Figure 34 Settin' chair illustrated in Henry Glassie, *Pattern in the Material Folk Culture of the Eastern United States* (Philadelphia: University of Pennsylvania Press, 1968), p. 230, fig. 66c. (Reprinted with permission of the University of Pennsylvania Press.) Glassie photographed this shaved chair while conducting field research in Gum Spring, Louisa County, Virginia, in 1966. Although he recalls seeing similar examples at that time, shaved settin' chairs are rare.

Antiquarianism and Art in Twentieth-Century Shaved Chairs

The premier expression of late post-and-rung seating in North America is the so-called "settin' chair" made throughout the American South (fig. 34). A few all-shaved examples are known, but they are rare compared with the characteristic model with turned posts. One of the most accomplished examples was reputedly found in an abandoned cabin in Burnsville, Yancey County, North Carolina (fig. 35). Its rear posts are shaved on their front faces above the seat, radically bent, and set on the bias to allow the maker

Figure 35 Side chair, probably western North Carolina, 1860–1920. Oak and ash. H. 30½", W. 18¾", D. 16¾". (Private collection; photo, Gavin Ashworth.) This chair was found in an abandoned cabin in Burnsville, Yancey County, in western North Carolina.

Figure 36 John D. Alexander Jr., side chair, Baltimore, Maryland, 2005. White oak and red oak. H. 33¼", W. 17½", D. 16¾". (Private collection; photo, Gavin Ashworth.)

to set the slats at different angles. The slats are surprisingly ergonomic, supporting the lumbar and thoracic regions of the back.

Because the seats of settin' chairs are typically level and made of inner bark, they do not provide an ergonomic slope. Although the practice has not been documented, some makers may have trimmed the bottoms of the rear posts to provide layback. Late-nineteenth- and twentieth-century photographs commonly depict sitters tipping back on the rear legs for comfort.[23]

With the assistance of wood scientist Dr. R. Bruce Hoadley, Alexander discovered the optimal moisture content for all the components of this seating form. In the chair illustrated in figure 36, the technology, lightness, and resilience of shaved post-and-rung construction were pushed to the limits of the medium. Alexander's classic chair design has also come to symbolize scholarly investigation of traditional green woodworking. As the modern seating illustrated in this article attests, the replication of period technologies offers insights into surviving objects and the people who made and used them.

ACKNOWLEDGMENTS For their help in researching and writing this article, the authors thank the late Joyce Alexander, Laszlo Bodo, Johanna Brown, Dennis Carr, Anne Cassidy, Sarah Fayen, Mark Ferguson, Pilar Garro, Henry Glassie, Norman J. Isler, Peter Kenny, Nathaniel Krause, Ethan Lasser, Robert Leath, Abigail Linville, Erin McGough, Susan Newton, Walter Peddle, Deanna Preston, Adrienne Sage, Nancy Sazama, Robert Blair St. George, Harry Mack Truax II, Dante Vallance, John Robert Vincent, Gerald W. R. Ward, and David Wood.

1. In 2008 John D. Alexander legally changed his gender and his name to Jennie Alexander. For the history of housing and other outbuildings at Plimoth Plantation, see James W. Baker, "As Time Will Serve: The Evolution of Plimoth Plantation's Recreated Architecture," *Old-Time New England* 74, no. 261 (Spring 1996): 48–74.

2. For more on early woodworking technology, see Herbert Cescinsky, *Early English Furniture and Woodwork*, 2 vols. (London: George Routledge and Sons, 1922), 1: 17–31, 103–75, 193–210, 231–370, 2: 1–209; Herbert Cescinsky, *English Furniture from Gothic to Sheraton* (Grand Rapids, Mich.: Dean-Hicks Co., 1929), pp. 1–31, 59–110; Robert Wemyss Symonds, "The Craft of Furniture Making in the XVIth and XVIIth Centuries," *Connoisseur* 99, no. 427 (March 1937): 130–37; Robert Wemyss Symonds, "Craft of the Joiner in Medieval England," *Connoisseur* 118, no. 501 (September 1946): 17–23 and 118, no. 502 (December 1946): 98–104; and Victor Chinnery, *Oak Furniture: The British Tradition* (Woodbridge, Suffolk: Antique Collectors' Club, 1979).

3. For more on the technology of post-and-rung chairmaking, see John D. Alexander Jr., *Make a Chair from a Tree: An Introduction to Working Green Wood*, rev. ed. (1978; Mendham N.J.: Astragal Press, 1994); and John D. Alexander Jr., *Make a Chair from a Tree* (DVD) (Baltimore: Green Woodworking, 1999). For more on techniques common to both shaved and turned chairs, see Peter Follansbee, "A Seventeenth-Century Carpenter's Conceit: The Waldo Family Joined Great Chair," *American Furniture*, edited by Luke Beckerdite (Hanover, N.H.: University Press of New England for the Chipstone Foundation, 1998), pp. 197–214. A seventeenth-century reference suggests that turners may have made both shaved chairs and turned chairs. On February 20, 1615, the Turners Company of London "directed that the makers of chairs about the City, who were strangers and foreigners, were to bring . . . [their chairs] to the Hall to be searched according to the ordinances. When they were thus brought and searched, they were to be bought by the Master and Wardens at a price fixed by them, which was 6s per dozen for plain matted chairs and 7s per dozen for turned matted chairs." A. C. Stanley-Stone, *The Worshipful Company of Turners of London: Its Origin and History* (London: Lindley-Jones & Brother, 1925), p. 121.

4. Benno M. Forman, "German Influences in Pennsylvania Furniture," in Scott T. Swank et al., *Arts of the Pennsylvania Germans* (New York: W. W. Norton & Co., 1983), pp. 107–12.

5. Court cases shed light on trade disputes in seventeenth-century London. In 1633 the court summoned the "Master & Warden of the comp[an]y of Turners" and the "Master & Warden of the Comp[an]y of Joyners" and noted:

> It appeareth that the Comp[an]y of Turners be grieved that the Comp[an]y of Joyners assume unto themselves the art of turning to the wrong of the Turners. It appeareth to us that the arts of turning and joining are two several & distinct trades and we conceive it very inconvenient that either of these trades should encroach upon the other and we find that the turners have constantly for the most part turned bed posts & feet of joined stools for the Joyners and of late some Joyners who never used to turn them on bedposts and stool feet have set on work in their houses some poor decayed turners & of them have learned the feate & art of turning which they could not do before. And it appeareth unto us by custom that the art of turning bedposts feet of tables joined stools do properly belong to the trade of a turner and not to the art of a Joyner and whatsoever is done with the foot as have treddle or wheele for turning of any wood we are of the opinion and do find that it properly belongs to the Turners and we find that the Turners ought not to use the [mortising] gage or gages, grouffe [groove] plaine or plough plaine or mortising chisels or any of them for that the same do belong to the Joyners Trade.

Henry Laverock Phillips, *Annals of the Worshipful Company of Joiners of the City of London* (London: privately printed, 1925), pp. 27–28.

Similarly, a 1632 decision regarding a suit between the joiners and carpenters led to a long and convoluted attempt to separate the two trades. E. B. Jupp, *An Historical Account of the Worshipful Company of Carpenters* (London: Pickering & Chatto, 1887), pp. 295–302. Chinnery cited these cases in *Oak Furniture*, pp. 42–43.

6. See a brief notice of French royal protection in Pierre Verlet, *French Royal Furniture* (London: Barrie and Rockliff, 1963), pp. 3–7. Before Colbert set up the *Garde-meuble* system under Louis XIV, French monarchs had offered informal protection and patronage to artists and artisans by housing them in the ground storey of the Louvre. Discussions of guilds in various German cities are found throughout Heinrich Kreisel, *Das Kunst des deutschen Möbels: Erster Band von den Anfängen bis zum Hochbarock* (Munich: C. H. Beck, 1963).

7. In 1608 the Turners Company of London instructed:

> The Master & Wardens together with so many of the Assistants as they shall appoint shall four times in the year or oftener if necessary at convenient times, enter into the Shops, Sollars, Cellars, Booths and Warehouses of any person using the Misterie who shall make, buy, or sell anything thereunto appertaining within the City or suburbs, either Free or Foreign, there to search & survey all manner of Bushel measures, Wood Wares, Works, and also their Journeymen, Servants & apprentices and all their staffs & workmanship and if in their search they shall find any shovels, scoops, busheltrees, washing bowls, chairs, wheels, pails, trays, truggers, wares, wooden measures or any other commodities belonging to the Misterie slightly or not substantially & workmanlike wrought with good and sound stuff or any other matter of abuse or misdemeanor, either in Master, Mistress, Apprentice, or Servants, it shall be lawful for those making the search, to seize and carry away the same faulty & deceitful wares, into their Common Hall, that the same may be considered & defaced if cause shall appear and the Master, Wardens & Assistants or the greater part of them may assess a reasonable fine upon the offender so as it exceed not 40 shillings for any one offense, so that others may be warned from making or selling deceitful ware to the discredit of the Misterie, and if any whether free or foreign, be found disobedient to the Master Wardens and Assistants or any three of them in any of their searches, he or they shall be fined not exceeding 40 shillings for every offence.

Stanley-Stone, *Worshipful Company of Turners,* pp. 264–65.

In 1631 London turner Nehemiah Willington bought shovel trees and trenchers that may have been made outside the city. Paul S. Seaver, *Wallington's World: A Puritan Artisan in Seventeenth-Century London* (Stanford, Calif.: Stanford University Press, 1985), p. 78. Among earlier-twentieth-century studies that have been influential on later scholars of green woodworking are George Sturt, *The Wheelwright's Shop* (Cambridge: Cambridge University Press, 1923); Walter Rose, *The Village Carpenter* (Cambridge: Cambridge University Press, 1937); H. Edlin, *Woodland Crafts in Britain: An Account of the Traditional Uses of Trees and Timbers in the British Countryside* (London: B. T. Batsford, 1949); and J. Geraint Jenkins, *Traditional Country Craftsmen* (London: Routledge and Kegan Paul, 1965). More recent monographs include Anton Viires, *Woodworking in Estonia: Historical Survey* (Jerusalem: Israel Program for Scientific Research, 1969); Fred Lambert, *Tools and Devices for Coppice Crafts* (Powys, Wales: Centre for Alternative Technology, 1977); Charles F. Hummel, *With Hammer in Hand: The Dominy Craftsmen of East Hampton, New York* (Charlottesville: University Press of Virginia, 1968); Raymond Tabor, *Traditional Woodland Crafts* (London: B. T. Batsford, 1994); Cecil A. Hewett, *The Development of Carpentry, 1200–1700: An Essex Study* (Newton Abbot: David & Charles, 1969); Cecil A. Hewett, *English Historic Carpentry* (London: Phillimore & Co., 1980); W. L. Goodman, *The History of Woodworking Tools* (London: G. Bell and Sons, 1964); and Robert Tarule, *The Artisan of Ipswich: Craftsmanship and Community in Colonial New England* (Baltimore: Johns Hopkins University Press, 2004).

8. The literature of the American "settin' chair" is discussed in n. 23 below. The various Canadian shaved chairs are discussed in Jean Palardy, *Les meubles anciens du Canada français* (Paris: Arts et Métiers Graphiques, 1963), nos. 280, 281, 283–91, 306, 318, 319, 323, 324, 326–29, 343–47, 352, 355, 361; W. John McIntyre, "Chairs and Chairmaking in Upper Canada" (master's thesis, University of Delaware, 1975), pp. 100–101; Walter W. Peddle, *The Traditional Furniture of Outport Newfoundland* (St. Johns, Newfoundland: Henry Cuff Publishers, 1983); Michael S. Bird, *Canadian Country Furniture, 1675–1950* (Toronto: Stoddart Publishing Co., 1994), p. 38, fig. 11; p. 153, figs. 159, 161; p. 179, figs. 223, 224; p. 180, fig. 226; p. 272, fig. 450; p. 292,

fig. 493; p. 307, fig. 521; p. 335, fig. 589; Donald Blake Webster, *Rococo to Rustique: Early French-Canadian Furniture in the Royal Ontario Museum* (Toronto: Royal Ontario Museum, 2000), pp. 177–99; and Michel Lessand, *Antique Furniture of Québec: Four Centuries of Furniture Making* (Toronto: McClelland & Stewart, 2002), pp. 126–35. Northern European visual sources consulted include Lilian M. C. Randall, *Images in the Margins of Gothic Manuscripts* (Berkeley: University of California Press, 1966); Linda A. Stone-Ferrier, *Dutch Prints of Daily Life: Mirrors of Life or Masks of Morals?* (Lawrence: Spencer Museum of Art, University of Kansas, 1983), p. 57, cat. no. 6; p. 65, cat. no. 9; p. 125, cat. no. 30; Christopher Brown, *Images of a Golden Past: Dutch Genre Painting of the 17th Century* (New York: Abbeville Press, 1984), pp. 69 and 74; Peter C. Sutton, *Masters of Seventeenth-Century Dutch Genre Painting* (Philadelphia: Philadelphia Museum of Art, 1984), p. 327, pl. 47, cat. no. 111; p. 355, pl. 48, cat. no. 124; Wayne E. Franits, *Paragons of Virtue: Women and Domesticity in Seventeenth-Century Dutch Art* (Cambridge: Cambridge University Press, 1993), p. 49, fig. 31b; p. 189, fig. 168; Michiel C. C. Kersten and Danielle H. A. C. Lokin, *Delft Masters, Vermeer's Contemporaries: Illusion through the Conquest of Light and Space* (Zwolle: Waanders Publishers, 1996), p. 165; *Jan Steen: Painter and Storyteller*, edited by Guido M. C. Jansen (New Haven: Yale University Press, 1996); Eddy de Jong and Ger Luitjen, *Mirror of Everyday Life: Genre Prints in the Netherlands, 1550–1700* (Amsterdam: Rijksmuseum, 1997); Peter C. Sutton, *Pieter de Hooch, 1629–1684* (New Haven: Yale University Press, 1998); *Gerrit Dou, 1613–1675: Master Painter in the Age of Rembrandt*, edited by Arthur K. Wheelock Jr. (New Haven: Yale University Press, 2000); Henk van Os, Jan Piet Filedt Kok, Ger Luijten, and Frits Scholten, *Netherlandish Art, 1400–1600* (Amsterdam: Rijksmuseum, 2000), p. 267; C. Willemijn Fock et al., *Het nederlandse interieur in beeld, 1600–1900* (Zwolle: Waanders, 2001), pp. 143, 152; Mariët Westerman et al., *Art and Home: Dutch Interiors in the Age of Rembrandt* (Denver: Denver Art Museum; Newark, N.J.: Newark Museum, 2001), pp. 33, 49, 58, 69, 99, 108, 125, 140; Wayne Franits, *Dutch Seventeenth-Century Genre Painting: Its Stylistic and Thematic Evolution* (New Haven: Yale University Press, 2004); *Senses and Sins: Dutch Painters of Daily Life in the Seventeenth Century*, edited by Joroen Giltaij (Rotterdam: Hatje Cantz Publishers, 2005), pp. 98, 105, 113, and 185.

9. Irving P. Lyon, "Square-Post Slat-Back Chairs," *Antiques* 20, no. 4 (October 1931): 210–16.

10. Peter Thornton, *The Italian Renaissance Interior, 1400–1600* (New York: Harry N. Abrams, 1991); *At Home in Renaissance Italy*, edited by Marta Ajmar-Wollheim and Flora Dennis (London: Victoria & Albert Museum, 2006); Dora Thornton, *The Scholar in His Study: Ownership and Experience in Renaissance Italy* (New Haven: Yale University Press, 1997); and Elizabeth Currie, *Inside the Renaissance House* (London: Victoria & Albert Museum, 2006). Peter Thornton consistently refers to shaved chairs as "rustic," but the uniformity and occasional elaboration of the Italian chairs across many urban centers suggest that they were a professional urban product.

11. Lyon, "Square-Post Slat-Back Chairs," pp. 210–16, fig. 4. Richard C. Nylander et al., *Beauport: The Sleeper-McCann House* (Boston: Society for the Preservation of New England Antiquities, 1990), pp. 38–46.

12. The Rochester chair belonged to Irving P. Lyon and is discussed in Lyon, "Square-Post Slat-Back Chairs," pp. 210–11, fig. 1.

13. The Thompson chair is discussed in ibid., pp. 210–11, fig. 2; and *The Concord Museum: Decorative Arts from a New England Collection*, edited by David F. Wood (Concord, Mass.: Concord Museum, 1996), p. 58, no. 23. *Caqueteuse* chairs are discussed in Peter Thornton, *Seventeenth-Century Interior Decoration in England, France and Holland* (New Haven: Yale University Press, 1978), pp. 186–87; and Chinnery, *Oak Furniture*, pp. 242, 244, 245, 451–54, 461–67.

14. The Wayland chair is discussed in Lyon, "Square-Post Slat-Back Chairs," p. 211, fig. 3.

15. The authors thank Peter Kenny for bringing the Senate House armchair to their attention. A New York slat-back armchair with convex ends on the shaved arms is on loan to the Walt Whitman House in Hempstead, New York, from the New York State Department of Parks, Recreation, and Historic Preservation (1974.26). The writers thank Erik Gronning for bringing that chair to their attention. Gronning is preparing a major study of New York slat-back chairs in the Dutch tradition.

16. Brian Cullity, *"A Cubberd, four joyne stools & other smalle things": The Material Culture of Plymouth Colony and Silver and Silversmiths of Plymouth, Cape Cod and Nantucket* (Sandwich, Mass.: Heritage Plantation of Sandwich, 1994), p. 121, figs. 127, 128.

17. Accession file 2004.13, Chipstone Foundation, Milwaukee, Wisconsin.

18. Lonn Taylor and Dessa Bokides, *New Mexican Furniture, 1600–1900: The Origins, Survival, and Revival of Furniture Making in the Hispanic Southwest* (Santa Fe: Museum of New Mexico Press, 1987).

19. Chairs with scalloped top edges to the crest rails and turned arms first appear in various regional centers circa 1810–1820. Mid-eighteenth-century banister-back and slat-back chairs associated with Massachusetts and New York also have scalloped upper edges with central cusps on the crests or slats. Shaved and bent posts first appear in Windsors circa 1805–1810 and were transferred to post-and-rung chairs somewhat later. For more on these developments, see Nancy Goyne Evans, *American Windsor Chairs* (Winterthur, Del.: Winterthur Museum, 1996). For more on the Keels chair, see Walter Peddle, *The Dynamics of Outport Furniture Design: Adaptation and Culture* (Gatineau, Québec: Canadian Museum of Civilization, History Division, 2002), p. 10.

20. Lyon, "Square-Post Slat-Back Chairs," fig. 30.

21. This chair was purchased in New England and has no provenance.

22. Research by Abigail Linville of the Museum of Early Southern Decorative Arts in Winston-Salem, North Carolina, suggests that the Moses Hall chairs date from the early twentieth century. See also Holly Hope, *For the Memorable Fight: Mosaic Templars of America Headquarters Building* (Little Rock: Arkansas Historic Preservation Program, 2004). Robert Pottage of Halifax, Virginia, brought the chairs to the attention of Robert F. Trent in the late 1970s. Trent donated examples to Winterthur Museum and the Museum of Early Southern Decorative Arts in 1990.

23. Literature on the American settin' chair is sparse. The earliest recognition of the form was Allen H. Eaton, *Handicrafts of the Southern Highlands* (New York: Russell Sage Foundation, 1937), pp. 147–61 and figs. opp. pp. 93, 197, 200. Eaton's interviews and questionnaires established that Appalachian chairmakers employed riving, shaving, heating and bending of posts and slats, and assembly with dry rungs driven into wet posts. Another source with technical information is "An Old Chairmaker Shows How," *Foxfire* 1 (1969): 128–38. Modern academic studies include John Robert Vincent, "A Study of Ozark Woodworking Industries" (master's thesis, University of Missouri at Columbia, 1962); Henry Glassie, *Pattern in the Material Folk Culture of the Eastern United States* (Philadelphia: University of Pennsylvania Press, 1968), pp. 230, 231, fig. 66; Michael Owen Jones, "Chairmaking in Appalachia: A Study in Style and Creative Imagination in American Folk Art" (Ph.D. diss., Indiana University, 1970); Michael Owen Jones, *The Hand Made Object and Its Maker* (Berkeley: University of California Press, 1975); Michael Owen Jones, *Craftsman of the Cumberlands: Tradition and Creativity* (Lexington: University Press of Kentucky, 1989); and Warren E. Roberts, "Turpin Chairs and the Turpin Family: Chairmaking in Southern Indiana," *Midwestern Journal of Language and Folklore* 7, no. 2 (Fall 1981): 55–106.

Daniel Finamore

Furnishing the Craftsman: Slaves and Sailors in the Mahogany Trade

▼ I HAVE READ *that the old Druid Priests taught the early Britons that if they cut the oak tree the spirit, which possessed its form, would cry out in protest; and as one sees the slaughter of those beautiful trees, one can almost imagine the spirits of the woods crying out in protestation against the ruthless destruction of tree-life. It is certainly a consolation to remember that the tree which is being robbed of its leafy bounty is destined to re-appear in a form where beauty and utility will combine. What an interesting story could be written on "The Romance of the Mahogany Log," relating its experience from its growth in a distant forest to its place of honour in a city mansion.*[1]

Lore and History
In the mid-1950s an unfinished mahogany plank measuring nine feet long by five feet wide by two and one half inches thick was discovered in the basement of a house in Salem, Massachusetts. The board had been used as a coal chute, but it still displayed the fiery, highly desirable grain pattern that forms on the trunk near the crotch of a branch. Clearly harvested from a very large, first-growth mahogany tree, this plank sheds light on the size of boards and billets that reached New England ports during the eighteenth and nineteenth centuries and provides a tantalizing glimpse into a trade that has gone little examined in the literature of decorative arts and maritime history. At the same time, the plank's intrinsic qualities provide little information as to its origin, extraction, processing, and transportation. Also difficult to ascertain is the human cost of the mahogany trade, since much of the labor that sustained it required the movement of populations over great distances, often against their will. With a deeper perspective on the processes that culminated in the delivery of wood to the craftsman's shop, mahogany furniture becomes central to the hegemonic discourse of the English slave-owning culture in the New World.

During the eighteenth and nineteenth centuries, ships transported large quantities of mahogany to and from many countries bordering on the North Atlantic. Because quantitative documentation of this trade has proved elusive, studies of furniture making typically begin in cabinetmakers' shops with the assumption that they had planks and other stock on hand. In their formal analyses, scholars typically identify the mahogany used in furniture arbitrarily as Jamaican, Honduran, Santo Domingan, or Cuban, through macroscopic visual assessment of color and physical appearance of grain. By incorporating this kind of questionable connoisseurship, furniture historians mythologize the exotic origins of the wood while further obfuscating the specific histories of the people and places of the mahogany trade.[2]

This essay combines historical and archaeological research to investigate in reverse sequence selected aspects of the process by which a living tree became an article of furniture. No single source offers a seamless chronology of data about the disparate and often little-documented phases of production, but each interpretative approach offers distinct insights that create a more holistic perspective than would be available from a single source alone. Sources utilized for this study include furniture that retains documentation or oral tradition regarding wood origins, archives with holdings pertaining to geographic, economic, and social factors of the mahogany trade, and the physical remnants of remote Central American forest encampments that contain artifacts of lives where subjugation was the norm and a voice in the archives is rare.

Though mahogany was harvested from around the Caribbean basin, research for this article focuses on the nation of Belize (fig. 1), which was known in the eighteenth century as the Bay Settlement, or simply Honduras, and from 1862 to 1973 as the colony of British Honduras. Belize is an ideal case study for the history of the mahogany trade because it existed for more than one hundred years as an informal British colony in a region claimed by Spain for the sole purpose of extracting wood for export. As a result, neither residents nor governments invested in political, social, or physical structures beyond those necessary for the efficient extraction and exportation of wood.[3]

Figure 1   Detail from "Spanish North America, Southern Part," (John Thomson, *A New General Atlas* [Edinburgh: John Thomson and Co., 1817].)

Figure 2 Chest attributed to the Symonds shops, Salem, Massachusetts, 1701. Oak, maple, mahogany, and red cedar (by microanalysis). H. 31¼", W. 47¾", D. 20⅝". (Courtesy, Concord Museum, Concord, MA, gift of Russell Kettell; photo, David Bohl.) The dated panel is mahogany.

Mahogany began entering English ports during the seventeenth century (fig. 2), but it was not widely used as a primary wood for cabinetmaking before the 1730s. Lore regarding the origins of the mahogany trade emphasizes the accidental nature of the wood's discovery, maintaining that mariners picked up entire trunks for use as ballast only to toss them overboard on arrival home, where they were "free for the taking" by cabinetmakers scavenging wood from the foreshore. The enormous size and weight of trees that would offer optimal timber for cabinetmaking and the significant amount of labor required to harvest, prepare, load, and unload the wood from a ship strongly suggests that the use of mahogany in furniture of this era was never accidental. A 1737 advertisement in the *Boston Gazette* announced the sale of "Ligmimviree, Box Wood, Ebony, Mohogony Plank, Sweet Wood Bark, and wild Cinnamon Bark," indicating that early on mahogany was a valuable commodity.[4]

Among the remarkably comprehensive array of furnishings, decorative arts, and documents relating to more than 150 years of business and daily life in Salem that make up the Ropes Family Collection at the Peabody Essex Museum is the account book of Judge Nathaniel Ropes. In an un-

Figure 3 Chest-on-chest possibly by Abraham Watson (1712–1790), Salem, Massachusetts, 1760–1770. Mahogany with white pine. H. 90", W. 44", D. 23". (Courtesy, Peabody Essex Museum Collection, R1120, bequest of Sarah Cheever, 1908.) Watson may have made this chest for Judge Nathaniel Ropes in exchange for unfinished mahogany.

dated entry, he gave cabinetmaker Abraham Watson 60 feet of mahogany in exchange for £18, a "desk and caseing," and possibly other furniture made from that wood (fig. 3). The judge may have acquired the mahogany through maritime trade or as payment for a debt owed locally, but there is no evidence that he imported wood as a business. The most likely scenario is that Ropes acquired the mahogany specifically to buy furniture at a savings. Transactions of this type were common during the period. From 1757 to 1759 Newport ship captain Joseph Arnold supplied cabinetmaker John Cahoone with 243 feet of mahogany and 13 feet of walnut in exchange for a desk and four tables. Arnold received these items over time and probably sold them as venture cargo.[5]

In some instances, the importer was also the end user of the wood. Generations of oral tradition maintain that the desk illustrated in figure 4 was part of ship captain James Chever's "wedding outfit" that he had made from Santo Domingo mahogany he had "brought home." Since Chever married in 1776, it is possible that the disruption of trade during the Revolutionary War had created a shortage of mahogany in Salem. Alternatively, he may have had access to better-quality wood at Hispaniola than what was arriving at Salem at the time. Chever may have saved a good deal of money by buying the mahogany at its source, rather than purchasing the best wood available in Salem. Decorative arts historian Dean Lahikainen has shown how several prominent Salem cabinetmakers formed a cartel to buy large quantities of mahogany logs, which were cut into planks locally. One of these artisans, Josiah Austin, also served as the surveyor of boards, plank, and timber for the town in 1799. By importing his wood directly from the source region, Chever may have circumvented competition from organized local interests to acquire better wood at a more reasonable price.[6]

Repositioning Wood: Transshipment and Regional Variation
The name "mahogany" is now used liberally to describe a variety of species in the Meliaceae family that grow in Africa, India, the Philippines, and elsewhere, but the historical range of the three species that constitute true mahogany is neotropical America from southern Mexico and the southern tip of Florida, into South America including much of the Amazon basin, as well as most of the Caribbean islands. Within this genus (*Swietenia*) there is considerable variability in density, color, and grain. Mahogany from well-drained, hilly, or rocky regions, particularly on the West Indian islands, has traditionally been recognized as slower growing, harder, and more figured—all qualities that cabinetmakers found desirable. Mahogany of the Central and South American mainland, and in particular the Caribbean coastal plain, was traditionally believed to grow slightly more rapidly, be somewhat softer, and have a more uniform grain. These qualities were considered to be the result of different growing conditions; not until 1886 were the trees from these two regions separated into different species.[7]

Historic terms that were geographic in allusion—"Jamaican mahogany," "Spanish mahogany," and "Honduras mahogany"—may also have referred to qualities perceived as characteristic of the wood from each area. However, the accuracy of such generalizations was often problematic at best. In 1802 New York cabinetmaking firm Samuel and William S. Burling reported that it had "on hand . . . at their mahogany-yard, St. Domingo, Cuba, [and] Bay Mahogany, in Logs, Plank, and Boards." Although cabinetmakers and lumber merchants used geographic terms for marketing, buyers were more concerned with the visual and physical characteristics of mahogany than with the origin of the wood. As early as 1757 a resident of the north coast of Honduras, then called the Mosquito Shore, speculated about the perceived superiority of Jamaican mahogany over Honduran:

Figure 4 Desk attributed to William King (b. 1754), Salem, Massachusetts, ca. 1776. Mahogany with white pine and brass. H. 43½", W. 40¼", D. 21½". (Courtesy, Peabody Essex Museum Collection, 101792, bequest of Sarah Cheever, 1908.)

> The reason probably is that what is now got in that island, grows in dry rocky ground, where it has been preserved to the last by the Difficulty of transporting it, and for want of soil is of a slow growth and close grain; but here it has been cut for convenience in low land near to the water side from which situation its growth is quick, and its grain open; but some cut on the high land is as good as any.

By the mid-eighteenth century, Jamaican mahogany was becoming scarce, and wood from other areas was too diverse to be indisputably associated with the highest quality. One importer noted that "Instances are not uncommon where a single ton increases the value of a whole cargo £500 and Mahy from the coast of Yucatan may be quoted from £6 to 100£/ton." In the end, the quality of the wood rather than the region of growth dictated price. Notwithstanding the obvious fact that high-quality mahogany was valued and sought out by certain consumers, the wood was only a relatively small component of the overall cost of furniture, the majority being the maker's labor. An advisor to the British Parliament in 1790 claimed, "It is of very little consequence to the community whether the manufacturer pays 15 or 2/6 per ft. for fine mahy because experience has shown that the price of fine furniture will be the same, it consisting not so much in the wood as in the finishing." The desire to generalize about wood from different regions extended even to small-scale topographic distinctions, but an advisor to the British government who visited Belize noted the difficulties inherent in such assumptions. "The Mahogany in this country differs considerably in grain, & consequently in durability, according to the soil on which it grows, and contrary to almost all other countries, the lower and more swampy the soil, the harder and closer grained the wood."[8]

The quantities of mahogany that entered North America in the eighteenth century will never be comprehensively accounted for, since the wood was loaded onto ships and recorded by shipmasters, merchants, and custom officials in many different forms: logs, log ends (short parts cut from a long log to fit into a hold), slabs, planks (probably thick and hand-shaped or cut in a saw pit), boards (thinner and probably cut at a sawmill), and pieces. Wood was recorded by weight, by the number of pieces, or by using a formula to determine board feet. The variability in reporting the volume of cargos renders quantitative analysis of imports and exports problematic. On October 2, 1764, the schooner *Speedwell* returned to Boston from a voyage to Puerto Rico, where she took on "218 pieces" of mahogany. Three years earlier the Bahamian-registered brig *Harriot* had arrived carrying three logs from New Providence, while on October 31, 1752, the Boston sloop *Sparrow* arrived from that port carrying 1,500 feet of wood in an unidentified state.[9]

Between late October 1752 and the end of September 1765, forty-nine ships carrying indeterminate quantities of mahogany arrived at Boston from New Providence, St. Thomas, Florida, Jamaica, the Mosquito Shore, Puerto Rico, Honduras, North Carolina, and New York. Additional shipments arrived at Salem from Jamaica, Maryland, South Carolina, and St. Eustatius. Of these ports, many are outside the region of mahogany growth, and others, though within it, were not commercial centers of extraction and export. These shipments could represent export from the source or transshipment of wood from a third location. Only a relatively small number of ships appear to have carried wood directly from the originating port into Boston and Salem. When specified, the state of the wood reported in a given shipment indicates whether it was a direct import from its origin or a transshipment from another port. Wood that arrived in board form had probably been processed for sale elsewhere, since most ports of origin, such as Belize and the Mosquito Shore, did not have sawmills, and their wood was exported exclusively in unfinished form, primarily as logs. It was common to transship wood through intermediate points, where it would sometimes be cut and then reloaded to ship out again.[10]

Surviving shipping records for colonial Massachusetts ports (fig. 5) suggest that most mahogany arrived there through multistaged voyages. Most

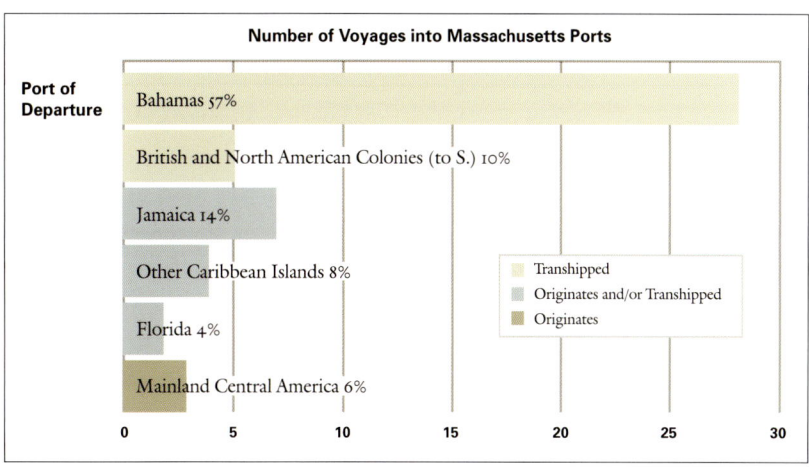

Figure 5 Mahogany Entering Massachusetts Ports, 1752–1765. (Derived from "Abstracts of English Shipping Records," Peabody Essex Museum.)

of the cargos that specified the form of the wood stated it as planks, and only one was said to contain logs. Over half of all voyages originated at New Providence in the Bahamas, an island group within the zone of mahogany growth but far too small to have been the sole source of such large quantities of wood. This port served as a primary center of transshipment because it offered convenient access to Atlantic traders entering and departing the Caribbean. Wood was also transshipped through smaller Caribbean islands as well as through British colonies to the south. Localities such as Jamaica acted both as primary extraction centers and transshipment points. Only a small percentage of wood can be said with confidence to have arrived directly from its source of extraction. With no record of a single importation of mahogany from Santo Domingo during these years, it even is possible that Captain Chever's later voyage was not to that island but to a transshipment center, where he may have had his choice of wood from a number of sources. His destination could even have been New York, where in 1797 George Shipley advertised "a cargo of choice St. Domingo Mahogany, very suitable for the French or English Market."[11]

Massachusetts was not the final destination for much of the wood that entered the colony's ports (fig. 6). In January 1764 the Boston brig *Katey* departed for Europe with a cargo of 183 mahogany logs and 673 mahogany planks. To sell the wood to best advantage, the shipmaster probably intended to visit several ports along the Atlantic coast or Mediterranean. That same year the Salem snow-rigged ship *Jenny* cleared customs and departed for the Isle of Jersey with 5,000 "boards & planks," plus 52 additional feet of plank. Between 1752 and 1765 thirty-three ships cleared outward from Boston and Salem customhouses. Most of these vessels headed for the British Isles, but one-third were bound for the Netherlands, Spain, and Portugal. An exceptionally large cargo of 35,000 boards and planks was destined for Newfoundland.[12]

Transshipping was advantageous for breaking up bulk cargos, preventing markets from becoming inundated, and avoiding excessive duties. Shippers often owed duty on the wood, especially when it was considered a foreign product. Even before mahogany became the primary export of Belize, entrepreneurial shippers of other woods had realized that the indeterminate political status of that settlement allowed them to sidestep the navigation laws and ship directly to New England and European markets since they were not technically traveling from one British colony to another or from a colony to a foreign country. This situation changed in the early 1770s, when the Crown allowed wood shipped from British colonies on British ships to be imported duty free. Custom agents in London understood, however, that wood from other ports was passing through duty-free entrepôts such as Jamaica or the Mosquito Shore. One official reported that port officers "have [wood] . . . viewed by persons who pretend to know the growth [origin] and it requires great firmness to stand out against them." Naturally, shippers felt that these "specialists," who assessed duties based on their determination of the wood's origin, often acted arbitrarily and unfairly. In 1770 London agents claimed that mahogany arriving there on the Rhode

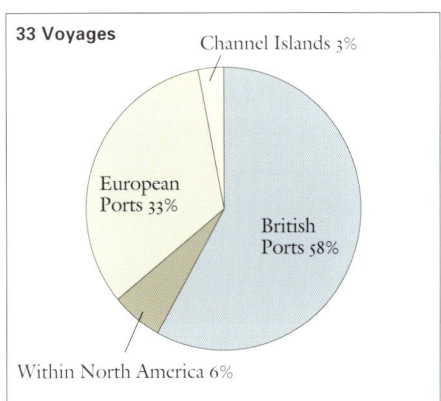

Figure 6 Mahogany Clearing Massachusetts Ports, 1752–1765. (Derived from "Abstracts of English Shipping Records," Peabody Essex Museum.)

Island ship *Hero* from the Mosquito Shore was actually from Belize and therefore foreign and dutiable because the certificate for the wood did not identify it as "the growth of that place." "This plan of our officers to make Honduras wood pay custom is owing to an information given by some busy persons. . . . All that came from our own colonies was supposed to be the growth of our colonies till now, and was in consequence admitted custom free." The notion that the source of mahogany could be identified through visual examination on the London docks was bitterly disputed by the Belize wood merchants.[13]

Though many logs were cut to fit spaces in a ship's hold, length influenced the desirability and price of wood in furniture making centers. In 1766 the Bristol agent for a prominent Newport, Rhode Island, merchant complained about receiving "very short Pieces [planks], which renders it of very little Value." Six years later the same agent complained about a shipment consisting of "a great deal of small, rather porus [wood], much shaken, and in general *too short*—especially the very large loggs—which are four feet shorter than they are coveted to be." In the initial stage of processing harvested trees, laborers "placed [the logs] in whatever position [would] . . . admit of the largest square being formed, according to the shape which the end of each log presents, and then reduced by means of an axe, from the round, or natural, form, into the square." To maximize the value of a squared log, one had to know how to cut it into useful lengths for manufacturing furniture, while minimizing waste. By the mid-nineteenth century, the logs most valuable to cabinetmakers were those that could be used in the manufacture of dining tables, which averaged 4½ to 5½ feet in length, and 22 to 30 inches wide. Logs that were even multiples of these lengths—5, 10, 15, or 20 feet plus or minus a few inches—could be cut most efficiently for this purpose. The best logs for chairs were at least 9 feet in length and 15 inches in diameter. Shorter logs of 7½ to 8½ feet could be used for bedposts.[14]

Superficial measurements were only estimates. Even after a log cleared customs, it was not possible to determine its exact monetary value, whether in board feet or quality of wood, until it was fully cut (fig. 7). Sales of logs were based on estimates of the usable wood they would produce. In 1843 Belize wood merchant Charles Craig reputedly had a log that weighed fifteen tons, measured 57 by 64 inches after being squared, and contained an estimated 5,168 board feet of wood. The ultimate job of processing that log and ascertaining the accuracy of those measurements was probably left to a well-financed wood merchant in Liverpool or London. Purchase of raw wood involved a certain amount of speculation, as illustrated by the optimistic assessments accorded one log in an 1823 newspaper account:

> The largest and finest log of mahogany ever imported into this country has been recently sold by auction at the docks in Liverpool. It was purchased by James Hodgson, Esq. for three hundred and seventy-eight pounds, and afterwards sold by him for five hundred and twenty-five pounds, and if it *open* well, it is supposed to be worth *one thousand pounds*. If sawn into veneers it is computed that the cost of labour in the process will be seven hundred and fifty pounds. The weight at the King's beam is six tons thirteen hundred weight.[15]

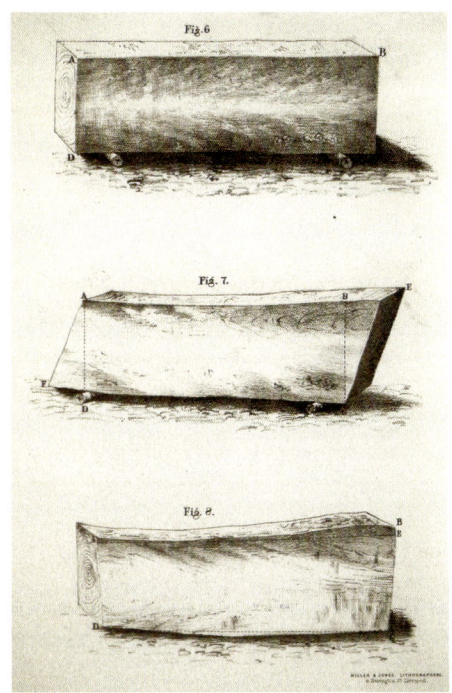

Figure 7 Assessing the contents of a squared log. (Chaloner and Fleming, *The Mahogany Tree* [Liverpool: Rockliff and Son, 1850].)

Although enormous logs occasionally generated public attention and could be exploited for promotional purposes, some lumber merchants felt that large logs yielded inferior timber. In 1771 Henry Drinker of Philadelphia complained to his Central American supplier: "We have repeatedly observed that you seem to set a high value on the largest wood which is in general a mistaken notion because it is not in common so good in quality as middle size and is larger than the consumers of that article generally require." Drinker requested planks and logs of four, eight, or twelve feet in length and sixteen to twenty-four inches in diameter to conform to the desires of Bristol cabinetmakers.[16]

Americans in the Mahogany Trade

North American cabinetmakers and woodlot operators had no direct contact with ports of origin in the mahogany trade, but that was not the case with shippers whose businesses hinged on relationships with Caribbean and Central American lumber merchants and their agents. Unlike most of their Massachusetts counterparts, who dealt in transshipped mahogany, shippers in Newport, Philadelphia, and New York endeavored to purchase wood as it emerged from the forests of Belize and the Mosquito Shore.

Harvesting and exporting wood typically involved partnerships between the woodcutters who staked claims to forest tracts and managed field operations and the financiers who arranged for the credit necessary to support a workforce and made arrangements for transportation and sale. Thus, both field managers and their agents were central players in the compulsory labor system of the mahogany trade. Immediately following emancipation of the slave population at Belize in 1838, the anticipated cost of operating a mahogany camp capable of producing 300,000 board feet in a seven-month season was £7,001, including labor, tools, trucks, livestock, watercraft, and provisions. Before emancipation, however, the costs would have been similar, owing to substantial investment in slave ownership, or the common practice of "hiring," or leasing, the slaves of another timber cutter.[17]

Among the most active mahogany traders in colonial America was Aaron Lopez (fig. 8), who immigrated from Portugal to Rhode Island in 1755 and worked with a network of business partners around the Atlantic to become Newport's most prosperous merchant. Lopez sent many ships to Belize with cargos of goods for forest-dwelling, timber-cutting laborers: barrels of dried and pickled foods, clothing, lanterns, cooking pots, saw blades, axes, and boat compasses. Much of the wood Lopez purchased at Belize was destined for the international market, although some of his mahogany went to Rhode Island via Jamaica. Lopez's correspondence with his London agent suggests that the mahogany trade was lucrative in good times but frequently subject to market saturation. Caribbean timber merchants were habitually indebted to Lopez, who was forced to accept wood in payment even though his London agent warned him in 1772 that the city had enough mahogany to last ten years. As part of a complex international market, mahogany prices were affected not only by supply and the cost of importing the wood but also by the shifting diplomatic and political landscape of the later eighteenth

Figure 8 Portrait of Aaron Lopez, unidentified artist. Oil on metal. Dimensions not recorded. (Courtesy, American Jewish Historical Society, New York, NY and Newton Centre, MA.)

century. Hurt by the nonimportation acts that were supported by colonists in certain cabinetmaking centers, Lopez's agent railed against "the Haughty Insolent Overbearing Arbitrary Rebellious Bostonians . . . [and] the Stiff foolish Obstinate Philadelphian Quakers," but reserved positive comments for the "Wise Good & Spirited" New Yorkers, who he apparently felt struck a balance between commerce and political ideology. At certain times, Lopez's profits on mahogany shipments were negligible, and it is possible that they were intended only to defray some of the expenses of the west-to-east transatlantic voyage, the majority of profits being made carrying European or North American goods into Jamaica.[18]

Belize was considered a remote corner of the Caribbean, not a destination for speculative voyages. Wood shipments were arranged in advance, since masters wanted to sail there only when they knew full cargos awaited them. As prices for mahogany declined during the 1760s and 1770s, even prominent shipowners became entangled in a growing web of insolvent and untrustworthy partners, undesirable cargos, and unpaid bills, which inspired many to invest elsewhere.

By 1771 Lopez's mahogany interests were unraveling rapidly, with problems extending well beyond the depressed price of that wood. One of his primary correspondents was John Newdigate, a Rhode Island shipmaster who lost Lopez's trust after failing in an important venture. As a result, Lopez sent Newdigate to the Sibun River valley of Belize to work off his debt by acquiring high-quality mahogany. In several letters, the banished shipmaster assured Lopez that he had secured large stocks of wood, which were "only waiting for a vessel to take it in." Newdigate implored Lopez to "send . . . down two vessels to carry it away," adding, "I want to come home." In separate letters, Newdigate begged Lopez's wife to intercede, indicating that his relationship with her husband extended beyond business. These arguments failed to sway Lopez, since he was simultaneously receiving negative reports concerning his former associate. Described as "a . . . weak Headed puffed up foolish fellow" with a head "as soft as a boiled turnip," Newdigate was accused of adultery, bigamy, misuse of funds, and other offenses.[19]

To make matters worse, Newdigate arranged for the Belize mahogany cutter Basil Jones to travel to Newport on Lopez's brigantine *Charlotte,* but the ship struck a reef called "the colloradoes" and had to divert to Charleston, South Carolina, for repairs. Shaken by the incident, Jones called the vessel "unfit for the seas" and insisted on having his wood offloaded. As bills for the ship mounted, Lopez turned to Jones to pay his portion of the freight, but the latter's wood remained unsold in Charleston, and Jones's health swiftly declined. Eight months later, Jones died of cancer and Lopez was left to recover the debt from the former's estate in Belize, which, ironically, was being managed by Newdigate. Whether Newdigate ever repaid his debt to Lopez or Lopez left him in Belize "to repent" of his "former misdeeds," the disgraced shipmaster eventually escaped his purgatory and resettled in Savanna, Georgia.[20]

Belize woodcutters were at the economic mercy of many distant parties:

the shippers who sent vessels to carry away their wood, port agents who measured it for freight and duty charges, and the market that decided its ultimate value. The attempts of one cutter to wrest a modicum of control over these forces illustrate the difficulties of life at that end of the export trade. William Tucker, a resident of the Sibun River valley in the southern portion of the Belize settlement, acquired a brig to ship his own mahogany. He made the ill-fated choice of New York merchant Henry Cruger, whose own business was in decline, to represent his overseas interests. Before Tucker's ship left Belize, Cruger complained that the "age of the brig Monkton and other defects" made securing insurance difficult. Tucker's ship sailed with only £2,000 of coverage and, when the brig arrived in New York, it was "hove down & narrowly inspected by two judicious old sea captains and two able ship carpenters," who estimated that repair costs would exceed the value of the ship. Because mahogany prices were low at that time, Cruger could not send the ship back to Belize for another cargo. Further, proceeds on the sale of Tucker's cargo yielded a loss of more than £250 after factoring in the costs of operating the *Monkton*. Tucker was forced to let Cruger sell the brig at auction. After purchasing the vessel for himself, Cruger requested an additional £55 from Tucker to settle their account.[21]

Between the financial centers of coastal North America and the hardscrabble settlements of mainland Central America, mariners like James Card (fig. 9) became acquainted with the more rigorous aspects of the mahogany trade. He was a Newport resident but spent several years in Belize representing the interests of other Rhode Islanders such as Oliver Ring Warner. Card transported wood for residents of Belize whom he knew personally, including his brother Jonathan. Following a lucrative slaving voyage to Senegal in 1760, James married the daughter of a mahogany trader from Guernsey and purchased a mahogany desk from Edmund Townsend for £203. Like their Rhode Island counterparts, merchants in the Channel Islands supported their business networks by interlinking them with family ties. With his Newport contacts and the Channel Island connections that his marriage brought, Card was well positioned to trade mahogany at different Atlantic ports.

In addition to trading in wood, Card transported slaves into the Bay of Honduras, as well as between Belize and the Mosquito Shore. One slave from the latter place had been convicted of stealing and was sentenced to be "transported from the shore for life." Card's client Warner had leased the labor of another slave named Newport to Card's Rhode Island relative William Cahoon. The slave, who had been born on Africa's Gold Coast, was intended for cutting mahogany in Belize. Cahoon died, leaving his entire estate to Card's brother Jonathan, and Newport slipped away to the Mosquito Shore. Although James Card followed with the intent of catching and selling him on Warner's behalf, an unidentified person tipped off Newport, and he disappeared into the backcountry.[22]

James and his brother Jonathan had a falling-out, which the former regularly lamented but never explained. Following James's death in Belize in

Figure 9 Portrait of James Card, unknown artist, medium, and dimensions. (Ex-collection, Rhode Island Historical Society. Current location unknown.)

1772, Jonathan wrote a cryptic letter to his sister-in-law Sarah, offering to send her the proceeds of her late husband's Belize business ventures. He also referred to "circumstances which may be necessary to be kept private from the ears of people in our place" and "paper" that should remain confidential for "your own security." The need for secrecy suggests that James's untimely death at age forty-two may not have been natural.[23]

Jonathan's attitude toward Belize was less exploitative than that of his brother. The former settled there permanently, raising two children "begotten on the body of a free Mustie woman named Dorothy Taylor." Before his death in 1788, Jonathan had freed several slaves, including one named Valentine "for divers good causes." His daughter Sarah married William Roach of New York City and moved from Belize, but Jonathan's son and namesake continued cutting mahogany at Spanish Creek and Poor Man's Rest along the Belize River. With a workforce of thirty-five slaves, the younger Jonathan became one of the most successful traders in the settlement. On receiving his father's inheritance, the younger Jonathan freed one of his father's slaves named Lucretia, along with her daughter Maria, whom he had probably fathered. Later in life, he expanded his business by supplying ships in the mahogany trade with turtle meat and other provisions.[24]

After the Revolutionary War, British timber merchants and shippers attempted to block American ships from the most lucrative aspects of the mahogany trade, but shorter coastwise voyages and the demand for products from the new republic gave her ships several advantages. In the two years before President Thomas Jefferson's 1807–8 embargo acts decimated maritime trade, forty-nine American vessels cleared the Honduras Settlement carrying mahogany. All were small ships with limited cargo capacity, the majority being unarmed brigs and schooners of between 46 and 225 tons with an average complement of only seven men. In contrast, British ships in the transatlantic trade usually weighed 300 to 350 tons and carried up to sixteen guns and thirty-six men. A law intended to reserve the best wood for British merchants ostensibly prevented American ships from exporting logs greater than twenty inches in girth, but enforcement proved largely ineffective.[25]

America's continued presence at Belize represented a tremendous advantage in the mahogany trade. On numerous occasions, settlers there were granted unrestricted trade with America in response to food shortages such as those that followed a gale in 1804 and a hurricane in 1805. One visitor noted that British ships often arrive in ballast (without inbound cargo), but not American ones: "For here, as it happens in our colonies generally, articles of American production are determined to be almost indispensably requisite." With most of the population engaged in the extraction of wood, rather than farming, settlers at Belize were dependent on imported food, especially for the logging camps. Between 1807 and 1812, most American ships left Honduras for, in order of frequency, New York, Portland, Charleston, Boston, Norfolk, Philadelphia, and Newport. Others sailed directly across the Atlantic, where they were frequently charged the same rate of duty as British ships.[26]

Upriver

Maritime merchants in the mahogany trade traversed the geographic and cultural divide between the worlds of the cosmopolitan cabinetmaker and the remote Central American frontier (fig. 10). Records of their business activities, though sparse, are far more prevalent and detailed than those pertaining to woodcutters and laborers.

The origins of the English settlement on the coast of Belize are shrouded in mystery, but in the turbulent era following the 1667 Treaty of Madrid, when England and Spain agreed to suppress piracy cooperatively, many British mariners went to the coast of Belize. Although the land was part of the Spanish Empire, there was almost no Spanish occupation. The logwood that grew there also attracted British mariners and merchants, since it was in considerable demand in Europe for dyeing textiles. When Dominican friar Joseph Delgado traveled through the country in 1677, pirates under the command of Bartholomew Sharpe, who were camped near the mouth of the Belize River, captured him. The settlement received newcomers from the 1680s on, such as the crew of Captain Coxon. Sent there to appease the Spanish government and evacuate the logwood cutters, Coxon's crew

Figure 10 Detail from "Mexico and Central States," (Sydney Hall, *A New General Atlas* [London: Longman, Brown, Green and Longmans, 1857].)

instead decided to mutiny and join them. The early years of this settlement were characterized by a cooperative approach to labor and a relatively egalitarian way of life, where sailors worked in small groups to cut logwood to sell to visiting shipmasters. Since the wood was to be chipped and boiled for use, it could be exported in any convenient form, so sailors usually cut it into lengths small enough to be carried on the back of a man.[27]

Though fiercely independent, many residents of the community had come from New England, and some still felt an affinity with home. For example, in 1726, when a group of sea captains proposed building a spire on Old North Church, presumably as an aid to navigation for those entering Boston Harbor, "Matthew Bond, Captain Richardson and others" donated cargos of logwood to be auctioned off to support the construction. Inside the church, a large double pew was inscribed "This Pew for the use of the Gentlemen of the Bay of Honduras 1727." Other cargos were donated between 1727 and 1743, during which time the pew was reduced in size by half for lack of use, and then increased in size again. The baymen's attendance at the church was intermittent, but their philanthropy remained focused. In 1754 the church sold the pew, presumably because the baymen were no longer using it. Logwood was no longer the primary economic force in Belize, and the residents had developed closer social ties with towns like Newport and New York, which were more deeply engaged in the mahogany trade.[28]

The emergence of the mahogany trade spelled both the end of the egalitarian lifestyle of the logwood cutters and the establishment of a new economic and social hierarchy. Given the size of the trees, mahogany extraction and preparation for shipment required large amounts of labor that had to be well organized into specialized activities. It was practically impossible for anyone without access to abundant sources of labor to participate in the acquisition of mahogany. Slaves began arriving in the settlement by 1724, and they outnumbered whites—"fifty white Men, and about a hundred and twenty Negroes"—by 1745. The growth in the slave population continued rapidly, and by 1779 slaves outnumbered nonslaves by approximately six to one. The economic primacy of mahogany had become solidified, and the settlement's transformation into a traditional colonial society with a strongly hierarchical social structure was complete. Unlike in the Caribbean islands and North American colonies, however, slaves at Belize lived not on plantations, but in relatively small groups in remote camps in the forest.[29]

Slaves who occupied the upriver mahogany camps were divided into groups according to the specialized jobs they did, including huntsman, axeman, path clearer, ox-team driver, and log trimmer. Such organized labor was essential, since mahogany trees grew to a height of eighty to one hundred feet, with a basal diameter ranging from four feet up to legendary thicknesses of twelve feet. If left to mature naturally, about one mahogany tree grows in a square mile of forest. Slaves spent nine to ten months of the year in the camps, heading out from the coast at the beginning of the dry season in January and returning with the wood during the heaviest flooding of the rainy season. The huntsman, who roamed vast expanses of forest,

Figure 11 J. McGahey, *Felling Mahogany*, Liverpool, England, ca. 1850. Lithograph. 6" x 9". (Courtesy, American Antiquarian Society.)

located suitable specimens by climbing the highest trees and looking out over the forest canopy during the time of year when mahogany leaves turned yellow. Being a huntsman offered some independence, since if treated poorly he could sell his information to the owner of a neighboring claim. Before the axeman felled a tree (fig. 11), path clearers identified the shortest route to move the log through the woods—avoiding slopes, swamps, and rocks—then built a rudimentary road. In the earliest years, human power alone moved the logs, limiting the size of tree that could be harvested, but by the 1780s teams of oxen became the norm (figs. 12, 13). During the height of the dry season, from February to May, the axemen would fell the trees, usually from a stage built eight to ten feet above the ground to avoid the huge root buttresses that protrude at the base. Once felled, the trees were cleared of their limbs, dragged to the river, and cut with a distinctive mark, often initials, to identify their owner. To avoid overheating the oxen, the most strenuous work was undertaken at night, using torches for light. Other laborers gathered edible leaves to feed these animals.

With the advent of heavy rains in July, workers threw the logs into the river, arranged up to two hundred in a large raft, and floated them down to the coast (fig. 14). By the early nineteenth century, woodcutters began capturing the floating logs near the end of the river with a large boom chain

Figure 12 Day and Son, *Cutting and Trucking Mahogany in Honduras,* Liverpool, England, 1850. (Chaloner and Fleming, *The Mahogany Tree* [Liverpool: Rockliff and Son, 1850].)

Figure 13 Manner of Trucking Mahogany in Honduras, attributed to William B. Annin and George G. Smith after Andrew Bayntun, Boston, 1826. Engraving on paper. 4" x 7". (*Honduras Almanack,* 1826.)

77 FURNISHING THE CRAFTSMAN

Figure 14 "Rafting mahogany logs down New River." (Standley and Record, *The Forest and Flora of British Honduras* [Chicago: Field Museum of Natural History, 1936], pl. 4.)

attached to huge anchors at each shore (fig. 15). Before boom chains came into use, workers simply steered logs toward shore at the river mouth or allowed them to float out into the harbor, where they were captured and sorted by owner. Either in the forest or on the coast, workers squared the logs to facilitate efficient lading into a ship's hold and marked them with an inventory code. The largest logs were almost invariably rough-squared in

Figure 15 Boom chain of undetermined date retrieved from the lower Belize River at the village of Burrell Boom. (Photo, Daniel Finamore.)

Figure 16 Wedge-shaped end of a squared mahogany log, used to prevent stacks of logs from rolling. (Photo, Daniel Finamore.) The author found this log in the Sibun River near Cedar Bank.

the forest to make them lighter and to prevent rolling (fig. 16). When ships arrived, laborers bundled logs into smaller rafts and lighters floated the rafts out into the harbor, where they were hoisted from the ship's spars into the hold through specially designed cargo doors at the stern (fig. 17).[30]

Figure 17 Charles Dashwood, *Merchant's House and Yard for Siding the Mahogany Trees before Putting Them on Board Ship for England, Belize*, ca. 1830. Graphite and ink on paper. 10¼" x 8¼". (Courtesy, Yale Center for British Art, Paul Mellon Collection.)

Archaeology of the Woodcutting Camps

Of the diverse populations who traversed land and sea in the mahogany trade, the least is known about those who lived at the wood's point of origin. No firsthand documentation of slave life survives, and descriptions by others are either cursory or obviously promotional of a particular point of view. For example, a medical doctor hired to report to the head of government on the health of the woodcutters found that "a more vigorous and fine looking lot of men is no where to be met with . . . which I am of the opinion is the natural consequence of salubrity of climate, a healthy occupation, and kind treatment." The doctor was a nineteen-year resident of Belize, and it is doubtful that he was unbiased.[31]

Principals in woodcutting operations probably invested little in the huts and camps in which their workers lived. Composed largely of slave labor, woodcutting camps moved periodically to exploit different parts of the forest (fig. 18). In 1790 a hut with "a thatched roof and inclosed with . . . Pimento sticks, tyed together with small yarns" attracted the attention of a traveler, who noted that it had been "built . . . to lodge the negroes at night, when attending mahogany." Similarly, an early almanac of Belize described a woodcutting camp as

> a small village on the bank of the river, the choice of situation being always regulated by the proximity of such river to the mahogany intended as the object of future operations. In the arranging and appearance of the habitations, much rural taste is often displayed, and it is highly gratifying to the curious to remark the different modes peculiar to the several Nations or Tribes of Africa, as also the improvement introduced by European experience in the construction of the houses. . . . We have frequently seen

Figure 18   Mode of Travelling of the Woodcutters in the British Settlement of Honduras, attributed to William B. Annin and George G. Smith after Andrew Bayntun, Boston, 1828. Engraving on paper. 4" x 7". (*Honduras Almanack,* 1828.)

houses of this kind completed in a single day, and with no other implement than an axe.[32]

Efficiency probably dictated social organization in most camps except when higher-status individuals, such as a foreman or owner, were in residence. With little documentation to shed light on everyday life, the author conducted an archaeological survey to locate and examine sites where woodcutters lived and worked. Because the surrounding forests were actively exploited during the eighteenth century, the survey encompassed the New River valley of northern Belize, from the river mouth in the north all the way to the New River Lagoon in the south. Documentary aids included a group of maps and a census that were drawn and compiled between 1786 and 1790. The maps gave the names of settlers and the locations of their landholdings along the various rivers, often designated by little huts with red roofs that pinpoint camp locations in relation to meanders along the rivers. The census for the settlement breaks down the population by heads of households and lists men, women, and children individually by name, identifying them as white, free, or slave. Integration of these data sets enabled the author to locate the riverside woodcutting claims held by the settlers during the 1780s and to determine the numbers and names of the slaves who lived there for most of each year.[33]

Only a limited portion of the New River is accessible by land, so most of the archaeological survey was undertaken from a skiff with a small outboard engine. Over a six-week period, the author surveyed approximately sixty kilometers of the New River and identified seventeen historic sites. Deposits ranged from a few fragments of bottle glass to several hundred ceramic, glass, and metal artifacts distributed over more than a hectare. According to the census, each of these sites was occupied seasonally by between sixteen and fifty-two woodcutters. Much of the riverbank was in high bush, posing significant challenges for surveying the ground surface, but other sites were located in sugar cane fields that had just been harvested, leaving mostly exposed, burned ground surface, where scatters of artifacts could be spotted easily. Because the New River rarely floods, making soil buildup scant, most of the artifacts were found lying on the surface.

The seventeen sites investigated offer rare insights into woodcutter life. Two sites yielded significant quantities of artifacts, indicating heavy occupation by slaves. One was in dense bush above the confluence of two branches of the New River, approximately twenty-six kilometers from the river mouth. This locality is identified on the 1787 survey map as the camp of Matthias Gale, a settler of considerable property who named his business Caledonia (figs. 19, 20). When staking a land claim, he typically nailed a stave "[cut] with the . . . [word] GALE" to a tree. Gale was a white settler whose household in 1790 included six white men, seven free men, twenty-

Figure 19 Tracing of a portion of David Lamb's *A Map of that part of Yucatan in the Bay of Honduras allotted to Great Britain for the cutting of Logwood*. Ink and watercolor on paper, 1787. The map, which is oriented with north at the bottom, shows Matthias Gale's Caledonia and the woodcutting claim of Robert Francis O'Brien. Caledonia was located on a wedge-shaped piece of elevated land, flanked on two sides by swamp and on the third by the New River. Densely forested today, it is several kilometers from the modern town of Caledonia. The site was carefully investigated through surface collection within a grid of meter-square units, yielding a large assemblage of eighteenth- and early-nineteenth-century ceramics, glassware, pipe fragments, and gunflints. O'Brien's site was discovered thirty-four kilometers south of the New River mouth, in a recently cut sugar cane field on a low ridge running parallel to the east bank. The site contained a thin scatter of artifacts ranging from buff-bodied slipwares of the early eighteenth century to hand-painted pearlwares of the 1810s and 1820s. The site appears to have been occupied longer than most of the others.

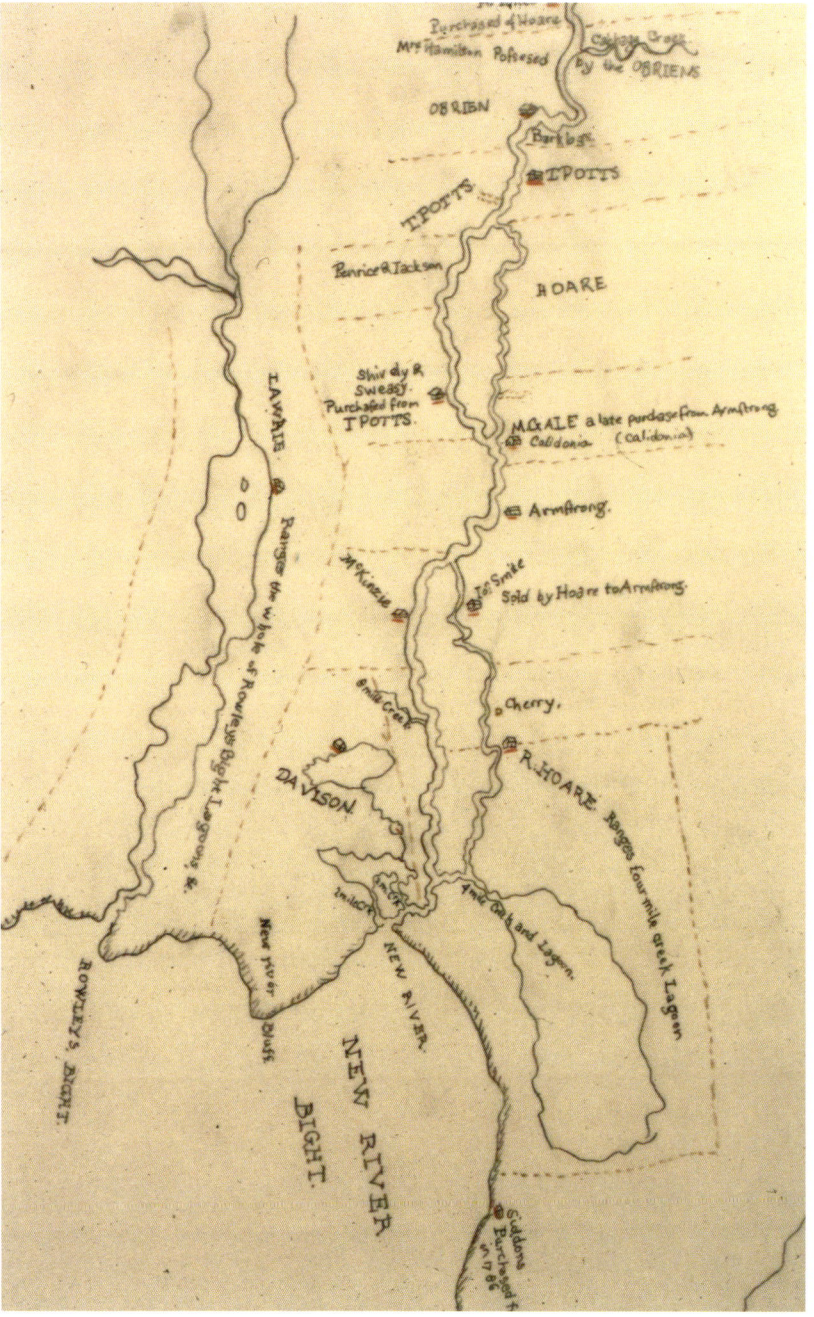

six male slaves, and four female slaves. He served terms as the Belize settlement's treasurer and conservator of the peace, in which capacity his duties ranged from acting as chief constable to presiding over marriages. Gale was apparently one of the settlement's most influential residents until his death about 1794. Since his official positions required him to spend much of his time in town, it is unlikely that Gale lived at Caledonia to any great extent.[34]

The other archaeologically rich site (fig. 19) corresponds with a camp of Robert Francis O'Brien, one of the wealthiest residents at Belize during the 1780s. He owned eighty-two slaves and had claims on the New River and Belize River to the south. Given the size and locations of his property, O'Brien probably quartered his slaves at more than one site and may have moved them from place to place as need arose. As was the case with Gale, O'Brien's slaves were equally unbalanced by gender, with sixty adult males, thirteen women, and nine children.

Like most of the artifacts recovered from woodcutting sites along the New River, those from Gale's and O'Brien's claims are largely associated with food preparation and communal consumption. Indeed, only a few rusty fragments of what appear to be machete blades relate to the dominant activities of cutting, shaping, and transporting wood. Most of the New River artifacts are plates and bowls. As one might expect, these objects are largely undecorated save for minimal shell-edge coloring and transfer printing on some later wares. An occasional teapot fragment suggests activities having

Figure 20 Site of Matthias Gale's woodcutting claim Caledonia. (Photo, Daniel Finamore.)

to do with individual choice or household decoration, but since teapots are also found in military camps, they cannot be interpreted as conclusive evidence of domestic family life.³⁵

The large number of storage vessel fragments recovered at O'Brien's site suggests that it was more permanent than most camps identified in this survey. The manager of his claim no doubt relied heavily on imported food. By contrast, investigation of Gale's Caledonia site revealed fewer storage vessel fragments and a higher percentage of gunflints; his workforce may have relied more on hunting for subsistence. Key artifact categories common to other British colonial sites but absent from those along the New River include glass lamp chimneys and lighting devices, household cutlery, window glass, house-construction nails, coins, and clothing buttons. Unlike plantations where hand-me-downs from the main house were common, the slaves working the New River sites had no access to manufactured goods other than what the claimholder or his agent transported upriver for their use.

Two artifacts from New River sites exhibit postmanufacture marks possibly denoting personal ownership (fig. 21). Such marks frequently appear on artifacts from contexts where objects are by necessity stored and treated as communal property, such as aboard ship or in frontier or military camps. Alternatively, marks could express deeply rooted cultural affiliations. Ceramic bowls inscribed with an "X," sometimes inside a circle, appear frequently in excavations of slave plantations in South Carolina. The consistency of such marks suggests that they did not denote personal ownership. It is difficult to envision the range of activities that might have taken place in these remote forest camps, but with a lack of first-person accounts of life there, it is easy to focus on the economic realm and overlook evidence that might hint at the social or even spiritual practices of the inhabitants. African American priests in modern Cuba inscribe a similar cruciform pattern on the bottom of vessels when they are creating charms, and art historians have traditionally recognized an "X" within a circle as a cosmogram of the Bakongo people of the southwest coast of Africa. Many people from that region were transported across the Atlantic during the slave trade, and Bakongo culture was so influential that other people adopted their practices in both Africa and the Americas. Like the slaves on South Carolina plantations, Belize laborers may have been using these inscribed vessels in Bakongo rituals that connected the living with the powers of the dead, traversing the earthly and spiritual horizons depicted in the cosmogram. These vessels and their sacred contents were not solely remnants of cultural practices fractured by slavery but may have represented the persistence of the slaves' worldview, one that varied significantly from that of those who enslaved them. As such, they could have been emblems of resistance to the way of life forced on these laborers by the seemingly incessant demand for mahogany.³⁶

For most people, the beauty of mahogany transcended the colonial hinterland and conveyed only an aura of richness and refinement that rendered it a desirable cabinetmaking material. Like his contemporaries, Newport merchant Aaron Lopez placed many orders for mahogany furniture with

Figure 21 Base of a pearlware bowl recovered from the O'Brien site. (Photo, Daniel Finamore.) The bowl is inscribed with an "X."

cabinetmaker John Goddard. In March 1770 Goddard billed Lopez for "2 pr. Roles [Torah rollers] for Moses's Law" at a cost of 13s. 8d. per pair. (In Hebrew, Torah rollers are known as *atsey chayim,* "trees of life.") Although it is possible that the rollers were for Lopez's personal use, it is more likely that they were to hold a Torah he had donated to Touro Synagogue in Newport several months earlier. Prominent individuals often donated decorative and functional objects to the temples and churches they attended, and the use of mahogany would have been a visible symbol of the donor's wealth and status.[37]

Today, Touro Synagogue displays a sixteenth-century Torah written on deer hide and fitted with rollers that appear to be mahogany. Although there is no evidence that these are the rollers created by Goddard and donated by Lopez, they were produced from the wood of choice for urban furniture of the eighteenth and early nineteenth centuries. Mahogany was, however, much more than just a desirable and expensive commodity. Its harvesting, transportation, marketing, and sale represented links in a long chain that bound the disparate lives of slaves, mahogany claim holders, mariners, British merchants, American traders, and furniture makers and their patrons on both sides of the Atlantic.

ACKNOWLEDGMENTS For assistance with this article the author thanks Patricia McAnany, Mary Beaudry, Dean Lahikainen, Josephine Carothers and George Schwartz.

1. Walter J. Gadsby, *On the Shores of the Caribbean Sea (Stories of Far-off British Honduras)* (London: J. W. Butcher, n.d. [1911]), pp. 53–54. At the invitation of Dean Lahikainen, the author presented a paper on the mahogany trade at the "Boston Furniture Symposium: New Research on the Federal Period," Peabody Essex Museum, November 14–16, 2003. I am grateful to the participants who made valuable suggestions for this published version.

2. Unfinished mahogany was shipped well beyond this region, to mainland Europe and beyond, but this study focuses primarily on the colonial and early American trade.

3. To date, no single volume adequately presents the unconventional history of the Bay Settlement, Colony of British Honduras, and independent nation of Belize. The best sources for the general reader are Nigel Bolland, *The Formation of a Colonial Society: Belize, from Conquest to Crown Colony* (Baltimore: Johns Hopkins University Press, 1977); and Narda Dobson, *A History of Belize* (London: Longman Caribbean, 1979).

4. Adam Bowett, "The Commmercial Introduction of Mahogany and the Naval Stores Act of 1721," *Furniture History* 30 (1994): 43–56. Robert F. Trent, "Chest with Drawer," in *The Concord Museum: Decorative Arts from a New England Collection*, edited by David F. Wood (Concord, Mass.: Concord Museum, 1996), pp. 6–7. Charles H. Foss, *Cabinetmakers of the Eastern Seaboard: A Study of Early Canadian Furniture* (Toronto: M. F. Feheley Publishers, 1977), p. 3. *Boston Gazette,* August 22–29, 1737, cited in *The Arts and Crafts in New England, 1704–1775,* compiled by George Francis Dow (Topsfield, Mass.: Wayside Press, 1927), p. 129.

5. Ropes Family Papers, undated entry at end of family shop account book, ca. 1760–1770, Peabody Essex Museum (hereafter cited as PEM), Phillips Library. Mack Headley, "Eighteenth-Century Cabinet Shops and the Furniture-making Trades in Newport, Rhode Island," in *American Furniture,* edited by Luke Beckerdite (Hanover, N.H.: University Press of New England for the Chipstone Foundation, 1999), p. 17.

6. Object file, acc. 101,792, American Decorative Arts Department, PEM. At some point in the early nineteenth century, the spelling of the family name changed from Chever to Cheever. Dean Thomas Lahikainen, "A Salem Cabinet-maker's Price Book," in *American Furniture,* edited by Luke Beckerdite (Hanover, N.H.: University Press of New England for the Chipstone Foundation, 2001), pp. 155, 194.

7. Paul Carpenter Standley and Samuel J. Record, *The Forests and Flora of British Honduras* (Chicago: Field Museum of Natural History, 1936). Peter L. Weaver and Oswaldo A. Sabido, *Mahogany in Belize: A Historical Perspective* (Rio Piedras, Puerto Rico: Institute of Tropical Forestry, 1997), p. 1. F. Lewis Hinckley, *Directory of Historic Cabinet Woods* (New York: Crown Publishers, 1960), pp. 118–38. Mainland mahogany is now known as *Swietenia macrophylla* and island mahogany as *Swietenia mahogani*. A third species grows only on the Pacific coast and is not relevant to this discussion.

8. *The Arts and Crafts in New York, 1777–1799*, compiled by Rita Susswein (New York: New-York Historical Society, 1954), p. 138. "The First Account of the State of That Part of America called The Mosquito Shore in the Year 1757," Public Record Office (hereafter cited as PRO), Kew, England, Colonial Office Records CO123/1. "Dyer to Your Lord," 1790, Nelson Papers, British Library, Add. 34,903 F.166-170. Report by George Hyde, February 2, 1836, R.2, p. 477, National Archives, Belize. Modern studies have found the rate and density of growth to vary based on a wide range of factors, including age, size, rainfall, and locality. Favorable conditions include fertile and well-drained soils that characterize large portions of modern Belize. K. Shono and L. K. Snook, "Growth of Big-Leaf Mahogany (Swietenia macrophylla) in Natural Forests in Belize," *Journal of Tropical Forest Science* 18, no. 1 (2006): 66–73.

9. "Abstracts of English Shipping Records Relating to Massachusetts Ports, from Original Shipping Records in the Public Record Office, London, 10 vols., compiled for the Essex Institute, Salem, Massachusetts," typescript, 1931, PEM.

10. Ibid. Jonathan Tomkyne, "An account of the quantities of Mahogany, satinwood, rose wood not including any dyeing woods imported into England from Christmas 1777 inclusive to Christmas 1783," April 11, 1785, PRO, T64/276B/417. One mid-nineteenth-century mahogany merchant stated that the best planks were at least eight to ten inches thick and as long as possible (not under twenty-seven feet) (E. Chaloner and W. Fleming, *The Mahogany Tree: Its Botanical Characters, Qualities and Uses, with Practical Suggestions for Selecting and Cutting It in the Regions of Its Growth, in the West Indies and Central America* [Liverpool: Rockliff and Son, 1850], p. 46). Daniel Finamore, "'Pirate Water': Sailing to Belize in the Mahogany Trade," in *Maritime Empires: British Imperial Maritime Trade in the Nineteenth Century*, edited by David Killingray, Margarette Lincoln, and Nigel Rigby (Rochester, N.Y.: Boydell Press, 2004), pp. 30–47. Although New Providence in the Bahama Islands is technically in a mahogany-growing region, its location as a transit point between Caribbean and North American colonial ports, its limited forested area, and the large quantities of wood exported indicate that the majority of wood reported to have arrived from there actually originated elsewhere. In the five years between January 1797 and June 1802, approximately 50 percent of mahogany exports of Belize went directly to the British Isles, 42 percent went to American ports, while 8 percent went to Jamaica or New Providence to be transshipped elsewhere.

11. Conversely, the vast majority of wood exported from primary extraction centers such as Belize was in the form of squared logs, with only enough wood in other forms to fill the interstitial areas of the cargo hold (Finamore, "'Pirate Water,'" pp. 44–45). *New-York Daily Advertiser*, November 16, 1797.

12. "Abstracts of English Shipping Records."

13. Dobson, *A History of Belize*, pp. 60–61. "Dyer to Your Lord." Hayley and Hopkins to Aaron Lopez, London, December 8, 1770, Aaron Lopez Papers, letters, box 652, book 631, pp. 42, 47, Newport Historical Society (hereafter cited as NHS).

14. *Commerce of Rhode Island, 1726–1800*, 2 vols. (Boston: Massachusetts Historical Society, 1914), 1: 386–87, 172. *Honduras Almanack* (Belize: The Magistrates, 1827), p. 12. Chaloner and Fleming, *The Mahogany Tree*, pp. 58–59.

15. Archibald Robertson Gibbs, *British Honduras: An Historical and Descriptive Account of the Colony from Its Settlement, 1670* (London: Sampson, Low, Marston, Searle & Rivington, 1883), p. 116, citing the *Honduras Observer*, 1843. Orlando W. Roberts, *Narrative of Voyages and Excursions on the East Coast and in the Interior of Central America* (Edinburgh: Constable Company, 1827), p. 302, citing the *Macclesfield Courier,* October 1823.

16. Henry Drinker to Capt. Oswald Eve, November 30, 1771, Drinker Letter Book, 1769–1772, p. 449, Historical Society of Pennsylvania, Philadelphia.

17. Angel Cal, "Rural Society and Economic Development: British Mercantile Capital in 19th-Century Belize" (Ph.D. diss., University of Arizona, 1991), pp. 128–29. Henry Gardiner, "Detailed Account of the Establishment and Expense of a Mahogany Gang," in Young Anderson, *Eastern Coast of Central America: Mr. Anderson's Report* (London: Manning and Mason, 1839), pp. 135–38, cited in Cal, "Rural Society," p. 132. Evidence for renting out the labor of

slaves for timber cutting and other work appears frequently in the Henley Papers, Caird Library, National Maritime Museum, Greenwich (hereafter cited as NMM). In 1809, for example, the master of the ship *Freedom* paid over £84 for 253 days of "negro hire" at 6s. 8d. per day (HNL/59/83), and in 1813 Capt. Robert Horry submitted a bill for 315 days' labor performed by Antonio, January, Joe Long, Ned Jones, Billy Hemming, Joe Lamb, Quam Edwards, Dick Edwards, John Morris, and Scotland Grant, who warped the ship *Lord Nelson* off the shore after she was driven up by a hurricane in 1813 (HNL82/38).

18. Account of Sales of Sundry goods shipped by Mr. Aaron Lopez on Board the Brig *Charlotte* in the Bay of Honduras, 1768, Papers of Aaron Lopez (hereafter cited as PAL), box 1, folder 9, American Jewish Historical Society, New York (hereafter cited as AJHS). Hayley and Hopkins to Aaron Lopez, September 19, 1772, PAL, box 14, folder 1, AJHS. William Robertson to Aaron Lopez, September 22, 1770, Aaron Lopez Papers, letters, box 652, book 631, NHS. Account of charges on the *Minerva* Capt. Samuel Clarke from the Bay of Honduras for account of Mr. Aaron Lopez, Hayley and Hopkins, April 30, 1773, PAL, box 2, folder 11, AJHS. On this voyage at least, the charges for lighterage, pierage, pilotage, small repairs, and clearance totaled more than the value of the cargo.

19. John Newdigate to Aaron Lopez, April 9, 1771, Aaron Lopez Papers, letters, box 652, book 632, NHS. Ron Potvin, "'A poor soft weak Headed puffed up foolish fellow': The John Newdigate Controversy," *Newport History* 68, no. 236 (1997): 137–42.

20. John Newdigate to Aaron Lopez, July 14, 1771, Aaron Lopez Papers, letters, box 652, book 632, NHS. Nathaniel Russell to Aaron Lopez, April 6, 1770, February 15, 1771, and March 29, 1771, Aaron Lopez Papers, letters, box 652, book 631, NHS. Virginia Steele Wood, personal communication, July 23, 2004.

21. Cruger to William Tucker, New York, August 9, 1766, and April 22, 1767, Henry Cruger Papers, letter book, 1764–1768, New-York Historical Society (hereafter cited as N-YHS).

22. James Card Papers, MSS9001C, box 1, Rhode Island Historical Society (hereafter cited as RIHS), including James Gourhty Sr. to Capt. Card, August 14, 1771, and Card to Warner, April 4, 1770. Private records book 1, 1774–1797, p. 299, National Archives, Belize.

23. Charles H. Card, "Richard Card and Descendents," typescript, 1996, RIHS. Jonathan Card to Sarah Card, July 2, 1772, Sarah Card Papers, RIHS.

24. Private records book 1, 1774–1797, pp. 84, 105, National Archives, Belize. List of the Inhabitants of Honduras, taken by His Majesty's Superintendent, in January and February 1790, CO123/11, PRO. Jonathan Card's Bill, HNL/86/4, Caird Library, National Maritime Museum, Greenwich, U.K.

25. George Henderson, *An Account of the British Settlement of Honduras* (London: R. Baldwin, 1811), pp. 33–35. Port of Belize Shipping Returns for 1807 and 1809 through 1812, CO128/1, PRO. Finamore, "'Pirate Water.'" Henderson, *An Account of the British Settlement of Honduras*, p. 34.

26. Sir John Alder Burdon, *Archives of British Honduras*, 3 vols. (London: Sifton Praed, 1931–1935), 2: 5. Henderson, *An Account of the British Settlement of Honduras*, p. 33. Standard commodities arriving on American ships included bread, flour, crackers, butter, vinegar, pitch, potatoes, sheep, turkeys, lumber and shingles, as well as preserved mackerel, pork, beef, onions, and codfish in hogsheads, kegs, and barrels. Port of Belize Shipping Returns for 1807 and 1809 through 1812, CO128/1, PRO. Memorial of the Committee of Merchants trading to Honduras on the subject of orders allowing American ships to import Mahogany & logwood into this country, July 13, 1797, PC 1/39/125, PRO.

27. Daniel Finamore, "A Mariner's Utopia: Pirates and Logwood in the Bay of Honduras," in *X Marks the Spot: The Archaeology of Piracy*, edited by Russell K. Skowronek and Charles Ewen (Gainesville: University Press of Florida, 2005), 64–78. Burdon, *Archives of British Honduras*, 1: 2, 57, 60. Gilbert M. Joseph, "John Coxon and the Role of Buccaneering in the Settlement of the Yucatan Colonial Frontier," *Belizean Studies* 17, no. 3 (1989): 2–21.

28. Charles Knowles Bolton, *Christ Church, Salem Street, Boston, 1723: A Guide* (Boston: Christ Church, 1944), p. 96. Mary Kent Davey Babcock, *Christ Church, Salem Street, Boston: The Old North Church of Paul Revere Fame, Historical Sketches, Colonial Period, 1723–1775* (Boston: Thomas Todd Co., 1944). The practice of donating wood to support causes has precedents in the region. In 1648 the Company of the Eleutherian Adventurers acknowledged support from Massachusetts settlers for their fledgling Bahamian community with a gift of ten tons of braziletto, which was sold in Boston for £124 and applied to the Harvard College Endowment Fund. See Zoe C. Durrell, *The Innocent Island: Abaco in the Bahamas* (Brattleboro, Vt.: Durrell Publications, 1972), p. 20.

29. Bolland, *The Formation of a Colonial Society,* p. 49. CO137/48, PRO. Bolland, *The Formation of a Colonial Society,* p. 50.

30. Henderson, *An Account of the British Settlement of Honduras,* pp. 56–64. Finamore, "'Pirate Water,'" pp. 30–47.

31. Dr. John Young to Supt. Reporting on the health and physical conditions of work of the mahogany cutters, August 8, 1836, 2R529-32, National Archives, Belize.

32. Thomas Graham, "Journal of my Visitation," 1790, CO123/9, PRO. *Honduras Almanack,* pp. 8–9.

33. The National Science Foundation funded the author's archaeological survey. Daniel Finamore, "Sailors and Slaves on the Woodcutting Frontier: Archaeology of the British Bay Settlement, Belize" (Ph.D. diss., Boston University, 1994). "A Map of that part of Yucatan in the Bay of Honduras allotted to Great Britain for the cutting of Logwood," by David Lamb, CO700 BH no. 14, 1787, PRO. "List of the Inhabitants of Honduras with their Families," 1790, CO123/9:256-262, PRO.

34. Private Records Book 1, 1774–1797, February 21, 1789, p. 120, National Archives, Belize.

35. Joyce M. Clements, "The Cultural Creation of the Feminine Gender: An Example from 19th-Century Military Households at Fort Independence, Boston," *Historical Archaeology* 27, no. 4 (1993): 39–64.

36. Olive R. Jones and E. Ann Smith, *Glass of the British Military, ca. 1755–1820* (Quebec: Parks Canada, 1985), p. 115. Leland Ferguson, "'The Cross is a Magic Sign': Marks on Eighteenth-Century Bowls from South Carolina," in *"I, Too, Am America": Archaeological Studies of African-American Life,* edited by Theresa A. Singleton (Charlottesville: University Press of Virginia, 1999), pp. 116–31. Leland Ferguson, *Uncommon Ground: Archaeology and Early African America, 1650–1800* (Washington, D.C.: Smithsonian Institution Press), 1992.

37. Aaron Lopez to John Goddard, 1760–1771, PAL, box 12, folder 10, AJHS. Stanley F. Chyet, *Lopez of Newport: Colonial American Merchant Prince* (Detroit: Wayne State University Press, 1970), p. 57. Torahs were not commonly owned for personal devotion, though they were held by some wealthy Americans of that era. Jonathan Sarna, personal communication, December 1, 2003. *Commerce of Rhode Island,* 2: 195, Jeremiah Osborne to Aaron Lopez, Graves End, March 31, 1767, "a sett of candle stick worth £36 I have on board from Enocks Mother for the Sinegoge." These candlesticks arrived on the ship *Pitt* from Lisbon, delivered by Capt. Osborne in 1767. Bert Lippincott, librarian, NHS, personal communication, April 2003.

Figure 1 Pier table, Philadelphia, Pennsylvania, 1825–1835. Mahogany with tulip poplar and white pine; marble, glass. H. 37", W. 42" D. 20". (Courtesy, Aileen Minor Antiques.)

Nicholas C. Vincent

Philadelphia Pier Tables and Their Role in Cultures of Sociability and Competition

▼ PIER TABLES WERE the epitome of stylish taste in early-nineteenth-century America. The materials used in their construction were often expensive and conspicuously ostentatious, placing them at the vanguard of stationary furniture forms. Pier tables were also opulent in function, serving both as glorified stands for lighting equipment and ornaments and, in most instances, as elaborate looking glass frames. Placed between windows, pier tables with mirrored backs worked in conjunction with pier glasses hanging above them to reflect light and create the illusion of doubled space.

Contrary to modern interpretations, pier tables were seldom bought in pairs, rarely used for dining or serving beverages, and almost never found in hallways. To be displayed effectively, these large architectural objects demanded a setting that was harmonious, expansive, and splendidly furnished. Consequently, the owners of pier tables in Philadelphia tended to be wealthy businessmen. With very few exceptions, patrons placed their tables in parlors. As this essay will demonstrate, owners used these objects not only to decorate their homes but also to enhance sociability and to facilitate business.

Although inspired by similar classical sources, Philadelphia and New York cabinetmakers produced empire-style pier tables that were regionally distinctive. Philadelphia rectangular pier tables often have upper rails with a cavetto molding, carved or turned wood front supports and applied rear pilasters, oil gilding, integral looking glass plates with decorative borders, and ogee-curved lower shelves with demilune, pie-wedge mahogany veneers (figs. 1, 2). By contrast, New York rectangular pier tables typically feature straight-sided rails, columnar marble front supports and applied rear pilasters, gilded cast brass ornaments, delicately shaded freehand gilding and bronze powder stenciling, integral looking glass plates with undecorated borders, simple incurved lower shelves, and carved, cornucopia brackets adjoining lion's-paw feet (figs. 3, 4).[1]

Most pier tables represent the work of multiple tradesmen, including joiners, turners, carvers, gilders, stonecutters, and glassworkers. By the second quarter of the nineteenth century, large manufactory warehouses dominated urban furniture production, consolidating the work of smaller specialized shops scattered throughout the city. Competing firms often purchased parts from the same specialized shops, resulting in a uniformity of design. In urban classical furniture, regionalism was largely a product of standardization and piecework production.

Philadelphia makers had access to the labor and materials necessary to copy New York pier tables, but they chose to distinguish their products

Figure 2 Pier table, Philadelphia, Pennsylvania, 1825–1835. Mahogany with unrecorded secondary woods; marble, glass. H. 39" W. 42" D. 20". (© Christie's Images Limited [2006].)

Figure 3   Pier table labeled by Michael Allison, New York City, 1816–1825. Rosewood with tulip poplar; brass, marble, glass. H. 37" W. 40" x D. 20". (Courtesy, Winterthur Museum.)

Figure 4   Pier table, New York City, 1820–1830. Rosewood with white pine; marble, glass. H. 39", W. 44", D. 19". (Courtesy, Winterthur Museum.)

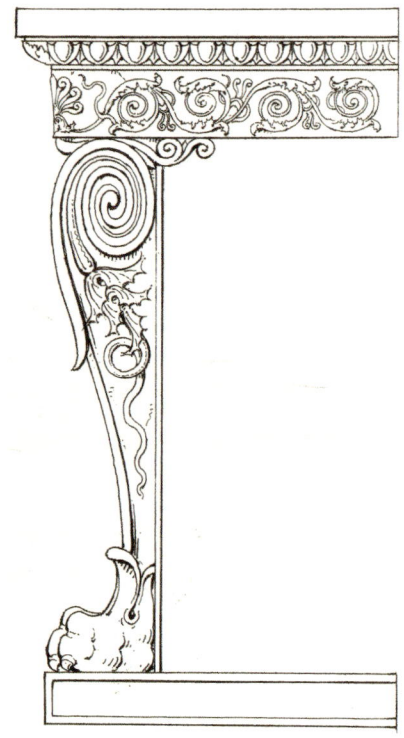

Figure 5 Composite illustration showing, (a) Crispijn van de Passe, *Oficina Arcularia* (Amsterdam, 1642) pl. 17 (Courtesy, Winterthur Library: Printed Book and Periodical Collection); (b) detail of the support on the pier table illustrated in fig. 30; (c) George Smith, *Ornamental Designs* (London, ca. 1812), pl. 30 (Courtesy, Winterthur Library: Printed Book and Periodical Collection); (d) William Smee and Sons, *Designs of Furniture* (London, ca. 1840), pl. 86 (Courtesy, Winterthur Library: Printed Book and Periodical Collection).

from those made in other urban centers. During the 1820s Philadelphia cabinetmakers adopted the carved scroll-and-paw support as a fashionable alternative to the marble columns favored in New York. As with most classical details, however, this "new" feature was actually the third or fourth revival of an earlier design (fig. 5).

With increasing competition, makers and retailers of pier tables had to be innovative to satisfy the demand for fashionable forms. At the same time, they had to standardize production to control costs and generate profit. Period price books and surviving objects indicate that makers and retailers resolved these opposing market forces by developing basic frame designs to which options could be easily added. *The Philadelphia Cabinet and Chair Makers' Union Book of Prices* (1828) lists a "plain pier table" with "four solid columns" at $4.50. "Two plain solid pilasters rabbetted to receive glass" cost twenty-five cents "extra from [the] start."[2]

Figure 6 Pier table, Philadelphia, Pennsylvania, 1820–1830. Mahogany with tulip poplar; marble, glass. H. 38", W. 34", D. 17½". (Courtesy, Historical Society of Delaware, permanent collection; photo, Gavin Ashworth.)

Dimensional variations among extant Philadelphia pier tables suggest many were commissioned rather than purchased from stock-in-trade. The example illustrated in figure 6 was almost certainly made for a small pier or recess, whereas the unusually large example shown in figure 7 was commissioned for a room with broad expanses of wall space. As was the case with earlier pier tables, some Philadelphia examples made in the classical style had ornamental details intended to echo or harmonize with interior architectural components (fig. 8).[3]

Figure 7 Pier table bearing the label of Anthony G. Quervelle, Philadelphia, Pennsylvania, 1825–1829. Mahogany with tulip poplar; brass, marble, glass. H. 37 3/4", W. 48", D. 22". (Courtesy, Athenaeum of Philadelphia.)

Figure 8 The Family of John Q. Aymar, attributed to George W. Twibill, New York City, ca. 1833. Oil on canvas. 30" x 40". (Private collection; photo, Gavin Ashworth.) No period images of a Philadelphia pier table in situ are known. In this New York interior, the pier table and the fireplace surround share complementary features such as gilt Ionic capitals. John Q. Aymar was a prominent China trade merchant; the ship masts in the distance symbolize the source of his family's wealth and social standing.

Figure 9 Design for a pier table in Jean le Pautre, *Livre de miroirs, tables et gueridons* (Paris, ca. 1660), pl. 3. (Courtesy, Winterthur Library: Printed Book and Periodical Collection.)

Genealogy of the Pier Table Form

Elaborately carved wood tables with marble tops were Italian renaissance inventions with roots in antiquity. Popularized by French King Louis XIV at his court at Versailles during the seventeenth century, marble-topped pier tables situated beneath looking glasses became status symbols in fashionable state apartments throughout Europe. Tastemakers such as Robert Adam began advocating lighter, more delicate variations suitable for both wood and marble tops during the 1760s, but French court designs under Napoleon Bonaparte soon returned to a more architectonic, archaeologically correct interpretation of ancient classical design. This included the "empire" pier table with a looking glass plate in the back and its many variants, which became fashionable in America during the first half of the nineteenth century.

The wall-oriented tables that originated in Italy during the late sixteenth century were highly sculptural, often designed by architects, and lavishly finished with carving and gilding. Imposing and expensive, these tables were ideally suited to formal French interiors of the late seventeenth century. As Carl Kaellgren has argued, the grand rooms at Vaux-le-Vicomte

Figure 10 Pier table attributed to William Buckland and William Bernard Sears, Richmond County, Virginia, 1761–1771. Cherry with beech; marble. H. 31 1/4", W. 45 3/8", D. 29 3/4". (Courtesy, Colonial Williamsburg Foundation; photo, Gavin Ashworth.)

and Versailles, used for formal and ceremonial activities, helped popularize and codify the form and presentation of side, pier, and console tables. By the mid-seventeenth century, pier tables were designed for specific architectural settings, often accompanied by a looking glass above and candlestands on either side (fig. 9).[4]

In America, "slab tables," or "sideboard tables," with marble tops came into use by the late 1720s. As the latter term implies, many of these examples were probably used in dining rooms. Their height, which was lower than that of classical pier tables, was well suited for displaying ceramics, glass, and plate, as well as serving food and drink. A notable exception, however, can be found in two marble-top tables commissioned for Mount Airy, Richmond County, Virginia, house of planter John Tayloe II (figs. 10, 11).

Figure 11 Sideboard table attributed to William Buckland and William Bernard Sears, Richmond County, Virginia, 1761–1771. Walnut; marble. H. 35", W. 42½", D. 25½". (Collection of the Museum of Early Southern Decorative Arts, Old Salem Museums & Gardens; photo, Gavin Ashworth.)

Figure 12 Pier or side table, carving attributed to Nicholas Bernard and Martin Jugiez, Philadelphia, Pennsylvania ca. 1765. Mahogany; marble. H. 34", W. 66", D. 30". (Courtesy, Philadelphia Museum of Art, purchased with the J. Stogdell Stokes Fund and the John D. McIlhenny Fund, 1953; photo, Gavin Ashworth.)

Figure 13 Pier table, Philadelphia, Pennsylvania, 1767–1770. Mahogany with yellow pine and walnut; marble. H. 32 3/8", W. 48 1/4", D. 23 1/4". (Courtesy, Metropolitan Museum of Art, John Stewart Kennedy Fund, 1918 [18.110.27]; photo, Gavin Ashworth, Image © Metropolitan Museum of Art.)

Although both objects are attributed to architect William Buckland and his carver William Bernard Sears, their stylistic disparity suggests that only one of the tables may have been used in a dining room. Similarly, the Philadelphia examples illustrated in figures 12 and 13 may have been intended as pier tables for use in a parlor. Indeed, the scroll-foot example was derived from a design for a pier glass and table illustrated on plate 152 in the third edition of Thomas Chippendale's *Director* (1762). Both follow grand European tradition in being solely the work of a carver.[5]

For the most part, American pier tables are a post-Revolutionary form. A few Philadelphia examples dating from the last quarter of the eighteenth century are in the early neoclassical style promulgated by Robert Adam, George Hepplewhite, and Thomas Sheraton (figs. 14, 15). Hepplewhite and

Figure 14   Designs for pier tables in Thomas Sheraton, *The Cabinet-Maker and Upholsterer's Drawing-Book* (London, 1793), pl. 4. (Courtesy, Winterthur Library: Printed Book and Periodical Collection.)

Sheraton associated pier tables with excessive decoration and specific use. As Sheraton noted in 1793, "pier tables are merely for ornament under a glass, they are generally made very light, and the style of finishing them is rich and elegant." The following year Hepplewhite wrote: "*Pier Tables* are become an article of much fashion; and not being applied to such general use as other Tables, admit, with great propriety, of much elegance and ornament."[6]

A pier table made by New York cabinetmaker Charles-Honoré Lannuier recalls Sheraton's designs in having cross-stretchers and an urn finial, but most American examples in the early neoclassical style stand on four straight legs with no stretchers or lower shelf. Excepting differences in their tops, some pier tables are difficult to distinguish from card tables. As the nineteenth century progressed, the design of pier tables became increasingly distanced from that of other tables. While this is consistent with the greater numbers of specialized forms that appeared from 1775 to 1850, it also suggests pro-

Figure 15 Designs for pier tables in George Hepplewhite, *The Cabinet-Maker and Upholsterer's Guide,* 3rd ed. (London, 1794), pl. 65. (Courtesy, Winterthur Library: Printed Book and Periodical Collection.)

gressively nuanced distinctions in the function of objects and the language used to describe them.[7]

By the second decade of the nineteenth century, the term "pier table" carried connotations that to most Americans were distinct from the form's closest cognate, the "console table." Scholars in Europe do not draw distinctions between pier tables and console tables because there the two forms were effectively synonymous. In America, the term "pier table" appears with much greater frequency than "console table." The Society of Journeymen Cabinetmakers' 1836 wareroom inventory lists a single "consul" table and seven "pier" tables. As understood here, a console table was attached to the wall and did not have a back frame or support.[8]

Perhaps the biggest change in the design of pier tables was the incorporation of a mirrored glass plate. As Sheraton noted:

Figure 16 Detail of pier table in Pierre de La Mésangère, *Collection de meubles et objets de goût* (Paris, 1802), pl. 10. (Courtesy, Metropolitan Museum of Art, Harris Brisbane Dick Fund, 1930 [30.80], Image © Metropolitan Museum of Art).

The glasses are often made to appear to come down to the stretcher of the table; that is, a piece of glass is fixed in behind the pier table, separate from the upper glass, which then appears to be the continuation of the same glass, and, by reflection, makes the table to appear double. This small piece of glass may be fixed either in the dado of the room, or in the frame of the table.

With the advent of the "antique taste" and its emphasis on massive, architectonic forms and columnar supports, plate glass was incorporated in numerous forms, including sideboards, dressing tables, and pier tables. The design and structure of late neoclassical furnishings facilitated and depended on the use of mirrored glass more than any preceding style (fig. 16). Thus, when Rudolph Ackermann illustrated a formal pier table in his *Repository of Arts* (fig. 17), he noted: "At the back is a looking-glass, in order both to lighten the design and to give an appearance of distance, where it would otherwise be heavy."[9]

Befitting Philadelphia's large and diverse population in the nineteenth century, the city's classical pier tables exhibit an eclectic mix of stylistic sources. Appropriately, the best-known pier table from that city is an intriguing early example made in the shop of Joseph B. Barry & Son for merchant Louis Clapier (fig. 18). Made under the supervision of Barry's foreman, George Wright, the table displays elements of both French and British design. The carved and pierced panel at the back derives from Sheraton's *Drawing Book,* whereas the spiral garlands on the front columns and gilt brass mounts have parallels in French and Italian work. Circa 1820 Barry produced another hybrid pier table—sporting the by now de rigueur glass plate in the back and a marble rather than wood top—for which there is no direct parallel (fig. 19). The robustly carved and gilt lion's-paw feet and their accompanying winged brackets recall fashionable New York pier tables, while the inset marble shelf and the scrolled gilt brackets along the apron provide visual interest and distinction to what is essentially a French Consulate form. Barry's "sampling" was the norm rather than the exception, reflecting the choices available to makers, who wanted more profitable and hence standardized production, and their patrons, who wanted distinctive if not quite unique pieces.[10]

Figure 17 Pier table illustrated on plate 17 in Rudolph Ackermann, *The Repository of Arts, Literature, Commerce, Manufactures, Fashion and Politics* (September 1828). (Courtesy, Winterthur Library: Printed Book and Periodical Collection.)

Figure 18 Pier table bearing the label of Joseph B. Barry & Son, Philadelphia, Pennsylvania, 1810–1815. Mahogany, satinwood, and amboina with tulip poplar and white pine; brass, marble, glass. H. 38", W. 54", D. 24". (Courtesy, Metropolitan Museum of Art, Friends of the American Wing Fund, Anonymous gift, George M. Kaufman gift, Sansbury-Mills Fund, gifts of the Committee of the Bertha King Benkard Memorial Fund, Mrs. Russell Sage, Mrs. Frederick Wildman, F. Ethel Wickham, Edgar William and Bernice Chrysler Garbisch, and Mrs. F. M. Townsend by exchange; and John Stewart Kennedy Fund and bequests of Martha S. Tiedeman and W. Gedney Beatty by exchange, 1976 [1976.324] Image © Metropolitan Museum of Art.)

Figure 19 Pier table attributed to Joseph B. Barry, Philadelphia, Pennsylvania, ca. 1820. Mahogany with unrecorded secondary woods; marble, glass. H. 40", W. 48", D. 20". (Courtesy, *Antiques* [May 1989], Brant Publications Inc.; photo, Wayne Gibson.)

Figure 20 Design for draperies in Pierre de la Mésangère, *Collection de meubles et objets de goût* (Paris, 1808), pl. 304. (Courtesy, Metropolitan Museum of Art, Harris Brisbane Dick Fund, 1930 [30.80] Image © Metropolitan Museum of Art.)

Cultures of Sociability

From their inception, pier tables in Europe were envisioned as an integral part of the enfilade—the prescribed progression of visitors from room to room. These tables were first encountered in passing as visitors made their rounds through the house. After touring the house and grounds, the party withdrew to the best parlor, where elaborate window draperies created a stage set within the home, with the pier table and pier glass serving as the centerpiece (fig. 20). On either side of these objects were large windows that looked out onto the estate (fig. 21). After dark, pier tables set with lighting fixtures and accompanied by looking glasses functioned as surrogate windows, providing a dramatic source of illumination. Like the owner's property, which had been visible through the flanking windows during the day, these furnishings also served as totems of wealth and social standing.[11]

This legacy of use continued in America, albeit on a smaller scale. Pier tables did not become fashionable in the United States before the widespread introduction of double parlors, an architectural innovation that evolved from the traditions of aristocratic and court custom in Continental Europe and Britain. By the second half of the eighteenth century, front and back parlors set next to a side entry and passage became the common urban town house form for the middling and upper classes in cities throughout the English-speaking world. Within this architectural setting, pier tables functioned en suite with lighting devices and looking glasses to reflect light throughout the room while creating the illusion of doubled space. Like the front parlors in which these tables were placed, their use was infrequent and formal, ideally suited to entertaining. As large, fixed, and brightly lighted objects, pier tables dictated guests' movement through the room and facilitated the discreet yet highly critical value judgments that characterized the culture of sociability. Thus, just as pier tables were part of an ensemble of furnishings, they also synchronized with an ensemble of human relationships.[12]

Pier tables are unusually tall and have no corresponding seating: they were designed for standing encounters. Pier tables with looking glass back plates almost always have marble tops, which, as the table's most visually

Figure 21 Design for a window curtain for a boudoir in Rudolph Ackermann, *The Repository of Arts, Literature, Commerce, Manufactures, Fashion and Politics* (April 1809), pl. 19. (Courtesy, Winterthur Library: Printed Book and Periodical Collection.)

accessible and prominent feature, connoted antiquity while signifying the object's massiveness, cost, and potential use. Stone tops were very durable, impervious to both liquid and fire, and comparatively easy to clean: these traits help explain why the popularity of marble-topped pier tables in America coincided with the advent of oil lighting. Following the invention of the Argand lamp in 1782, owners could light their homes more brightly than ever before, facilitating increased nighttime entertaining and complementing reflective surfaces. Yet in addition to being a fire hazard, the Argand lamp and its many offspring—astral, solar, and sinumbra lamps—were relatively fixed lighting devices, as an 1811 Philadelphia publication lamented:

> It has been a strong prejudice against the use of [Argand] lamps, that they can only be used for stationary or fixed lights, as being moved by hand, they are liable either to go out or spill the oil; to prevent this inconvenience, I would recommend, that a common tin hand-lamp be used.[13]

The growing popularity of stationary oil lamps as major lighting components for the home made the size and immobility of pier tables a functional asset rather than a liability. The successful use of expensive oil lamps also suggested a well-managed household; such lamps were fickle, prone to extinguishing, and required constant maintenance. According to *The House Servant's Directory*: "Lamps are now so much in use for drawing-rooms, dining-rooms, and entries, that it is a very important part of a servant's work to keep them in perfect order, so as to show a good light." Thus, pier tables, looking glasses, and oil lamps were costly luxuries that worked together to reflect their owner's status (fig. 22).[14]

Pier tables were not as common as the number of surviving examples would seem to suggest. Because these objects were sturdily built, endured little physical use, and usually belonged to families of means, they have survived in larger numbers and in better condition than perhaps any other table form. Philadelphia inventories reveal that at least 59 individuals owned pier tables between 1830 and 1839, and that number increased to 155 between 1840 and 1850. These figures reflect the greater popularity of the pier table form and the city's expanding market base. Indeed, between 1800 and 1850

Figure 22 Augustine Edouart, *Family in Silhouette,* New York City, 1842. Sepia wash with black paper cutouts. 19" x 28⅛". (Courtesy, Winterthur Museum.)

Table 1 Population of Urban Places (1800–1850)

	1800	1810	1820	1830	1840	1850
New York	60,515	96,373	123,706	202,589	312,710	515,547
Philadelphia	51,938	73,596	108,809	161,271	220,423	340,045
Baltimore	26,514	46,555	62,738	80,620	102,193	169,054
Boston	24,937	33,787	43,298	61,392	93,383	136,881

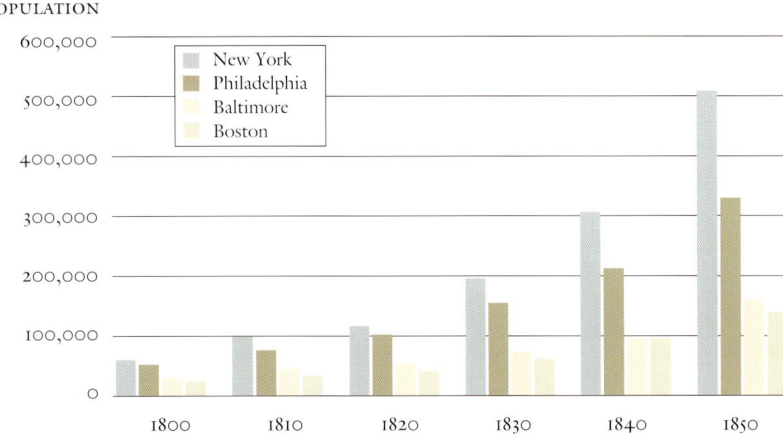

Modified from Campbell Gibson, "Population of the 100 Largest Cities and Other Urban Places in the United States: 1790 to 1990," June 1998, Population Division Working Paper, no. 27. U.S. Bureau of the Census.

Table 2 Pier Tables: Percent Ownership by Year (1830–1850)

	1830	1835	1840	1845	1850
	%	%	%	%	%
Pier tables	2.3	3.7	8.0	9.0	13.0
Card tables	35.0	27.0	28.0	21.0	19.0
Breakfast tables	32.0	17.0	21.0	11.0	11.0
Pembroke tables	1.5	0.7	0.0	1.1	0.0
Tea tables	2.3	5.9	1.8	0.0	0.0
Center tables	0.0	3.7	10.0	14.0	18.0
Dining tables	39.0	33.0	20.0	22.0	22.0
Dressing tables	4.6	3.7	4.9	3.4	3.7
Side tables	1.5	0.7	3.1	1.1	3.7
Sideboards	24.0	26.0	29.0	19.0	24.0
Sofas	18.0	22.0	31.0	26.0	35.0
Pianos	5.4	4.4	5.5	11.0	8.8

Philadelphia's population increased by a factor of six (Table 1). Although pier tables are often displayed in pairs today, the majority (78 percent) of Philadelphia owners had a single table in their best parlor.[15]

Between 1830 and 1850 from 2.3 percent to 13 percent of the population of Philadelphia owned pier tables, but these figures must be examined within the larger context of table ownership and home furnishings. For instance, pier tables appear with much less frequency than sofas, even though their average appraised values were similar. Previously owned pier tables were well within the financial reach of many consumers, yet for reasons of practicality and comfort, most opted to invest in sofas (Tables 2, 3). The comparative rarity of pier tables in Philadelphia suggests that few families were willing or able to allocate the time, space, and money to procure one. As luxury items, pier tables held certain meanings for their owners that were not shared by the populace at large (Table 4).

During the first part of the nineteenth century, most owners of pier tables in Philadelphia were professionals whose success depended on social and business networks and the exchange of information (Table 5). They tended to be wealthy and to live and work along the city's major thoroughfares near the Delaware River—the heart of Philadelphia's economy. In addition to shared proximity, many owners also had in common old claims to property rights within Philadelphia County.[16]

Table 3 Pier Tables: Average Value by Year (1830–1850)

	1830 $	1835 $	1840 $	1845 $	1850 $
Pier tables	11.38	18.75	14.39	12.83	9.05
Card tables	3.64	5.14	4.41	7.02	6.02
Breakfast tables	3.25	3.54	3.90	2.91	2.67
Pembroke tables	7.67	3.50	0.00	7.50	0.00
Tea tables	8.50	2.43	0.92	0.00	0.00
Center tables	0.00	16.60	9.95	11.54	9.96
Dining tables	6.16	9.02	7.20	6.65	5.40
Dressing tables	1.42	10.20	10.94	10.22	4.88
Side tables	1.00	3.00	4.54	5.50	2.56
Sideboards	13.63	16.39	12.69	14.20	6.33
Sofas	9.22	16.16	15.53	13.70	11.19
Pianos	44.29	147.86	80.56	112.78	90.50

Source: Wills, County of Philadelphia, Philadelphia, Pennsylvania, 1682–1875. Downs Collection, Winterthur Library.

Table 4 Comparative Wealth of Pier Table Owners in Philadelphia (1830–1850)

	1830	1835	1840	1845	1850
House Goods Average All	535.83	1,385.38	820.27	662.15	598.15
House Goods Average with Pier Table	2,156.21	3,145.66	1,251.66	1,628.68	698.62
Total Worth Average All	10,696.0	15,951.30	7,974.94	12,648.49	10,949.85
Total Worth Average with Pier Table	176,906.53	81,579.05	12,743.16	39,690.98	10,023.6

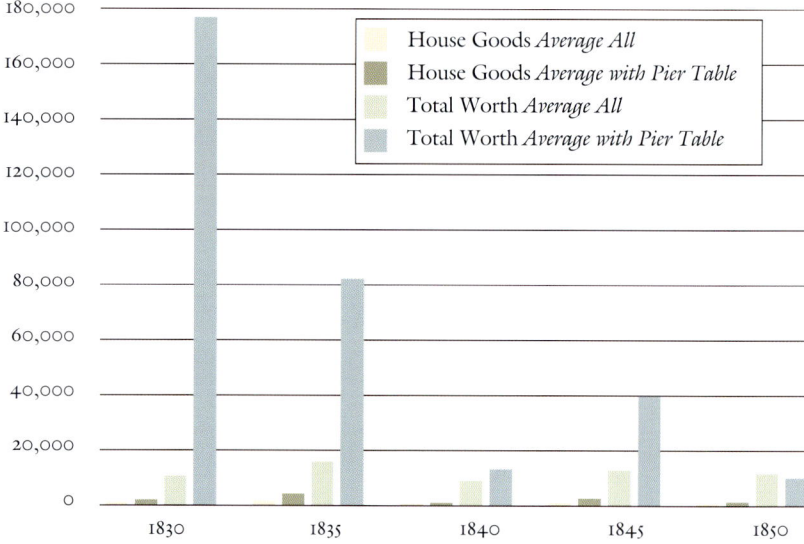

Table 5 Occupations of Pier Table Owners (1830–1850)

	1830–1835	1836–1840	1841–1845	1846–1850
Unknown (Businessman?)	5	28	24	27
Merchant	5	8	15	10
Gentleman / woman	0	7	6	13
Lawyer / Esquire	1	2	2	5
Auctioneer	1	0	1	0
Spinster	1	0	0	1
Accountant	1	1	2	0
Doctor	1	0	3	0
Broker	1	1	0	0
Silversmith	1	0	0	0
Tailor / Clothier	0	2	1	0
Grocer	0	1	2	0
Bookseller / Bookbinder	0	3	0	0
Waiter	0	1	0	0
Smith / Farrier	0	1	0	0
Engraver	0	1	0	0
Teacher	0	0	1	0
Printer	0	0	2	0
Confectioner	0	0	1	0
Judge	0	0	1	1
Bricklayer	0	0	1	2
Ship captain	0	0	2	1
Chevalier	0	0	1	0
Manufacturer	0	0	1	0
Druggist	0	0	2	0
Mast maker	0	0	1	0
Carpenter	0	0	0	2
Cabinetmaker	0	0	0	1
Skin dresser	0	0	0	1
Innkeeper	0	0	0	1
County commissioner	0	0	0	1
Cooper	0	0	0	1
Tobacconist	0	0	0	1
Clerk	0	0	0	2
Stevedore	0	0	0	1
Marble mason	0	0	0	1
Paper hanger	0	0	0	1

Due to the distinctive character of ground rent, the system of land tenure in Philadelphia, in which renters paid a perpetual annual rent of 6 percent of the lot's value at the time of the deed, property did not change hands often. Although the ground rent system virtually eliminated capital barriers and brought buying a house within the reach of many Philadelphians, property ownership remained largely in the hands of landed elites, the beneficiaries of inheritance. The ground rent system also meant that those who aspired to wealth but did not have the luxury of inherited land were forced to rely on property owners for credit. Pier table owners ensured the cultural capital of their extended families via property ownership within an urban setting. For instance, skin dresser and businessman George Schryer, whose will lists a "mahogany pier table, marble top and mirror" valued at ten dollars, also owned more than a dozen houses and lots, all located on the same street. In his will, Schryer bequeathed property to his extended family, thus ensuring the continuation of his dynasty. The extraordinary landholdings of most owners of pier tables suggest a link between the form and its old world connotations, wherein power was often based on hereditary land rights.[17]

People who owned pier tables were also characterized by the diversification of their investments. Stephen E. Fotterall—listed as a "gentleman" living at 152 South Third Street in the 1839 city directory—had real estate valued at $243,745.50, stocks and loans at $374,620.02, ground rents at $168,264.70, cash and gold at $1,290.00, bank assets at $401,335.00, and property for sale at $89,550. With approximately one-third of his assets invested in low-risk real estate, Fotterall (who owned two pier tables appraised at $40.00 each) had a security blanket to offset ventures of higher risk. In Philadelphia, owning a pier table was a sign that the owner likely had a substantial portion of his assets invested in ground rents, a guaranteed source of income and an effective tool for securing credit.[18]

Class distinction was not easily discernible in Philadelphia's architecture, where both rich and poor lived in town houses that looked similar from the street. Given Philadelphia's architectural homogeneity, it is not surprising that probate inventories follow a strikingly similar progression. Most begin in the front parlor, where in well-to-do households valuable and prized furnishings impressed visitors' senses: sight (through lighting devices, sparkling mirrors and ornaments, exotic woods, lustrous fabrics), touch (soft fabrics on furniture, cold and hard stone tops and sculpture) and sound (mantel clocks ticking, plush carpets that dampened noise). In the second quarter of the nineteenth century, a typical upscale Philadelphia parlor had one or two sofas, between six and twelve chairs, one or two card or pier tables, and a center table. Lighting devices, glass ornaments, and fireplace equipment were also standard. Appraisers next moved into a second or back parlor, then on to the dining room. The second and potentially third stories, whether rented or not, consisted almost entirely of bedchambers, with an occasional drawing room, followed by the garret/attic. The kitchen was often the last room surveyed because of its location in the cellar. Although testators presumably chose the most logical course through the dwellings, the similarities among room-by-room inventories reveal a predetermined architectural procession. It is no coincidence that pier tables, when they do show up, are often among the first items catalogued. They were part of a family's public presentation, a starting point from which testators departed for the quotidian.[19]

Only two of the 214 individuals who owned pier tables in Philadelphia between 1830 and 1850 used them in rooms other than the front parlor. In seven instances pier tables are listed in the front parlor and in another room. This pattern of use should come as no surprise, given that parlors were the locus for display and site for creating first impressions. However, this does not explain why pier tables are so rarely found in other seemingly appropriate spaces, such as the dining room (marble tops were ideal serving surfaces) and entry halls (a popular location for slab tables in the eighteenth century). Since other rooms had piers, what was it about the parlor that made it so suitable for pier tables?

Henry Sargent's *The Dinner Party* (1821) and *The Tea Party* (1824)—two

Figure 23 Henry Sargent, *The Tea Party*, Boston, Massachusetts, ca. 1824. Oil on canvas. 64 3/8" x 52 3/8". (Courtesy, Museum of Fine Arts, Boston, gift of Mrs. Horatio Appleton Lamb in memory of Mr. and Mrs. Winthrop Sargent, 19.12; photo © Museum of Fine Arts, Boston.)

of the best-known depictions of fashionable early-nineteenth-century American interiors—provide clues. Although the paintings are set in Boston and neither depicts a pier table, they show how architectural spaces and household furnishings influenced social activity. The paintings make visible what one scholar has called "the material culture of genteel ambition," which demanded the display of social knowledge through polite conversation and the complex rituals of sociability. By elucidating the distinctive character of parlor behavior, these paintings hint at how and why pier tables were ideally suited to the parlor but less so to other rooms.[20]

Parlors facilitated social flow. People interacted with quick, superficial contacts and convenient exits. In *The Tea Party* (fig. 23), guests are clustered around center tables, rows of chairs, and hearths. The arrangement of furnishings prompted the guests to move about, conducting conversations with their neighbors while keeping an eye on the larger scene. In such settings, indirect glances and discreet observation were not only possible but also encouraged by the strategic placement of lighting devices and reflective surfaces.[21]

The source of light in *The Tea Party* radiates from the center table in the parlor, blocked at the painting's midpoint by a cluster of two women and a man standing together. The resulting triangular shape of light and shadow is a shrewd artistic device that leads the viewer's eye into the back parlor, where a large crowd stands between the center table and the pier glass (fig. 24). The reflective quality of the large pier glass suggests the presence of another strong light source, perhaps resting on an unseen pier table, in addition to that on the center table. As Elisabeth Garrett has argued, in the parlors of wealthy, early-nineteenth-century Americans, artificial light, looking glasses, gilded edges, and polished surfaces created drama and facil-

Figure 24 Detail of the painting illustrated in fig. 23.

itated social entertainment. Pier tables embodied all these elements in a single form by supporting lighting devices and having polished surfaces, carving, gilding, metal mounts, and mirrored backs. The tables functioned as a microcosm of the parlor, providing brilliant contrasts between light, color, and surfaces.[22]

Although the outward tone is one of leisure, such parties provided an important avenue for the dissemination of information and power. In a period when credit was still largely based on personal relationships, one's social reputation was a strategic investment that could open avenues of credit. Household possessions, in addition to economic capital, signified social capital—an investment in the acquisition and display of reputation. In *The Tea Party*, paintings serve as the major ornaments. The front parlor doubles as a gallery, encouraging close inspection and critical judgments of the paintings: yet such judgments required a large degree of social capital and were confirmed or disavowed in conversation with others. Although the notion of paintings and ornaments as "conversation pieces" is correct, in these outwardly frivolous dialogues people's reputations could be made or destroyed.[23]

In contrast to the shifting impermanence of parlor sociability, *The Dinner Party* (fig. 25) depicts a comparatively static environment wherein guests sat in a fixed position throughout the courses of the meal. The food service and servers changed and impressed, but the sitters' company remained constant. In such a setting, functional side or serving tables were more appropriate than decorative pier tables. Indeed, contemporary domestic guidebooks advised "solid, unpretentious furniture" for the dining room, noting that food, not the furnishings, was the showcase.[24]

Sargent's paintings elucidate the link between furniture forms and the activities that take place within the architectural space. Compared with the transient male-female exchanges within the double parlors of *The Tea Party*, the exchanges of the male diners in *The Dinner Party* are more measured and constant. Pier tables were appropriate to the social conventions of parlors because they provided a fixed arena for the exchange of information. Like the fireplace, pier tables attracted guests by providing light sources such as astral lamps; ornaments such as vases, flowers, shells, and clocks; and glittering reflections produced by the glasses above and below the stone top that created a mini-stage within the home. Unlike chairs and most other table forms, pier tables could not be pulled out from the wall to accommodate guests. Rather, people were forced to negotiate pier tables as they made their rounds, engaging the forms in a superficial manner similar to the pleasantries with which they greeted various guests.

Sargent's images may be set in Boston, but the culture of sociability he depicted was an international standard. Elite Philadelphians would have understood the rituals as well as prominent Bostonians or, for that matter, Europeans. *The Dinner Party* depicts the final stage of a dinner party: the tablecloth has been removed for the fruit course. Both the universality of this image and the ubiquitous culture of snap judgments are demonstrated in Robert Waln's 1819 account of a dinner party in Philadelphia: "By the

Figure 25 Henry Sargent, *The Dinner Party*, Boston, Massachusetts, ca. 1821. Oil on canvas. 61⅝" x 49¾". (Courtesy, Museum of Fine Arts, Boston, gift of Mrs. Horatio Appleton Lamb in memory of Mr. and Mrs. Winthrop Sargent, 19.13; photo © Museum of Fine Arts, Boston.)

time the cloth was removed, a few almonds cracked, and an orange or two quartered; I observed glances short, quick, stolen, and expressive, continually passing from the eyes of the guests, to that end of the table where the lady of the house presided." Fixed exchanges gave way to brief critical encounters in the houses maintained by people of means. Pier tables functioned within this larger performance of gentility, which masked competition behind a veil of manners. Sidney George Fisher alluded to the theatricality of dinner and tea parties among Philadelphia's elite when he reflected, in 1841, on a small party at Mrs. Israel Pemberton Hutchinson's "fine new house in Spruce above 10th." After noting that "their rooms are the most beautiful I ever saw. . . . *All* the furniture from Paris of the most costly description and in admirable taste and keeping," he turned his attention to the disjuncture between the lofty architectural setting and the party's guests:

> The furniture in short . . . is just such as you see in palaces in Europe, but the *company* is very different. Instead of the courtly & high bred crowd, who have been accustomed to this splendor all their lives, you see here merchants & lawyers, who work all day in countinghouses & offices & when then they go into such a house stare about them & seem out of their element. Here it is a show, there the habitual scene of daily life.[25]

Similarly, although pier tables are generally characterized by elaborate decoration and the lavish use of expensive materials, on many American examples much of the effect is superficial. Freehand gilding and stencils substituted for ormolu brass; thin veneers of exotic woods were glued to cheap secondary woods; black paint emulated ebony; bronze powder gave the illusion of gilt surfaces; and green and gold paint simulated the patina on antique bronze. When combined with looking glasses and lighting devices, the whole arrangement produced a dazzling effect—the illusion of space, wealth, and light.

A major function of pier tables was to facilitate the small talk or gossip essential to business and social advancement (sociability), but what, specifically, did that entail? Because trade centered on personal credit and was an inherently risky endeavor, merchants saw significant financial incentives in having intimate knowledge of their peers. Merchants and businessmen were constantly sizing up one another, trying to determine who was or was not a good credit risk. According to historian Thomas Doerflinger, "In such appraisals the man and the merchant were inseparable . . . not only were the liquidity and net worth of a trader taken into account but also many details about his business and private life." Punctuality and prudence were the most significant attributes that made someone credit-worthy: a trader/businessman was deemed successful if he paid his debts on time (punctuality) and always had cash on hand to be able to seize new investment opportunities (prudence).[26]

Pier tables helped their owners look and act the part of a successful and, more important, dependable professional. Pier tables can be understood as highly charged social symbols that worked on multiple levels: the material, in which they conveyed status while facilitating critical glances and determining movement within a room; and the symbolic, in which they evoked financial security and hereditary distinction. Status was not a birthright in republican America, and thus self-performance was crucial to securing credit and encompassed everything from one's house to one's deportment. Indeed, as articles of consumption became increasingly available, it was not enough merely to look the part; one had to act the part as well.[27]

This helps explain why ownership of pier tables correlates so closely to ownership of pianos despite the fact that pianos were consistently valued forty to one hundred percent higher than pier tables (see Table 3, fig. 26). Pianos and pier tables had several things in common: as luxury items, they were not only important elements in entertaining while imparting a degree of social panache but also key instruments in courtship. In Philadelphia, marriage was the fastest means to join the highest strata of society, particularly because so much property ownership was inherited. A father's one-hundred-dollar investment in a pianoforte might be a shrewd investment if it enabled his daughter to marry well. Though they operated in a less overt way, pier tables functioned in this arena as well, as is illustrated in a story published in Philadelphia in 1831:

Figure 26   Loud & Brothers, upright piano, Philadelphia, Pennsylvania, 1831. Mahogany. H. 76 1/8", W. 50", D. 28". (Courtesy, Metropolitan Museum of Art; Rogers Fund, Alice M. Hufstader gift, Richard B. Kellam gift, Crosby Brown Collection of Musical Instruments, by exchange, and funds from various donors, 1976 [1976.317.1] Image © Metropolitan Museum of Art.)

> Mr. Nathaniel Doolittle was a grocer in the upper part of the city.... One would have judged from an inspection of the premises, that Nathaniel drove but a small business—sufficient barely to support a bachelor of moderate pretensions. But appearances are frequently deceitful—the door that led out of the shop, opened into as pretty a parlour as any in Broadway. On one side were a mirror and a pier table—opposite, reclined a sofa, flanked by a couple of rocking chairs; on a third side, stood an upright piano of the latest fashion.

The protagonist, a bachelor intent on winning Mr. Doolittle's daughter, ascertains the family's status from a brief glance around the parlor, which is furnished in the most up-to-date style. Nonetheless, he still feels compelled to talk with brokers to determine Mr. Doolittle's commercial standing, hinting at the limitations of material display. In other words, one needed the entire package of cultured refinement—furnishings, manners, property, and contacts—to establish one's reputation. As this story implies, owning a pier table did not conclusively demonstrate a person's financial stability. However, these objects were important tools in the performance of sociability that secured one's financial and social standing.[28]

Given that merchants, accountants, lawyers, and other professionals were in the business of personal transactions, a furniture form that facilitated brief, indirect evaluations of others was suitable, if not mandatory. With a single glance at the quality and condition of a pier table's marble top, a visitor could register key information about the owner's financial and cultural status and draw a positive or negative conclusion. In 1850, for example, a Mrs. Swisshelm offered a biting critique of the furnishings in the East Room at the White House: "The centre and pier tables, the sofas and chairs would suit a second rate ice cream saloon." Similarly, a story in an 1853 periodical conveyed the heroine's faded circumstances by highlighting the decrepit state of her formerly elegant drawing room, signified when "a slovenly man servant in a ragged shirt and trousers" brought in "a guttering tallow candle stick in a mildewed silver candlestick, which he sat upon a dusty, stained, and spotted marble pier table." The author cites material indicators of a downturn in wealth and status: a noxious and smoky tallow candle sits on the pier table's dirty marble top, where presumably once a bright oil lamp shone on a gleaming, elegant marble surface. The use of a derelict pier table is a particularly potent device given the form's associations with elegance, wealth, and permanence.[29]

Cultures of Competition
Pier tables were a component in the display of status, yet their efficacy depended and built on several forms of capital. Jacob Eichholtz (1776–1842) provides an instructive case study, for, with the help of pier tables, he literally transplanted Philadelphia elite society into the hinterlands. An established portrait painter in his native town of Lancaster, Pennsylvania, Eichholtz moved to Philadelphia in 1823 in search of more patrons and greater acclaim. Starting out in rented quarters, he quickly prospered and began acquiring property. By 1831 Eichholtz owned at least three houses, one of which he rented to his son-in-law. In this regard, he was typical of many wealthy

Philadelphians who found rental property a reliable and profitable source of income that supported other, riskier entrepreneurial ventures.[30]

When he returned to Lancaster in 1832, Eichholtz utilized his associations with Philadelphia to impress the locals. He moved his family into a brick row house modeled on the prevailing fashions in Philadelphia and furnished it in the latest style. No household object better communicated Eichholtz's intimate knowledge of urban fashion than his pier table. Writing from Lancaster to his daughter in Philadelphia in 1832, he noted: "The pier table is much admired by . . . all who have seen it. I now appear to take precedence in all matters of taste here."[31]

A pier table (fig. 27) that descended in Eichholtz's family is likely the one mentioned in his letter. It displays classic Philadelphia features: a cavetto molding on the apron; turned wood columns and applied rear pilasters; ogee-shaped lower shelf; pie-wedge mahogany veneers within a gilt semicircular border; turned rear feet; and a gadrooned ring above lion's-paw front feet. As was proper custom in Philadelphia, Eichholtz placed the table in the window pier of the front parlor. In his lifetime the flanking windows looked across open fields toward Philadelphia, not only the location of the pier table's manufacture but also the source of Eichholtz's standing in Lancaster.[32]

Eichholtz may not have grown up with pier tables, but he learned about them from his important patrons. For instance, a pier table features prominently in his 1827 portrait of Mrs. John Frederick Lewis of Philadelphia, completed only a few years before Eichholtz wrote to his daughter about the reception of his own pier table in Lancaster (fig. 28). Though the staging follows the prevailing portraiture conventions of the period, Mrs. Lewis's

Figure 27 Pier table, Philadelphia, Pennsylvania, 1825–1832. Mahogany with tulip poplar; marble, glass. H. 38", W. 38", D. 20". (Courtesy, James Buchanan Foundation, Lancaster, Pennsylvania.)

Figure 28 Jacob Eichholtz, *Mrs. John Frederick Lewis*, Philadelphia, Pennsylvania, 1827. Oil on canvas. 36" x 28½". (Courtesy, Pennsylvania Academy of the Fine Arts, Philadelphia, gift of Mrs. John Frederick Lewis [John Frederick Lewis Memorial Collection].)

silk dress and the pier table on which she leans were likely her own possessions. The pier table's white marble top, gilt decoration, and polished Ionic columns would have made it a fashionable and desirable object in 1827.[33]

The sitter's husband, John Frederick Lewis, was an auctioneer and East India merchant. His personal and professional success depended on an intimate knowledge of international markets and the ability to grant and secure credit and contacts. Both Lewis and Eichholtz were emblematic of professionals and businessmen in competitive trades: each used pier tables to convey cosmopolitan taste, financial security, and well-managed households, all key factors in securing credit. These tables evoked not just a world of elites but also of professionals engaged in trade.[34]

The most famous and best-documented Philadelphia pier table commission occurred in 1829, when Andrew Jackson ordered four pier tables with white Italian slabs and three center tables with black and gold marble slabs from cabinetmaker Anthony G. Quervelle (fig. 29). Jackson used the tables to furnish the newly finished East Room in the White House, which, as the

Figure 29 Pier table bearing the label of Anthony Quervelle, Philadelphia, Pennsylvania, 1829. Mahogany with tulip poplar; marble, glass. H. 43", W. 66", D. 26". (Courtesy, White House Historical Association; photo, Bruce White.)

major audience or reception room, was the largest room in the building and required suitably fashionable and awe-inspiring furnishings to simultaneously impress and intimidate visitors.[35]

From a cabinetmaking perspective, Quervelle's White House commission offers an intriguing business model. Faced with the challenge and honor of supplying the president's furnishings, Quervelle had significant incentive to deliver pieces that were both stylish and distinctive. He chose scrolled monopodia front supports embellished with an eagle's head at the top in direct reference to the Great Seal of the United States. The original bill of sale lists the four pier tables at $700.00 and the three center tables at $335.00. By comparison, in 1830 the household furnishings of a typical Philadelphia family totaled $535.00 (see Table 4). The pier tables stood under "4 Pier Looking-glasses, in rich gilt frames, 108 by 54 inches" that cost an astounding $2,400.00. A visitor to the newly furnished East Room in 1830 reported:

> Each pier is filled with a beautiful pier table, richly bronzed and gilt, corresponding with the round tables—each table having a lamp and pair of French china vases with flowers and shades agreeing with those on the mantels. The curtains are of blue and yellow moreen, with a gilded eagle, represented as holding up the drapery, which extends over the piers.[36]

If the White House examples were unusually large for American pier tables, their dimensions were in keeping with comparable European forms. The East Room provided one of the few architecturally appropriate settings for pier tables in America, akin to the long, formal drawing rooms of state apartments and royal palaces in Europe. Congressman Levi Lincoln made just this point in 1840, in defense of the expenditures for White House furnishings: "the spacious halls and lofty ceilings of such a mansion require much, which would be suited to no other residence."[37]

Figure 30 Pier table, Philadelphia or Pittsburgh, Pennsylvania, 1830–1835. Mahogany with tulip poplar and white pine; marble, glass. H. 37", W. 40", D. 19". (Private collection; photo, Gavin Ashworth.)

On a more domestic scale is a pier table with ties to the Wilkins family of Pittsburgh (fig. 30). A lawyer by trade, William Wilkins (1779–1865) served as a judge, a United States senator, and secretary of war under President Zachary Taylor. Wilkins's success, like that of many pier table owners, was based on personal connections and his ability to grant and receive credit. Wilkins was one of the original financial backers of the Pittsburgh Manufacturing Company, which became the Bank of Pittsburgh in 1814. His marriage four years later to Mathilda Dallas, daughter of politician and judge Alexander J. Dallas of Philadelphia, further strengthened his economic position while providing key political clout. Mathilda brought to the marriage an enormous family fortune, and her family ties and subsequent cultural affiliations with Philadelphia may have prompted the Wilkinses to purchase a Philadelphia-style pier table for their home in Pittsburgh during the late 1820s or early 1830s.[38]

The Wilkinses' prominent family ties and political associations made them ideally suited to pier table ownership, for the form conveyed cosmopolitan taste, financial security, and ambitious hospitality. Furthermore, it is possible that William Wilkins bought a pier table in an explicit attempt to align himself politically with the White House. The scroll-paw front supports on his table are similar to (albeit less refined than) those on the White House tables. Wilkins was elected to the Senate in 1831, and he would have been familiar with Quervelle's tables by that time at the latest. He also supported

Figure 31 Pier table attributed to Barry and Krickbaum, Philadelphia, Pennsylvania, ca. 1837. Mahogany; marble, glass. (Courtesy, The Hermitage: Home of President Andrew Jackson, Nashville, Tennessee; photo, Bill Lafevor.)

President Jackson's controversial decision to withdraw federal deposits from the Second Bank of the United States in 1832, severing ties with the bank's president, Nicholas Biddle, in 1834. The next year, Wilkins acknowledged his loyalty to Jackson with the construction of Homewood, an enormous Greek revival mansion in Pittsburgh. The conceptual model was The Hermitage, the mansion built outside Nashville by Andrew Jackson, who himself owned a pair of Philadelphia pier tables by the firm Barry and Krickbaum (fig. 31).[39]

Both the Wilkinses' table (fig. 30) and the table illustrated in figure 19 are distinguished by lower shelves with an inset marble well. One theory holds that the recess was intended to receive a wine cooler. However, no Philadelphia inventory between 1830 and 1850 lists bottle or liquor chests near pier tables. It is reasonable to conclude that the waterproof marble recess was meant for urns, flower vases, and other "ornaments," which are listed next to pier tables in inventories and depicted in design books and interior scenes.[40]

According to tradition, the pier table illustrated in figure 32, a mate, and a matching center table with carved dolphin supports were made for the Nashville, Tennessee, home of Henry Middleton-Rutledge and his wife, Septima Sexta Middleton. At forty-four inches high, the table is unusually tall, intended for a large-scale Greek revival interior. The Rutledge table is meant to dazzle; it was as much a showpiece for the warehouse that made it as it was for the patron. The cornucopia brackets under the apron are an explicit reference to abundance and wealth. Similarly, the elaborately carved and gilt dolphin supports—a classical reference to success and safety at sea—identify this table as a distinctive and therefore expensive commission.[41]

The Rutledge table represents the combined efforts of several different and highly specialized crafts. It took at least one cabinetmaker to construct the frame and apply the exotic wood veneers; carvers to produce the lion's-paw feet, dolphin front supports, acanthus pilasters, scrolled cornucopia brackets, and gadrooned moldings; various specialists to create the gilded and *vert antique* decoration; and still others to import and finish the glass plate and marble slab top. This table represents the consolidation of several different trades, thus explaining why pier tables were overwhelmingly produced in or around urban centers.[42]

Owing to the number of hands and specialist shops involved, construction practices vary even among labeled pieces. Many Philadelphia cabinetmaking firms were large enough to employ specialized tradesmen, but some found it cheaper to purchase components and services from the numerous smaller shops located in the lower-rent districts away from the Delaware waterfront and Philadelphia County. Consequently, a large shop could acquire turned and carved components from specialized shops around the city, add the top, apply gilding, *vert antique,* and other decorative finishes, and market the table as its own.[43]

By the 1830s commentators noted the ease with which fashionable furniture could be procured. In Philadelphia, this was the result of several separate but related factors: improvements in transportation, increased furniture production, growing population, the construction of Greek revival buildings with larger interiors and double parlors, and more public auctions at which consumers could procure fashionable goods secondhand. The latter phenomenon was the subject of an 1832 article:

Figure 32 Pier table, Philadelphia, Pennsylvania, 1825–1835. Mahogany and rosewood with tulip poplar; marble, glass. H. 44", W. 50", D. 24". (Courtesy, Winterthur Museum.)

If men or women are anxious to spend money in a very agreeable way, in a large city like Philadelphia they have only to attend the auctions. . . . It is surprising what a change of household commodities there is in Philadelphia. A housekeeper may go out any morning and buy a new sofa or pier table at auction, have it home before dinner, and the old one at the store ready for sale the next day. Thus she can have two *excitements*—one in buying, and the other in bidding up her cast off furniture—nay, a third, for in the afternoon she can admire her purchase, and if not perfectly satisfied, call a hand-barrow and whisk it off to the next "great sale." This is the secret of those never ending advertisements of furniture.

Figure 33   John Henry Belter, étagère, New York City, 1840–1860. Rosewood; marble, glass. H. 88", W. 59", D. 22". (Courtesy, Winterthur Museum.)

The ease with which large forms such as pier tables and sofas could be transported is notable, as is the sheer abundance of goods in the city. Philadelphia was, after all, a major manufacturing center in the first half of the nineteenth century.[44]

During the early 1800s chairmakers and cabinetmakers in urban areas looked beyond local markets to sustain operating costs. With higher rents and overhead in the city, it was imperative to produce readily salable goods, or to make salable what had already been produced. Large firms held periodic auctions to clear out their inventory and storage rooms, while other makers shipped goods on venture and attempted to sell them at public auction in distant markets. New York makers of pier tables dominate the extant auction notices in Southern locales, reflecting both the larger scope of the New York cabinetmaking trade and the tight connections between New York cotton merchants and Southern planters. The coastal shipping records for Philadelphia reveal that chairs dominated the export trade, whereas tables constituted only a tiny fraction of the total. Unable to compete directly with New York's coastal trade, Philadelphia makers seem to have focused on inland markets, sending their wares west and then down the Ohio and Mississippi rivers.[45]

Pier tables passed out of favor after midcentury, replaced in form and terminology by curvilinear console tables, which often did not incorporate mirrors. The later form whose function most closely approximated that of pier tables was the étagère or whatnot—a large, opulent, and almost purely decorative object (fig. 33). Three related factors contributed to the demise of the pier table. The advent of gas lighting fixtures in the late 1830s and early 1840s, which were attached directly to the wall or ceiling, reduced the tables' function as a glorified lighting stand. Similarly, the stone tops long associated with the form became more common as marble production increased, thus lowering both the cost and distinctiveness of stone tops. Finally, improvements in glass plate production increased the availability of larger pier glasses that extended almost from the ceiling to the floor (fig. 34).

Figure 34 "Fashion Plates for Decorating Parlor Windows," *Godey's Magazine and Lady's Book* 49 (July 1854). (Courtesy, Winterthur Library: Printed Book and Periodical Collection.) The pier/console table is low in height and does not have an integral glass plate since an extended pier glass hangs above.

Large plate glass was available in America by the late 1830s, and according to an observer several decades later, that commodity spelled the end of pier tables with mirrors in America. The authors of *Beautiful Homes: or, Hints in House Furnishing,* published in 1878, reflected:

> Parlor tables, thirty years back, consisted in the inevitable "center-table," and what was termed a "pier-table,"; the latter being a sort of ornamental stand with three sides and a plain back, placed flat against the wall beneath the "pier-glass," which the long, narrow mirror was termed. This table was some four feet in height, with marble slab, and generally richly ornamented with carving and gilding, but it was an exceedingly stiff and ungraceful looking piece of furniture. A few years later, the "pier-table" was superseded by the gilded and marbletopped mirror-bracket, introduced for the accommodation of the now extended mirror which reached from the ceiling to the floor, but the popular center-table still held its place.[46]

The study of material culture boils down to a single question: Why do things look the way they do? In the early nineteenth century, pier tables served an important ceremonial function: they simultaneously signified hospitality and business, equality and competition. It is no coincidence that the form remains in currency within the hotel industry, where hospitality and business collide (fig. 35). Similarly, among private residences, the use of wall-oriented tables with accompanying mirrors and lighting devices persists even in the age of electric lighting. When today's homeowners and decorators place a fixed table against the wall beneath a mirror with lamps or candles on top, they are continuing—like pier table owners in the first half of the nineteenth century and whether they know it or not—a tradition that has its roots in French and Italian court culture.

Pier tables make little sense in the world of modernism, where utility, sleek proportions, and mobility are treasured. The fact that these tables are so out of place in modern society helps convey just how different the world for which they were created was from our world today. The sheer size and weight of pier tables are major inhibitors today, yet their size and immovability were precisely what made these tables so desirable to their original owners. These tables of sociability are products of an entirely different time, aesthetic, and ideology. Though their massiveness and materials staked claims to order, stability, and permanence, their ornament and use encouraged fleeting encounters and quickly made judgments. In this last regard, pier tables are perhaps victims of their own success: few people today give them a second thought.

ACKNOWLEDGEMENTS For assistance with this article the author thanks J. Ritchie Garrison, Morrison Heckscher, Peter Kenny, and Amelia Peck.

Figure 35 Lobby of the Omni William Penn Hotel, Pittsburgh, Pennsylvania. (Courtesy, Omni William Penn Hotel; photo, Laura Libert.)

1. Pier tables also exhibit some regional variations in construction. In New York pier tables, the rear stiles often join the top and bottom rails via a single large dovetail, while in Philadelphia, mortise-and-tenon joints were favored. See Charles L. Venable, *American Furniture in the Bybee Collection* (Austin: University of Texas Press, 1989), pp. 106–7, 124–25; and Robert C. Smith, "The Furniture of Anthony G. Quervelle, Part I: The Pier Tables," *Antiques* 103, no. 5 (May 1973): 984–94.

2. Venable, *American Furniture in the Bybee Collection,* p. 123. Peter M. Kenny, Frances

F. Bretter, and Ulrich Leben, *Honoré Lannuier, Cabinet Maker from Paris: The Life and Work of a French Ebéniste in Federal New York* (New York: Metropolitan Museum of Art, 1998), p. 45. *The Philadelphia Cabinet and Chair Makers' Union Book of Prices* (1828) diagrams card, breakfast, and loo (center) table feet, but there is no mention of pier tables. Presumably, feet for pier tables were interchangeable with feet for other tables, yet their absence in the price book indicates that the form remained rarefied in the late 1820s. Also see Alexandra Alevizatos Kirtley, "Philadelphia Furniture in the Empire Style," *Antiques* 171, no. 4 (April 2007): 92–101.

3. *The Philadelphia Cabinet and Chair Makers' Union Book of Prices* lists a plain pier table frame as 40" high. Also see Kenny, Bretter, and Leben, *Honoré Lannuier*, p. 81. Both Jacob Eichholtz and Andrew Jackson owned Philadelphia pier tables with wood Ionic columns that corresponded to the marble Ionic columns on their parlor fireplace surrounds.

4. Carl Peter Kaellgren, "Stately and Formal: Side, Pier and Console Tables in England, 1700–1800" (Ph.D. diss., University of Delaware, 1987), pp. xxi, 31, 32; Peter Thornton, *Authentic Décor: The Domestic Interior, 1620–1920* (New York: Viking Press, 1984), pp. 52–53; and Elisabeth Donaghy Garrett, *At Home: The American Family, 1750–1870* (New York: H. N. Abrams, 1989), pp. 153–55.

5. For more on the Buckland tables, see Luke Beckerdite, "Architect-designed Furniture in Eighteenth-Century Virginia: The Work of William Buckland and William Bernard Sears," in *American Furniture,* edited by Luke Beckerdite (Hanover, N.H.: University Press of New England for the Chipstone Foundation, 1994), pp. 37–43. For more on the Philadelphia tables, see Luke Beckerdite and Alan Miller, "A Table's Tale," in *American Furniture,* edited by Luke Beckerdite (Hanover, N.H.: University Press of New England for the Chipstone Foundation, 2004), pp. 34–35; and Morrison H. Heckscher and Leslie Greene Bowman, *American Rococo, 1750–1775: Elegance in Ornament* (New York: Metropolitan Museum of Art, 1992), pp. 191–93.

6. Thomas Sheraton, *The Cabinet-Maker and Upholsterer's Drawing-Book* (London, 1793–1802; reprint, New York: Dover Publications, 1972), p. 152; and George Hepplewhite, *The Cabinet-Maker and Upholsterer's Guide,* 3rd ed. (London, 1794; reprint, New York: Dover Publications, 1969), p. 12.

7. The Lannuier pier table retains its original casters, suggesting that it was mobile and hence doubled as a serving table. It is illustrated and discussed in Kenny, Bretter, and Leben, *Honoré Lannuier,* pp. 50, 69–70. For Baltimore examples, see William Voss Elder III and Jayne E. Stokes, *American Furniture, 1680–1880, from the Collection of the Baltimore Museum of Art* (Baltimore: Baltimore Museum of Art, 1987), pp. 159–62. For a Boston example in which slight differences in the table's construction, not the overall form itself, signify its intended use as a pier table, see Robert D. Mussey, *The Furniture Masterworks of John and Thomas Seymour* (Hanover, N.H.: University Press of New England, 2003), p. 289.

8. The 1836 catalogue of the John Hare Powel sale clarifies the period terminology in America. In the saloon were "2 Massive Pier Table, entirely of breschia marble, supported by carved consols, with mirror backs and ebony frames, made in Paris." See Kathleen Catalano, "Cabinetmaking in Philadelphia, 1820–1840" (master's thesis, University of Delaware, 1972), p. 107; Kenny, Bretter, and Leben, *Honoré Lannuier,* p. 81; and *Catalogue of the Household Furniture, Part of the Books, Plate, Wine, &c. of Col. J. Hare Powel, to be Sold at Public Sale . . . April 19, 1836,* Historical Society of Pennsylvania, no. 1582, box 23, folder 19.

9. Sheraton, *Drawing-Book*, pp. 141–42. The phrase "antique taste" is taken from Pierre de la Mésangère, *Collection de meubles et objets de goût* (1802). Rudolph Ackermann, *The Repository of Arts, Literature, Commerce, Manufactures, Fashion and Politics.* 12, no. 69 (September 1828): 182.

10. On the Barry pier tables, see Catherine Ebert and Alexandra Alevizatos Kirtley, "From Apprentice to Master: The Life and Career of Philadelphia Cabinetmaker George G. Wright," in *American Furniture,* edited by Luke Beckerdite (Easthampton, Mass.: Antique Collectors' Club for the Chipstone Foundation, 2007), pp. 113–19; and Donald L. Fennimore and Robert F. Trump, "Joseph B. Barry, Philadelphia Cabinetmaker," *Antiques* 135, no. 5 (May 1989): 1212–25. On the polyglot character of American classical furniture, see Donald L. Fennimore, "American Neoclassical Furniture and Its European Antecedents," *American Art Journal* 13 (Autumn 1981): 49–65. For sources of classical inspiration, see Wendy A. Cooper, *Classical Taste in America, 1800–1840* (New York: Abbeville Press, 1993), pp. 26–73, 130, 142. Also see Joan Woodside, "French Influences in American Furniture as Seen through Pierre de la Mésangère's *Meubles et objets de goût*, 1802–1835" (Ph.D. diss., University of Chicago, 1986).

11. I am indebted to Elizabeth White for this observation. For a pictorial survey of pier groupings, see Samuel J. Dornsife, "Design Sources for Nineteenth-Century Window Hangings," *Winterthur Portfolio* 10 (1975): 69–99.

12. J. Ritchie Garrison, *Two Carpenters: Architecture and Building in Early New England, 1799–1859* (Knoxville: University of Tennessee Press, 2006), p. 98. Also see Bernard L. Herman, *Town House: Architecture and Material Life in the Early American City, 1780–1830* (Chapel Hill: University of North Carolina Press, 2005), pp. 3–4.

13. As testament to the durability of stone tops, Eliza Leslie advised: "Tables, &c., with marble tops, though the most costly at first, will be found, perhaps, cheapest in the end. They are easily kept clean, by merely wiping them every day with a soft cloth, and a flannel; they require no cloth to cover them, and there is no danger of their splitting or warping with the heat." Miss Leslie, *The House Book: or, a Manual of Domestic Economy for Town and Country* (Philadelphia: Carey & Hart, 1841), p. 192. *Archives of Useful Knowledge, a Work Devoted to Commerce, Manufactures, Rural and Domestic Economy, Agriculture, and the Useful Arts* 2, no. 2 (October 1811): 207.

14. *The House Servant's Directory* (Boston, 1828), as quoted in Major L. B. Wyant, "The Etiquette of Nineteenth-Century Lamps," *Antiques* 30, no. 3 (September 1936): 114. Also see Garrett, *At Home*, pp. 140–62.

15. The percentages and averages given are based only on usable inventories, meaning that the inventory included information about the owner's wealth and/or furnishings. Inventories suggest that outdated tables were moved upstairs and, likely owing to their water-resistant stone tops, reused as dressing or toilet tables. I have only counted references to "pier" tables as conclusive evidence of ownership. This almost certainly omitted some pier tables listed under another heading, such as "marble top table" or "side table," but I believe pier tables were such a distinctive form that they were rarely conflated with generic tables. For urban population statistics, see Campbell Gibson, "Population of the 100 Largest Cities and Other Urban Places in the United States: 1790 to 1990," June 1998, Population Division Working Paper No. 27, U.S. Bureau of the Census. My table is a modified version of these data, which are available at http://www.census.gov/population/www/documentation/twps0027.html (accessed March 29, 2007). The "Philadelphia" population includes that for Kensington, Southwark, Northern Liberties, Spring Garden, and Moyamensing, all of which are represented in the probate inventory sample.

16. Thomas M. Doerflinger, *A Vigorous Spirit of Enterprise: Merchants and Economic Development in Revolutionary Philadelphia* (Chapel Hill: University of North Carolina Press, 1986), pp. 11–69.

17. Donna Rilling, *Making Houses, Crafting Capitalism: Builders in Philadelphia, 1790–1800* (Philadelphia: University of Pennsylvania Press, 2001), pp. 7, 42–49. Wills, County of Philadelphia, Philadelphia, Pennsylvania, 1682–1875, will no. 45 (1847): Mic 959-135, Downs Collection, Winterthur Library.

18. Wills, County of Philadelphia, Philadelphia, Pennsylvania, 1682–1875, will no. 197 (1839): Mic 959-1355, Downs Collection, Winterthur Library. Many owners of pier tables invested heavily in burgeoning transportation networks. See David Meyer, *The Roots of American Industrialization* (Baltimore: Johns Hopkins University Press, 2003), pp. 28–29; and Bruce Laurie, *Working People of Philadelphia, 1800–1850* (Philadelphia: Temple University Press, 1980), pp. 8–9.

19. Beatrice B. Garvan, *Federal Philadelphia, 1775–1825: The Athens of the Western World* (Philadelphia: Philadelphia Museum of Art, 1987), p. 15.

20. Charlotte Gere, *Nineteenth-Century Decoration: The Art of the Interior* (New York: H. N. Abrams, 1989), p. 153; Garrett, *At Home*, pp. 46–47; Cooper, *Classical Taste in America*, pp. 38–39; and Herman, *Town House*, p. 36.

21. On parlor sociability, see Garrett, *At Home*, pp. 39–77.

22. Ibid., p. 46.

23. Herman, *Town House*, p. 201.

24. William Parkes, *Domestic Duties, or, Instructions to Young Married Ladies: On the Management of Their Households and The Regulation of Their Conduct in the Various Relations and Duties of Married Life* (New York: J. & J. Harper, 1829), p. 173.

25. Both *The Tea Party* and *The Dinner Party* were exhibited in Philadelphia. See Cooper, *Classical Taste in America*, p. 92. Garrett, *At Home*, p. 82. Robert Waln Jr., *The Hermit in America on a Visit to Philadelphia*, edited by Peter Atall (Philadelphia: M. Thomas, 1819), p. 102. Nicholas B. Wainwright, ed., *A Philadelphia Perspective: The Diary of Sidney George Fisher Covering the Years 1834–1871* (Philadelphia: Historical Society of Pennsylvania, 1967), pp. 116–17.

26. Doerflinger, *A Vigorous Spirit of Enterprise*, p. 18.

27. At the 1819 dinner party in Philadelphia, a guest discreetly informed Robert Waln about another member of the party: "He belongs to a pretty numerous class, existing in our city, which, by birth, is entitled to hold a situation in the first ranks of society. Nor are its mem-

bers wanting in the education and polish so essential to the finished gentleman. Presuming upon these qualities, birth, education, and fortune,—they take (and, what is worse, are permitted to take) liberties in conversation with ladies, which no birth, no talents, no gold can warrant, or excuse." Waln, *The Hermit in America*, pp. 115–16. On self-performance and manners, see David Shields, *Civil Tongues and Polite Letters in British America* (Chapel Hill: University of North Carolina Press, 1997), pp. xxvi–xxvii, 275–307; Richard L. Bushman, *The Refinement of America: Persons, Houses, Cities* (New York: Alfred A. Knopf, 1992), pp. 79–80; and C. Dallett Hemphill, *Bowing to Necessities: A History of Manners in America, 1620–1860* (New York: Oxford University Press, 1999), pp. 84–85.

28. "Extract from the Diary of a Bachelor," *Philadelphia Album and Ladies' Literary Portfolio* (October 15, 1831): 5, 42. For more on credit, see Rosalind Remer, *Printers and Men of Capital: Philadelphia Book Publishers in the New Republic* (Philadelphia: University of Pennsylvania Press, 1996), pp. 50, 100–101.

29. "The White House," *Saturday Evening Post* 29 (May 18, 1850); and "Mark Sutherland: or, Power and Principle," *National Era* 5, no. 342 (June 21, 1853): 113.

30. Thomas R. Ryan, "Defining Jacob Eichholtz," in *The Worlds of Jacob Eichholtz: Portrait Painter of the Early Republic,* edited by Thomas Ryan (Lancaster, Pa.: Lancaster County Historical Society, 2003), p. 12.

31. Ibid., pp. 14–16.

32. In the 1940s a "Leaman" gave the pier table to the James Buchanan Foundation for the Preservation of Wheatland in memory of her father—most likely rifle manufacturer Henry Eichholtz Leman (1812–1887) of Lancaster, who was Jacob Eichholtz's nephew. See object file, James Buchanan Foundation, Lancaster, Pennsylvania. Ryan, "Defining Jacob Eichholtz," p. 19.

33. For more on the relationship between comportment and gentility, see Bushman, *Refinement of America*, pp. 61–69.

34. Ryan, ed., *The Worlds of Jacob Eichholtz*, p. 122. According to the household inventory taken at her death in 1865, "Eliza Lewis, widow of John F. Lewis," had two marble-top tables in her parlor, valued at $45.00 and $12.00, respectively. The $12.00 table is most likely the ca. 1827 pier table in Mrs. Lewis's portrait, while the table valued at $45.00 is probably a newer model. Also listed in the inventory is a solitary "framed portrait" valued at $2.00, which could be the Eichholtz portrait. Wills, County of Philadelphia, Philadelphia, Pennsylvania, 1682–1875, will no. 406, 1865 (bk. 55, p. 549), August 19, 1865, Downs Collection, Winterthur Library.

35. In furnishing the East Room with pier tables, President Jackson continued a tradition started by James Madison, who purchased an elaborate gilt pier table by French cabinetmaker Pierre-Antoine Bellangé in 1817. For more on Quervelle's White House commission, see Betty C. Monkman, *The White House: Its Historic Furnishings and First Families* (New York: Abbeville Press, 2000), pp. 63, 82–83.

36. The author thanks Melissa Naulin and William G. Allman for sharing the object file with condition notes on the Quervelle pier table at the White House. An engraving in *Gleason's Pictorial* from May 6, 1856, and a ca. 1861 lithograph offer early depictions of the East Room and provide clear evidence of Quervelle's pier tables with scrolled front supports. They are reproduced in Monkman, *The White House*, pp. 181–82. For Quervelle's White House commission, see Robert C. Smith, "Philadelphia Empire Furniture by Antoine Gabriel Quervelle," *Antiques* 86, no. 3 (September 1964): 304–9; Monkman, *The White House,* p. 286; and Catalano, "Cabinetmaking in Philadelphia," pp. 56, 113. For the White House furnishings, see "Speech of Mr. Ogle: From Lewis Vernon & Co. Voucher No. 6. Private Office," *Investigator and Expositor (1839–1840),* September 1, 1840, 0,_1, http://o-www.proquest.com.library.metmuseum.org:80/ (accessed March 3, 2008). For the 1830 visitor's full report on the East Room, see "The East Room," *Nile's Weekly Register (1814–1837),* January 2, 1830, 290, http://o-www.proquest.com.library.metmuseum.org:80/ (accessed March 3, 2008). For a splendid critique of the White House furnishings, see Mrs. Swisshelm, "Article 5—No Title," *Saturday Evening Post (1839–1885),* May 18, 1850; 0_002, http://o-www.proquest.com.library.metmuseum.org:80/ (accessed March 3, 2008).

37. Speech of Mr. Levi Lincoln of Massachusetts, April 16, 1840, as quoted in Monkman, *The White House,* p. 94.

38. The current owner purchased the table from a member of the Pleasants family. The Pleasants married into the Wilkins family in the twentieth century. See John A. Garraty and Mark C. Carnes, eds., *American National Biography,* 24 vols. (New York: Oxford University Press, 1999), 23: 399.

39. Ibid. Homewood was demolished in 1924. See Franklin Toker, *Pittsburgh: An Urban Portrait* (University Park: Pennsylvania State University Press, 1986), p. 221. According to Marsha Mullin, Chief Curator/Director of Museum Services at the Hermitage, the pier tables were probably purchased in Philadelphia from the firm of Barry and Krickbaum in February 1837, when the Jacksons were refurnishing the Hermitage mansion after a fire. The February 9, 1837, invoice from Barry and Krickbaum for two pier tables at $60.00 each is published in *Correspondence of Andrew Jackson,* edited by John Spencer Bassett, 7 vols. (Washington, D.C.: Carnegie Institution of Washington, 1926–1935), 5: 459.

40. Most bottle chests are far too large to fit on the inset marble recess occasionally found on pier tables with mirror backs. See Alexandra Alezivatos Kirtley, "A New Suspect: Baltimore Cabinetmaker Edward Priestly," in *American Furniture,* edited by Luke Beckerdite (Hanover, N.H.: University Press of New England for the Chipstone Foundation, 2000), pp. 100, 119–21; Fennimore and Trump, "Joseph B. Barry," p. 1223.

41. Object file, acc. 1975.191, Winterthur Museum. The Middleton-Rutledge House was converted into apartments in the 1920s, but the chair rails in surviving sections indicate the original grand proportions. For a view of the present-day first-floor hallway, see http://mywebpages.comcast.net/jimrv6/index.html (accessed March 3, 2008).

42. For lists of cabinetmakers working in Philadelphia during the early nineteenth century, see Catalano, "Cabinetmaking in Philadelphia"; Deborah Ducoff-Barone, "The Early Industrialization of the Philadelphia Furniture Trade, 1800–1840" (Ph.D. diss., University of Pennsylvania, 1985); Deborah Ducoff-Barone, "Philadelphia Furniture Makers, 1800–1815," *Antiques* 134, no. 5 (May 1991): 982–85; and Deborah Ducoff-Barone, "Philadelphia Furniture Makers, 1816–1830," *Antiques* 145, no. 5 (May 1994): 742–55. For features associated with Quervelle, see Smith, "The Furniture of Anthony G. Quervelle, Part I," pp. 984–94. On the dangers in attributing furniture to Quervelle, see Thomas Gordon Smith, "Quervelle Furniture at Rosedown, in Louisiana," *Antiques* 160, no. 2 (May 2001): 772; and Anna Tobin D'Ambrosio, ed., *Masterpieces of American Furniture from the Munson-Williams-Proctor Institute* (Syracuse, N.Y.: Syracuse University Press, 1999), p. 59.

43. A significant number of small shops manufactured, but did not market, their own wares, and most specialist carvers and turners worked for several different cabinetmakers. See Ducoff-Barone, "Early Industrialization," pp. 23, 46, 62–63.

44. "The Town Tatler—no. 27," *The Ariel: A Semimonthly Literary and Miscellaneous Gazette (1827–1832),* June 9, 1832, 50, http://0-www.proquest.com.library.metmuseum.org:80/ (accessed March 3, 2008). To transport these heavy forms, cabinetmakers employed furniture cars with attendants. Private citizens could also rent cars from cabinetmakers when moving household furniture or taking goods to or from public auction. See Ducoff-Barone, "Early Industrialization," p. 181. Perhaps the best indication of the dramatic changes experienced by the Philadelphia furniture industry in the antebellum period is the fact that the 1850 city directory lists almost as many furniture warerooms (65) as individual cabinetmakers (79). John Downes, *Bywater's Philadelphia Business Directory and City Guide for the Year 1850* (Philadelphia: Maurice Bywater, 1850). For more on Philadelphia's industrial and banking prowess in the nineteenth century, see Doerflinger, *A Vigorous Spirit of Enterprise,* p. 5; and Sam Bass Warner, *The Private City: Philadelphia in Three Periods of Its Growth* (Philadelphia: University of Pennsylvania Press, 1987), pp. 47–160.

45. For coastal shipping records of Philadelphia export furniture, see Catalano, "Cabinetmaking in Philadelphia," app. 6. On Philadelphia classical furniture in the South, see Jason T. Busch, "Furniture Patronage in Antebellum Natchez," *Antiques* 158, no. 2 (May 2000): 804–13; and Smith, "Quervelle Furniture at Rosedown," pp. 770–79.

46. Henry T. Williams and Mrs. C. S. Jones, *Beautiful Homes: or, Hints in House Furnishing* (New York: Henry T. Williams, 1878), pp. 174–75.

Nancy Goyne Evans

The Written Evidence of Furniture Repairs and Alterations: How Original Is "All Original"?, Part II

Figure 1 Detail of a desk interior, northeastern Massachusetts or New Hampshire, 1770–1800. Maple with white pine. H. 41⅜", W. 37¼" (feet), D. 20¼" (at feet). (Courtesy, Winterthur Museum, bequest of Henry Francis du Pont, acc. 58.2224.)

▼ THE EXTENSIVE DATABASE that forms the foundation of this study has been described in part 1, published in 2007. The material, which has a broad geographic range, covers locations both urban and rural and, for the most part, dates from the immediate pre-Revolutionary years to the mid-nineteenth century. At best, craftsmen's accounts are short on description, flexible in the language of object identification, and often highly original in orthography. Records of repairs and alterations to case furniture constitute the largest section of part 2. Included are desks, chests, and storage cupboards in their variety, followed by a brief discussion of clock case repairs. Notes on repairs to looking glasses form a separate short section. Completing the study are remarks on the maintenance of minor household equipment and personal items made of wood or with wooden parts.

Desks
Most desks deposited for repairs in the shops of American craftsmen from the mid-eighteenth century through the early decades of the nineteenth century were of the type often described today as a "slant-front desk" (fig. 1).

The form was current in England in the early eighteenth century, although its popularity in large urban centers appears to have waned after midcentury. Thomas Sheraton, writing in his *Cabinet Dictionary* of 1803, provided a description of this desk form, noting that in England the term "bureau" usually was "applied to common desks with drawers under them, such as are made very frequently in country towns." Continuing, he stated,

> They run from 3 to 4 feet long, and have three heights [tiers] of common drawers under them, the upper one divided into two in length. The desk flap turns down to 30 inches perpendicular height from the ground, or a little less, for sitting to write at. The inside of the desk part is fitted up with small drawers, and holes for letters. These pieces of furniture are nearly obsolete in London.

Considerably more popular in urban settings in late-eighteenth-century England was the slant-front case surmounted by a bookcase. Of particular note, English designers, including Thomas Chippendale, William Ince and John Mayhew, and George Hepplewhite, labeled this case form a "Desk and Bookcase" rather than a bureau.[1]

In America the cost of general repairs to the low desk could vary from as little as 16½¢ (1s.) to $9.00 or more. A general survey suggests that repairs priced at $1.00 (6s.) or more, $1.00 being equivalent to a day's pay for many craftsmen, were perhaps two times as common as repairs that cost less than $1.00. The desk was a popular furniture form. It served as a small commercial center and reflected a degree of social standing. Perhaps that is why, on occasion, householders paid a local cabinetmaker to restore an "old" desk, a process referred to at times as "fitting up [an] old Desk." The *Oxford English Dictionary* defines the term "fitting up" as "bring[ing] into a suitable condition."[2]

The terms "repair" and "mend" appear to have been in about equal use to describe repair work to desks. Whatever the word choice, a shop usually was consistent in its use of the term. On rare occasions craftsmen substituted the words "fix" or "work at" to describe the general repair process. Wood identification appears to have been more common in desk repair than in the repair work discussed in part 1, which included bed frames, tables, and stands. Named in records as primary desk woods are pine, maple, cedar, cherry, black walnut, and mahogany, mahogany and maple being mentioned most frequently. Desk size appears to have been fairly consistent because the descriptors "large" and "small" rarely occur. A single reference only describes an uncommon desk form introduced in the federal period. In 1808 Fenwick Lyell of Middletown, New Jersey, made note of "Repairing a Cylender fall Desk" for £1.4 ($4.01).[3]

Records cite specific desk repairs only on occasion, unlike the identification of new desk parts. Mentioned most frequently in named repairs is work to the board that forms the writing surface, a component Sheraton termed a "flap" because of its hinged structure. Among American craftsmen two other terms were common. Jeduthern Avery of Bolton/Coventry, Connecticut, described mending "A lid to [a] Desk" in 1830 and charged 15¢. Samuel Douglas identified a similar repair in western Connecticut and also supplied a lock, all for 25¢. "Hanging a Desk Lid" was a task Chapman Lee undertook at a comparable price early in the century at Charlton, Massachusetts. In "Reparing [a] Desk Fall" in 1809, John Sager of Bordentown, New Jersey, identified another term for the writing board. Ten years later Job E. Townsend of Newport, Rhode Island, performed work for Captain John Bigley that included "Mending and Hanging a Desk fall and fitting a

Key to the Lock," charging 50¢. Drawer repairs were less common. Of two recorded for 1792, Job Danforth of Providence repaired a drawer in a desk belonging to pewterer Gershom Jones. At Williamsburg, Virginia, William Pigget undertook the same work for St. George Tucker, a lawyer. Charges for both jobs were less than 50¢, as was the work of "gluen feet on a desk" for Captain William Bartlett of Beverly, Massachusetts, completed in 1772 by Sewell Tuck.[4]

New desk parts in greatest demand at cabinetmakers' shops were "trimmings," the metal fittings that made interior access possible and brightened exterior surfaces (fig. 1). How much retrimming work was necessitated by normal wear and tear versus updating the style of the hardware is unknown. When Luke Houghton repaired and varnished a desk for a customer at Barre, Massachusetts, in 1821, he also refurbished the case with "one set of trimmings" for $1.00 and "five esscouchings" (escutcheons), the metal shields surrounding the keyholes, for 20¢. Decades earlier Job Townsend Jr. of Newport, Rhode Island, had placed a "handle" on a customer's desk. The specific reference to a single handle and the substantial cost of the hardware at 7s. ($1.17) suggest this was a large lifting handle of a type sometimes placed on the sides of cases to facilitate moving. Townsend's son, Job E. Townsend, employed alternative terms for case hardware and often named the structural material of the desk under repair: "To mending a black Wollnot Desk and finding New Brasses for Ditto" (1786); "To Putting firnuture on a old mapol Desk" (1791); "To mending a Mohogony Desk and Putting on New firnature" (1799); "To Mending & Plaining over a Cherry Desk and fixing on New firnature" (1824). At Philadelphia Daniel Trotter also used the term "new furnitor" when repairing a desk for merchant Stephen Girard. Desk repairs made at Boston in 1785 by Alexander Edwards were followed a few years later by the installation of new "Brasses and Locks." On occasion, Job E. Townsend was employed in "Cleaning the Brasses for a Desk" rather than mounting new hardware. When a craftsman fitted a desk with new furniture and brass locks, he sometimes provided "Nubs," probably the diminutive brass knobs used as pulls on the small drawers in the writing cabinet. An alternative material for desk trimmings was wood, although it appears to have been uncommon. Miles Ward of Salem, Massachusetts, made note in 1756 of "tunig [turning] 8 boles [balls] for desk."[5]

Almost as common as trimming a desk was the installation of locks, of which many appear to have been new fixtures, where none existed previously. The many single locks installed on desks without further comment likely were intended to secure the writing cabinet, or "desk head" as it sometimes was identified. More specific are references such as that penned at North Stonington, Connecticut, in 1798 by Oliver Avery: "To [a] desk fall lock." A rarity is James Gere's reference to installing "Drawer Locks" for a customer at Groton. Isaiah Tiffany's work for a client at Norwich suggests some of the same activity. Constant use of the desk subjected the fall, or writing board, to damage at the attachment points with the case. When David Evans repaired a desk for Rachel Atmore at Philadelphia in 1777, he also supplied "a Pair of Desk Hinges" for 2s. 6d. (42¢). More expensive at 75¢ were the "large size butts hinges" Hiram Taylor placed on a desk for a customer in Chester County, Pennsylvania. As noted by Elisha Harlow Holmes at Essex, Connecticut, the installation of a pair of butt hinges required "1 doz screws."[6]

The number of customer calls at cabinet shops for new desk lids, or falls, was perhaps about the same as that for drawers. The cost of replacing a lid was variable, depending on the type and quality of wood required, although craftsmen's accounts seldom identify materials. In 1780 Job E. Townsend of Newport, Rhode Island, charged a customer 6s. ($1.00) for "making a fall for a Desk." The same year he charged another customer 13s. 6d. ($2.25) for "mending a Desk and making a New fall." In neither case is the wood specified. Some householders required new baize, a napped woolen cloth usually green in color, for the writing surface of their desk. Reed and Hollis of Salem, Massachusetts, charged John Devereaux, Esq., $2.00 in 1835 for "Finding Cloth & putting the same on Desk." Philip Warren provided more detail a few years earlier at Philadelphia, when he billed Thomas Cadwalader for "Repairing and Tacking a Cloth on a Desk, Green Binding, Tacks &c."[7]

The records of Job E. Townsend describe other activity in desk repair, when in 1783 he provided a client at Newport with "a Drawer for the head of the Desk," or writing compartment. Other requests at this shop appear to have been for full-size drawers. Townsend's father, Job Townsend Jr., made a "Draw to a Desk" eighteen years earlier for John Wanton, "mariner" and member of a prominent Rhode Island family. Sometimes drawer work was coupled with other tasks, as described in 1808 by Fenwick Lyell of Middletown, New Jersey, who put "Castors & Drawers to a Desk" and charged £4.10 ($15.03), a sum that suggests the wood was mahogany.[8]

Desk feet were subject to damage and destruction. Work carried out at Boston in 1781 by Alexander Edwards for his client Daniel Crosby involved "fixing up desk New feet & fall &c." The £2 charge ($6.68) reflects the status of the desk. A job undertaken at Providence two decades later by Job Danforth at a cost of £1.1 ($3.51) may describe a desk of similar quality: "To Plaining over & Putten too [two] new feet to a Desk." A single account appears to address a variant of the fall-front desk over a full case of drawers. The alternative form, known today as a desk-on-frame, was identified by a shop patron of Fenwick Lyell at Middletown, New Jersey, who engaged the cabinetmaker to put "Brackets on a Desk frame" at a cost of 14s. ($2.34). These small ornamental embellishments fit the angles between the tall legs and the case frame. Thomas J. Moyers and Fleming K. Rich pursued a more utilitarian task at Wytheville, Virginia, in 1837, when "reparing & putting backboard on [a] desk" with a full case of drawers.[9]

Surface treatments requested by householders when having their desks repaired or refurbished ran the gamut. Craftsmen's records identify thirteen single or combination procedures. As indicated in part 1 of this study, technical language at times is variable. In the present case, planing and dressing a wood surface describe the same activity. Similarly, scraping and cleaning can be equated. In enumerating customer options in desk finishes, the list moves from preliminary to final treatments: *planing*—alone, with stain, with stain and polish, with polish alone, or with varnish; *scraping*—with varnish; *staining*—alone, with planing (as above), with planing and polish (as above), with polish alone, or with varnish; *varnish*—alone, or with other procedures (as above); *painting*—alone; *coloring*—alone.

Finish work on desks, which, as described, ranged from simple to complex procedures, is recorded for all locations, rural and urban. Charges varied from as little as 25¢ to the equivalent of a full day's pay, or more, for an average working man. The records of Job E. Townsend of Newport, Rhode Island, are more complete and comprehensive than those of most craftsmen whose records exit. The cabinetmaker identified the wood of many refinished desks. In 1779 he recorded "Playning and Poillishing a mohogony Desk," followed two years later by staining and polishing a maple desk. Late in his career Townsend recorded "Plaining over" a cherry desk. In rural New Ipswich, New Hampshire, Josiah P. Wilder debited the account of James Bancroft in 1838 for scraping and varnishing a pine desk. The varnish could well have been toned with pigment to a medium or dark wood color. Two decades later Robert Rantoul of Beverly, Massachusetts, paid William Raymond for "Repairing & painting a large desk," possibly one used for record keeping in his extensive drug business. *Coloring* a desk with size and pigment probably was not much practiced beyond the opening years of the nineteenth century, when Oliver Avery of North Stonington, Connecticut, refinished a desk in this manner for which he was paid 42¢, while working in the shop of Gilbert Sisson.[10]

Craftsmen's records identify several desk forms of specialized function, of which one is the "portable desk." John Marshall, cabinetmaker, advertised "Portable Writing Desks" from his shop in Meeting Street, Charleston, South Carolina, on February 17, 1796. These desks have several forms. An early design is a diminutive imitation of the head of a standard desk, complete with slanted façade above a shallow drawer, with an interior of small drawers and pigeonholes. Dating to the post-Revolutionary period, a rectangular, hinged-lid style includes a hinged writing board in the interior that fits into the lid, with compartments for writing equipment and supplies in the bottom section. Another federal-period portable case has an arched, tambour-top closure at the back behind a slanted façade above a shallow front drawer. The interior contains a folded, baize-covered writing board and storage compartments (fig. 2). Most, if not all, portable desks have carrying handles mounted on the side panels.[11]

Ten references to the repair of this small portable center of business and social interaction have emerged from the body of records consulted for this study. Half are for unnamed repairs carried out in the shops of Silas E. Cheney (Litchfield, Connecticut, 1802), John Hockaday (Williamsburg, Virginia, 1807), Jacob Brouwer (New York City, 1808), and Elisha Harlow Holmes (Essex, Connecticut, 1829, two customers). At Kennebunk, Maine, Paul Jenkins undertook a moderately expensive job when he repaired, scraped, and varnished a portable desk and then installed a lock, $2.08 being the sum of charges. Two dollars was Thomas Boynton's charge for "scraping

Figure 2 John Brewster Jr., *James Prince and Son, William Henry*, 1801. Oil on canvas. 60⅜" x 60½". (Courtesy, Historical Society of Old Newbury, Newburyport, Massachusetts, gift of William Andrews Currier.)

and varnishing a portable Desk" at Windsor, Vermont, in 1814 for Frederick Pettes, proprietor of an inn that also served as a "Stage House." The small desk likely received good custom from his patrons. At Middletown, New Jersey, Fenwick Lyell cleaned and polished a portable desk for one customer and installed a "New Lock" on a desk for another patron, both jobs completed just after 1800. Two decades later Elizur Barnes supplied a new portable desk lock for a client at Middletown, Connecticut. Aside from his repair work, Fenwick Lyell provided insight on the accessories and cost of a new portable desk: "1 Portable Desk with Ink & Sand Glasses" at £4.12 ($15.36).[12]

When first encountered in records, the term "writing desk" appeared to this author to be an alternative term for the slant-front desk with drawers. The periodic recurrence of the term and the nature of some repair work, however, began to suggest that something more was indicated. Ultimately, the records of Fenwick Lyell of Middletown, New Jersey, shed light on the elusive form. On May 22, 1805, Lyell debited the account of Charles R. Camman for "Puting 4 Ledges on the flaps of a Writing Desk," identifying a type of work station for a counting room, office, or store that accommodated one or more persons. Most writing desks probably were elevated on a plain, open frame to a height suitable for either sitting or standing. The frame supported a slant-top box of appropriate width with hinged "flaps" to afford access to interior storage. Near the outside bottom of each flap was a "ledge," or cleat, to support a ledger or other document. The writing desk could be single-sided or double-sided, and it might contain a row of small drawers and pigeonholes, even a bookcase, across the back or at the division between two sides (fig. 3). The book *Prices of Cabinet and Chair Work* published at Philadelphia in 1772 describes both a double and a single desk on a frame for a "Store," with a row of drawers and pigeonholes at the back, the whole constructed of walnut or pine.[13]

Complementing Fenwick Lyell's work on a writing desk are entries from the accounts of three other shops for constructing writing-desk frames at prices ranging from 75¢ to $4.75. Job Danforth built "a fraim to a Righting

Figure 3 Edward S. Russell, *Office of Humphrey Hathaway, at the Head of Rotch's Wharf,* New Bedford, Massachusetts, 1819–1873. Pencil sketch, as published in Horatio Hathaway, *A New Bedford Merchant* (Boston: privately printed at Merymount Press, 1930). (Anonymous collection © The New Bedford Whaling Museum.) In this scene writing desks are depicted in the middle ground and background.

Dask" in 1796 for Philip Crapo, a merchant of Providence, Rhode Island. Hezekiah Healy's work a few years earlier at Windsor, Vermont, was for Isaac Greene, a storekeeper. Most expensive was Abner Taylor's job of building "a writing desk botom with a drawer" at Lee, Massachusetts. Nicholas Low, a merchant of New York City, required merely a "new brace to [a] desk frame" in 1824, which he acquired from Abraham S. Egerton. Aside from information in the Philadelphia book of prices, the wood used in writing desks is named only twice in the records consulted for this study. Dr. Isaac Senter of Newport, Rhode Island, engaged Walter Nichols in June 1784 to construct a "maple writing desk and frame" for $8.00. Pine was used in a new desk built for $6.00 in 1833 by William Webb IV for Joseph G. Waters, a lawyer of Salem, Massachusetts.[14]

Several craftsmen made additions to existing writing-desk frames. Silas E. Cheney of Litchfield, Connecticut, billed Isaac Baldwin $1.17 in 1809 for "puting shelf to writing Desk." A "Book frame for writing Desk," costing $1.00, was supplied at Cooperstown, New York, in 1830 by Robert C. Scadin. Priced somewhat higher at $1.50 was a writing-desk drawer, as indicated in a bill of 1792 from Seth R. Kneeland to James Beekman, a merchant of New York City. Only four months earlier Kneeland had supplied Beekman with nine stools. Sometimes all that was required for a writing desk was a lock, as noted by Hezekiah Healy in Vermont. Job E. Townsend's work at "Mending and Cleaning a Righting Disk and Book Case" in 1795 at Newport, Rhode Island, indicates that bookcases were part of some writing-desk structures. At Providence Job Danforth twice recorded "putting [a] Cupboard to [a] Writing Desk" for 15s. ($2.51). The enclosed space may have served the same function as a bookcase. Another reference to a bookcase illuminates the subject of finish. In 1806 Stephanus Knight of Enfield, Connecticut, made note of "Painting [a] Boockcase and Writeing desk." Eight years earlier Knight had painted a writing desk for another customer, an activity also recorded at Windsor, Vermont, by Thomas Boynton and at Kennebunk, Maine, by Paul Jenkins.[15]

A series of transactions between Stephen Girard, an eminent merchant of Philadelphia, and cabinetmaker Henry Connelly introduces another form to this discussion, the writing table. In June 1810 Connelly undertook to repair a table of this description and to cover it with "green cloth," probably baize, at a total cost of $6.25. The simple baize-covered frame in figure 2 may illustrate this table form, as well as a table William Webb IV repaired and covered with cloth for Joseph G. Waters, Esq., at Salem, Massachusetts. By November 1811 Connelly was again at work on Girard's writing table, this time engaged at "altering mouldings." A new cover was required again in May 1812, at which time Connelly also constructed a "New Drawer" for a table and installed a "patent Lock." The baize-covered table may have been replaced in 1817, when Girard purchased from Connelly a new writing table with a "writing flap" for $28.00. A decade later Elisha H. Holmes of Essex, Connecticut, enhanced the functionality of a client's writing table by making a "secretary," that is, a series of small drawers, and possibly pigeonholes, at the back of the frame.[16]

The slant-front desk fitted with a bookcase above the writing compartment is termed a "desk and bookcase" in eighteenth-century and early-nineteenth-century records (fig. 2). Bookcase tops are flat or pedimented. The doors fronting the bookcase shelves show greater variety, being plain, paneled, arched, scalloped, or sashed. Records provide little information either about design or the exact nature of repairs. Descriptions in eighteenth-century accounts are particularly spare. After "mending a Desk and Book Case" at Newport, Rhode Island, in 1783, Job E. Townsend finished the job by "fitting the Locks." A few years later he mended and "cleaned" a desk-and-bookcase for another client, although there is no evidence that he applied any type of finish. During the 1780s Daniel Ross "polished" a desk-and-bookcase at Ipswich, Massachusetts, charging his client 6s. ($1.00). The size of the two-part desk-and-bookcase may have been a deterrent to carting it off to a cabinet shop for any but essential work.[17]

Early-nineteenth-century evidence of repairs to the desk-and-bookcase is slightly more common and descriptive, probably because by this period the form was aging. A customer engaged Perez Austin at Canterbury, Connecticut, in 1823 to "fit" his desk-and-bookcase, a job that likely rehabilitated an older piece of furniture for new service. Work carried out by Elizur Barnes for a patron at Middletown two years earlier may describe some of the tasks also performed by Austin: "To Repairing, Cleaning & Varnishing Desk & Book Case." Barnes charged $3.50 for his work; Austin's bill was higher at $7.00. Allen Holcomb's work at New Lisbon in central New York State in the 1820s included varnishing a desk-and-bookcase for Dr. Walter Wing.[18]

A small group of records relative to the desk-and-bookcase describes an alteration/conversion that likely was relatively common, especially in the federal period. First mention in records consulted for this study is in 1774, when Robert Cockburn, who worked in Orange County, Virginia, charged a customer £2 ($6.67) for making "one Wal[nu]t Bookcase and mending the ould Desk." A dozen years later Townsend Goddard of Newport, Rhode Island, performed similar work for merchant Christopher Champlin, again using walnut and charging £2.2. Converting a desk to a desk-and-bookcase was relatively simple, and in these two jobs the material of the desk likely dictated that of the bookcase. In 1808 Jonathan Peckham paid Edward Slead of Dartmouth, Massachusetts, $2.00 for "colouring and fixing a desk," which was followed by "making a book case for the Desk" for $5.00. When, several years later, Albert C. Greene engaged Stephen Sweet of East Greenwich, Rhode Island, to build a bookcase, his desk required only some "Bracing." Work to a desk, described in 1821 as "fixing a desk," was a prelude to Daniel Downing's acquisition of a bookcase for his desk at the shop of Thomas Safford in Canterbury, Connecticut. As late as 1833 John Wolferspergen bespoke similar work, which was spelled out in detail by John Ellinger of Palmyra, Lebanon County, Pennsylvania: "To mending and old Desk [and] Varnish'g and Making Book Case on and Cleaning old Mountings" (hardware). The transaction, which serves to illuminate the conservative nature of the German community in Pennsylvania, also demonstrates that it was never too late to convert something old into something new and useful.[19]

In distinguishing the secretary-and-bookcase from the desk-and-bookcase, George Hepplewhite noted in his *Cabinet-Maker and Upholsterer's Guide* (1794) that the secretary "differ[s] in not being sloped in front." He went on to explain that "the accommodations . . . for writing are produced by the face of the upper drawer falling down by means of a spring and quadrant, which produces the same usefulness as the flap to a desk." Descriptions of the secretary-and-bookcase in craftsmen's records are few. Therefore, it

Figure 4 William Appleton, secretary-and-bookcase, Salem, Massachusetts, 1795–1804. Mahogany and mahogany veneer with white pine, ebony, and holly. H. 97½" (finial), W. 43¼", D. 24⅜". (Courtesy, Winterthur Museum, museum purchase with funds provided by Lammot du Pont Copeland, acc. 53.57.)

usually is not possible to know the exact form of the double case: whether the lower case was close to the floor or elevated on tall legs; whether it was filled with drawers or a combination of drawers and cabinets; whether the writing surface was a drawer with a drop front or a fold-out board at the top of the lower case. The type of writing surface also dictated the style of the upper case. The drop-front drawer has a fitted case at the back containing small drawers and pigeonholes, and the upper case is a full bookcase, usually glazed (fig. 4). The small drawers and pigeonholes accompanying the fold-out board are concealed at the bottom of the upper case behind cupboard doors, a tambour, or small solid panels in the glazed doors.[20]

Craftsmen rarely distinguished between the low secretary and the secretary-and-bookcase. Internal evidence, such as repair costs and named furniture parts, indicates that the two terms were interchangeable in most cases. The secretary was a new form in America in the federal period, and, indeed, most repair work noted by craftsmen falls in the 1820s and 1830s, a period when many cases had accrued sufficient age to require attention by the local cabinetmaker. Many repairs are anonymous. In one unusual circumstance Elisha H. Holmes of Essex, Connecticut, noted, "Going to Deep river & repairing secretary." The 75¢ charge would have included the time spent going to and coming from Deep River, a community on the Connecticut River about 3½ miles distant from Essex. More specific is Allen Holcomb's record of "Reparing a Secretary Drawer" for 50¢ at New Lisbon in central New York State. Of particular note is work undertaken in 1810 by Silas E. Cheney at Litchfield, Connecticut, for his client Joseph L. Smith. Each task in the extensive job is listed and priced separately, the total amounting to $4.56: "to puting feet to seckretary" ($2.00); "to fixing locks & hanging Dores & altering quadrents" ($1.25); "to Varnishing seckretary & book case" (50¢); "to 2 handles for [secretary]" (50¢); "to 5 kee hole etscutions [escutcheons]" (31¢). The "quadrants" Cheney speaks of are the curved metal straps supporting the drop front of the writing drawer, as identified in Hepplewhite's *Guide* (fig. 4).[21]

The varnish finish noted by Cheney was, by far, the more common of the two surface finishes noted in craftsmen's records for the secretary-and-bookcase. In 1827, when Michael Bouvier, a cabinetmaker of Philadelphia, repaired a secretary for Stephen Girard, he identified "polish" as the alternative surface coating. Bouvier completed the job by "Putting Knobs On Secretary," although the material of the new knobs is uncertain. More specific is a reference in the accounts of Thomas J. Moyers and Fleming K. Rich of Wytheville, Virginia, who in 1837, after "reparing & varnishing [a] secutary and book case" for James R. Miller, installed "1 set glass knobs." Glass was a new medium for furniture trimmings by the second quarter of the century, made possible by technological advances in the rising American glass industry. Moyers and Rich completed their job for Miller by "painting glass," an apparent reference to coating the back surfaces of the panes in the bookcase doors in lieu of installing interior hardware and curtains.[22]

New trimmings were a frequent addition to repaired and refurbished secretaries-and-bookcases. Unfortunately, most trimmings are not identified beyond the knobs installed at Philadelphia and Virginia, and Silas E. Cheney's handles and escutcheons for a Connecticut client. In 1807 John Collins trimmed a secretary belonging to Richard Blow of Portsmouth, Virginia, using "10 handles," and twelve years later Friedrich Bastian recorded "Putting Mountins [mountings, or hardware] on a Secretary" in central Pennsylvania. Thomas Boynton supplied hardware of another type at Windsor, Vermont, in this period, when he debited the account of Charles Marsh, Esq., $2.00 for "3 Balls for a Secretary," identifying spherical finials for the pediment.[23]

A reference to "Repairing a Ladies Cabinet," a new, specialized furniture form in the federal period, is a rarity among records consulted for this study. Fenwick Lyell carried out the work in 1809 for a client at Middletown, New Jersey. If Lyell's terminology is accurate, the form he referred to is described and illustrated in Sheraton's *Cabinet-Maker and Upholsterer's Drawing-Book* (1793) as well as in his *Cabinet-Makers' London Book of Prices* for 1793. Basically, the form is a small rectangular writing table with a fold-out board supported when open on lopers or on a shallow drawer in the frame. At the back of the table rises a shallow, two-tier case fitted variously with a bookshelf, small cabinets with drawers, nests of drawers, "letter holes," and open recesses. Lyell's shop at Middletown was located near the northern Jersey coast, within easy sailing distance of lower Manhattan, the business center of New York City. Lyell would have been familiar with the latest furniture fashions in the urban center, given his location in New Jersey and his earlier business experience in Manhattan between 1797 and 1799 at his shop in Beaver Street.[24]

Bookcases

When considering repairs to the freestanding bookcase, references cannot always be taken at face value. Undoubtedly, some bookcases identified without further description actually formed the top section of a desk-and-bookcase rather than a stand-alone case. Examples of this ambiguity include Isaac Vose's record of "work on [a] book case" at Boston in 1791 and Joel Mount's note of "reparing [a] bookcase" half a century later at Juliustown, New Jersey. By contrast, a job at "Fitting up Book cases" undertaken by Reed and Hollis at Salem, Massachusetts, for John Devereux, Esq., appears to identify the independent form more clearly.[25]

Regardless of the independent or dependent status of the bookcase, structural repairs to the form were similar. John G. Hopkins repaired a "Shelf to [a] book Case" in 1830 at Providence, Rhode Island, for as little as 20¢. Felix Huntington's work for Colonel Joshua Huntington at Norwich, Connecticut, in the late 1770s included "new hanging [a] Book Case," that is, rehanging the doors. The cabinetmaker also indicated that he supplied the new "hinges & screws." "Putting [a] pice [piece] on a book case" was all that was required to refurbish a case for Doctor B. Smart at Kennebunk, Maine. Paul Jenkins further accommodated the doctor by moving the case and "putting up [an] old one." At Middletown, New Jersey, Fenwick Lyell made repairs to "the Lower part of a Book Case," charging his client 7s. ($1.17).[26]

More activity revolved around the actual replacement of bookcase parts. Phillip Filer supplied a new shelf for a client's bookcase at or near Rome, New York, whereas David Pritchard of Waterbury, Connecticut, made a new bookcase back. In an unusual credit arrangement Elizur Barnes of Middletown, Connecticut, permitted one of his woodworking customers to offset part of his debt by "making [a] bottom to [a] bookcase" for another of Barnes's customers. From Vermont to Virginia woodworkers were kept busy installing new locks on bookcases or replacing old ones. A relatively complete, although unusual, job of providing hardware was recorded by Pennell Beale in 1791 at Philadelphia. Beale charged General Henry Knox 7s. 6d. ($1.25) for "Rectifying [putting right] a Book Case" and then itemized the additional hardware and installation charges: "1 Stocklock" 11s. 3d., "putting it on the Doore" (2s. 6d.), "1 Small Lock" (1s. 6d.), "putting it on" (6d.), "4 Screws and putting a Lock on" (1s. 6d.). The total additional charge was 17s. 3d. ($2.88). As described in the *Oxford English Dictionary*, a stock-lock is a mechanism enclosed in a wooden case and usually fitted on an outer door. The secondary locks in this order appear to have secured internal drawers or cupboards. Other bookcase work focuses on the doors. Both Howard Smith of New Haven, Connecticut, and Nathaniel Holmes of Kingston, Massachusetts, may have supplied doors where none existed previously. Holmes's $1.00 charge also included priming. Fenwick Lyell of Middletown, New Jersey, supplied one pane of glass for a door, whereas Robert Kennedy carried out more extensive work at Philadelphia for merchant William Barrell by "Glazeing 12 lights" and painting the entire bookcase, all for 12s. ($2.00).[27]

Paint was the surface finish on at least two other bookcases, as recorded by Thomas Boynton at Windsor, Vermont, and William G. Beesley at Salem, New Jersey. Polish was requested at Litchfield, Connecticut, and Newport, Rhode Island, by customers of Silas E. Cheney and Walter Nichols, respectively. A varnish finish was the more common selection, however. Before varnishing a bookcase for a client, Elizur Barnes of Middletown, Connecticut, first "cleaned" the surface. In this process he either removed all of a former finish or smoothed the surface in some manner so that the varnish coat he applied made the case look as good as new. When work on the bookcase was finished, Barnes recorded "Sending it home." The wording implies that the owner had previously directed the cabinetmaker to make the transportation arrangements. A description of work undertaken by Daniel Trotter at Philadelphia in 1787 for Benjamin Thaw was more focused. When completed, the cabinetmaker recorded "mending & varnishing the head of a Bookcase" for 7s. 6d. ($1.25). The term "head" identified a pediment or a substantial molding that formed an ornament at the top of the case.[28]

Chests
The term "chest" when first encountered in craftsmen's records appears to be an ambiguous word. A study of pertinent references indicates, however, that in most cases this term identified a box-form chest with a hinged lid at

the top accompanied at times by one or more tiers of drawers at the bottom (fig. 5). The relevant evidence includes many references to mending or replacing a chest "lid," or "top," the frequent installation of a single lock, the occasional mention of a chest till or a chest with one drawer, and the extensive use of paint as a surface finish.

Figure 5 Chest with lid, Nassau County, Long Island, New York, 1770–1800. Pine with brass and iron. H. 38¼", W. 41¾", D. 19¾". (Courtesy, Winterthur Museum, acc. 70.440.)

"Mend," "repair," and "fix" were terms craftsmen employed to describe the process of returning a chest to a sound structural state. The word "mend" appears in the records more often than "repair" and "fix" combined. On occasion the terms "old" or "large" are part of the description. When working for widow Mary Norris of Philadelphia in 1778, Thomas Tufft named the construction material in "mending a Walnut Chest" at a charge of 10s. ($1.67). Solomon Cole of Glastonbury, Connecticut, identified the function of a chest he refurbished in 1801 as a repository for clothes. Structural repairs varied in cost from as little as 10d. to well over £1. In the decimal-based currency adopted in the United States in the 1790s, this represented a range of 14¢ to $4.00.[29]

On occasion, craftsmen identified actual structural repairs and replacements. Most common was work involving the "lid" or "top" of the chest, a job described sometimes as "hanging a Chest." Part of the same task might be other structural repairs or replacements and the repair or installation of a lock. A typical entry, recorded in 1797 at Ridgefield, Connecticut, by Elisha Hawley, reads: "to Chest Lid for Josiah & puting Lock." Job E. Townsend of Newport, Rhode Island, used alternative language in 1790 when identifying the basic job as "a New top to a Chest" for his customer Daniel Weatherly. No money exchanged hands. Instead, Weatherly bartered "fish Sounds" (air bladders) and fish to pay for the work. Second on the list of structural work was the repair, replacement, or addition of a drawer or drawers. Again, Townsend's records provide comprehensive insights into the nature of this work and the scope of related activity. On August 22, 1818, Townsend charged Isaac Stoddard 17¢ for "Mending the Drawers of his Chest." This appears to have been the same chest for which Townsend had made a "New Till & Draws and Perticeans" (partitions) eight months earlier, charging Stoddard $2.00 for the work. In the 1780s Townsend had accommodated another customer, J. Hill, by "making a New Bottom and two Drawers to a Large Chest" for 9s. ($1.50). Whether this was replacement work or an alteration to an otherwise drawerless chest is unclear, although the cost of Townsend's work for Stoddard and for Hill indicates that both jobs, including materials, required more than a day's labor. Still another structural repair is identified in the accounts of Peter Ranck, a Pennsylvania German craftsman of Jonestown, Lebanon County. In 1795 Ranck recorded "putting feet to one chest and one lock and painting it."[30]

Hardware for lidded chests is an item of considerable note in craftsmen's accounts. Lock work, whether a repair or the installation of a new or replacement lock, was the most common request. Nine pence (12½¢) was the amount Samuel Durand charged Henry Bull at Milford, Connecticut, in 1814 for "mending [a] Chest lock." The supply and installation of a new lock appears to have cost in the range of 1s. 4d. to 4s. (22¢ to 67¢). A simple installation of a lock in hand usually cost less than 1s. When putting a lock on a chest in 1770, Timothy Loomis of Windsor also noted the use of "nails." Some jobs were more extensive. After mending a chest at Wallingford in 1806, Titus Preston put on both a lock and hinges. More complete information occurs in the records of George Claypoole of Philadelphia, who in 1773 recorded the installation of hardware on a chest belonging to Samuel Meredith: "to a lock & hinges" (2s. 2d.), "to a hasp & two staples" (1s.), "to puting the above to a Chest" (1s. 6d.). The various charges ranged from 16½¢ to 36¢.[31]

At times the installation of hardware accompanied repainting the exterior surface of a chest. Titus Preston provided considerable detail in 1819, when describing work he carried out for a client in Connecticut: "painting & puting brasses on a chest which with the necessary preparations [for painting] & going over it 5 times took me over 8 hours beside finding oil paints & varnish and puting on a lock." Preston's charge was 8s. ($1.34). More modest in cost at 41¢ was a job Samuel Douglas undertook for Miss Mary Embry in 1812 in the area of New Hartford and Canton, when "puting Lock on Chest, hanging lid [and] painting Mahogany Couler." Paint was the popular finish for the lidded chest, far exceeding all other options combined. Aside from mahogany color, Douglas recorded "painting [a] Chest with oran[ge]" three years later. At the beginning of the century Stephanus Knight of Enfield had recorded "Painting a Chest Blew."[32]

A few householders elected to have their chest recolored, a relatively cheap surface treatment utilizing pigment suspended in size. This was the option of several customers at the shop of Oliver Avery in North Stonington, Connecticut, in the late eighteenth century, a period when David Haven of Framingham, Massachusetts, also recorded "Collaring a Chist with one Draw" for a resident of Hopkinton, a community located about nine miles to the west. Of unusual nature is a customer entry of 1764 in the accounts of John Durand of Milford, Connecticut: "by Coming up to your hous and Colering a Chest." Only rarely did a craftsman undertake repair work or refurbishing at a client's home. Furniture delivery and pickup were the responsibility of the customer. In this case Durand's customer paid handsomely for the service at 8s. 6d. ($1.42). Other options for refurbishing a chest surface were staining, as recorded by Abner Taylor circa 1814 at Lee, Massachusetts, and varnishing, a task Jeduthern Avery completed on an "old Chest" for 15¢ in 1824 at Bolton/Coventry, Connecticut.[33]

Chests of Drawers
The storage form consisting of a set of drawers within an open box-style frame was identified by one of three names in the eighteenth and early nineteenth centuries. Most common was the term "case of drawers" (also called a case "with" or "and" drawers), which was used far more often than the second and third choices combined, "drawers" and "chest of Drawers" (fig. 6). Two cabinetmakers identified the primary wood of chests of drawers they

Figure 6 Designs for chests of drawers illustrated in pl. 52 in George Hepplewhite, *Cabinet-Maker and Upholsterer's Guide,* 3rd ed. (London, 1794). (Courtesy, Winterthur Library, Printed Book and Periodical Collection.) The date on the engraved plate is 1787.

repaired. Job E. Townsend named mahogany at Newport, Rhode Island, and John Hockaday cited walnut at Williamsburg, Virginia.[34]

General references to chest-of-drawers repair work occur as early as the 1740s in materials supporting this study. In 1743 Joseph Lindsey recorded "repairing a Case of Drawers" for a customer at Marblehead, Massachusetts. Another repair is of interest because of the nature of the customer's barter goods. When Job Townsend Jr. of Newport, Rhode Island, completed work on Thomas Weaver's "Case [of] Drawers" in late December 1767, he already had recorded partial payment on December 24 in the form of "one Turkey 8 [pounds]." A small group of documents provides specific insights into structural work. Silas E. Cheney put a "Back to Case with Draws" in 1808 at Litchfield, Connecticut. A contemporary, Reuben Loomis, who worked in the area of Suffield, accommodated a client by "puting a top to an old case of draws." Two craftsmen installed new legs on customer's chests. William Proud of Providence, Rhode Island, charged 1s. 6d. (25¢) in 1776 for "torning a Seatt [set] of . . . Case of D[r]aws Legs." The date, the nature of fabrication, and the low cost suggest these were feet for an early-eighteenth-century chest. Samuel Davison's job of "makeing a leg for draws" at the same price in 1801 at Plainfield, Massachusetts, appears to describe work to a chest with bracket feet. Four years later Jacob Sass of Charleston, South Carolina, recorded "Gluing a Chest of Drawers Bracket [foot] and putting on a set of new Castors" for a client at a charge of $3.50. Most of the expense lay in the cost of the casters. More extensive work at "Rep'g [repairing] the under part of a chist of draws" required "2 days" of Alexander Low's time in 1798 at Freehold, New Jersey. To the 16s. charge for labor Low posted a charge of 2s. for "glew, wood & sprigs."[35]

Constant use or a desire for enhanced efficiency led other householders to request repairs to the drawers of their chests. Two craftsmen, Silas E. Cheney of Litchfield, Connecticut, and Job E. Townsend of Newport, Rhode Island, replaced "Sliders on a Set of Drawers" at charges of 17¢ and 39¢, respectively. Job Danforth of Providence charged 33¢ for a new "Draw Bottom." "Puting partitions in [a] Drewer" was more costly at 50¢ and 60¢, as recorded by George Merrifield at Albany, New York, and Luke Houghton at Barre, Massachusetts.[36]

Repaired or replaced hardware was the focus of other customer requests at the local cabinet shop. When "mending a Case of Drawers" in 1788 for merchant Samuel Coates of Philadelphia, Daniel Trotter also altered the lock. Craftsmen identified case hardware by several names: "brasses," "trimmings," "mountings," and "furniture." Replacing the hardware on a chest of drawers often accompanied more extensive work, as when Titus Preston mended, painted, and put "Brasses" on a "case with draws" in 1798 for a customer at Wallingford, Connecticut. In the same decade Asa Jones completed work for James Perkins at Bridgewater, Massachusetts, by "Repairing a Case of Drawers, plaining and Staneing and polishing," then noting, "found Brasses." Somewhat later, Friedrich Bastian of Dauphin County, Pennsylvania, recorded mending and varnishing a chest of drawers and "Puting on monnlings" (mountings). By the 1820s and 1830s customers were requesting fashionable "knobs for draws," as indicated in the records of Daniel Ross of Ipswich, Massachusetts, and George Merrifield of Albany, New York.[37]

Customer options for resurfacing the chest of drawers were broad. Surface smoothing was accomplished by planing, as identified by Asa Jones at Bridgewater, Massachusetts, or scraping, a task noted at Litchfield, Connecticut, by Silas E. Cheney, who then put varnish on the new surface of a double case (chest-on-chest). Varnishing sometimes accompanied mending a case, as indicated on several occasions in the 1820s by Moses Parkhurst of Paxton, Massachusetts. Painting the surface of a chest of drawers may have been almost as popular. Three craftsmen working during the first quarter of the nineteenth century recorded "painting a Chest of Drawers," or "Low

Figure 7 High chest of drawers, Boston, Massachusetts, 1730–1750. Maple with ash, white pine, and yellow poplar. H. 69⅜", W. 40½" (at cornice), D. 22¹¹⁄₁₆" (at feet). (Courtesy, Winterthur Museum, bequest of Henry Francis du Pont, acc. 52.255.)

Chest" as it was identified at times, at charges ranging from 33¢ to 42¢. Included in this group are Oliver Moore and Samuel Douglas of Connecticut and Allen Holcomb of New York State. Like the varnished chest, cases to be painted were repaired on occasion. Other householders deposited their chests of drawers with a woodworker for the purpose of having the surface polished. In one instance, in 1795, Elisha Hawley of Ridgefield, Connecticut, identified the polishing agent as "wax." The material and job cost 2s. 9d. (46¢). In 1748 Joseph Symonds of Salem, Massachusetts, posted the earliest reference in this study to polishing "a cas[e] of Draws." Of about equal popularity with polishing was coloring the surfaces of a case. Lemuel Tobey and Edward Slead of Dartmouth recorded "Cullering [a] Cais Draws" in 1774 and 1801, respectively. Staining a surface, as undertaken by Asa Jones at Bridgewater, appears to have been an infrequent option.[38]

Tall chests received attention from furniture craftsmen in proportion to their more limited frequency in clients' homes. Job E. Townsend of Newport, Rhode Island, recorded making an inexpensive 12½¢ repair to a "High Case of Drawer[s]" (fig. 7) in the immediate post-Revolutionary years. Several decades later at Framingham, Massachusetts, Abner Haven undertook "fixing a high Case of draws," whose greater age appears reflected in the $11.00 charge for repairs. Surface coating accompanied some general repairs, which Townsend noted on several occasions in the late eighteenth century. In 1785 he recorded staining and polishing "a high Case of Drawers." Polish, alone, had accompanied "mending a Pair of hy Case of Drawers" almost three years earlier. Varnish was the surface coating applied in 1831 to a "highcase of Draws" in Lancaster County, Pennsylvania, by Jacob Bachman.[39]

In terms of structural repairs, more descriptive information emerges from records for the chest-on-chest of drawers (fig. 8). Silas E. Cheney spent the better part of three days at Litchfield, Connecticut, in 1801 "peasing and mending [a] Chest on chest." Another day, or more, was devoted to scraping and varnishing the case. Equally enlightening is a lengthy job carried out a few years earlier by Alexander Low at Freehold, New Jersey, described as "Rep'g a chist on chist 3 days work." Low's labor charge of £1.4, or 24s., suggests that his usual daily wage was 8s., a figure considerably higher than the common 6s. wage, or less, although Low's figure may reflect working days of extra length. In itemizing the materials he supplied, Low described, in part, what the work entailed: "To a lok & key 2s., one handel 1s., rep'g lokes 4s." for a total of 7s.; the "sprigs & Glew" he supplied cost another 3s. Somewhat unclear is work undertaken for Christopher Champlin in 1786 at Newport, Rhode Island, by Townsend Goddard, who recorded "To Carkes [carcass] & Repairs on a Chest on Chest of Draws."[40]

Equally current with entries for repairs in craftsmen's accounts are references to alterations to the various chest forms described above. Many alterations made to the low chest of drawers (fig. 6) are unidentified, and the adjective "old" occurs with frequency. Jeduthern Avery of Bolton/Coventry, Connecticut, provided some insight in 1824, when he

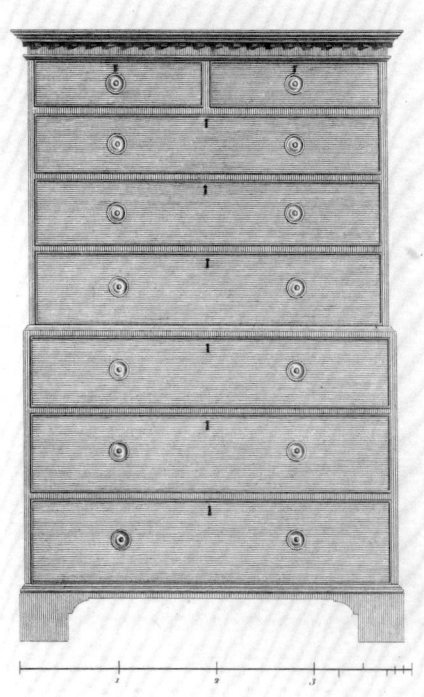

Figure 8 Design for a double chest of drawers (chest-on-chest) illustrated in pl. 53 in George Hepplewhite, *Cabinet-Maker and Upholsterer's Guide*, 3rd ed. (London, 1794). (Courtesy, Winterthur Library, Printed Book and Periodical Collection.) The date on the engraved plate is 1787.

recorded "Altering old Draws & trimings." His charge was $4.00. The records of two other craftsmen, who posted similar charges, are more enlightening. Elizur Barnes of Middletown charged Mary Bement for "Altering & varnishing [a] Case Draws," "Cleaning Handles," and providing a "sett [of] Locks." Oliver Moore of East Granby described the final product in 1818, when debiting George Griswold's account for "altering your old Case of Drawers into a Bureau." A more explicit record is that of Nathaniel Dominy V of East Hampton, Long Island, who in 1819 noted a job for Jeremiah Miller: "To cut off old drawers, make new top, feet &c. to D[itt]o." Dominy's substantial charge of £1.16 ($6.01) indicates that he spent most of a work week at the job. His description suggests that the "old drawers" were of tall form, five or six drawers high, lowered to a four-drawer chest and updated with a new style top and feet.[41]

A number of high chests underwent significant alteration. On two or more occasions high chests of drawers (fig. 7) became "a Berew [bureau] & Dressing table." Alexander Low recorded this work in 1799 at Freehold, New Jersey, followed by James Francis in the 1820s at Wethersfield, Connecticut. When Job Danforth of Providence, Rhode Island, made "two beaurows out of a case of draws" for 48s. ($8.02) in 1801 and provided "trimmings" for one of them, he identified another tall form, the chest-on-chest (fig. 8). The following year Silas E. Cheney of Litchfield, Connecticut, was employed at "aultearing [a] Chest on Chest into two burose" for prominent jurist Tapping Reeve. When undertaking a similar alteration a few years later, Cheney identified the resulting bureaus as "Large Size." Polishing followed some structural work, which Job E. Townsend undertook following repairs to "a Case of Drawers and Putting feet to the Top Part."[42]

To begin a discussion of the bureau form, it is necessary first to define the term as it was understood and used in American society at the end of the eighteenth century and later. In French and British use "bureau" identifies a desk, the word derived from the French term "bure," the name for the woolen baize used to cover the writing surface. In America the word "bureau" appeared in a published notice of New York City origin as early as 1777, when a public auction offered household furnishings that included mahogany desks, "buroes," and chests of drawers, the list suggesting strongly that the bureau was not a desk and in some way could be distinguished from a chest of drawers. Another city auction, held in 1783, offered chests of drawers and "fine Buroes." More particularly enlightening are several advertisements of John Marshall, a cabinetmaker of Charleston, South Carolina, who in 1795 was prepared to supply "Ladies commode chests of drawers, of different forms" and "[Ladies] plain straight [chests of drawers]." Marshall shortened the first item to "Ladies Commodes" when advertising the following year. His use of the term "Commode" appears to have had special meaning, which is further amplified by the *Oxford English Dictionary* in identifying the term as "a chest of drawers . . . of the decorative kind." Few American craftsmen used the term "commode," however, preferring to use "bureau," as demonstrated in 1793 by Jonathan Gostelowe, a Philadelphia cabinetmaker, who advertised that he had on hand "a few

Figure 9 Bureau, attributed to Jonathan Gostelowe, Philadelphia, Pennsylvania, 1780–1793. Mahogany with yellow poplar and pine. H. 36", W. 47¼", D. 26⅝". (Courtesy, Winterthur Museum, bequest of Henry Francis du Pont, acc. 59.631.)

Mahogany Bureaus" (fig. 9). Four months later Gostelowe held a public auction, offering "Circular and plain Bureaus," suggesting that "bureau" had become a generic term describing any new chest of drawers in a current style. As for the vintage styles, craftsmen still identified repairs to chests of drawers as late as the 1840s.[43]

Like the short studies of repairs to other case forms, an investigation of bureau repairs comes up short on description. Without particular information about structure and style, it is difficult to envision that cases with drawers that passed through the repair shops of American cabinetmakers from the post-Revolutionary years until the 1840s were anything more than plain rectangular chests. Fortunately, a group of documents mentioning furniture repairs also contains information on new work, often in more detail, thus providing greater insight. Bureaus with four, six, and seven drawers are identified, the latter two cases containing at least one tier of narrow drawers at the top. Case façades are described as "straight," "circular," "round," "swelled," "elliptic," "sweep front," and "commode style," with some terms likely overlapping. To this list is added the "undulating serpentine façade," identified in both the London price book of 1793 and Hepplewhite's *Guide* (1794).[44]

New cases with paneled ends are first mentioned in 1814 in documents used in this study. "Colum[ne]d" bureaus appear in the records as early as

Figure 10 Levi Ruggles, bureau, Boston, Massachusetts, 1813–1816. Mahogany, mahogany veneer, and birch veneer with pine, glass, brass, and copper. H. 75", W. 38½", D. 23¼". (Courtesy, Winterthur Museum, bequest of Henry Francis du Pont, acc. 57.567.)

1795 and 1796, although these quarter-column cases are different from later bureaus with three-quarter columns continuous with the feet (fig. 10) and the even later cases with freestanding columns, or pillars. References in this study to the last two styles date from 1817 to 1841. A variation of the full-column bureau was the half-column case. Several records cite bureaus specialized for "dressing," also described as having a "drassor top" or a "Case on the top." Features may have included a fitted dressing drawer, a dressing glass, and/or a tier of narrow setback drawers on the case top (fig. 10). A "back Board" of a type extending above a case top appears in two records dating to 1827, one board described as "ornamented." The second bureau also had a "prospect front," a term suggesting that the front of the case had cupboard doors or a cupboard below a drawer. Joseph Meeks and Sons' well-known broadside advertisement produced in 1833 at New York includes tiny images of two "Mahogany Bureaus" with cupboards in the case. From 1829 into the 1830s several cabinet shops produced bureaus with a front "projection," that is, a case with a top drawer extending forward of the lower drawers. Nathaniel Knowlton of Eliot, Maine, provided a particularly complete description: "a Bureau, mahog[any] front, Top projected, turned & reeded pillars."[45]

Craftsmen's records also describe a small number of nonstructural ornamental embellishments that might be present on a bureau deposited at a cabinet shop for general repair. Cock beading bordered many drawer fronts, and some feet were carved. Crossbanding and stringing offered other visual diversity. Relatively new in the 1820s and 1830s were "Glass Triming[s]," more particularly described as "Cut glass Knobs."[46]

Wood choice for bureaus describes a moderate selection. Mahogany was the decided preference as a primary wood, although the "mahogany front bureau" was more common than the full mahogany case. Cherry "ends" accompanied some mahogany façades. The all-cherry bureau was the next most popular choice. A new maple or curled maple case was an occasional selection by householders. Pine was more popular in this era of painted furniture, one example described as "ornamented." Birch and butternut cases appear to have been rarities. Whitewood (yellow poplar) ends framed at least one case, although whitewood was more common as a secondary material, as described in 1829 by James Gere of Groton, Connecticut: "Cherry, pine, and whitewood for mohagany front bureau."[47]

Whether craftsmen recorded fixing, mending, or repairing a bureau, the records are almost uniformly silent on the exact nature of the work. The most comprehensive description is that recorded by William Rawson in 1836 at Killingly, Connecticut. His labor cost was $1.00, suggesting that the craftsman spent a day or less at the work. His itemized list of materials describes the nature of the work: "8 feet [of] Boards @ 3 [cents]" (24¢), "4 Bureau feet" (50¢), and "8 [Bureau] Knobs" (70¢). The board length was about right to supply a new horizontal two-board backing to the case. The new bureau feet, which were cheaper than the eight turned knobs, may have been of simple bracket form. The eight knobs would have accommodated a four-drawer case. Rawson completed the job by varnishing the case. In reviewing other, briefer, citations focused on the fabrication of new parts, it is possible to enlarge on vulnerable construction features. Several shops made a new "top for [a] burow," among them that of Moyers and Rich at Wytheville, Virginia. In 1834 the partners charged a client $14.00 for the work, almost half the price of a new "mahogany front bureau" purchased at the shop the same year by another customer for $30.00. Constructing this new bureau top involved more than simply supplying and finishing a top board. At a minimum the work involved building a tier of setback drawers and an ornamental backboard. More likely, given the cost, the new top board and drawers were accompanied by a vertical structure supporting a dressing glass of the general type illustrated in figure 10, with the supports possibly updated to the period. It is unclear whether the work represented the replacement of a damaged structure or an alteration to enhance an older case. Most jobs involving case tops were less extensive. For example, when

Nathaniel Dominy V of East Hampton, Long Island, made a "Top to [a] Bureau" for a customer in 1819, his charge of £1.4 ($4.01) also included smoothing (probably scraping), coloring, and trimming the case. The new top likely was no more than a new board shaped on the edges and attached to the case. At the Middletown, Connecticut, shop of Elizur Barnes a client requested a new or replaced ornamental backboard for his bureau. "Vaneering a Bureau top" was a task carried out at Eliot, Maine, some years earlier by Nathaniel Knowlton at a modest charge of 37¢.[48]

The cost of a complete new drawer for a bureau varied with size and material. In 1807 George Short of Newburyport, Massachusetts, charged a customer as little as 50¢. At the Virginia shop of Moyers and Rich "4 new drawers for [a] bureau" cost a substantial $6.00 several decades later. All, or most, of these drawers were of large size and possibly made of mahogany. Fifty cents was the charge at the same shop to another customer who required "new sides in [a] bureau drawer." Other cabinet shops recorded work to the case feet. On several occasions during the 1810s Friedrich Bastian of Dauphin County in central Pennsylvania charged customers for "Meaking feet on . . . Bearow." John T. Ball carried out related work in 1809 at New York City for merchant and land developer Nicholas Low. Of more specific nature is Solomon Sibley's record at Ward (Auburn), Massachusetts, of "Putting on Bracket feet to Buro." A related, although probably more extensive, job was undertaken at Petersburg, Virginia, in 1814 by Alexander Taylor for Richard Blow. The "new apron & feet" Taylor supplied for the Virginia merchant's mahogany bureau likely describes work to a case with French bracket feet (fig. 6, bottom). In another type of work, dating to 1830, Providence, Rhode Island, craftsman John G. Hopkins accommodated Richard W. Greene, United States attorney for Rhode Island, by supplying two sets of "Brass Socket Casters," one priced at $1.25, the other at $1.50. Hopkins's charge for "putting them on Buerows" was 50¢.[49]

Of the cabinet shops that undertook some type of bureau work, half recorded the replacement or repair of hardware. A typical general account entry, as recorded by Elisha H. Holmes at Essex, Connecticut, in 1828, reads, "Repairing and triming [a] cherry bureau." Oliver Moore of East Granby provided a more specific explanation when he described "taking off old trimmings from a Bureau and puting on new ones." Elijah Sanderson of Salem, Massachusetts, Benjamin Ellery of Gloucester, and True Currier of Deerfield, New Hampshire, described the same work as "putting on new brasses." Job E. Townsend of Newport, Rhode Island, preferred the term "New firnature." Individual items are further described in some accounts as handles, escutcheons, and locks and keys. Two craftsmen recorded polishing hardware, although they used other terms. Thomas Boynton of Windsor, Vermont, referred to the process as "cleaning," whereas Pennell Beale of Philadelphia used the word "rubing." Knobs were a feature of some bureaus, whether of wood, metal, or glass. Paul Jenkins of Kennebunk, Maine, supplied "8 mahogany knobs for [a] Bureau" in 1838 at a cost of 45¢. Elizur Barnes of Middletown, Connecticut, described a "Sett of Knobs" for $1.50 in 1821, suggesting by the price that the material was brass.[50]

Varnish was the common finish for the bureau when the surface was refurbished. Abraham S. Egerton of New York City recorded "repairing & varnishing 4 bureaus" in 1824 for the household of Nicholas Low. "Varnishing [a] Burua twice" was the request of a customer at the shop of Silas E. Cheney at Litchfield, Connecticut, some years earlier. James Gere of Groton recorded the cost of materials for coating a bureau once: "Varnish for Bureau," 25¢, and "Turpentine," 3¢. Varnishing preceded by planing or scraping surfaces was the second-most common consumer option. Elizur Barnes undertook either procedure, as requested, for his customers at Middletown. Staining and varnishing a surface was an occasional choice among householders and the finish selected by several customers at the Hartwick, New York, shop of Leonard R. and James R. Proctor. Sometimes a surface was intact and needed only to be polished. Few bureaus were repainted. Thomas Boynton, a chairmaker and painting specialist of Windsor, Vermont, described a job at his shop as "painting Bureau Draws mahog[any] Im[itation]." Use of the term "imitation" virtually guarantees that the case was grain-painted; the charge was 50¢.[51]

Cupboards

The term "cupboard" as used in the eighteenth and early nineteenth centuries may be defined as an architectural "recess or piece of furniture with a door [or doors] and usually shelves for storing crockery, provisions, or other small items." This was not the only name for the form, however. On occasion craftsmen alternatively employed "closet," "bofet" (buffet), and "dresser," the last named form containing a superstructure of open shelves set at the back of the frame. Although most references to cupboard repairs are general in nature, the chance descriptor provides insights into cupboard use, placement, and specific form. Some cupboards were repositories for cheese or pewter, some stood in a kitchen, and others were fitted into the corner of a room. A highly specialized cupboard was the wardrobe for clothing, also called a "press." A few wardrobes made of mahogany were more than utilitarian in nature.

More often than not, craftsmen used general terms when citing repairs to the tall, closed, single-stage or two-stage cupboard of broad or narrow form (figs. 11, 29, left). Abner Haven of Framingham, Massachusetts, charged Levi Metcalf 15¢ in 1810 for "fixing a Cheese cupboard," the charge a typical one for a general repair. Another craftsman, Peter Ranck of Jonestown, Pennsylvania, identified the place where a cupboard stood: "mending a kitchen cupboard." Among named repairs, the most common one was reattaching a cupboard door. When "hanging cobbard doors" for Asa Rogers in 1809, Scolley and White of Newtown, Connecticut, may have spent as long as half a day at the work, judging by their 50¢ charge. Even more common was the fabrication and installation of new doors. Two craftsmen, Perez Austin of Canterbury, Connecticut, and Elias Savage of Windsor, Vermont, each recorded "making a paniel [panel] Cubboard Dore" for a customer, although whether the panels were recessed (fig. 11) or raised (also fielded, fig. 13) is not indicated. "Two small cubard Dors" supplied by "Skipper" Lunt of Newbury, Massachusetts, in 1767 refurbished Lemuel Fowler's piece of furniture. More extensive work was undertaken in 1840 in Lancaster County, Pennsylvania, by Jacob Bachman, who installed "Cupboard Doors, Locks and Hinges" for David Graff. The function of another cupboard was indicated in 1756, when Peter Emerson of Reading, Massachusetts, provided "Doors for [a] Puter Closet" in the home of his father.[52]

Rather than locks, some cupboard doors were secured by bolts, as recorded in 1833 near Canton, Connecticut, by Samuel Douglas. Another option was the "Cupboard turn," a small pivoting bar of wood attached to the cupboard frame next to a door. The device was supplied to customers in Massachusetts in the 1820s by Luke Houghton of Barre and Moses Parkhurst of Paxton (fig. 13). Other cupboard work was of large scale. "A Camesh [cornice, cornish] for a Cupe boord" was the focus of a 5s. (83½¢) job in 1801 at the Freehold, New Jersey, shop of Alexander Low. Two other shops, those of Luke Houghton in Massachusetts and Moyers and Rich in Virginia, recorded "puting on back on cupboard." In 1816 Nathaniel Bassett sought the services of Abner Taylor at Lee, Massachusetts, for "putting

Figure 11 Closed rectangular cupboard, Berks County, Pennsylvania, 1775–1800. Yellow poplar, maple, and pine with glass and brass. H. 84½", W. 78" (at cornice), D. 19" (at top of lower case). (Courtesy, Winterthur Museum, bequest of Henry Francis du Pont, acc. 64.1895.)

Figure 12 Corner cupboard, Pennsylvania, 1790–1830. Pine and yellow poplar. H. 84", W. 44½", D. 22½". (Courtesy, Winterthur Museum, gift of Mr. and Mrs. Henry Pleasants, acc. 94.11.)

Figure 13 Dresser, or open rectangular cupboard, Pennsylvania, 1750–1800. American black walnut with yellow poplar. H. 81¼", W. 62¾", D. 21⅛" (feet). (Courtesy, Winterthur Museum, bequest of Henry Francis du Pont, acc. 65.2750.) The cupboard turns, or turn buckles, are replacements.

a shelf in a Cupboard." The modest charge for the work was 17¢. Less clear is the nature of Chapman Lee's work for Orlean Prince in 1820 at Charlton, when "puting an End on [a] Cupboard." The 41¢ charge seems low for the structural work involved in replacing an entire end panel. Work to the lower parts of cupboards is described in account entries of two other craftsmen. Job E. Townsend recorded "Laying a floor" in a cupboard in 1789 at Newport, Rhode Island, and five years later Elisha Hawley made a "Cleat for [a] Cubbard" at Ridgefield, Connecticut. The cleat, priced at only a few pennies, may have been a trestle-style foot secured beneath a side panel of the case (fig. 13). Some cupboards had solid doors in the upper stage, whereas others were glazed. As early as 1735 Miles Ward of Salem, Massachusetts, recorded "Glasing a Bofatt" (buffet) for Captain Ebenezer Bowditch (fig. 11).[53]

Paint was the common surface coating for refinishing the cupboard. Prices for the work indicate the job took anywhere from half a day or less to more than one day. Enos Reynolds of Boxford, Massachusetts, charged the low sum of 66¢ in 1815 for painting a customer's cupboard and table. At the

high end was Charles C. Robinson's bill of $1.50 for painting a cupboard at Philadelphia the previous year. Prices would have reflected the size of the cupboard and the number of coats applied. Of particular note is a job recorded by Abberley and Hartley of New York City in 1839 for Miss Sophia Roorbach. The partners charged Roorbach $2.00 for "Painting & Grain'g [graining a] Cubbard" (fig. 11). Repairs sometimes accompanied the work of repainting. Judging by the single reference in this study to "staining [a] Cupboard," that method of recoating a surface appears to have been a limited option. Oliver Moore of East Granby, Connecticut, recorded the job in 1809 at the low cost of 25¢.[54]

Few entries in craftsmen's accounts make specific reference to the corner cupboard (fig. 12). Undoubtedly, some structures were identified merely as "cupboards" and others were termed "buffets," as suggested in the accounts of Miles Ward of Salem, Massachusetts: "to Dowrs [doors] for Bofut & Cobard." Some corner cupboards were part of the architecture of a room rather than freestanding. Peter Emerson of Reading, Massachusetts, near Boston, completed "work in ye Corner Closet" for his father in 1756 and charged him £2 ($6.68). That sum seems high and may reflect the currency problems of the region at the time. During the early nineteenth century both William G. Beesley of Salem, New Jersey, and Friedrich Bastian of Dauphin County, Pennsylvania, recorded "painting a corner copbord" for $1.50, a charge similar to that for a rectangular closed cupboard.[55]

The cupboard with recessed, open shelves above an enclosed base was termed a "dresser" in the eighteenth and early nineteenth centuries (fig. 13). Some cases were of broad form; others were narrow. Dressers were particularly common among the Pennsylvania Germans, although the form was known in New England as well. References in this study identify dressers in New Hampshire, Massachusetts, Rhode Island, New Jersey, rural Pennsylvania, and a Quaker household in Philadelphia. Some of the common wares stored in the dresser for everyday use were pewter dishes, plates, and spoons; knives and two-tined forks; wooden trenchers (platters or plates); lighting devices; coffeemills; and crocks containing foodstuffs.[56]

Records cite general repairs to three dressers in rural Pennsylvania households, of which two dressers are identified as standing in the kitchen. The kitchen also was the location of a dresser in the Philadelphia home of merchant Stephen Collins. The only named repair is one made at Newport, Rhode Island, by Job E. Townsend in 1785 for Robert Taylor, Esq.: "To mending the Dresser, a floar." The charge was 7s. ($1.17), representing about a full day's work. Like the closed rectangular cupboard, the common surface coating of the refurbished dresser was paint. John Sager painted a dresser in 1810 at Bordentown, New Jersey. When Jacob Bachman carried out the same work several decades later in Lancaster County, Pennsylvania, he again identified the place where the open cupboard stood as the kitchen. On two occasions Moody Carr of Rockingham County, New Hampshire, identified the material used in refurbishing a dresser. He charged John Mudget 2s. 9d. (46¢) in 1807 for "paint for Dressers 2¾ lb." and another 1s. 6d. (25¢) for "putting the paint on myself." The previous year he had supplied paint for a dresser to another customer, who apparently did the work himself. When David Haven of Framingham, Massachusetts, undertook a job of painting "your Dressers" for Levi Metcalf in 1789, the modest charge of 1s. 2d. (19½¢) probably identified cupboards of small size.[57]

A cupboard alteration recorded in 1818 by Chapman Lee at Charlton, Massachusetts, could apply to any of the cupboard forms discussed so far: "to Cutting Cupboard in two &c." The work cost 25¢ and likely divided the case into separate upper and lower sections. The purpose of the work is not indicated. The owner may have desired more flexibility in moving the tall case, especially through doorways, or he may have wanted to use the two parts of the case independent of one another. An upper cupboard section could have been placed against a wall at the back of a large rectangular table.[58]

The nature of references to the wardrobe form in craftsmen's accounts and the cost of the work described there indicate that most framed cases used for this purpose were more sophisticated in style and material than the cupboards discussed above (fig. 14). Mahogany is identified as the primary

Figure 14 Clothespress, attributed to Michael Allison, New York City, 1800–1815. Mahogany, mahogany veneer, and satinwood veneer with yellow poplar, white pine, and brass. H. 99¾" (finial), W. 52½" (cornice), D. 24" (cornice). (Courtesy, Winterthur Museum, bequest of Henry Francis du Pont, acc. 57.921.)

wood of several wardrobes included in this study. The desirability of fine materials for this furniture form is emphasized in a letter written in 1802 by John Hewitt, a cabinetmaker of New York City who at that time was a temporary resident of Savannah, Georgia, to his supplier Matthias Bruen in New York: "I shall take it a particular favour if you will send me as many vineers as will answer for a wardrobe that I have on hand." Hewitt apparently had constructed the carcass and awaited suitable finishing materials, described as "four vineers 4 f[oot] 4 I[nches] Long & 12 Inches wide." Hewitt also indicated that if Bruen "should see a handsome pair of pannels" he "should be glad to have them." Although Hewitt did not indicate what he intended to do with the panels, it is likely he wanted two book-matched veneers for use on the doors of the same wardrobe or another that he intended to build.[59]

In 1792 Daniel Trotter of Philadelphia repaired "a Mahogany Cloths press" for Stephen Girard, thereby identifying an alternative term for this storage cupboard. A brand-new mahogany wardrobe purchased a few years later, in 1805, by St. George Tucker of Williamsburg, Virginia, from John Hockaday was returned the following month for "Extree work" to the drawers, described as "Extree locks, Escutcheons, screws, &c." Because of the size and delicacy of a fine wardrobe, Richard W. Greene of Providence, Rhode Island, elected to have S. and J. Rawson come to the "House" in 1839 to repair his case; the complete charge was $2.00. Just the business of "Hawling [a] Wardrobe," probably at a time of moving eight years earlier, had cost James J. Skerrett, Esq., of Philadelphia $2.50. Skerrett's cabinetmaker, Charles H. White, also charged $1.25 for "Taking Down & Putting up [the] Wardrobe." Two other craftsmen supplied new parts for their clients' wardrobes. David Pritchard provided a "Back for [a] Wardrobe" in 1837 at Waterbury, Connecticut. Four decades earlier George Claypoole of Philadelphia had supplied "a lock for a Cloths press" belonging to merchant Samuel Meredith. Surface refurbishing is addressed in two accounts. On the eve of the Revolution William Savery of Philadelphia charged Joseph Pemberton 5s. (83½¢) for "polishing & Mending a Cloaths Press." More than half a century later J. A. Moricet of New York City repaired, varnished, and "put up a wardrob[e]" for Arthur Bronson for the substantial sum of $16.00.[60]

Sideboards

The sideboard was a new furniture form in America in the federal period (fig. 15). Repairs to the case, as indicated in materials collected for this study, are recorded from 1781 to 1845. Two references of early date describe alternative serving equipment or furniture. Twice in 1782 Felix Huntington, a cabinetmaker of Norwich, Connecticut, mended a "Server" for his prosperous kinsman Colonel Joshua Huntington. Rather than a sideboard table, the precursor of the sideboard, this item may have been a serving tray; the repairs cost a modest 8d. (11¢) the first time and 1s. 6d. (25¢) later in the year. Clouding the picture, however, is the same 1s. 6d. charge made by Walter Nichols at Newport, Rhode Island, early in 1790 for "mending [a]

Figure 15 Design for a sideboard illustrated in pl. 29 in George Hepplewhite, *Cabinet-Maker and Upholsterer's Guide,* 3rd ed. (London, 1794). (Courtesy, Winterthur Library, Printed Book and Periodical Collection.) The date on the engraved plate is 1787.

side board table" for Dr. Isaac Senter. Little more than a year later, Senter purchased what likely was his first sideboard from Samuel Ward of New York City. Rather than a serving and display piece only, the sideboard, with its drawers and cupboards, added a storage function to the household furnishings.[61]

The cost of general repairs to the sideboard varied from as little as 17¢ to a substantial $7.00. Information illuminating the nature of sideboard work is somewhat more plentiful than for many other furniture forms. Cupboard doors may have received more attention than other parts of the sideboard. Philemon Robbins of Hartford, Connecticut, and Elizur Barnes of Middletown undertook this work. Barnes recorded "mending [a] Side Board Dore & hanging at house" in 1821 at a charge of 34¢ to his client Mrs. Esther Williams. As furniture craftsmen did not ordinarily undertake work at a client's home, Barnes may have made the repairs when he returned to Williams a table for which he had made a new leg. After repairing a door in Nicholas Low's sideboard in January 1798, Jacob Brouwer of New York followed the work a month later by "blocking the side board draw[er]s." The nature of this work is unclear, although Brouwer may have added glue blocks to the underside of the drawers to better secure the bottoms. Four years later Peter Douglass of Philadelphia made a minor repair to "a Side board leg" for merchant Samuel Meredith.[62]

Several craftsmen identified modest structural additions or improvements to their clients' sideboards. At New York Robert McConachy fitted two sideboards with "Back Boards" in 1808 for merchant and entrepreneur Nicholas Low and charged him $10.00. The price indicates these were ornamental pieces fixed to the upper back edges of the furniture. Three years earlier Fenwick Lyell of Middletown, New Jersey, a cabinetmaker who began his career in New York City, had carried out similar work on a client's sideboard, charging him $3.00. About this time Job Danforth of Providence,

Rhode Island, was called upon by James Burrel Jr., Esq., to put "a board in [a] sideboard for decanters." This was a much simpler structure than the rectangular partitions for bottles fitted into sideboard drawers (fig. 15, right detail). The single horizontal board pierced with rectangular or, more likely, circular holes probably was fitted over a narrow ledge inside a drawer. The charge was a low 2s. 6d. (42¢), reflecting the simplicity of the task. Comparable in price at 39¢ was Elizur Barnes's job of "altring shelves in [a] Side Board" for a client at Middletown, Connecticut.[63]

Considerable activity centered on repairing, replacing, or adding hardware to the sideboard. Several general references to "Triming [a] Sideboard" at a low cost, including one recorded by Robert C. Scadin at Cooperstown, New York, may have identified wooden knobs or, at best, a few circular metal pulls. "Puting New Handles on a Side Board" often accompanied general or other repairs, as indicated in the accounts of Fenwick Lyell of Middletown, New Jersey, and John Collins of Portsmouth, Virginia. A significant amount of sideboard work involved the locking mechanisms and closing devices common to this furniture form. Elizur Barnes of Middletown, Connecticut, mended a "brass lock" in 1823 and reattached it to a customer's sideboard. Other craftsmen supplied new locks, as recorded by Elisha Adams at Boston in 1809 in his accounts with David S. Greenough. In New York City Walter Livingston required only a new "kee" for his sideboard, which Gifford and Scotland supplied for 4s. (67¢). Other closing fixtures varied from bolts to ketches to turn buckles. Casters provided a measure of mobility for the sideboard, as desired in some households. In 1805 Jacob Sass of Charleston, South Carolina, fitted "a set of Castors" to a sideboard owned by his client Peter Trezevant.[64]

Polishing and varnishing are the two treatments named in refurbishing the surfaces of the sideboard. Polishing a sideboard could cost as little as 50¢, as recorded at Philadelphia by Pennell Beale, or as much as $3.00, reflecting several days' work, as charged by Philemon Robbins in 1834 at Hartford, Connecticut. The more common request among customers was for a coat of varnish, which usually accompanied repairs. Paul Jenkins of Kennebunk, Maine, undertook this work, as did craftsmen on the North Shore of Massachusetts—Thomas Needham and Henry Hubon of Salem and Porter Russell of Newburyport. In New York State George Merrifield varnished customers' sideboards at Albany, and Robert C. Scadin performed similar work at Cooperstown. The combined jobs of repairing and varnishing a sideboard completed at Philadelphia by the firm of Barry and Krickbaum in 1836 cost John Cadwalader, Esq., $5.00. Some measure of surface protection for a new sideboard or a newly polished or varnished one was realized through the use of a sideboard cloth. Elizabeth de Hart Bleecker McDonald, when a new bride in 1800 at New York, chose instead to have a Mrs. Germond come to the house "to fix an Oil Cloth on my Side Board."[65]

In another dimension to sideboard work, two cabinetmakers who worked at Philadelphia identified tasks that involved an accessory to the sideboard found in some households, the knife case for storing cutlery.

Isaac Ashton completed a job for General Henry Knox in 1793 described as "Varnishing 1 Knife Case." Some years later, in 1820, Richard Alexander undertook more extensive work in the city, when "Repairing and Varnishing a pair of Knife Cases" for Mrs. John Francis at a charge of $6.00. The records of Nicholas Low, a successful New York City merchant of the early federal period, provide further insight by identifying a series of household purchases and maintenance work that focuses on sideboards and knife cases. Low's first sideboard may have been the mahogany case purchased from David F. Lanny in December 1794 at a cost of £18. The records are silent on the acquisition of a knife case, although one appears to have been introduced to the household following the purchase of the sideboard because Jacob Brouwer submitted bills to Low for "mending a knife case" in January 1796 and again in June and August 1797. Low added a second sideboard to his furnishings sometime following this work and before November 1808, when Robert McConachy provided ornamental backboards for two sideboards, as described previously. Meanwhile, Brouwer had already submitted bills for "Repairing two knife casses" in July and November 1807. Circumstances in the Low household likely describe related activity in the domestic settings of other affluent families. Knife cases of the early nineteenth century frequently took the form of an urn or an upright box with a slanted lid. A number of skilled craftsmen in London specialized in making this accessory, and it is likely that many cases identified in American settings were imported from that center of fashion. Other records indicate that some knife cases were of domestic origin. Fenwick Lyell, a cabinetmaker who pursued his craft at Middletown, New Jersey, in the early nineteenth century, had some years earlier conducted business in New York City, where he advertised "knife cases made to contain any Number of Knives, forks, or spoons."[66]

Whether a sideboard was new or in need of repair, it was transported at times to the customer or to a local cabinet shop in a specially constructed packing case to protect the surface and structure during travel by road or water. When John Bunnel bought a new sideboard for £26 ($87.00) from Fenwick Lyell at Middletown, New Jersey, in 1808, he ordered that it be wrapped in a mat and packed in a box for delivery. The further cost for this service was $4.34. At Middletown, Connecticut, Elizur Barnes charged a customer $1.75 for "making Box for Side Board & Packing it at your house" before sending it off in a wagon to the shop. Not all packing was substantial enough to withstand the rigors of sea travel, as John Hewitt found to his dismay at Savannah, Georgia, where he had traveled at the turn of the nineteenth century to retail furniture shipped to him by Matthias Bruen and others from New York City and vicinity. In a letter of 1801 to Bruen, Hewitt stated, "I must get you to send me three sideboards tops for those streat [straight] fronted sideboards that you sent Last, for the tops are split from one end to the other, so that I cannot sell them till there is new tops made for them." Hewitt then added a postscript, advising, "You had better make the sideboard tops with you [at your shop], the sise of them must be five foot Eleven Inches Long when finished By two feet wide outside."[67]

There were times when even a brand-new sideboard did not quite suit after a few months' use, and the owner took steps to remedy the situation. In August 1794 James Beekman of New York City bought a new sideboard from McEvers and Barclay for £8 ($26.72). By December Beekman had engaged a Mr. Hoes for the work of "altering a side Board bot of McEvers & Barclay" at the cost of another $16.70.[68]

Clock Cases

Records in this study that provide information on the repair of clock cases indicate that as many as one-fifth of the craftsmen who made case repairs also undertook work on the movement itself. References recording work on the case of a clock are clear-cut. When work on a "clock" is recorded, internal evidence is necessary to determine whether the case or the movement was the subject of repair. The practice of cabinetmakers repairing clock movements appears to have been relatively common in Connecticut, although woodworking craftsmen in New York State and Massachusetts also recorded this activity.

Among Connecticut craftsmen, a straightforward reference to repairing a clock mechanism is that penned in 1837 by Alexander H. Gilbert at Chester: "To mending movement of clock & cleaning $1.34." Samuel Durand of Milford provided clarity in another way: "To repairing clock and case & varnishing." At Wallingford two craftsmen, Titus Preston and John Doolittle, recorded "regulating" and "Cleaning" a clock, respectively. Reuben Loomis performed another type of job for a client in 1801 at Windsor by "altering the clock face & the clock," a job that took "one Day." Seven years later Loomis permitted an indebted customer to earn credit by "Cleaning my Clock & a spindle."[69]

In Massachusetts Robert Cowan of Salem cleaned a clock in 1802 for Aaron Wait and then finished his work by varnishing the case. The entire job cost $3.00. One of John Roulstone's clients at Boston was merchant Caleb Davis, for whom in 1787 he performed the work of "Clean'g an Eaight Day Clock that Stands on the Stairs" and for which he provided "a new line." Roulstone later accommodated his customer by "Cleaning the Clock in the parlour." Work undertaken by several craftsmen in New York State was comparable. William Bentley of Butternuts (Gilbertsville), Otsego County, repaired a clock movement in 1812 for Cornelius Jenny and charged him 50¢. On occasion Nathaniel Dominy V of East Hampton, Long Island, recorded cleaning a clock. William Kip's work for Robert R. Livingston at Red Hook, along the Hudson River, was more detailed. In May 1833 Kip charged Livingston $1.75 for "Reparing Musical and Hall Clock[s]." He followed this job in November with "Rep'g Parlour and Musical and Hall clocks" for an additional $2.25.[70]

Craftsmen identified general repairs to clock cases using a variety of terms (fig. 16, fig. 29, right). Most familiar are the words "mend," "repair," and "fix." For example, Slover and Taylor of New York City charged merchant Nicholas Low $1.00 in 1805 for "repairing a Clock Case." In the same period Stephanus Knight of Enfield, Connecticut, and Solomon Cole of Glaston-

Figure 16 Nathaniel Dominy V, tall clock case with movement by Nathaniel Dominy IV, East Hampton, Long Island, New York, 1799. Mahogany with white pine and cherry. H. 92", W. 17" (cornice), D. 9" (cornice). (Courtesy, Winterthur Museum, acc. 57.34.1.)

bury employed the phrase "To Work on a Clock Case." Earlier, Jonathan Gavit of Salem, Massachusetts, recorded "a Jobb at your Clock case" and charged Timothy Orne 2s. 4d. (38¢). "Glueing [a] Clock Case" was a simple and inexpensive repair carried out in the 1820s by William Capron at East Greenwich, Rhode Island, and by Miles Benjamin at Cooperstown, New York, who charged 12½¢ for the work. Other calls focused on the case doors. Silas E. Cheney of Litchfield, Connecticut, recorded "aultering dores" in 1800 for his client Elijah Wadsworth. Several craftsmen, including Job Townsend Jr. of Newport, Rhode Island, made general door repairs. At Philadelphia William Savery specifically identified the hinge sites of a door as the location of damage to a clock case owned by merchant Joseph Pemberton. Records indicate that considerable activity also centered on the glass-faced areas of the hood. The work is expressed in several ways. Thomas Boynton of Windsor, Vermont, spent part of a day in 1836 "glazing [a] Clock Door." Paul Jenkins of Kennebunk, Maine, and Titus Preston of Wallingford, Connecticut, recorded "setting glass." At Plymouth, Connecticut, Philemon Hinman identified "putty" as one of the essential materials in completing this work. When "Repairing ye head of a Clockcase" for Major Thomas Jones of Northumberland County, Virginia, for the sum of 10s. ($1.67), Henry Mann of Richmond identified a part of the clock case that was the focus of attention by other craftsmen.[71]

The "head" referred to that part of the clock case identified today as the hood, or bonnet (fig. 16). Craftsmen recorded the replacement of entire heads, although the cost of that work usually was lumped into a more extensive job that encompassed repairs, surface coating, or both. For example, when Moyers and Rich of Wytheville, Virginia, constructed a "new Clock case head" for Daniel Wiseley in 1834, they also varnished the entire case. Two decades earlier at Wallingford, Connecticut, Titus Preston supplied Jotham Tuttle with a new "clock head" and included in the charge "repairing and painting the other part and setting it up." Moving down the case to the waist, or midsection, Abner Taylor of Lee, Massachusetts, completed a simple job in 1818, when "putting a cupboard turn in [a] Clock case." The waist section, top or bottom (fig. 16), may have received the "Moulding round a Clock Case" installed for Matthew Cozzens in 1757 at Newport, Rhode Island, in the shop of Job Townsend Jr. Richard Johns's record of "making a Bottom to the Clock Case" a decade later at Philadelphia for Deborah Morris was not an unusual repair. The interior lines supporting the weights of the movement broke on occasion, causing the heavy metal to crash through the bottom of the lower chamber. Nathaniel Dominy V of East Hampton, Long Island, sought to avoid this mishap in 1842, when "puting a new line in his clock" for Nathaniel Hunting.[72]

Case feet also were subject to damage. On occasion a single new "Clock Case foot" sufficed, as replaced in 1825 for 50¢ by Thomas Boynton at Windsor, Vermont. At other times a complete new set of supports was required. Job E. Townsend of Newport, Rhode Island, charged Captain William Gardner 7s. 6d. ($1.25) in 1801 for "Raising his Clock Case with New feet." Although the language was different, the outcome was the same when David Evans of Philadelphia charged a client 12s. 6d. ($2.09) in 1778 for "making a Set of New Clock Case Brackets." Less clear is Benjamin Baker's record of a "mehogni Base for Clock case" made in 1774 at Newport. The cost, recorded in inflated currency, provides little help in determining whether Baker replaced the entire box below the waist section or merely the feet and related structure at the bottom. For the top of the case, three accounts identify new trimmings, or finials, all described as "balls." Silas E. Cheney of Litchfield, Connecticut, charged Daniel Huntington $1.34 in 1807 for "3 Brass Balls for [a] Clock Case" (fig. 16). That sum was on the high side of many a workingman's daily wage. A charge of $1.25 covered another "set of clock ball[s]" in 1824 at the Barre, Massachusetts, shop of Luke Houghton. Three finials priced at 12s. ($2.00) cost somewhat more from Job E. Townsend at Newport in 1801, although the material of all the finials likely was the same.[73]

Varnish is named slightly more often than paint as the coating material of the refurbished clock case, as indicated in records informing this study. Labor and material charges for varnishing or painting likely were comparable, when circumstances were similar. Jeduthern Avery's bill for "varnishing [a] Clock Case" at Bolton/Coventry, Connecticut, in 1834 was 40¢. At Chester, Alexander H. Gilbert charged only 34¢ for both "cleaning" (probably scraping) and varnishing a case. The cost of "Rubing and Varnishing a Clock Case" at Fenwick Lyell's Middletown, New Jersey, shop several decades earlier was substantially higher at 8s. ($1.34), reflecting the greater amount of labor involved. Frequently, charges for individual tasks were buried in the cost of a larger job, as when Paul Jenkins of Kennebunk, Maine, varnished a clock case for Captain Isaac Downing after setting a glass and making general repairs.[74]

In 1813 Elihu Harvey, who at that time was boarding with craftsman Jonathan C. Loomis at Whately, Massachusetts, was credited 25¢ for "painting [a] clock case." Based on other records, that figure appears to have been close to the basic charge for this activity. In pursuing that assumption, Thomas Boynton's price of $6.00 for "painting a clock Case" at Windsor, Vermont, for Leonard Spaulding in 1813 is at first difficult to explain. Because Boynton was a chairmaker and a painting specialist, it appears that the charge covered some highly ornamental work, such as grain painting and perhaps simulated inlay. Two other craftsmen recorded another type of work requested on occasion. In 1772 Benjamin Baker, a cabinetmaker of Newport, Rhode Island, debited a local clockmaker, Thomas Claggett, for "polishing [a] Clock Case." Almost two decades later David Evans repaired and polished a walnut clock case for a client at Philadelphia, charging 7s. 6d. ($1.25).[75]

One chore that regularly brought the furniture maker to the home of his client was that of assembling a clock case and movement. Job E. Townsend, of Newport, Rhode Island, charged a Mr. Martinberry 2s. (33¢) in 1783 for "Setting up a Clock in house." Another local cabinetmaker, Benjamin Baker, used a more common term for this work, when in the same year he charged merchant Jacob Rodriguez Rivera 50¢ for "puting up [a] Clock." As late as 1836 Nathaniel Appleton of Salem, Massachusetts, still employed this term. Jacob Brouwer described a more extensive job at New York in 1814 as "Taking down & putting up a clock" for Nicholas Low. Alternative terminology in the records of Silas E. Cheney at Litchfield, Connecticut, under the date 1800 describes "fastening up [a] Clock" for Elijah Wadsworth. Whether the term "fastening" also identified the process of assembling the case and regulating the clock or described instead a method of securing the case to the interior architecture is unclear. Several reasons are apparent for the need to reassemble a timepiece: repairs made to the case or movement that required disassembly; changing one's place of residence; receiving a timepiece as a bequest; or simply a desire or need to relocate the timepiece to another part of the house. Both Job E. Townsend of Newport and Job Danforth of Providence recorded "moveing [a] clock" for a client. On occasion a timepiece other than the tall case clock is the subject of a written record. In work completed for Thomas Baker in 1825, Nathaniel Dominy V of East Hampton, Long Island, described "seting up Clock and making shelf for it."[76]

Looking Glasses
Many looking glasses repaired by craftsmen during the late colonial and federal periods were imported from Europe. Merchants found looking glasses a salable item, along with imported textiles, ceramics, metalwares, tea, spices, and other household necessities, although shipping conditions at times were less than ideal. In 1776 Owen Biddle, a Quaker merchant of Philadelphia, engaged David Evans to mend "a Parcel of Looking Glasses" he had imported. Similarly, looking glasses offered for sale by the proprietors of looking glass stores in America were not necessarily of their own manufacture. Two well-known craftsmen in this business advertised imported merchandise in 1784 at Philadelphia. John Elliott Jr. offered a "very neat assortment of LOOKING GLASSES in mahogany frames" from London, and James Reynolds stocked "a great variety of English, French, and Dutch Looking-Glasses." A decade earlier Reynolds was engaged by merchant Samuel Powel III to make repairs to two groups of looking glasses at a cost of £13.5. and £7.7.6, respectively. The high figures suggest these were imported glasses that had suffered considerable damage rather than furnishings from Powel's own home.[77]

Most household looking glass repairs recorded in this study were of a modest scope and priced under $1.00, the average cost being less than 50¢ (fig. 17). Few minor repairs are described, although gluing a frame was a recurring task at cabinet shops. John Spurlock made note of "1 Days work glueing a lo[o]king glas & other jobs" at 5s. (83½¢) in 1791 for Major Thomas Jones, a resident of Northumberland County, Virginia. If gluing a

Figure 17 Elisha Tucker, looking glass, Boston, Massachusetts, 1815. Mahogany with white pine and glass. H. 17½", W. 11½", D. ⅝". (Courtesy, Winterthur Museum, acc. 55.92.1.)

frame was insufficient to address a repair problem, the next step might be "fixing [an] iron on [a] looking Glass," as recorded by Nathaniel Dominy V in 1815 at East Hampton, Long Island. Fixed in place with screws, this metal strip could secure a crack or add structural strength to a delicate element, such as a headpiece. Job Danforth recorded a more complete job fourteen years earlier at Providence, Rhode Island, for Jabez Bowen, a wealthy public official and chancellor of Brown University: "To putting a back to a looking glass, to finding screws, to putting up, & gluing frame." The charge was a reasonable 6s. ($1.00). The looking glass could well have been imported; however, the new backing would have been fabricated from a native American wood. In addition to screws, Daniel Trotter of Philadelphia also named "hooks" as a necessary accessory, following the repair of a looking glass for merchant Stephen Girard. A particularly fragile part of a looking glass frame named in a number of accounts is the pediment, or "top." Job Townsend Jr. of Newport undertook to construct "a Top for a Looking glass" in 1752 for a member of the prominent Wanton family at Newport, Rhode Island. At Canaan, Connecticut, Jonathan Gillett referred to the same task several decades later as "Making a Crown to a Looking glass" and charged 9s. ($1.50). Of more specific nature is Jonathan Kettell's record of "Carving a peice for [the] Top [of] your glass" for a customer at Newburyport, Massachusetts.[78]

Several circumstances dictated the need to frame or reframe a piece of silvered reflecting glass. When Luke Houghton set about "framing [a] looking glass" in 1817 at Barre, Massachusetts, he may have framed either a new or a recycled piece of glass. His charge of 50¢ suggests that the frame was a basic one, little more than a picture frame. This type of work is better detailed in charges posted in 1768 by John Elliott Sr. to the account of the Philadelphia firm of Hollingsworth and Rudolph. The job included "a new Glass put in a frame" and "framing the broken Glass," the charges being £2.14. ($9.02) and 9s. ($1.50), respectively. The cost of the new glass suggests an imported plate of some size. The craft of silvering glass plates was still in its infancy in America, and the resulting products often were imperfect. Because of the cost of silvered glass, broken plates were regularly trimmed and put into new frames. Other framed glasses were altered to fit a special need, as when Philemon Robbins of Hartford, Connecticut, added "pillars & feet to [a] looking glass." The 75¢ charge identifies a small glass altered to stand independently on the top of a chest of drawers or dressing table or a new superstructure for the top of a small dressing box.[79]

The "supports for looking glasses" that Abraham S. Egerton supplied in 1824 to the household of Nicholas Low in New York City for $2.00 appear to have been another item altogether. Likely these were small stamped or cast brass cloak pins with long shanks, which doubled at times as looking glass supports at the bottom of a frame. Large, heavy glasses, such as the "Pier Glass" and "Chimney Glass" mended by John Elliott Sr. of Philadelphia in 1772 for the wealthy John Cadwalader, were prime candidates for this type of extra support. Elliott appears to have carried out the repair work at his shop rather than at Cadwalader's home because he supplied "A Case

& packing D[itt]o" for 10s. ($1.67) to transport the glasses. The chimney glass likely was of horizontal form to hang above a mantelpiece and the pier glass of vertical form to fit the wall space between two windows.[80]

Several general references to looking glass repair demonstrate further how specialists in this field at Philadelphia and New York City interacted with prominent clients in the 1770s and the early nineteenth century. John Penn, a governor of Pennsylvania and a grandson of the founder, paid James Reynolds 7s. 6d. ($1.25) at Philadelphia in 1771 "for mend'g a Looking Glass." John Elliott Jr., a second-generation looking glass specialist in the city, altered "the frame of a Glass" in 1779 for Hannah Morris, member of a prominent Quaker family. When Charles Del Vecchio of New York City billed James L. Brinckerhoff $10.00 in 1816 for "Repairing Mirrors," he may have described something other than flat-surfaced glasses. Thomas Sheraton commented on the term "mirror" in his *Cabinet Dictionary* of 1803, calling it "a particular kind of glass, either of convex or concave surface." Today the term "girandole" generally applies to this form, which may also be fitted with candle arms, or "branches." In elucidating further on the subject, Sheraton described how these glasses collected reflected rays of light "into a point, by which the perspective of the room in which they are suspended, presents itself on the surface of the mirror and produces an agreeable effect." As early as 1796 Nicholas Low of New York City owned a pair of girandoles, which he had the firm of Cumberland and Beazor regild "with new branches" for £6 ($20.04).[81]

Sometimes a looking glass required only a surface coating of varnish on the frame to restore the original luster. The price varied with the size and delicacy of the frame. Elisha H. Holmes of Essex, Connecticut, charged a customer 25¢ in 1826 for "varnishing [a] looking glass frame," a job that required a quarter of a day or less of the craftsman's time. Allen Holcomb's fee was the same at New Lisbon, New York, about a decade earlier for both mending and varnishing a glass. Regilding a frame, sometimes accompanied by varnishing, was another surface treatment requested by clients. This could be an expensive job, depending on the size of the looking glass frame. Charles N. Robinson of Philadelphia repaired and regilded two frames in 1830 for Charles Wistar at a charge of $7.00 apiece. Joshua Ward paid the same price at Salem, Massachusetts, in 1809, when he engaged P. Vannuck, a looking glass specialist, to gild and varnish an "old Looking Glass frame," and again the following year, when Barnard Cermenati gilded another looking glass frame. The firm of Cumberland and Beazor of New York City regilded an elegant pier glass frame in 1796 for merchant Nicholas Low. The charge of £12 ($40.08) also included the installation of a "pannell ornamental top." Without further description it is impossible to know whether the panel was a reverse-painted glass tablet or a board embellished with wooden or composition ornament.[82]

Miscellaneous Objects

The many small utilitarian and personal items scattered throughout a household that were the province of the woodworker, from fabrication to repair, often are overlooked in furniture studies. This section will highlight a number of those objects, as detailed in craftsmen's accounts when returned to the shop for repairs or refurbishing or when the subject of reinstallation in the client's home. The seven subtopics in this section form somewhat arbitrary groups of objects, the purpose of the divisions being to create more manageable units and to establish reasonable relationships for purposes of discussion within a diverse body of material. The subject matter includes general household objects, kitchen and laundry equipment, handles and gunstocks, hearth equipment, textile equipment, small containers, and personal items.

General Household Objects

The open wooden frame enclosing visual material to be hung on a wall was commonly identified by craftsmen in general terms as a "picture frame," most of the contents subject today only to speculation (fig. 29, center). Specific references in this study identify a map, several portraits, and a group of prints. Most frame repairs probably were of modest scope, although determining factors, such as frame size and degree of embellishment, are usually unknown. William Sherman of Philadelphia noted "1 picture frame Repeared" in 1824 for merchant Stephen Girard at a modest cost of 50¢. The brothers Daniel and Samuel Proud of Providence, Rhode Island, charged a customer a mere 6¢ for "Glewing [a] picture frame." Another type of repair was described by Job E. Townsend of Newport as "framing one Picktur Broking Glass," the cost being 1s. (16½¢). Paint was a common surface finish for a frame. Charles C. Robinson charged 18½¢ in 1821 for "painting a map frame" for a customer at Philadelphia. Four years later Thomas Boynton of Windsor, Vermont, charged only 1¢ more to paint "3 picture frames," although their collective dimensions could have equaled that of the map. A larger job recorded by Moyers and Rich of Wytheville, Virginia, and credited to the account of one E. M. D. Reed in 1837 was that of "painting 6 portrait frames" at an allowance of 2s. 3d. apiece, for a total credit of $2.25. Painting a frame sometimes was accompanied by other surface coatings. Stephanus Knight's charge for "painting and guilding a Picture frame" in 1803 for a customer at Enfield, Connecticut, was 1s. 6d. (25¢). A sizable job at Providence in 1789 for Rev. Enos Hitchcock called for Grinnel and Taylor to gild sixteen picture frames, although the individual charge per frame was only 1s. (16½¢). These could well have been small profile, or silhouette, frames. Another job for the cleric involved "Painting, gilding and varnishing a picture frame" for 4s. (67¢). Executed in stages because of the nature of the work, the job took the shop a total of one-half to three-quarters of a day to complete, based on the cost.[83]

More sophisticated work, again as determined by cost, was undertaken by specialists in the framing and gilding business. In 1815 Charles Del Vecchio of New York City completed an expensive job at $15.00, when "regilding a frame" for Robert L. Livingston, member of a prominent local family. Other specialists were residents of Philadelphia. Charles N. Robinson, a looking glass and picture frame manufacturer, regilded a picture frame for

Figure 18 Trade card of Robert Kennedy, engraved by James Smither, Philadelphia, Pennsylvania, 1765–1770. Printed laid paper. 10⅜" x W. 8⅜". (Courtesy, Winterthur Museum, acc. 60.729.)

$5.50 in 1836 for Judge John Cadwalader. David Kennedy's charge for "Regilding a Rich portrait frame" in 1821 for John Francis was slightly higher at $7.00. Other work undertaken in the city is of eighteenth-century date. During the 1770s James Reynolds gilded a frame for wealthy Samuel Powel III, who became the first mayor of the city following adoption of the Constitution. Reynolds's contemporary Robert Kennedy (fig. 18) also served Powel and several other prominent citizens of the city: James Hamilton, a provincial governor of Pennsylvania; Edmund Physick, attorney to John Penn, grandson of the founder; and William Barrell, a Quaker merchant. Aside from glazing, gilding, and varnishing clients' picture frames, Kennedy also repaired, cleaned, and glazed their framed prints.[84]

Window blinds were desirable covers for controlling the heat of the summer sun and assuring privacy year-round. Thomas Sheraton identified two types of blinds in use in his *Cabinet Dictionary* of 1803: "a plain rolling blind," likely made of canvas, and a "Venetian blind." The early Venetian blind, a European accessory composed of wooden slats, appears to have been of fixed position until 1757, when a French craftsman advertised a movable blind. Ten years later, in 1767, John Webster, an upholsterer who emi-

Figure 19 Venetian blind, Philadelphia, Pennsylvania, 1791–1810. Cherry with pine, cotton, and silk. L. 70⅝", W. 52½". (Courtesy, Winterthur Museum, bequest of Henry Francis du Pont, acc. 67.557.1.)

grated from London to Philadelphia, advised that he retailed "the newest invented Venetian sun blinds for windows . . . stained to any color, moves to any position, so as to give different lights, screens from the scortching rays of the sun, draws a cool air in hot weather, draws up as a curtain, and prevents from being overlooked [provides privacy], and is the greatest preserver of furniture of anything of the kind ever invented." Most material in this study referencing the repair of blinds appears to refer to the Venetian blind. Initially that blind was something of a luxury item, but by the second quarter of the nineteenth century expanded production and mechanization made the product more affordable. The Venetian blind illustrated in figure 19 is an original window cover from the residence of John Imlay, a Philadelphia merchant who retired and built a house at Allentown, New Jersey, sometime between 1790 and 1794.[85]

As early as 1775 William Savery of Philadelphia recorded a charge of 10s. ($1.67) against the account of Joseph Pemberton for "Peicing 2 Window Blinds & fixing them & 4 hooks for D[itt]o" followed by "Painting D[itt]o." The nature of the work and the cost indicate that the window covers were more than plain, rolling blinds. Piecing was necessary to repair wooden slats that had broken. Adding new wood dictated that all the slats be painted because paint still was hand-mixed by the job and exact matches were difficult to achieve. More than two decades later David Evans of the city left no doubt about the nature of work he completed for Ann Head: "Repair'd . . . 2 Venetian blinds, Painted & new hung with tossils &c." Handsome embellishments, such as tassels, were readily available in the city, as advertised in 1797 by C. Alder, an upholsterer: "Fringes, linens and tassels imported and manufactured as usual." Within several years Fenwick Lyell of Middletown, New Jersey, completed a job of "New Hanging and Painting 2 Sets of Blinds" for Jane Micheau for which he also provided "2 tossels." The charges for Evans's and Lyell's work at $12.53 and $5.34, respectively, support the reality that Venetian blinds were indeed luxury goods. By the 1820s and 1830s the cost of owning and refurbishing Venetian blinds was more moderate. Robert C. Scadin of Cooperstown, New York, recorded painting and trimming blinds for $2.75, the trimming probably describing new tapes. Even more reasonably priced at 92¢ was a job that Elisha H. Holmes undertook at Essex, Connecticut, for widow Polly Hayden, when "Makeing 22 pieces for venitian blinds" and providing six brackets.[86]

A complement to some blinds, and to some window curtains, was a cornice. In 1806 Jacob Sass of Charleston, South Carolina, repaired a cornice for Peter Trezevant, although most general cornice work appears to have focused on restoring the surface with paint. This was the type of work carried out by Timothy and John Minott in 1796 at Boston and by George Landon in 1818 at Erie, Pennsylvania. Prices per cornice varying from 50¢ to more than $1.00 indicate that not all cornices were plain-painted. Thomas Boynton, when working in Boston early in his career, described "ornamenting and varnishing a set of cornices," although the nature of the ornament is not indicated. Charles N. Robinson of Philadelphia identified another type of ornament in 1825, when he recorded "Regilding & repairing Cornices" for James J. Skerrett.[87]

A variety of miscellaneous household items received the attention of the worker in wood and related materials. Many recorded jobs represent single references only, such as Richard Johns's note made at Philadelphia in 1767 of "fixing up the Shell Work" for Deborah Morris. This may have been a boxed ornament to hang on the wall, with or without a candle arm. Another infrequent call is represented in Michael Allison's record of "Repairing [a] Hat Stand" at New York in the early nineteenth century. When Grinnell and Taylor refurbished the surface of another household item at Providence, Rhode Island, they described the work as "Painting a Wine Cooler twice over." Close, if not similar, in form and function was the wine cistern repaired at New York in 1797 by Jacob Brouwer. Both objects were receptacles for wine in the bottle. When the terms "cooler" and "cistern" were not used interchangeably, the cooler may have been distinguished by the presence of a cock to drain water from the tub-shaped or chest-shaped form. The wine cooler, or cistern, was at times an accompaniment to the sideboard and stood on the floor beneath the center section.[88]

Kitchen and Laundry Equipment

The kitchen, and adjacent areas in some households, was the principal center of domestic activity during the period covered by this study. The repair and maintenance of household equipment were well within the scope of the woodworking craftsman, whether in a rural or urban location. Because breadmaking was an activity central to most homes, craftsmen's records identify a variety of pertinent equipment. Essential to the breadmaking process was the "bread trough," also known as a "kneeding trough" and a "dough tray," a large box with canted sides that was placed on a table or supported independently on long legs (fig. 20). Some dough troughs had

Figure 20 Bread trough or dough tray, probably Pennsylvania or the South, 1750–1825. Walnut. H. 25⅞", W. 38⅛" (top), D. 22⅜" (top). (Courtesy, Winterthur Museum, bequest of Henry Francis du Pont, acc. 65.2748.)

wooden covers that also served as surfaces for shaping the bread loaves and preparing other baked goods. Aside from general repairs to the bread trough, which many shops reported, Abner Taylor of Lee, Massachusetts, identified the common task of "putting [a] Bottom to [a] Bread trough." His charge of 17¢ for the job was comparable to that of John Durand at Milford, Connecticut, for similar work. Another craftsman, Luke Houghton, supplied a "cover to [a] bread trough" for widow Abigail Wheeler at Barre, Massachusetts, again at a nominal charge. Of related form to the board-type cover, if not the entire dough box, was the "Break [brake] for to make bread upon" repaired in 1757 for the household of Jacob Rodriguez Rivera at Newport, Rhode Island, by Job Townsend Jr. Some bread troughs appear to have been placed in service without a finish on the wood; others received a coat of paint. Hiram Taylor of Chester County, Pennsylvania, painted a customer's bread trough in 1835 following unnamed repairs.[89]

The miscellany of other breadmaking equipment noted in craftsmen's accounts includes the peel, a flat, long-handled, shovel-like implement used to insert and remove loaves of bread and other baked goods from a masonry oven. Elisha Hawley mended a peel for a customer at Ridgefield, Connecticut, in 1787 and charged him 3s. (50¢). A few years earlier Daniel and Samuel Proud of Providence, Rhode Island, provided a customer with "an Oven led [lid] for [the] bakehouse," probably to replace a broken or charred one, at a time when the brothers also supplied a "Lage Led [large lid] to a Chest for the Bake House." A "Bread tray" figures in craftsmen's accounts on occasion. William Lander of Salem, Massachusetts, repaired one as early as 1739 for Captain Joseph Bowditch. Many years later, in 1804, Reuben Loomis noted a similar job at Suffield, Connecticut. Thomas Boynton of Windsor, Vermont, recorded another type of work, when in 1827 he was

Figure 21   Tray, United States, 1800–1850. Wood. L. 19⁷⁄₈", W. 10¹³⁄₁₆". (Courtesy, Winterthur Museum, bequest of Henry Francis du Pont, acc. 67.719.)

Figure 22   John Conger (carver), gingerbread board or mold, retailed by James Y. Watkins, New York City, 1830–1835. Mahogany. H. ¹⁵⁄₁₆", W. 7¹⁄₈", D. 4¹⁄₈". (Courtesy, Winterthur Museum, bequest of Henry Francis du Pont, acc. 61.1704.)

asked to "ornament [a] Bread tray." At a cost of 17¢, the design likely was as simple as that illustrated in figure 21, which decorates a tray that may have served at times as a bread tray. In the early nineteenth century two Massachusetts craftsmen, Lewis Chandler Jr. of Bernardston and Daniel Ross of Ipswich, made repairs to a specialized baking accessory, the "gingerbread board," or "mould" (fig. 22). Housewives and bakers used these carved, ornamental boards to impress a design into a type of gingerbread that was rolled flat and baked hard, perpetuating a tradition brought from Europe. The gingerbread board illustrated in figure 22 originated in New York, a city that even in the early nineteenth century retained strong elements of its Dutch heritage.[90]

Somewhat more substantial than the tasks of repairing and supplying parts for breadmaking equipment was the craftsman's work on another household fixture—the churn. Of the many references informing this study, only one may refer to the rotary churn, a barrel-shaped chamber elevated on legs, with a handle or crank at one end. Hiram Taylor, a craftsman of Chester County, Pennsylvania, recorded "turning [a] handle for Churn" in 1836 for a female customer. Craftsmen directed major attention instead to the upright churn, a tapered cylindrical, stave-formed container with a central hole in the top to accommodate a "staff" fitted with a "dasher," or "dash," at the bottom for agitating milk or cream in the butter-making process. Three components of the upright churn, the top (also called a "cover"), the staff, and the dasher were the focus of repairs and replacements recorded by woodworkers.[91]

Three Connecticut craftsmen, Elisha Hawley of Ridgefield, Samuel Douglas of New Hartford/Canton, and Titus Preston of Wallingford, along with two Rhode Island woodworkers, Job Danforth and Job E. Townsend, recorded making a replacement top for the churn. Only Preston noted a specific charge of 6d. (about 8½¢) for the top alone. The staff, basically a cylindrical stick, appears to have been more durable, as there are few references to its replacement. In one instance Reuben Loomis, when working at Suffield, Connecticut, in 1820, recorded making a "churn staff & dasher for [a] stone[ware] churn" at a cost of 38¢. The dasher was the focus of most of the reported work to the churn. Craftsmen in Massachusetts, Connecticut, Rhode Island, and New Jersey repaired or replaced this component. Aaron Ogden of Newark, New Jersey, recorded a job in 1817 "to fix [a] Churn Dash" at a cost of 1s. 3d. (21¢). Jesse Tuttle's charge for this work at North Haven, Connecticut, a year earlier was only 9d. (12½¢). Like the bread trough, some churns were painted. The cost of this work in the early nineteenth century varied significantly, suggesting that size could be a factor—the small upright churn versus the large rotary model. Josiah P. Wilder painted a churn at New Ipswich, New Hampshire, for 13¢, whereas John Ellinger's charge at Palmyra in eastern central Pennsylvania was 25¢. George Landon, a woodworker at Erie in the far northwest of the state, charged 50¢ for the job.[92]

The use of trays in the home frequently revolved around the service of tea (fig. 29, center). That focus is reinforced in Sheraton's description of these serving pieces as "boards with rims round them on which to place glasses, plates, and tea equipment." Sheraton further noted that tea trays were of "various shapes and sizes." Craftsmen's records indicate that repairs to "tea bords" were not uncommon. Nehemiah Munroe of Boston mended two boards in 1788 for Major William Erving of neighboring Roxbury at a cost of 2s. (33¢). More specific tasks included a "Tea board Glued & Clined [cleaned]" at Portsmouth, Virginia, in 1791 by Robert Borland and the work of Job Townsend Jr. in "Pollishing a Large Tea Board" at Newport, Rhode Island. One craftsman, Thomas Boynton of Windsor, Vermont, referred to this serving form as a "tea waiter" when billing a customer in 1816 for repainting.[93]

Trays or traylike forms were used for other purposes. Job E. Townsend of Newport made note in 1821 of "Making a New Bottom to [a] Chopping Tray" for 25¢. The word "voider," a term dating from the Middle Ages although still in use in the eighteenth century, often identified a tray of some size used particularly in clearing away dirty dishes, utensils, and waste food from the table. In 1790, shortly after joining the new federal government at New York, General Henry Knox paid a visit to the shop of Isaac Nichols, where he purchased "one uncommon Large mahogany voider" for £1.10 ($5.00) and a smaller one in mahogany for 18s. ($3.00). Mrs. Knox thought better of the purchase, however, as described by Nichols in his accounts: "To altering the large voider and making Two of it by order of Mrs. Knox." The further charge was 8s. ($1.34). The large tray may well have proven awkward and heavy for servants, when in service.[94]

Woodenware containers met various needs in the home. To extend the life of these utensils and perhaps for the sheer joy of adding color to ease the drudgery of daily life, many examples were painted and repainted. Reuben Loomis applied paint to a pail (fig. 23) and a washtub in 1811 for a customer at Wethersfield, Connecticut. Three years later James Gere of Groton posted 12¢ to a customer's account for painting a keg. During the 1820s Luke Houghton of Barre, Massachusetts, and Allen Holcomb of New Lisbon, New York, each charged a customer for painting a bowl, the charges being 6¢ and 12½¢, respectively. Houghton's work also included repainting a pail for 17¢. A request for an alteration was described by Job E. Townsend of Newport, Rhode Island, as "making two Washing Tubbs out of a Barrell."[95]

Aside from washtubs, a variety of laundry equipment was part of the large miscellany of domestic items repaired or refurbished by the woodworker. Of some consequence in the early nineteenth century, given the number of repairs recorded, was the "washing machine," a piece of household equipment that received considerable attention from would-be patentees. These early "machines" consisted of a large tub with a drain, which was elevated on legs or placed on a low table. Agitation was produced through the use of a cranked handle or some type of spring action. Repairs might cost 1s. (16½¢) or less, as recorded by Jesse Tuttle at New Haven, Connecticut, or as much as $2.50, the charge made by Nathan Lucas at Kingston, Massachusetts, for "repairing a Wash Machine." Other laundry equipment in need of attention on occasion was the clotheshorse, a rack for drying garments indoors. Both urban and rural craftsmen made repairs. George Claypoole mended a clotheshorse at Philadelphia for merchant Samuel Meredith; Phillip Filer undertook similar work at his shop near Rome, New York. At Litchfield, Connecticut, a center of county government, Silas E. Cheney recorded "painting [a] close hors white." Another craftsman, Job E. Townsend of Newport, Rhode Island, was engaged by a customer to

Figure 23 Pail, possibly Shaker community of Mount Lebanon, New York, 1850–1900. White pine with iron. H. 7⅛", Diam. of top: 10³⁄₁₆". (Courtesy, Winterthur Museum, gift of Robert E. P. Hendrick, acc. 62.50.)

repair an "Ironing Board," typically a length of padded board placed for use on the surface of a table. The Philadelphia book of prices for 1772 describes ironing boards from four feet to six feet in length, with the option of purchasing a pair of "trussels," or trestles, for support.[96]

Householders requested that local woodworkers repair a variety of equipment useful in the kitchen in the preparation of food and drink. One of the most consistent requests was to repair a coffeemill (fig. 29, lower right). Most repairs were of nominal cost and unspecified nature. An exception is Nathaniel Dominy V's "repair [of a] Coffe mill" in 1818 for Sarah Gardiner at East Hampton, Long Island, at a cost of 4s. (67¢), suggesting that the damage was significant. More descriptive is the work of two Rhode Island cabinetmakers, both jobs completed in 1798 and each at a cost of 1s. 6d. (25¢). Job Danforth of Providence supplied "a bottom to a Coffee mill," whereas Job E. Townsend of Newport dealt with the mechanism in "Sharping" a coffeemill. Some years earlier, in 1780, Townsend had made a "Coffemill Box" for another customer. The 3s. (50¢) charge suggests that Danforth's later use of the term "bottom" described a replaced part rather than the entire wooden structure.[97]

Danforth and Townsend also directed their attention to the repair of a kitchen gadget popularly named "Squash Squeezers," a piece of hand equipment for squeezing juice from lemons and limes for use in cooking, baking, and the preparation of punch drinks. Alternatively identified as lemon or lime squeezers, the implement could be simple in from—a two-part hinged block shaped on the interior with a hemispherical dome opposite a complementary hollow, each part of the block having a handle extending from the end opposite the hinge for applying pressure when squeezing—to the more complex equipment illustrated in figure 24. This platform squeezer, with interior space for a bowl, introduced greater efficiency to the process, especially when juice in quantity was required. Two Pennsylvania craftsmen made repairs to other equipment of general or special use in the kitchen. Abraham Overholt, who worked in the area of Bedminster, Bucks County, "repaired a pair of butter molds" in 1798 for Karla Zelner. John Ellinger's work centered on "Mending [a] Pealing Machine" for Jacob Early at Palmyra, Lebanon County.[98]

Several repair jobs describe other domestic activity in the kitchen. In 1822 Elizur Barnes of Middletown, Connecticut, recorded "putting Leggs to [a] Bottle Drainer" at 25¢ for a local customer. More than a quarter century earlier, Daniel and Samuel Proud of Providence, Rhode Island, accommodated a client by "fixing [a] Rowl [roll] for [a] towell." At Newport Samuel Mosers sought the services of Benjamin Baker in 1770 for the repair of a "Candil Mold," a reminder that in the pre-Revolutionary period candlemaking was as much an urban as a rural household task.[99]

Handles and Gunstocks
The large number of references in craftsmen's accounts to the replacement of teapot handles describes the vulnerability of this appendage. Unknown is the exact style of any given pot or handle and, with a few exceptions, the

Figure 24 Lemon squeezer, United States, 1800–1900. Wood with iron. H. 15⅞", W. 7³⁄₁₆", D. 7". (Courtesy, Winterthur Museum, bequest of Henry Francis du Pont, acc. 65.2102.)

metal of fabrication. References range geographically from Vermont to Virginia, with both rural and urban locations represented. The reference period extends from 1741 to 1829, with all but a few dates falling before 1800. The price range of most handles was 12½¢ to 50¢, although three-quarters of the handles in this group actually were priced on the low side, between 12½¢ and 25¢. Of the three silver teapots identified, the cost of new handles for two of them falls on the high side in this general group. At Newport, Rhode Island, Job E. Townsend charged Mary Collins 2s. (33¢) in 1795 to replace the wooden handle in her silver teapot. Job Danforth of Providence recorded "putting [a] handle to [a] Silver Pot" in 1804 for Jabez Bowen at a cost of 2s. 6d. (42¢). Among Danforth's other clients were two local pewterers, William Billings and Gershom Jones, for whom he provided teapot handles during the 1790s, presumably for new pots, priced at 1s. (16½¢) and 1s. 6d. (25¢), respectively. Given those prices, it would appear that many teapots taken to woodworkers' shops for replacement handles were made of pewter. Metal handles for teapots, either of pewter or silver, were uncommon before the 1810s.[100]

Craftsmen shaped handles for teapots to various profiles. Basic is the C-shape (or ear shape, fig. 25), sometimes modified by an angular top. The S-

Figure 25 Jacob Hurd, teapot, Boston, Massachusetts, ca. 1750. Silver with fruitwood. H. 6⅛", W. 9⁵⁄₁₆". (Courtesy, Winterthur Museum, gift of Henry Francis du Pont, acc. 61.937.)

shape profile is still more complex and varies in length with the design of the pot. Small spurs, or carved projections (fig. 25), often embellish either shape. At a cost of 7s. 5d. ($1.24), "a kink teapot handle" made by Joshua Delaplaine in New York City for a Dr. Brownjohn in 1741 appears to have been the most expensive type. The kink handle was formed either with a compound curve, consisting of a long S-shape profile at the top and a short reverse C-shape at the bottom, or an S-curve with an angular return at the bottom into the lower handle socket. Almost certainly Dr. Brownjohn's teapot was made of silver. Another "handle for [a] Silver tea pot" made half a century later, in 1791, at Portsmouth, Virginia, by Robert Borland cost merchant Richard Blow 6s. ($1.00). A second replacement part for a teapot is described in the records of Job Townsend Jr. of Newport, Rhode Island, both as "a Nub for the Top" and "a Top of a Tea pot."[101]

A few references identify handles for coffeepots. Some are priced in a low range below 1s. (16½¢). An entry in the accounts of Daniel Trotter, "To fixing a handle in a Coffee pot" for Philadelphia merchant Stephen Girard in 1790, suggests by the wording and the cost at 1s. 3d. (21¢) that the handle was not new but simply refastened in its sockets. A handle made for a coffeepot by another Philadelphia craftsman, Samuel Matthews, for merchant and public official Charles Norris and a handle made by Samuel Cheever of Salem, Massachusetts, for merchant John Derby likely were installed on silver pots, given the charges of 5s. (83½¢) and 75¢, respectively. Support for those identifications exists in the work of Henry Mann of Richmond, Virginia, who put "a Handle to a Silver Coffee pott" for the sum of 6s. ($1.00). Size, embellishment, and material would account for the differences in price between these three new handles.[102]

Besides the teapot and coffeepot, a variety of other domestic equipment required new handles from time to time. Craftsmen recorded a moderate business in producing long, turned handles for warming pans (fig. 26). The usual cost varied from 12½¢ to 39¢, although one example was priced as high as 83½¢. Choice of wood, degree of turned embellishment, and the extent of correlated repair work dictated the cost. As recorded in this study, craftsmen from New England to the South engaged in this work. In 1762 John Durand recorded "puting a handle into a warming pan" for 1s. 6d. (25¢) at coastal Milford, Connecticut. During the period of the Revolu-

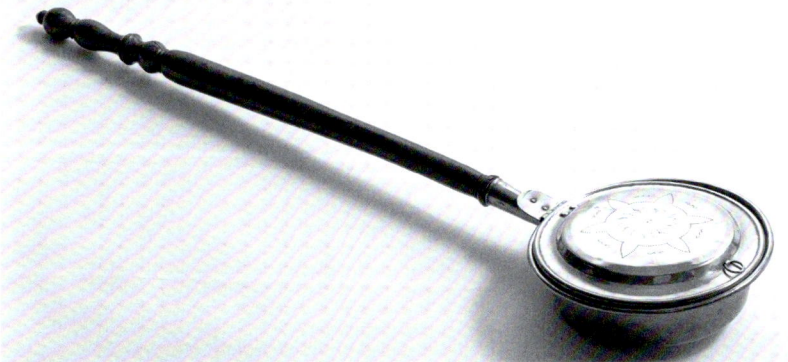

Figure 26 Warming pan, attributed to William C. Hunneman, William C. Hunneman Jr., or Samuel H. Hunneman, Boston, Massachusetts, 1799–1825. Copper, wood, and iron. H. 3⅝", L. 41½", Diam. of pan 10½". (Courtesy, Winterthur Museum, acc. 60.186.)

tionary War, General John Cadwalader of Philadelphia sought the services of Jacob Falconer in rural Kent County, Maryland, on the Chesapeake Bay for putting "one handl in a warming pann." Even as late as 1829 George Landon answered a request for a "warming pan handle" at Erie, Pennsylvania, a gateway to the western states and territories.[103]

Craftsmen installed handles on a miscellany of other domestic utensils. Most handles discussed here were turned to form and of nominal cost, 18¢ and less. Heading the list is the dipper, a type of ladle, frequently of large size. The Rhode Island shops of Daniel and Samuel Proud and Job E. Townsend replaced handles on dippers in the 1790s and later. Townsend's father, Job Townsend Jr., had earlier provided a customer with "a Punch Laddle Handle." In the early post-Revolutionary period several households required handles for chafing dishes. Daniel Ross responded by providing a customer at Ipswich, Massachusetts, with four handles. At Dartmouth, Lemuel Tobey recorded "Turning 2 Chafin Dish handles" for John Blackwell, a customer who earlier had acquired a new teapot handle at the shop. The most expensive handle purchase recorded in this study was that of Christopher Bubier of Marblehead, who paid 5s. (83½¢) in 1745 for "a Handle for a Frying pan" at the shop of Joseph Lindsey.[104]

Apart from domestic repairs, individuals approached the woodworker, whether in rural or urban locations, to undertake work on their firearms, namely the "gun" (fig. 29, upper right) and the "pistol." Few records provide more than a basic description of the work. Typical is that of James Gillingham of Philadelphia, who charged merchant William Barrell 15s. ($2.50) in 1766 for "Repairing [a] gunstock." Job E. Townsend provided somewhat more information at Newport, Rhode Island, in 1779, when "Mending a gun and Making a ramer for Ditto," which cost William Roberson 7s. ($1.17). Other records include repairs made by Elisha Hawley at Ridgefield, Connecticut, and Nathaniel Heath at Warren, Rhode Island. In one instance, Judkins and Senter of Portsmouth, New Hampshire, described their repair work as "peicing [a] Gun Stock." On other occasions the work required completely "new Stocking a Gun," as recorded by Shaw and Chisholm at Annapolis, Maryland. When Samuel Douglas of New Hartford/Canton, Connecticut, undertook to polish a gun for Arnold Crane in 1813, the work may have included both the wooden and metal parts of the firearm. Requests for pistol repairs were fewer than those for the gun. Daniel Ross mended "a pistol Stock" at Ipswich, Massachusetts, in 1786 for Aaron Smith for the modest sum of 8d. (11¢). The previous year Ross had mended a gunstock for the same client. More detailed is Titus Preston's record of work performed at Wallingford, Connecticut, in 1814 for Samuel Cook. Preston apparently was concerned that his customer would question the 3s. (50¢) charge. Consequently, he took the unusual step of including an explanation in his account book: "by peicing a pistol stock & making a rammer which took me more than four hours steady labor."[105]

Hearth Equipment
References in this study identify repair work to the fire screen between 1784 and 1810, although each reference is without further description. Whereas most repair costs were minimal, identification of the screens' owners, who resided from New England to Virginia, suggests that all the screens were relatively sophisticated pole stands supported on tripod bases to which was attached some type of adjustable shield to protect the face from the heat of the hearth. At Boston David S. Greenough, Esq., engaged Elisha Adams to mend a "fire screne." Job E. Townsend carried out related work at Newport, Rhode Island, for Captain John Oldfield. In western Connecticut Silas

E. Cheney mended a fire screen for Tapping Reeve, founder of the Litchfield Law School. Prominent Philadelphia cabinetmaker Thomas Affleck made repairs to a fire screen for General John Cadwalader in 1784 as well as to the general's basin stand. Cadwalader purchased no fewer than five fire screens during the early 1770s, one from Robert Jewell at a cost of £3 ($10.00) and four others from Affleck described as "Mahogany" and priced individually at £2.10 ($8.35). The Philadelphia book of prices for 1772, which lists a fire screen at Affleck's price, identifies the form as having claw feet "with leaves on the knees." Circa 1789 Richard Blow, a merchant of Portsmouth, Virginia, paid Robert Borland to mend a fire screen. Perhaps this was one of the two screens Blow purchased in 1785 from George Seddon and Son of London, whose invoice describes "2 face screens on Claws green silk mounts" (screens).[106]

In addition to the fire screen, craftsmen's accounts identify a piece of hearth equipment of a more ordinary stamp termed a "fireboard," also known today as a chimney board (fig. 27). Construction consisted of either

Figure 27 Fireboard, probably Massachusetts, 1790–1830. White pine. H. 30", W. 39½", D. 1¼". (Courtesy, Winterthur Museum, bequest of Henry Francis du Pont, acc. 67.1859.)

an open frame stretched with a piece of canvas or two or more horizontal (or vertical) boards butted together. The references at hand appear to describe board construction. Fireboards were made to fit into a hearth opening or provided with some type of support at the bottom to stand independently on the hearth. The purpose of a fireboard was to cover a hearth opening in a parlor or chamber during the summer months, when there was no fire. The board helped to secure a room, and the house, against the intrusion of birds, insects, dampness, and soot. Undoubtedly, some boards were plain painted. Many more, perhaps, were hand decorated or stenciled with a variety of ornament, including pots of flowers, flowering trees, fruits, animals, birds, land-, marine-, and townscapes, classical motifs, and trompe l'oeil subjects, some depicting ceramic tiles.[107]

Making a new fireboard, painting it, and adding decoration could cost almost half the price of a new mahogany fire screen. Elisha Adams's charge for a fireboard made in 1811 at Boston for David S. Greenough, Esq., was $4.00. Although there is no indication how Greenough's board was embellished, the records of John Derby of neighboring Salem provide some insight. In 1791 the merchant engaged Robert Cowan, an artist of Scottish birth, to paint a landscape on a fireboard, probably provided by Derby, and paid him £1.9.7 ($4.94) for the work.[108]

Several craftsmen recorded "Mending [a] fire Bord," including Benjamin Bardine of East Greenwich, Rhode Island, and Phillip Filer, near Rome, New York. Both men charged 1s. (16½¢) for their work. The need for an alteration to a fireboard prompted Dr. Charles Dyer to seek the services of Elizur Barnes in 1823 at Middletown, Connecticut. Barnes charged Dyer 25¢ for a "Job at house Plaining Flore & Sawing Fire board for handiron" (andirons). Two spaced slots at the bottom of a board permitted the use of andirons as a support for the heavy hearth cover, when it was not fitted into the hearth opening. Several craftsmen refurbished the surfaces of fireboards with paint or varnish. Thomas Boynton of Windsor, Vermont, recorded charges in the 1810s of 25¢ to 33¢, representing in time, perhaps, something less than a quarter of his working day. This may have been sufficient time to undertake some modest decoration, or touch up, given that the typical working day could have been as long as ten hours. Allen Holcomb of New Lisbon, New York, also recorded painting several fireboards, one identified as green.[109]

A miscellany of references identifies repairs to other objects identified with the hearth. The hand bellows is the subject of several notations. Silas E. Cheney mended a "pare [of] blelloses" in 1799, as he entered business at Litchfield, Connecticut. David Evans, a Quaker craftsman of Philadelphia, made a handle for a bellows belonging to Benjamin Rittenhouse and charged him 2s. 6d. (42¢). Somewhat more expensive at 4s. (67¢) was the "new top to a Mohogony Bellosses" that Job E. Townsend of Newport, Rhode Island, made in 1783 for John Bass. Another accessory for the hearth was the fire fender George Landon painted green for a customer at Erie, Pennsylvania. Although not strictly an accessory of the hearth, the "foot stove" (foot warmer) that George Merrifield repaired at Albany, New York, for H. B. Haswell utilized coals from the hearth as its heat source.[110]

Textile Equipment
A survey of textile equipment repaired by woodworkers indicates that the spinning wheel received the most attention. Of the two types of wheel in use, the flax, or little, wheel was the subject of repair more than twice as often as the wool, or great, wheel. In neither case is the material of fabrication indicated. References to wheel repair appear in accounts in the New England and the Middle Atlantic regions. Lack of insight on Southern activity is merely a shortcoming of the data collected for this study. Unlike the wool wheel, the flax wheel was known by many names (fig. 28): "little wheel," "linen wheel," "Dutch wheel," "foot wheel," "chair wheel," and

Figure 28 Jonathan Tyson, flax, or spinning, wheel, Philadelphia, Pennsylvania, ca. 1807–1816. Ash with maple, oak, leather, and iron. H. 51", L. 18" (table), W. 6⅝" (table). (Courtesy, Winterthur Museum, acc. 72.163.)

"spinning wheel." Of the group, "spinning wheel" was the common generic term. "Linen" describes the spun thread of the spinning wheel, which when woven produced linen cloth. "Dutch" describes the general European inspiration for the apparatus, with its prominent tilted table. "Foot" and "chair" describe the operation of the wheel; the spinner put into motion a foot treadle while seated in a chair.

Data for the study of flax-wheel repairs cover more than one hundred years, from 1731, when Jacob Hinsdale of Harwinton, Connecticut, provided Robert Webster with "a head for [a] Wheal" (possibly a wool wheel) at 8d. (11¢), to 1843, when Josiah P. Wilder made general repairs to a "spinning wheel" for Nathan P. Cummings at New Ipswich, New Hampshire. Because the flax wheel was essential to the domestic economy of many households, it was in frequent use, resulting in high demand for repair work. Charges ranged from a low of 4d. (6¢) to a high of more than $2.00, although forty-two percent of the priced jobs cost the customer 25¢ or less. Raising the upper limit of priced repairs to 50¢, or about a half day's work, represents fifty-nine percent of the total recorded in this study. Most expensive at 13s. ($2.17) was a job undertaken in 1800 by Jonathan Dart at New London, Connecticut, for George Daniels: "to Repairing foot wheel, all new but the Rim, Crank, and spindle." In carrying out this work, the wheel rim, made of several curved sections (felloes) butted together and secured with internal pins, or tenons, would have been disassembled to install a new nave and supporting spokes. The crank, a small, curved iron piece keyed to the end of a shaft through the nave, imparted motion to the wheel when a long stick, called a footman, was activated by the foot treadle. The spindle is a short, horizontal spool mounted between two short, upright posts forward of the wheel. Basically, Dart delivered his customer a new spinning wheel. The reconstruction cost compares closely with the cost of new flax wheels at 13s. 4d. ($2.23) supplied in 1763 and 1769 by Robert Crage of Leicester, Massachusetts, and a spinning wheel priced at $2.00 made by Nathan Lucas of Kingston in 1823.[111]

Because spinning wheel nomenclature used by craftsmen was variable, it is not always possible to determine exactly what part was repaired or replaced. Fortunately, the confusion is limited to the spinning mechanism forward of the wheel, consisting of two short, turned, upright posts (maidens) supporting between them a turned cross member (the bobbin) and a large C-shaped piece known as the flyer. The flyer both spins the flax into thread and winds it on the bobbin. In his accounts for 1811 Abraham Overholt of Bedminster, Pennsylvania, recorded the following work: "I made a large spinning wheel flyer for Philiph Kraut and turned two spools [and] two maidens." "Spool" was an alternative term for the bobbin, along with "quill" and, on occasion, "spindle." Some years later, in 1828, Overholt recorded a related job: "I turned six spools and put leather into the maidens for David Hoch" at a cost of 7¢. The leathers formed the connection between the maidens and the spool. Samuel Fithian Ware of Cape May County, New Jersey, a contemporary of Overholt, identified another part of the spinning mechanism, when he recorded "to turning whirl to wheel" and charged his customer 12½¢. The whorl, a small cleft disk adjacent to one end of the bobbin, or spool, provided the track that enabled the driving cord from the wheel to transfer power to the spinning mechanism.[112]

Another vulnerable part of the spinning wheel was the wheel itself. Thomas Boynton of Windsor, Vermont, and his contemporary Titus Preston of Wallingford, Connecticut, provided one or more new "spokes" for clients' wheels in the early nineteenth century at a unit cost of 8¢ to 13¢. In the same period Moody Carr of Rockingham County, New Hampshire, recorded "mending [a] rim to a wheel." John Paine's work for Ezra L'hommedieu at Southold, Long Island, was of greater scope in supplying both "1 spoke [and] 1 feler" for 4s. 6d. (75¢). The feler, or felloe, was one of the several curved sections that form the rim of a wheel. Repair or replacement of the foot assembly engaged other craftsmen. Robert Crage of Leicester, Massachusetts, pursued this work in 1763, and Job E. Townsend of Newport, Rhode Island, noted calls in 1787 and 1791 for making or mending a "foot to a Wheal." At East Hampton, Long Island, Nathaniel Dominy V had many requests for mending or supplying a "footboard." One request called for more extensive work in providing a "transum & footboard to [a] Dutch wheel." The transom is the transverse piece of the treadle assembly at either side of the footboard.[113]

The wool, or great, wheel is a much simpler and larger machine than the flax wheel. Its large wheel rim is formed of splint, a thin, wide supple strip of wood bent to form. An upright post forward of the wheel accommodates a simple head with a horizontal spindle for spinning woolen yarns. In lieu of a treadle, the standing spinner turns the wheel by hand. Whereas Robert Crage of Leicester, Massachusetts, charged 13s. 4d. ($2.23) for his flax wheels in the pre-Revolutionary years, the cost of his wool wheels in that period was about half the figure, at 6s. 8d. ($1.11).[114]

Repairs to the great wheel, when specified, involved new parts more commonly than the repair of damaged components. Among actual repairs, Samuel Douglas of New Hartford/Canton, Connecticut, identified work on the "head of a Great Wheel." John Paine of Southold, Long Island, repaired a wheel rim for each of two customers. Perhaps his work paralleled that of Abraham Overholt of Bedminster, Pennsylvania, who made two splints for the rim of a wool wheel owned by Henrich Meyer.[115]

The majority of newly fabricated parts for the wool wheel were for the wheel itself. Nathaniel Dominy V recorded newly "riming a Woolen Wheel" at East Hampton, Long Island, where in the 1810s he also installed new "axeltrees" in wheels for several other customers. Alexander Low of Freehold, New Jersey, was one of a number of craftsmen to supply "spoks to a wool whell." The fabrication method was turning, as identified by Abraham Overholt of Bucks County, Pennsylvania. Another turned part supplied by Overholt was "a pulley for a wool wheel," a part identified as a "whorl" by Dominy and by Job E. Townsend of Newport, Rhode Island. Dominy also is the only craftsman who indicated that he fabricated a new leg for a wool wheel.[116]

Craftsmen's records identify a variety of devices used to reel yarns into skeins for dyeing and storage before winding into balls for handwork or onto bobbins for weaving. Although many repaired reels are not further identified, a small body of material relates to repairs to the clock reel. This upright apparatus supported on a low platform has a box at the top of the vertical shaft on which is mounted a wheel nave containing from four to six turned, radiating, T-shaped arms. Interior gearing operates a small external clock hand mounted over a paper or painted clock face used to count the wheel revolutions, thereby measuring the yardage, whether a skein (560 yards) or lesser amount of yarn. Philip Deland of West Brookfield, Massachusetts, identified the cost of a new apparatus in 1839, when charging a customer $2.50 for making a "Clock real first rate." The price in this rural setting likely was equivalent to about three days' pay for a journeyman woodworker. The cost of actual repair work, as recorded in this study, varied from 3¢ to 50¢, although with one exception the nature of the work is unidentified. The exception is Titus Preston's work in 1803 in "puting an arm to a reel" for a customer at Wallingford, Connecticut, at a charge of 21¢. The clock reel had a long life in the domestic setting. Early repair records include those of circa 1735 for Thomas Pratt at Malden, Massachusetts, and for Isaiah Tiffany in 1757 at Norwich, Connecticut. An alternative method to skeining yarn on the upright reel, with or without a clock mechanism, was by using a "hand Reel," as identified in a New York City bill of 1792 from Gifford and Scotland to Walter Livingston for cleaning and polishing the apparatus. The woodworking partners likely described a niddy noddy, which has cross arms set at right angles to each other at the ends of a short rod. The device is turned and rotated by hand to wind yarn into skeins or shorter lengths.[117]

The records of three craftsmen identify repairs to the swift. This revolving cage, which stands on the floor or is mounted on a table edge, followed the reel in use. In mounting skeins on the frame, the process of winding wool into balls for knitting or onto bobbins for weaving was simplified. Some swifts are collapsible in the manner of an umbrella. Samuel Davison of Plainfield, Massachusetts, and Job Danforth of Providence, Rhode Island, each recorded mending a swift. Job E. Townsend's work at Newport involved "Mending a Pair of Swifts" at a unit cost of 6d. (8½¢).[118]

The quill wheel identified in the accounts of several craftsmen resembles the wool wheel in appearance, but its function is different. The quill wheel enabled householders to wind bobbins mechanically by attaching yarn mounted on a swift directly to the bobbin (also called a spool, quill, or spindle), which is positioned forward of the wheel between a pair of upright maidens. Samuel Durand of Milford, Connecticut, recorded "work at [a] quill wheel" in 1818 for Sarah Newton. Other records provide more insight. In 1790 Joseph Stone of East Greenwich, Rhode Island, fabricated "ten Spokes and a hub to a Quill wheel" belonging to the household of Captain William Arnold. On occasion, Abraham Overholt also undertook spoke repair at Bedminster, Pennsylvania. Several woodworkers, including Stone, directed their attention to making a "whirl on [a] Quill wheel spindle." Nathaniel Dominy V charged 6d. (8¢) for that job at East Hampton, Long

Island, and Job Townsend performed similar work at Newport, Rhode Island. The whirl, which accommodates the drive cord from the wheel, is mounted at one end of the bobbin adjacent to a maiden. The "Spooling Whele," identified by both Townsend and Overholt, is the same machine as the quill wheel.[119]

Of several miscellaneous textile-related accessories identified in craftsmen's records, the quilting frame appears most frequently (fig. 29, left). The simple frame consisted of four rails, or bars, that overlapped at the corners, where they could be lashed together for easy adjustment. The fabric to be quilted was stretched within the frame. The frame could be supported on trestles, or flat-top chairs could be placed at the four corners. The charge for "making a quilting frame" was nominal, as demonstrated in the records of Isaiah Tiffany of Norwich, Connecticut, from whom John Elderkin purchased a new frame for 1s. 8d. (28¢) in September 1755. By January 1756 Elderkin sought repairs to what was likely the same frame and paid Tiffany 7d. (10¢) for the work. The price of a new frame appears to have risen by the early nineteenth century. When individual customers of Joseph Griswold at Buckland, Massachusetts, and Luke Houghton at Barre required "2 pieces to a quilting frame" in 1821–1822, they paid 35¢ and 25¢, respectively.

Figure 29 John Lewis Krimmel, *The Quilting Frolic*, Philadelphia, Pennsylvania, 1813. Oil on canvas. 16⅞" x 22⅜". (Courtesy, Winterthur Museum, acc. 53.178.2.)

Figure 30 Tape loom, Boston, Massachusetts, or Philadelphia, Pennsylvania, 1760–1775. Cherry. H. 11⅛", L. 13½", D. 5⅛". (Courtesy, Winterthur Museum, museum purchase with funds provided by Henry Francis du Pont, acc. 56.72.)

Three shillings (50¢) was Fenwick Lyell's charge at Middletown, New Jersey, in 1806, when a customer needed "2 laths for a Quilting frame."[120]

A single reference to "Mending a Tape Lomb" (loom) describes the presence in some households of a more sophisticated piece of textile equipment (fig. 30). When Job E. Townsend repaired this small loom for a customer at Newport, Rhode Island, in 1799, he recorded a charge of 25¢. The loom illustrated in figure 30, one of a variety of designs, is of particular interest because John Singleton Copley included a virtually identical table loom in his well-known double portrait of Mr. and Mrs. Thomas Mifflin, painted in 1773 at Boston. As the Mifflins, who were Philadelphians, were merely visiting Boston, the loom perhaps can be ascribed to either city. In later years Thomas Mifflin became governor of Pennsylvania (1792–1800). Another textile accessory associated with a refined lifestyle was the tambour frame, consisting of two circular hoops, one inside the other, used to strain a piece of fabric for purposes of embroidery. Fenwick Lyell repaired tambour frames in 1807 and 1815 for clients at Middletown, New Jersey.[121]

Small Containers: Boxes, Cases, Chests, and Trunks

The term "container" as used in this study is a general word describing a broad group of small receptacles identified variously in craftsmen's records as "boxes," "cases," "chests," and "trunks." Many descriptions go a step further and identify the exact function of the receptacle. Why craftsmen distinguished between a case and a chest is not readily apparent without first consulting a dictionary and then reviewing function-specific examples in the records. Basically, a case is a box or container fitted to receive a specific object, whereas a chest is a box of strong construction, or at least one containing a lock, for the storage of articles of value. As it happens, the materials gathered for this study fit perfectly with those definitions, as will be demonstrated.

Wig boxes received the earliest attention of the woodworker. Charles Norris of Philadelphia engaged Samuel Matthews in 1761 to make "2 wig box tops" at a complete charge of 1s. 6d. (25¢). The low cost of the replacement lids describes the utilitarian nature of the boxes. Two New England craftsmen, Joseph Symonds of Salem, Massachusetts, and Job Townsend Jr. of Newport, Rhode Island, made general repairs in 1752 and 1770, respectively. Townsend's client was Colonel Joseph Wanton, who, like Norris, owned two wig boxes and, presumably, two wigs. Many wigs, particularly those that simulated natural hair, were stored and transported in bags. More genteel types of wigs fared better in box storage. During the late eighteenth century, however, the formal wig gradually faded from fashion.[122]

Boxes for other uses also commanded the attention of the woodworker. In the pre-Revolutionary years John Durand of Milford, Connecticut, recorded mending a "Candle Box" for 3s. (50¢). A few years after the war Elisha Hawley described mending a "Shugar Box" at Ridgefield. More attention appears to have been paid to the pipe box (fig. 31). Lemuel Tobey of Dartmouth, Massachusetts, and Job E. Townsend, of Newport, Rhode Island, repaired pipe boxes for their respective clients in the late eighteenth

Figure 31 Pipebox, probably Pennsylvania or the South, 1760–1810. Walnut. H. 21¼", W. 5¼", D. 4". (Formerly in the collection of the Winterthur Museum.)

century, and both men, when called upon, supplied a "Pipe Box Draw[er]" at a modest charge. In 1791 St. George Tucker, a prominent jurist of Williamsburg, Virginia, engaged Richard Booker to repair his "ink Box," a form at times also fabricated of metal.[123]

Changing lifestyles, especially among middle-class consumers, mark the post-Revolutionary years. Fashionable headgear was best protected in a suitable container. Tapping Reeve, Esq., of Litchfield, Connecticut, paid Silas E. Cheney 1s. (16½¢) in 1800 to put "a lid to a bunet [bonnet] box" for a female member of the family. To the north, in Windsor, Vermont, Thomas Boynton identified boxes for related purposes. The bandbox, made of wood or pasteboard, might serve as a storage container, a work box, or even a traveling valise for lightweight garments, in which case a fabric bag with drawstring handles to contain the box was a useful accessory. Some bandboxes were covered with ornamental paper. Boynton identified a wooden box, when he recorded "painting a Band Box verry handsome." His charge of $1.25 for the work indicates that he hand decorated the container. The price is in striking contrast to the 25¢ he charged another customer for "painting A work box." If that price reflected more than a surface coat of paint, the ornament was minimal. On another occasion Boynton recorded "making a top to a work Box."[124]

Work on unidentified boxes sheds additional light on the activity of the woodworker. At Providence, Rhode Island, Job Danforth recorded "putting tops to 2 Boxes," although there is no indication of box shape or whether the tops were hinged lids or separate covers. Glue was all that was required when Rookesby Roberts repaired the top of a box for St. George Tucker in 1795 at Williamsburg, Virginia. A rectangular box shape is implicit in the work of Elijah Barnes in the 1820s, when "putting [a] Bottom & Back to [a] Box." For another Middletown, Connecticut, customer Barnes installed "2 partitions in [a] Box." Exterior surfaces, when not repainted, were coated with varnish, as executed by Thomas Boynton in Vermont and Mark Pitman at Salem, Massachusetts. On occasion, craftsmen provided a general indication of box size. Job E. Townsend of Newport, Rhode Island, and Jonathan Kettell of Newburyport, Massachusetts, each completed work at "Mending a Small Boox" in the early post-Revolutionary period.[125]

Craftsmen who lived in close proximity to the seacoast had occasional calls to fabricate or repair a receptacle to house a quadrant, an instrument used for navigation in the period of this study. Job Danforth recorded one such request in 1799 from Benjamin Gladding of Providence, Rhode Island: "To manding Quadren case for Son." The bottle case, a fixture of some households, was the subject of other repair work. In 1775 Joseph Pemberton, a Philadelphia merchant, engaged William Savery to mend a "Bottle Case," a request also made after the turn of the century to two New England craftsmen, Job E. Townsend of Newport, Rhode Island, and Benjamin Ellery of Gloucester, Massachusetts. In the same general period (1799), William Wragg, Esq., of Charleston, South Carolina, who had ordered "a large liquor case" from Nicholas Silberg for the sum of £2.5 ($7.52), changed his mind and had his purchase altered to "a paper Case with two inside

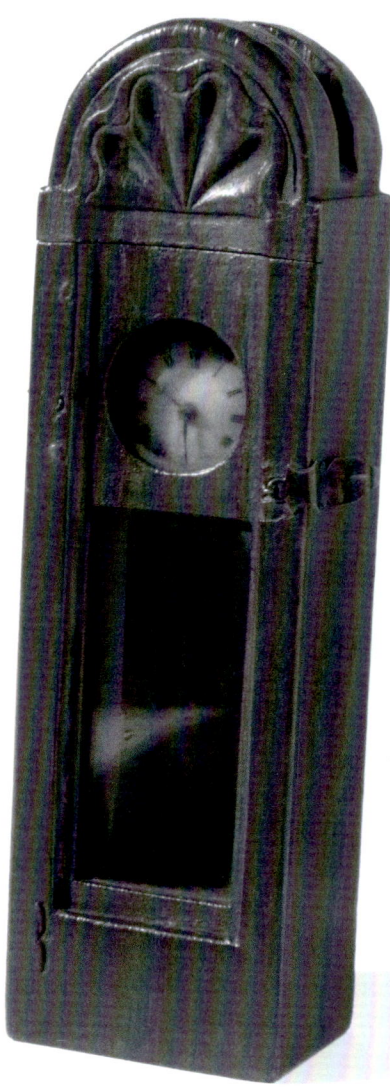

Figure 32 Watch case, New England, 1750–1800. Pine; glass, brass. H. 10 1/4", W. 3", D. 2 1/4". (Courtesy, Winterthur Museum, museum purchase with funds provided by Henry Francis du Pont, acc. 59.4.17.)

Boxes" for an additional £1 ($3.34). Other cases repaired by woodworkers for clients had more personal associations. William Guier of Philadelphia paid Davis Evans in 1801 for "painting a watch case," a box in which to hang a watch when not on the owner's person (fig. 32). Of unusual circumstance is a job of "Repairing a Music Case," which was a request to the firm of Hodghton and Son of Lima, Peru, in 1832 by Samuel Larned, a Providence merchant, who at that date was in the diplomatic service in South America. Of the cases identified here, all have a feature in common. Each was fitted to house a specific object.[126]

The two chests, or containers for storing valuable items, named in this study are identified in craftsmen's accounts as a tea chest and a medicine chest. References focused on the tea chest are the most numerous, and, with one exception, all date to the third and fourth quarters of the eighteenth century, a time when tea was still an expensive, precious commodity (fig. 33). For the most part, repairs to the tea chest are without further description, although several references provide some insight. Alexander Edward of Boston recorded "mending [a] tea chest & Lock" in 1785 for Grant Webster. In "puting a lid to a tea chest" for Captain Phineas Pond at Wallingford, Connecticut, Titus Preston either supplied a new top for the chest or, more likely given the 1s. 2d. (19 1/2¢) charge, rehung the original lid. A finishing task was that of "Varnishing a Tea chest," as executed by James Poupard in 1773 for General John Cadwalader at Philadelphia. The locations of other craftsmen who made repairs to the tea chest describe the heavy urban focus of ownership: William Jenkins at Salem, Massachusetts; Joseph Lindsey at Marblehead; Job Townsend Jr. at Newport, Rhode Island; James Linacre at Albany, New York; and Richard Johns, William Savery, and Daniel Trotter at Philadelphia.[127]

By the nature of its contents, ownership of a medicine chest was limited. When Dr. Jonathan Easton of Newport, Rhode Island, purchased a chest in February 1798 from Job E. Townsend for 15s. ($2.50), the cabinetmaker carefully recorded the specifications of the new box: "A medeson Chest 20 Inches Long and 14 Inches Wide & 7 Deepe . . . [and] 12 Partings" (partitions). Something in the design of the chest proved unsatisfactory because the doctor returned the chest to Townsend's shop in May for alterations at a cost of 3s. (50¢). Two years later, in 1800, Townsend was approached by a Dr. Turner of the frigate *General Green* (probably named for the American general Nathanael Green, 1742–1786) with a request to put a "Lock on the Meddecion Chest." To the north in Beverly, Massachusetts, in 1806, Robert Rantoul, a young druggist and merchant, required a new "Hinge on [a] midicin Chest." This may have been one of two "Medicine Box[es]" Rantoul purchased from Ebenezer Smith Jr. in 1796–1797, when he commenced business.[128]

The trunk, described succinctly by the *Oxford English Dictionary* as "a large box, usually with a hinged lid, for carrying clothes and other luggage when traveling," was also within the scope of repair work undertaken by the woodworker. Dressed skins, smooth or with hair, often covered the wooden foundation of the trunk. Sometimes covered surfaces were orna-

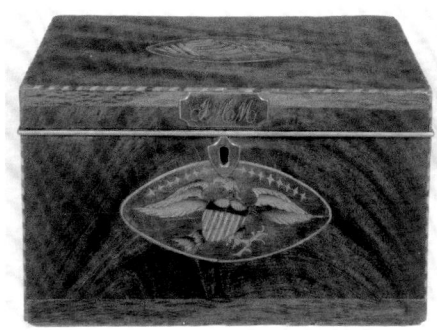

Figure 33 Tea chest, possibly New York City, 1790–1810. Mahogany and mahogany veneer with yellow poplar, white pine, silver, tin, and baize. H. 5⅛", W. 8¹³⁄₁₆", D. 5". (Courtesy, Winterthur Museum, gift of Henry Francis du Pont, acc. 61.1690.) Silver plaque at front of lid engraved with initials "J [or I] McM."

mented with brass-headed nails, and metal straps and corners could be introduced to provide reinforcement. Paper linings were common on the trunk interior to protect clothing and other possessions from damage by wooden splinters. A trunk lock was essential for security. Both Moses Parkhurst of Paxton, Massachusetts, and Fenwick Lyell of Middletown, New Jersey, recorded "putting on 1 trunk lock" in the early nineteenth century. Other vulnerable metalwork on the trunk was the hinges. "New hinges for trunk & putting on" are described in the accounts of G. and D. Cleveland of Providence, Rhode Island, and Titus Preston of Wallingford, Connecticut, the work priced between 22¢ and 25¢. The utility of a trunk could be enhanced by the addition of interior drawers and a till, a job undertaken in 1794 by Job E. Townsend at Newport, Rhode Island. A complete refurbishing of the exterior and interior of a trunk, described as "Covring, papring, and triming a trunk" was recorded in 1797 by Stephanus Knight of Enfield, Connecticut, who charged the sum of 5s. (83½¢).[129]

Personal Items

Musical instruments loomed larger in the lives of American families in the federal period than they do today. The piano, or pianoforte, stood at the top of the hierarchy, a ranking that is reflected in the financial and social standing of the owners who sought repair work or other accommodation from a woodworking craftsman or a specialist in instruments. Included in this owner's group are Colonel Benjamin Tallmadge, a merchant of Litchfield, Connecticut; Nicholas Low and James L. Brinckerhoff, merchants of New York City; General Henry Knox, a resident of Philadelphia when secretary of war in the first federal government; and James J. Skerrett, a wealthy Philadelphian, who also owned a country seat.[130]

Named repairs to the piano focus principally on the legs. Philemon Robbins of Hartford, Connecticut, charged 42¢ in 1834 for "repairing [a] piano leg." Elizur Barnes supplied casters to a client at Middletown a decade earlier, when he also constructed a new "musical Stool" that cost $2.25. The "New Caps on a Piano Forte" installed by Fenwick Lyell for a client at Middletown, New Jersey, in 1809, likely were cup casters. Two years later at Litchfield, Connecticut, Silas E. Cheney himself, rather than a shop journeyman, varnished Benjamin Tallmadge's piano, suggesting, perhaps, the delicacy and prestige of the job. Unspecified repairs made by Duncan Phyfe to James L. Brinckerhoff's piano in 1816 were accompanied by a new "Covering [for the] Piano Stool." The total job cost Brinckerhoff $13.00, the equivalent of about two weeks' pay for a journeyman furniture maker. Rather than repair work, James J. Skerrett's request to Loud and Brothers of Philadelphia in April 1832 was for "Removing a Piano Forte out of Town" to his country seat, where the instrument remained until November 1833, when Skerrett gave the order for "Removing a Piano from the Country." The moves cost Skerrett $4.00 and $5.00, respectively.[131]

Stringed instruments, specifically the violin (also called a "fiddle") and the double bass (known in the federal period as a "bass viol"), were the subject of broader ownership. With one exception, repairs to the violin identify only general mending (fig. 29, right). John Green of Southampton, Long Island, described a simple job for a customer in 1791 as "Gluing Your fidle." Making unnamed general repairs were Thomas Boynton of Windsor, Vermont, Jonathan Kettell of Newburyport, Massachusetts, and Job E. Townsend of Newport, Rhode Island. Boynton also identified a job for another customer as "glueing [a] Bass violl," for which he charged a modest 25¢. Repairs to a double bass in the shop of Elisha H. Holmes at Essex, Connecticut, were accompanied by the job of "making [a] bow." George Short of Newburyport, Massachusetts, recorded the most comprehensive account of work to the double bass: "to 2 bassviol pins, 1 bridge & foot piece for d[itt]o." Again the charge was 25¢.[132]

The umbrella, an item of personal convenience offering protection from rain or sun, was the subject of public notices in the late colonial and federal periods, thereby providing insight into the materials and general appearance of this accessory during the period covered by this study (fig. 34). Isaac Greenwood, a turner of Boston, could supply umbrellas "with Ivory or Bone Sockets and Sliders, and Mehogany Sticks." A retailer of house furnishings in the city described the cover when offering "a variety of silk and oyl cloth Umbrillos for Ladies." The owner of an umbrella lost in New York City identified the color of that example as "Scarlet." The cost of repairs, as reported in craftsmen's accounts, ranged from less than 10¢ to almost 50¢. Job E. Townsend of Newport, Rhode Island, put "a wire in [an] umberiller" in 1799 for as little as 6d. (8½¢). A new handle at the Erie, Pennsylvania, shop of George Landon in 1817 cost a customer 25¢. The price suggests that the wooden piece was turned. Several craftsmen undertook the work of replacing the "stick," or "staff," in an umbrella, among them Titus Preston of Wallingford, Connecticut, who charged 2s. 3d. (38¢), and Nathaniel Dominy V of East Hampton, Long Island, who priced his work at 2s. (33¢).

Figure 34   Detail of an umbrella, United States, 1800–1875. Cotton, wood, brass, and iron. L. 39". (Courtesy, Winterthur Museum, bequest of Henry Francis du Pont, acc. 58.2864.)

Umbrella repairs were as much in demand in urban areas as in rural locations, as demonstrated in the accounts of Samuel Matthews and Samuel Benge, Philadelphia craftsmen whose clients included Charles Norris, Stephen Girard, and Henry Knox.[133]

Globes mounted in stands appear to have been uncommon, except in homes of the affluent and at some educational institutions. In the pre-Revolutionary years two Philadelphia merchants, Joseph Pemberton and Charles Norris, owned stands with globes, which they placed in the hands of William Savery and Samuel Matthews, respectively, for repairs to the stands. There followed a similar request by General Thomas Cadwalader of the city in 1823, when patronizing craftsman Philip Warren.[134]

Figure 35 C. W. Wirths and Brothers, ice skates, Remscheid, Germany, ca. 1833, probably imported into Philadelphia, Pennsylvania. Wood, iron, and leather. L. 13 3/16", W. 2 9/16". (Courtesy, Winterthur Museum, bequest of Henry Francis du Pont, acc. 65.1978.1 and .2.) The Smithsonian Institution owns a related pair of skates with acorn-tipped scrolls at the front and also stamped by Wirths and Brothers. Research indicates that the Wirths Company exported 600 pairs of skates to Christian Hesser in Philadelphia on August 12, 1833. Skates of similar design are visible in Dutch and Flemish genre paintings of village life. Early Dutch and Flemish paintings of rural winter scenes with skaters illustrate similar curved-prow skates.

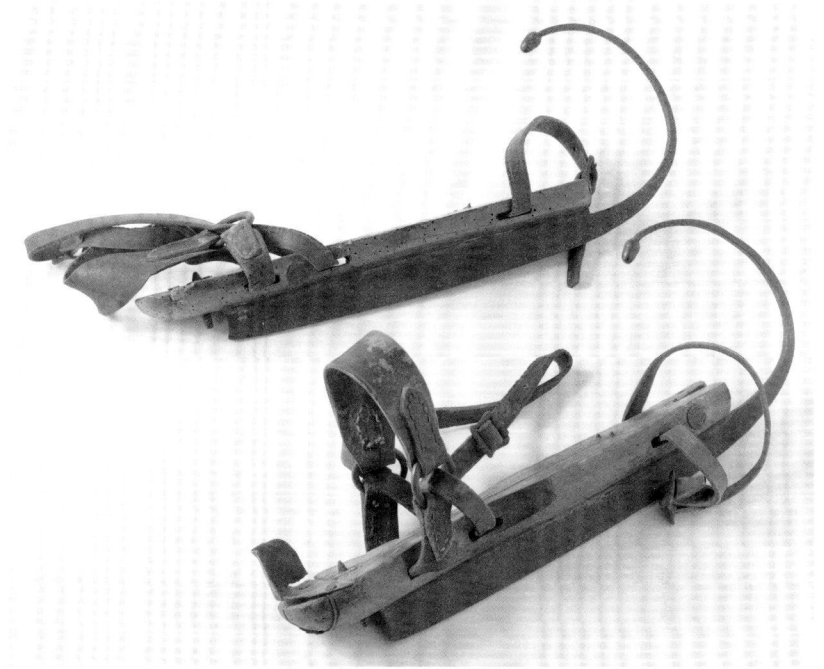

Equipment used for games and sports required periodic attention. When acquiring "two Bowlen Pins" from Job Townsend Jr. at Newport, Rhode Island, in 1757, Jacob Rodriguez Rivera took two other pins to the shop to be altered, presumably to match the new ones. Rivera's pins likely were for use in the game of ninepins, suggesting that somewhere in the area there were one or more outdoor alleys. Half a century later, in 1808, Richard J. Tucker carried a backgammon board to the shop of Fenwick Lyell at Middletown, New Jersey, for repairs that cost 2s. (33¢). Shops equipped with a lathe could also supply the gamesmen, or checkers, used in board games. A different type of request was made by Joseph Ailsworth, who in 1823 sought the services of Job E. Townsend at Newport for "Wooding [a] Pair [of] Skates" (fig. 35). The ice skates may have been refurbished for a son in the family, although it was not unusual for both children and adults to skate, when winter conditions permitted.[135]

The accommodation of a pet was the concern of other patrons of the woodworker's shop. Sometime before July 27, 1797, William Douglas visited the shop of Job. E. Townsend at Newport, Rhode Island, requesting that he make "a Squirrill Cage" at an agreed-upon price of 7s. ($1.17). In less than a month Douglas returned the cage to the shop for an alteration that Townsend described as "Cutting a Door in his Squirell Cage" at a cost of another shilling. Receiving more attention from the woodworker were enclosures described in an advertisement of 1759 as "Cages for Parrots and other Birds," which could be fabricated of wood, ivory, metal, or other material (fig. 29, upper right). Townsend and his father, Job Townsend Jr., each recorded "Mending a Bird Cage." George Merrifield engaged in similar work at Albany, New York, and Charles C. Robinson of Philadelphia undertook a related task described as "painting [a] bird Cage." Native birds, such as cardinals and mockingbirds, were prized, although some individuals preferred the more exotic parrot. In some homes parrots were released from their cages on occasion and given free rein of the household, often to the annoyance of visitors. A bird owned by John Girard, brother of Stephen Girard, may have had that freedom. In 1788 Girard visited the shop of Daniel Trotter in Philadelphia for the purpose of obtaining a "Board for a parrot Stand" for which he paid 3s. 5d. (75¢).[136]

Furniture-making shops active during the late colonial and federal periods offered a broad range of services to their patrons. A substantial part of their business consisted of repairing and refurbishing household furniture, whether of utilitarian or formal design, and a wide variety of domestic objects composed wholly or partly of wood. Charges were reckoned in pounds until the 1790s and the introduction of the dollar as the national monetary unit. Although circulating specie was scarce into the early nineteenth century, business flourished because an active barter economy permitted householders to exchange products and services to meet their domestic needs.

1. Thomas Sheraton, *The Cabinet Dictionary*, 2 vols. (1803; reprint, New York: Praeger, 1970), 1: 111; Thomas Chippendale, *The Gentleman and Cabinet-Maker's Director* (1762; reprint of 3rd ed., New York: Dover Publications, 1966), pls. 107–12; William Ince and John Mayhew, *The Universal System of Household Furniture* (1762; reprint, Chicago: Quadrangle Books, 1960), pls. 16, 17; and [George] Hepplewhite, *The Cabinet-Maker and Upholsterer's Guide* (1794; reprint of 3rd ed., New York: Dover Publications, 1969), pls. 40–42.

2. Benjamin and George Bardine Bill to William Arnold, East Greenwich, Rhode Island, ca. 1780s, A. C. and R. W. Greene Collection, Rhode Island Historical Society, Providence (hereafter cited as RIHS).

3. Fenwick Lyell Account Book, Middletown, New Jersey, 1800–1813, account with John G. Coster, August 5, 1808, Monmouth County Historical Association, Freehold, New Jersey (hereafter cited as MCHA).

4. Sheraton, *Cabinet Dictionary*, 1: 111. Jeduthern Avery Account Book, Bolton/Coventry, Connecticut, 1811–1855, account with Shubael Brewster, June 1830, Connecticut Historical Society, Hartford (hereafter cited as CHS). Samuel Douglas Account Book, New Hartford/Canton, Connecticut, 1810–1858, account with R. and H. Douglas, May 26, 1833, Connecticut State Library, Hartford (hereafter cited as CSL). Chapman Lee Ledger, Charlton, Massachusetts, 1799–1850, account with Nathaniel Blood, January 1802, Old Sturbridge Village, Sturbridge, Massachusetts (hereafter cited as OSV). John Sager Daybook, Bordentown, New Jersey, 1805–1817, account with Thomas Lawrence, September 8, 1809, Historical Society of Pennsylvania, Philadelphia (hereafter cited as HSP). Job E. Townsend Daybook, Newport, Rhode Island, 1803–1828, account with Capt. John Bigley, ca. March 1819, Newport Historical Society, Newport, Rhode Island (hereafter cited as NHS). Job Danforth Ledger, Provi-

dence, Rhode Island, 1788–1818, account with Gershom Jones, December 13, 1792, RIHS. William Pigget Bill to St. George Tucker, Williamsburg, Virginia, August 23, 1792, Tucker-Coleman Collection, Swem Library, College of William and Mary, Williamsburg, Virginia (hereafter cited as W&M). Sewell Tuck Bill to Capt. William Bartlett, Beverly, Massachusetts, November 27, 1772, Papers of William Bartlett, Beverly Historical Society, Beverly, Massachusetts (hereafter BHS).

5. Luke Houghton Ledger, Barre, Massachusetts, 1816–1827, account with John Bacon, June 25, 1821, Barre Historical Society, Barre, Massachusetts. Job Townsend Jr. Ledger, Newport, Rhode Island, 1750–1778, account with Matthew Cozzens, October 28, 1751, NHS. Job E. Townsend Ledger, Newport, Rhode Island, 1778–1794, accounts with Mrs. Ann Harrison, September 8, 1786, and Constant Taber, July 1, 1791, NHS; Job E. Townsend Daybook, Newport, Rhode Island, 1778–1803, account with Capt. Simon Davis, September 3, 1799, NHS; J. E. Townsend Daybook, 1803–1828, account with Solomon Southwick, October 30, 1824. Daniel Trotter Bill to Stephen Girard, Philadelphia, June 21, 1787, Girard Papers, American Philosophical Society, Philadelphia. Alexander Edwards Bills to Daniel Crosby, Boston, May 21, 1781, and April 28, 1785, Greenough Papers, Massachusetts Historical Society, Boston (hereafter cited as MHS). J. E. Townsend Ledger, 1778–1794, account with Edward Stanhope, May 17, 1786, and Daybook, 1778–1803, account with Rouse Potter, September 14, 1786, and Daybook, 1803–1828, account with Lydia Barney, October 18, 1809 (nubs). Miles Ward Ledger, Salem, Massachusetts, 1751–1771, account with John Petman (Pitman?), October 13, 1756, Peabody Essex Museum, Salem, Massachusetts (hereafter cited as PEM).

6. Oliver Avery Account Book, North Stonington, Connecticut, 1789–1813, account with Nathaniel Hewitt, February 3, 1798, Joseph Downs Collection of Manuscripts and Printed Ephemera, Winterthur Museum, Winterthur, Delaware (hereafter cited as DCM). James Gere Ledger, Groton, Connecticut, 1822–1852, account with George Harvey, September 13, 1831, CSL. Isaiah Tiffany Account Book, Norwich, Connecticut, 1746–1767, account with Matthew Simpson, January 21, 1758, CHS. David Evans Daybook, Philadelphia, 1774–1781, account with Rachel Atmore, November 27, 1777, HSP. Hiram Taylor Account Book, Chester County, Pennsylvania, 1828–1855, account with John Tucker, August 8, 1836, DCM. Elisha Harlow Holmes Daybook, Essex, Connecticut, 1825–1830, account with Bela Comstock, December 18, 1826, CSL.

7. J. E. Townsend Daybook, 1778–1803, account with William Harrison, August 11, 1780; J. E. Townsend Ledger, 1778–1794, account with Mr. or Mrs. Brown, March 10, 1780. Reed and Hollis Bill to John Devereux, Esq., Salem, Massachusetts, September 14, 1835, Waters Family Papers, PEM. Philip Warren Bill to Thomas Cadwalader, Philadelphia, February 14, 1824, Cadwalader Papers, Gen. Thomas Cadwalader, HSP.

8. J. E. Townsend Ledger, 1778–1794, account with John Hadwen, May 31, 1783. John Townsend Jr. Daybook, Newport, Rhode Island, 1762–1778, account with John Wanton, June 16, 1765, NHS. Lyell Account Book, account with John G. Coster, October 25, 1808.

9. Alexander Edwards Bill to Daniel Crosby, Boston, May 21, 1781, Greenough Papers. Danforth Ledger, account with Isaac Pearce, July 8, 1804. Lyell Account Book, account with Lenox and Matland, May 4, 1804. Thomas J. Moyers and Fleming K. Rich Account Book, Wytheville, Virginia, 1834–1840, account with Robert Kent, May 3, 1837, DCM.

10. J. E. Townsend Daybook, 1778–1803, accounts with Thomas Roberson, February 10, 1779, and John Perry, May 19, 1781; J. E. Townsend Daybook, 1803–1828, account with Solomon Southwick, October 30, 1824. Josiah P. Wilder Daybook and Ledger, New Ipswich, New Hampshire, 1837–1861, account with James Bancroft, May 30, 1838, private collection (typescript, Visual Resources Collection, Winterthur Museum). William Raymond Bill to Robert Rantoul, Beverly, Massachusetts, March 1819, Papers of Robert Rantoul, BHS. O. Avery Account Book, account with Gilbert Sisson, October 30, 1807.

11. Advertisement of John Marshall, *City Gazette and Daily Advertiser* (Charleston, S.C.), February 17, 1796, as quoted in *The Arts and Crafts in Philadelphia, Maryland, and South Carolina, 1786–1800,* compiled by Alfred Coxe Prime (Topsfield, Mass.: Walpole Society, 1932), pp. 190–91.

12. Silas E. Cheney Ledger, Litchfield, Connecticut, 1799–1817, account with Tapping Reeve, January 26, 1802, Litchfield Historical Society, Litchfield, Connecticut (hereafter cited as LHS). John Hockaday Bill to St. George Tucker, Williamsburg, Virginia, January 12, 1807, Tucker-Coleman Collection. Jacob Brouwer Bill to Nicholas Low, New York, December 6, 1808, Nicholas Low Collection, Library of Congress, Washington, D.C. (hereafter cited as

LC). Elisha Harlow Holmes Ledger, Essex, Connecticut, 1825–1830, account with Ezra Marther, October 15, 1829, CHS; E. H. Holmes Daybook, 1825–1830, account with Capt. Mason, August 10, 1829. Paul Jenkins Daybook, Kennebunk, Maine, 1836–1841, account with Barnabas Palmer, December 27, 1838, DCM. Thomas Boynton Ledger, Windsor, Vermont, 1810–1817, account with Frederick Pettes, July 18, 1814, Dartmouth College Library, Hanover, New Hampshire (hereafter cited as DC). Lyell Account Book, accounts with Ezra Sargeant, November 1, 1809, Robert R. Golet, January 18, 1804, and Henry A. Coster, July 11, 1808. Elizur Barnes Account Book, Middletown, Connecticut, 1821–1825, account with William Woodward, July 13, 1822, Middletown Historical Society, Middletown, Connecticut. Lyell Account Book, account with Henry A. Coster, July 11, 1808.

13. Lyell Account Book, account with Charles L. Camman, May 22, 1805; *Prices of Cabinet and Chair Work* (1772; reprint, Philadelphia: Philadelphia Museum of Art, 2005), p. 31.

14. Danforth Ledger, account with Philip Crapo, November 7, 1796. Isaac Greene (storekeeper) Ledger, Windsor, Vermont, 1788–1800, account with Hezekiah Healy (woodworker), July 29, 1790, Nathan Stone Collection, Vermont Historical Society, Montpelier. Abner Taylor Account Book, Lee, Massachusetts, 1806–1832, account with James Whiton, April 16, 1816, DCM. Abraham S. Egerton Bill to Nicholas Low, New York, March 10, 1824, Low Collection. Walter Nichols Bill to Dr. Isaac Senter, Newport, Rhode Island, June 1784, as published in Joseph K. Ott, "Recent Discoveries among Rhode Island Cabinetmakers and Their Work," *Rhode Island History* 28, no. 1 (February 1969): 8. William Webb IV Bill to Joseph G. Waters, Salem, Massachusetts, August 29, 1833, Waters Family Papers.

15. Silas E. Cheney Daybook, Litchfield, Connecticut, 1807–1813, account with Isaac Baldwin, September 16, 1809, LHS. Robert C. Scadin Ledger, Cooperstown, New York, 1829–1831, account with Damon Hatch, October 20, 1830, New York State Historical Association, Cooperstown, New York (hereafter cited as NYSHA). Seth R. Kneeland Bills to James Beekman, New York, January 30, 1792, and October 1, 1791, White-Beekman Papers, New-York Historical Society, New York (hereafter cited as N-YHS). I. Greene Ledger, account with Hezekiah Healy, August 27, 1790, Stone Collection. J. E. Townsend Daybook, 1778–1803, account with Joshua Crandel, July 24, 1795. Danforth Ledger, accounts with Rufus Waterman, March 18, 1805, and April 18, 1806. Stephanus Knight Account Book, Enfield, Connecticut, 1795–1809, accounts with Henry Terry, July 27, 1806, and Samuel Reynolds, December 12, 1798, CHS. Boynton Ledger, 1810–1817, account with Eliakim Spooner, May 14, 1813. Jenkins Daybook, account with Nathaniel Jeffords, May 9, 1840.

16. Henry Connelly Bills to Stephen Girard, Philadelphia, June 22, 1810, November 12, 1811, May 26, 1812, and May 30, 1817, Girard Papers. William Webb IV Bill to Joseph G. Waters, Salem, Massachusetts, November 19, 1831, Waters Family Papers. E. H. Holmes Daybook, 1825–1830, account with Alvin I. Whitmore, March 5, 1827.

17. J. E. Townsend Daybook, 1778–1803, account with John Hadwen, May 28, 1783. J. E. Townsend Ledger, 1778–1794, account with Constant Taber, March 14, 1791. Daniel Ross Account Book, Ipswich, Massachusetts, 1781–1804, account with James Burnham, June 27, 1787, PEM.

18. Perez Austin Account Book, Canterbury, Connecticut, 1811–1832, account with Thomas B. Pellit, September 1823, CHS. Barnes Account Book, account with G. W. Hanley, Esq., October 1, 1821. Allen Holcomb Account Book, New Lisbon, New York, 1809–ca. 1828, account with Dr. Walter Wing, June 16, 1825, Metropolitan Museum of Art, New York.

19. Robert Cockburn Account Book, King George County and Orange County (1773 and later), Virginia, 1767–1777, account with Mr. Smith, February 1774, DCM. Townsend Goddard Bill to Christopher Champlin, Newport, Rhode Island, August 11, 1786, Wetmore Papers, MHS. Edward Slead Account Book, Dartmouth, Massachusetts, 1797–1827, account with Jonathan Peckham, December 19, 1808, Baker Library, Harvard University, Cambridge, Massachusetts (hereafter cited as BL). Stephen Sweet Bill to Albert C. Greene, East Greenwich, Rhode Island, March 28, 1815, Greene Collection. Thomas Safford Ledger, Canterbury, Connecticut, 1807–1835, account with Daniel Downing, June 8, 1821, CSL. John Ellinger Account Book, Palmyra, Lebanon County, Pennsylvania, 1823–1845, account with John Wolferspergen, May 10, 1833, Landis Valley Museum, Lancaster, Pennsylvania.

20. Hepplewhite, *Guide*, p. 9.

21. E. H. Holmes Daybook, 1825–1830, account with H. Mather, November 14, 1826. Holcomb Account Book, account with Willard Coy, August 10, 1825. Cheney Daybook, 1807–1813, account with Joseph L. Smith, June 4, 1810.

22. Michael Bouvier Bill to Stephen Girard, Philadelphia, October 7, 1827, Girard Papers.

Moyers and Rich Account Book, account with James R. Miller, March 1, 1837. Arlene Palmer, *Glass in Early America* (New York: W. W. Norton for the Winterthur Museum, 1993), p. 397.

23. John Collins Bill to Richard Blow, Portsmouth, Virginia, December 12, 1807, Richard Blow Papers, W&M. Friedrich Bastian Account Book, Bethel Township, Dauphin County, Pennsylvania, 1802–1829, account with Miss Thompson(?), July 15, 1819, DCM. Boynton Ledger, 1810–1817, account with Charles Marsh, Esq., July 10, 1816.

24. Lyell Account Book, account with Samuel Ogden, April 6, 1809. Thomas Sheraton, *The Cabinet-Maker and Upholsterer's Drawing-Book* (1793; reprint, New York: Dover Publications, 1972), pl. 50 and p. 407; and *The Cabinet-Makers' London Book of Prices and Designs of Cabinet Work* (1793; reprint of 2nd ed., Leeds, Eng.: Furniture History Society, 1982, as volume 18 of *Furniture History Journal*), pl. 23, right, and pp. 85–87. Advertisement of Fenwick Lyell, *New-York Gazette and the General Advertiser,* March 22, 1797, as quoted in *The Arts and Crafts in New York, 1777–1799,* compiled by Rita Susswein Gottesman (New York: New-York Historical Society, 1954), p. 123.

25. Isaac Vose Bill to Caleb Davis, Boston, May 10, 1791, Caleb Davis Papers, MHS. Joel Mount Ledger, Juliustown, New Jersey, 1829–1865, account with Samuel Ellis, November 19, 1842, HSP. Reed and Hollis Bill to John Devereux, Esq., Salem, Massachusetts, September 14, 1835, Waters Family Papers.

26. John G. Hopkins Bill to Richard W. Greene, Esq., Providence, Rhode Island, July 16, 1830, Greene Papers. Felix Huntington Account Sheet, Norwich, Connecticut, 1775–1784, account with Col. Joshua Huntington, February 24, 1777, DCM. Jenkins Daybook, account with Dr. B. Smart, May 10, 1839. Lyell Account Book, account with Thomas L. Ogden, May 15, 1804.

27. Phillip Filer Account Book, near Rome, New York, 1798–1839, account with Matthew Brown, March 5, 1802, DCM. David Pritchard Jr. Account Book, Waterbury, Connecticut, 1827–1838, account with [first name unknown] Bisby, September 18, 1837, Mattatuck Museum, Waterbury, Connecticut. Barnes Account Book, account with Samuel Starr, December 30, 1823. (Vermont) I. Greene Ledger, account with Hezekiah Healy, November 15, 1790, Stone Collection; (Virginia) John Hockaday Bill to St. George Tucker, Williamsburg, Virginia, October 25, 1806, Tucker-Coleman Collection; Pennell Beale Bill to Gen. Henry Knox, Philadelphia, September 24, 1791, Henry Knox Papers, Maine Historical Society, Portland (hereafter cited as MeHS). Howard Smith Account Book, New Haven, Connecticut, 1844–1849, account with Seth Calhoun, April 31, 1844, CHS. Nathaniel Holmes Account Book, Kingston, Massachusetts, 1801–1813, account with Jedidiah Holmes, Esq., January 5, 1803, DCM. Lyell Account Book, account with Thomas Liddle, December 21, 1805. Robert Kennedy Bill to William Barrell, Philadelphia, ca. early 1770s, Stephen Collins Papers, LC.

28. Boynton Ledger, 1810–1817, account with Eliakim Spooner, September 4, 1812. William G. Beesley Daybook, Salem, New Jersey, 1828–1841, account with Benjamin Archer, December 21, 1829, Salem County Historical Society, Salem, New Jersey. Cheney Ledger, 1799–1817, account with Frederick Wolcott, April 15, 1801. Walter Nichols Bill to Dr. Isaac Senter, Newport, Rhode Island, June 1790, as published in Ott, "Recent Discoveries," p. 8. Barnes Account Book, account with William Williams, July 12, 1823. Daniel Trotter Account Sheet, Philadelphia, 1785–1798, account with Benjamin Thaw, July 20, 1787, DCM.

29. Thomas Tufft Bill to Mary Norris, Philadelphia, August 1778, Norris of Fairhill Manuscripts, Family Accounts, HSP. Solomon Cole Account Book, Glastonbury, Connecticut, 1794–1809, account with George Talcott, October 31, 1801, CHS.

30. Samuel Davison Ledger, Plainfield, Massachusetts, 1795–1824, account with Psalter Searles for "hanging a Chest," February 1796, Pocumtuck Valley Memorial Association, Deerfield, Massachusetts. Elisha Hawley Account Book, Ridgefield, Connecticut, 1781–1805, account with Capt. James Scott, April 31, 1797, CHS. J. E. Townsend Ledger, 1778–1794, account with Daniel Weatherly, October 23, 1790. J. E. Townsend Daybook, 1803–1828, accounts with Isaac Stoddard, August 22, 1818, and December 11, 1817. J. E. Townsend Daybook, 1778–1803, account with J. Hill, March 19, 1785. Peter Ranck Account Book, Jonestown, Lebanon County, Pennsylvania, 1794–1817, account with George Merk, 1795, account book as published in *The Accounts of Two Pennsylvania German Furniture Makers,* edited and translated by Alan G. Keyser, Larry M. Neff, and Frederick S. Weiser, Sources and Documents of the Pennsylvania Germans, no. 3 (Breinigsville, Pa.: Pennsylvania German Society, 1978), p. 49.

31. Samuel Durand Daybook, Milford, Connecticut, 1806–1838, account with Henry Bull, November 15, 1814, Milford Historical Society, Milford, Connecticut (hereafter cited as MiHS). Timothy Loomis Account Book, Windsor, Connecticut, 1768–1804, account with

Hannah Moore, 1770, CHS. Titus Preston Ledger, Wallingford, Connecticut, 1795–1817, account with Jared Alling, April 3, 1806, Sterling Memorial Library, Yale University, New Haven, Connecticut (hereafter cited as SL). George Claypoole Bill to Samuel Meredith, Philadelphia, April 10, 1773, Clymer-Meredith-Read Papers, New York Public Library, New York City (hereafter cited as NYPL).

32. Titus Preston Ledger, Wallingford, Connecticut, 1811–1842, account with Samuel Tuttle, January 1819, SL. Douglas Account Book, accounts with Miss Mary Embry, July 28, 1812, and Benjamin Palmiter, March 21, 1815. Knight Account Book, account with Zebulon Pease, November 1, 1802.

33. O. Avery Account Book, accounts with Gilbert Smith Jr., July 5, 1793, and Rachel Frishy, June 29, 1789. David Haven Account Book, Framingham, Massachusetts, 1785–1800, account with Richard Smith, January 1797, DCM. John Durand Account Book, Milford, Connecticut, 1760–1783, account with Mr. Lounsbery, April 18, 1764, MiHS. A. Taylor Account Book, account with Jonathan Foot, ca. 1814. J. Avery Account Book, account with Percy Haskins, June 1824.

34. J. E. Townsend Daybook, 1778–1803, account with Robert Taylor, August 27, 1783. John Hockaday Bill to St. George Tucker, Williamsburg, Virginia, May 20, 1807, Tucker-Coleman Collection.

35. Joseph Lindsey Ledger, Marblehead, Massachusetts, 1739–1764, account with Christopher Bubier, January 12, 1743, DCM. J. Townsend Jr. Daybook, 1762–1778, account with Thomas Weaver, December 29, 1767. Cheney Daybook, 1807–1813, account with Daniel Huntington, May 20, 1808. Reuben Loomis Account Book, Windsor/Suffield, Connecticut, 1796–1836, account with John W. Hanchett, June 1811, CHS. William Proud Ledger, Providence, Rhode Island, 1770–1779, account with Joseph Martin, March 7, 1776, RIHS. Davison Ledger, account with Samuel Brown, December 1801. Jacob Sass Bill to Peter Trezevant, Charleston, South Carolina, January 11, 1805, as quoted in Bradford L. Rauschenberg and John Bivins Jr., *The Furniture of Charleston, 1680–1820,* Frank L. Horton Series, 3 vols. (Winston-Salem, N.C.: Old Salem/Museum of Early Southern Decorative Arts, 2003), 3: 1207. Alexander Low Account Book, Freehold, New Jersey, 1784–1826, account with Gordon Forman, July 6, 1798, MCHA.

36. Cheney Ledger, 1799–1817, account with Caleb Bacon, January 2, 1801. J. E. Townsend Daybook, 1778–1803, account with John Hadwen, March 31, 1783. Danforth Ledger, account with Amos Throop, May 2, 1798. George Merrifield Account Book, Albany, New York, 1831–1847, account with D. Lathrop, March 16, 1837, DCM. Houghton Ledger, account with Dr. Samuel Gates, October 13, 1824.

37. Daniel Trotter Bill to Samuel Coates, Philadelphia, January 3, 1788, Reynell and Coates Collection, BL. Preston Ledger, 1795–1817, account with Caleb Parsons, July 19, 1798. Asa Jones Account Book, Bridgewater, Massachusetts, 1790–1840, account with James Perkins, February 17, 1795, DCM; Bastian Account Book, account with James Wetch (Welch?), March 7, 1814. Ross Account Book, account with Samuel Wade, December 15, 1823. Merrifield Account Book, account with N. Sanford, December 4, 1832.

38. Jones Account Book, account with James Perkins, February 17, 1795. Cheney Ledger, 1799–1817, account with John Allen, Esq., November 2, 1801. Moses Parkhurst Account Book, Paxton, Massachusetts, 1814–1839, accounts with Samuel Slade, May 3, 1821, and Capt. David Davis, March 17, 1817, OSV. Oliver Moore Account Book, East Granby, Connecticut, 1808–1821, account with Benjamin Harger, April 1810, CHS. Douglas Account Book, account with Josiah Goodsell, May 12, 1823. Holcomb Account Book, account with Benjamin Hull(?), July 5, 1819. Hawley Account Book, account with Mr. Burnet, March 12, 1795. Joseph Symonds Account Book, Salem, Massachusetts, 1738–1766, account with Joseph Hogars(?), August 4, 1748, PEM. Lemuel Tobey Daybook, Dartmouth, Massachusetts, 1773–1785, account with Capt. Thomas Hathaway, September 22, 1774, OSV. Slead Account Book, account with John Smith, March 28, 1801.

39. J. E. Townsend Daybook, 1778–1803, account with Theophilus Topham, March 23, 1789. Abner Haven Account Book, Framingham, Massachusetts, 1809–1830, account with Aaron Coolidge, April 1821, DCM. J. E. Townsend Ledger, 1778–1794, accounts with John Franklin, March 31, 1785, and Capt. James Webb, December 7, 1782. Jacob Bachman Daybook, Lancaster County, Pennsylvania, 1822–1861, account with Isaac McCalister, May 6, 1831, DCM.

40. Cheney Ledger, 1799–1817, account with John Allen, Esq., November 2, 1801. Low Account Book, account with Gordon Forman, July 6, 1798. Townsend Goddard Bill to Christopher Champlin, Newport, Rhode Island, November 18, 1786, Wetmore Papers.

41. J. Avery Account Book, account with Archibald Barrett, December 1824. Barnes Account Book, account with Mary Bement, August 28, 1821. Moore Account Book, account with George Griswold, January 16, 1818. Nathaniel Dominy V Account Book and Daybook, East Hampton, Long Island, New York, 1798–1847, account with Jeremiah Miller, October 4, 1819, DCM (all Nathaniel Dominy references, courtesy of Charles F. Hummel).

42. Low Account Book, account with Elisha Walton, February 8, 1799. James Francis Account Book, Wethersfield, Connecticut, 1797–1835, account with Nathan W. Pelton, ca. 1822–1826, CHS. Danforth Ledger, account with Stephen Jackson, June 17, 1801. Silas E. Cheney Daybook, Litchfield, Connecticut, 1802–1807, account with Tapping Reeve, July 14, 1802, LHS. Cheney Daybook, 1807–1813, account with Benjamin Tallmadge, April 20, 1811. J. B. Townsend Daybook, 1778–1803, account with Samuel Simpson, September 11, 1802.

43. Public auction advertisements, *New-York Gazette, and the Weekly Mercury,* October 6, 1777, and August 18, 1783, as quoted in Gottesman, comp., *Arts and Crafts in New York, 1777–1799,* pp. 132, 134. Advertisements of John Marshall, *South Carolina State Gazette* (Charleston), October 31, 1795, and *South Carolina Gazette* (Charleston), July 12, 1796; and advertisements of Jonathan Gostelowe, *Pennsylvania Packet* (Philadelphia), January 16, 1793, and *Independent Gazetteer* (Philadelphia), May 18, 1793, both as quoted in Prime, comp., *Arts and Crafts in Philadelphia, Maryland, and South Carolina, 1786–1800,* pp. 190–91 and 179–80, respectively.

44. *London Book of Prices* (1793), as reproduced in *Furniture History* (1982): 5–9. Hepplewhite, *Guide,* pls. 76 (top), 77.

45. Bureau forms are described in documents surveyed for this study as follows. A paneled-end case is in Nathaniel Knowlton Account Book, Eliot, Maine, 1812–1831, account with Benjamin Lamson, August 18, 1814, MeHS. Columned bureaus are in Samuel Ashton Account Book, Philadelphia, 1794–1803, credit listings for Richard Sweden, May 9 and June 6, 1795, DCM; in Henry Connelly Bill to Stephen Girard, Philadelphia, August 5, 1817, Girard Papers; and in Scadin Ledger, inventory of property assigned to William H. Averell, December 30, 1830. A half-columned bureau is in H. Taylor Account Book, credit listing for John Baldwin, January 4, 1836. A dressing bureau is in Scadin Ledger, 1829–1831, inventory of property assigned to William H. Averell, December 30, 1830. A bureau with a dresser top is in Jenkins Daybook, account with William Russell, September 4, 1839. Bureaus with a case on top, an ornamented backboard, or a front projection are in Knowlton Account Book, accounts with Joseph Nash, April 28, 1830, Capt. John Smith, April 14, 1827, and Samuel Hill, June 11, 1829, respectively. A prospect-front bureau is in Holcomb Account Book, credit listing for Ezra Bryan, November 24, 1827. The Joseph Meeks and Sons broadside advertisement is illustrated in *Art and the Empire City: New York, 1825–1861,* edited by Catherine Hoover Voorsanger and John K. Howat (New York: Metropolitan Museum of Art, 2000), p. 517.

46. Ornamental embellishments on bureaus are described in documents surveyed for this study as follows. Cock beading and stringing are in S. Ashton Account Book, credit listings for Richard Sweden, May 9, 1795, and Samuel Howel, ca. March 1802, respectively. Carved feet are in Robert C. Scadin Daybook, Cooperstown, New York, 1829–1831, credit listing for Joseph Shipley, July 21, 1831, NYSHA. Crossbanding is in Knowlton Account Book, account with Benjamin Lamson, October 5, 1812. Glass trimmings are in Gere Ledger, account with Giles Gallup, March 21, 1834. Cut-glass knobs are in H. Taylor Account Book, account with David Rickabaugh, April 29, 1836.

47. Wood choices for bureaus are described in documents surveyed for this study as follows. A full mahogany bureau is in Nathaniel Safford Bill to Robert Rantoul, Salem, Massachusetts, March 11, 1801, Rantoul Papers. A mahogany-front bureau is in Moyers and Rich Account Book, account with John Johnston, May 10, 1834. A mahogany bureau with cherry ends is in Scadin Ledger, 1829–1831, inventory of property assigned to William H. Averill, December 30, 1830. A cherry bureau is in Boynton Ledger, 1810–1817, account with N. Perkins, July 21, 1813. A curled maple bureau is in J. Avery Account Book, account with Ezekiel Richardson, April 1815. An ornamented pine bureau is in Barnes Account Book, account with Chauncey Whittlesay, July 22, 1824. A birch bureau is in Knowlton Account Book, account with Capt. John Smith, April 14, 1827. A butternut bureau is in Cheney Daybook, 1807–1813, account with Joel Munger, December 21, 1812. A whitewood-end bureau is in Barnes Account Book, credit listing for Samuel Starr, November 1, 1823. Gere Ledger, account with Moses A. Peirce of Norwich, August 3, 1829.

48. William Rawson Account Book, Killingly, Connecticut, 1835–1841, account with Ezekiel Mowrey, July 6, 1836, OSV. Moyers and Rich Account Book, account with John C. Crockett,

May 3, 1834. Dominy Account Book and Ledger, account with Jeremiah Miller, May 10, 1819. Barnes Account Book, account with Sylvester Willcox, November 24, 1823. Knowlton Account Book, credit listing for Benjamin Lamson, July 5, 1814.

49. George Short Account Book, Newburyport, Massachusetts, ca. 1807–1821, account with Mrs. Phyllis Small, August 11, 1807, PEM. Moyers and Rich Account Book, accounts with Robert Kent, January 23, 1839, and James R. Miller, March 6, 1839. Bastian Account Book, accounts with Matthew McClure, March 30, 1813, and Washington Russell, April 22, 1819. John T. Ball Bill to Nicholas Low, New York, November 30, 1809, Low Collection; Solomon Sibley Ledger, Ward, Massachusetts, 1793–1840, account with Adolphus Edson, January 24, 1805, OSV. Alexander Taylor Bill to Richard Blow, Petersburg, Virginia, March 12, 1814, Blow Family Papers, W&M. John G. Hopkins Bill to Richard W. Greene, Esq., Providence, Rhode Island, May 25, 1830, Greene Collection.

50. E. H. Holmes Ledger, 1825–1830, account with Selah Griswold, July 20, 1828. Moore Account Book, account with Harvey Thrall, April 28, 1820. Elijah Sanderson Bill to Ezra Northey, Salem, Massachusetts, October 30, 1821, Northey Family Papers, PEM. Benjamin Ellery Bill to Estate of Eliakim Prindall, Gloucester, Massachusetts, May 1820, Papers of Daniel Rogers Jr., PEM. True Currier Account Book, Deerfield, New Hampshire, 1815–1838, account with Oliver Nichols of Kingstown, February 1819, DCM. J. E. Townsend Daybook, 1778–1803, account with Capt. William Gardner, September 3, 1799. Handles listed in Cheney Daybook, 1807–1813, account with Benjamin Tallmadge, April 20, 1811. Escutcheons, key, locks, and a set of knobs listed in Barnes Account Book, account with John Bound, September 20, 1821. Boynton Ledger, 1810–1817, account with Ishmael Tukesbury, July 21, 1814. Pennell Beale Bill to Gen. Henry Knox, Philadelphia, September 24, 1791, Knox Papers. Jenkins Daybook, account with John B. Taylor, September 25, 1838.

51. Abraham S. Egerton Bill to Nicholas Low, New York, February 16, 1824, Low Collection. Cheney Daybook, 1807–1813, account with Benjamin Tallmadge, April 20, 1811. Gere Ledger, 1822–1852, account with Capt. Park Avery, April 26, 1824. Barnes Account Book, accounts with George W. Stanley, September 9, 1821 (cleaning and varnishing), and Capt. Horace Clark, May 15, 1823 (planing and varnishing). Leonard R. and James R. Proctor Ledger and Daybook, Hartwick, New York, accounts with John T. Cause, August 26, 1835, and Elizur Smith, August 25, 1835, NYSHA. Thomas Boynton Ledger, Windsor, Vermont, 1817–1847, account with Uriel Cummings, April 16, 1844, DC.

52. A. Haven Account Book, account with Levi Metcalf, October 1810. Ranck Account Book, account with Henry Frank, December 17, 1802, as published in Keyser et al., *Accounts of Two Pennsylvania German Furniture Makers*, p. 205. John Scolley and Josiah L. White Account Book, Newtown, Connecticut, 1808–1811, account with Asa Rogers, June 20, 1809, DCM. Austin Account Book, account with Walter Eaton, February 1831. I. Greene Ledger, account with Elias Savage, March 2, 1791, Stone Collection. "Skipper" Lunt Account Book, Newbury, Massachusetts, 1736–1772, account with Lemuel Fowler, October 1767, PEM. Bachman Account Book, account with David Graff, June 14, 1840. Peter Emerson Daybook, Reading, Massachusetts, 1749–1759, account with his father (unnamed), March 22, 1756, Boston Public Library, Boston, Massachusetts.

53. Douglas Account Book, account with R. and H. Douglas, January 14, 1833. Houghton Ledger, accounts with Dr. Anson Bates, September 15, 1820 (cupboard turns), and widow Abigail Wheeler, July 14, 1824 (cupboard back). Parkhurst Account Book, account with Nathaniel Lakin (Larkin?), February 4, 1825. Low Account Book, account with Job Emmons, February 11, 1801. Moyers and Rich Account Book, account with Nicholas Ogilsby, July 25, 1834. A. Taylor Account Book, account with Nathaniel Bassett, January 23, 1816. Lee Ledger, account with Orlean Prince, April 24, 1820. J. E. Townsend Ledger, 1778–1794, account with Thomas Mumford, January 1789. Hawley Account Book, account with Moses Ingersoll, August 14, 1794. M. Ward Ledger, account with Capt. Ebenezer Bowditch, September 1735.

54. Enos Reynolds Daybook, Boxford, Massachusetts, 1793–1840, account with Jonas Reynolds, July 31, 1815, PEM. Charles C. Robinson Daybook, Philadelphia, 1809–1825, account with Christian Young, March 30, 1814, HSP. Sophia Roorbach Receipt Book, New York, 1810–1852, account with Abberley and Hartley, April 8, 1839, Duykinck Collection, NYPL. Moore Account Book, account with Henry Kent, January 1809.

55. M. Ward Ledger, account with Capt. Benjamin Pickman, August 1832; Emerson Daybook, account with his father (unnamed), March 22, 1756. Beesley Daybook, account with Elizabeth Hopman, May 20, 1834. Bastian Account Book, account with Reven (the Reverend?) McClure, October 27, 1819.

56. Dressers and their contents are discussed in Benno M. Forman, "German Influences in Pennsylvania Furniture," in *Arts of the Pennsylvania Germans,* edited by Catherine E. Hutchins (New York: W. W. Norton for the Winterthur Museum, 1983), pp. 155–56; and Nancy Goyne Evans, "Everyday Things: From Rolling Pins to Trundle Bedsteads," in *American Furniture 2003,* edited by Luke Beckerdite (Hanover, N.H.: University Press of New England for the Chipstone Foundation, 2003), pp. 30–31.

57. Dressers located in the kitchen are identified as follows. Ranck Account Book, account with Valentine Schaufler, July 20, 1798, as published in Keyser et al., *Accounts of Two Pennsylvania German Furniture Makers,* p. 93. Bastian Account Book, account with Henry Arfen (Arson?), April 2, 1814; and Robert Parrish Bill to Stephen Collins, Philadelphia, 1769, Collins Papers. J. E. Townsend Ledger, 1778–1794, account with Robert Taylor, June 23, 1785. Sager Daybook, account with Moore Edwards, July 10, 1810. Bachman Daybook, account with Jacob Smith, February 23, 1827. Moody Carr Account Book, Rockingham County, New Hampshire, 1800–1815, accounts with John Mudget, June 30, 1807, and Benjamin Choate, May 24, 1806, OSV. D. Haven Account Book, account with Levi Metcalf, June 1789.

58. Lee Ledger, account with George W. Eddy, December 1818.

59. Letter from John Hewitt, Savannah, Georgia, to Mathias Bruen, New York, January 30, 1802, Hewitt Letters, DCM.

60. Daniel Trotter Bill to Stephen Girard, Philadelphia, July–October 1792, Girard Papers. John Hockaday Bills to St. George Tucker, Williamsburg, Virginia, June 22 and July 24, 1805, Tucker-Coleman Collection. S. and J. Rawson Bill to Richard W. Greene, Esq., Providence, Rhode Island, April 19, 1839, Greene Collection. Charles H. White Bill to James J. Skerrett, Philadelphia, November 15, 1831, Loudoun Papers, Papers of James J. Skerrett, HSP. Pritchard Account Book, account with [first name unknown] Bisby, September 18, 1837. George Claypoole Bill to Samuel Meredith, Philadelphia, November 9, 1790, Clymer-Meredith-Read Papers. William Savery Bill to Joseph Pemberton, Philadelphia, January 10, 1775, Pemberton Papers, HSP. J. A. Moricet Bill to Arthur Bronson, New York, November 1, 1839, Bronson Papers, NYPL.

61. Huntington Account Sheet, accounts with Col. Joshua Huntington, June 10 and November 12, 1782. Walter Nichols and Samuel Ward Bills to Dr. Isaac Senter, ca. February 1790 and June 1, 1791, respectively, as published in Ott, "Recent Discoveries," pp. 8, 9.

62. Philemon Robbins Account Book, Hartford, Connecticut, 1833–1836, account with Timothy Sheldon, CHS. Barnes Account Book, account with Mrs. Esther Williams, October 18, 1821. Jacob Brouwer Bills to Nicholas Low, New York, January 18 and February 17, 1798, Low Collection. Peter Douglass Bill to Samuel Meredith, Philadelphia, October 2, 1802, Clymer-Meredith-Read Papers.

63. Robert McConachy Bill to Nicholas Low, New York, November 8, 1808, Low Collection. Lyell Account Book, account with John B. Graves, February 18, 1805. Danforth Ledger, account with James Burrel Jr., Esq., August 2, 1802. Barnes Account Book, account with Josiah Williams, May 4, 1822.

64. Scadin Daybook, 1829–1831, account with B. Sparrow, June 6, 1829. Lyell Account Book, account with John B. Graves, February 13, 1805. John Collins Bill to Richard Blow, Portsmouth, Virginia, December 12, 1807, Blow Papers. Barnes Account Book, account with Josiah Williams, January 9, 1823. Elisha Adams Bill to David S. Greenough, Boston, January 1809, Greenough Papers. Gifford and Scotland Bill to Walter Livingston, New York, March 12, 1792, Livingston Papers, N-YHS. A bolt is listed in Abraham S. Egerton Bill to Nicholas Low, New York, February 16, 1824, Low Collection. Ketches are listed in Barnes Account Book, account with Josiah Williams, January 9, 1823. Turn buckles are listed in Pennell Beale Bill to Gen. Henry Knox, Philadelphia, September 24, 1791, Knox Papers. Jacob Sass Bill to Peter Trezevant, Charleston, South Carolina, June 11, 1805, as quoted in Rauschenberg and Bivins, *Furniture of Charleston,* 3: 1207.

65. Pennell Beale Bill to Gen. Henry Knox, Philadelphia, September 24, 1791, Knox Papers. Robbins Account Book, account with John A. Tainter, June 13, 1834. Jenkins Daybook, account with William Lord, December 28, 1837. Thomas Needham Bill to Robert Manning, Salem, Massachusetts, January 8, 1825, Papers of Robert Manning, PEM. Henry Hubon Bill to Mrs. Barton, Salem, Massachusetts, January 10, 1821, Papers of Samuel and John Barton, PEM. Porter Russell Bill to Capt. Edmund Kimball, Newburyport, Massachusetts, March 30, 1818, Kimball Family Papers, PEM. Merrifield Account Book, account with Mr. Ferguson, May 2, 1832. Scadin Ledger, 1829–1831, account with Calvin Graves, August 18, 1830. Barry and Krickbaum Bill to John Cadwalader, Esq., Philadelphia, June 11, 1836, Cadwalader Papers,

Judge John Cadwalader. Elizabeth de Hart Bleecker Diary, New York, 1799–1806, entry for August 14, 1800, NYPL.

66. Isaac Ashton Bill to Gen. Henry Knox, Philadelphia, January 16, 1793, Knox Papers. Richard Alexander Bill to Mrs. John Francis, Philadelphia, April 28, 1820, Cadwalader Papers, Gen. Thomas Cadwalader. Bills to Nicholas Low, New York: David F. Lanny, December 11, 1794; Jacob Brouwer, January 9, 1796, June 20, 1797, August 10, 1797, July 15, 1807, and November 19, 1807; and Robert McConachy, November 8, 1808, all in Low Papers. Advertisement of Fenwick Lyell, *New-York Gazette and the General Advertiser,* March 22, 1797, as quoted in Gottesman, comp., *Arts and Crafts in New York, 1777–1799,* p. 123.

67. Lyell Account Book, account with John Bunnel, July 27, 1808. Barnes Account Book, account with James H. S[co]tch(?), November 24, 1821. John Hewitt, Savannah, Georgia, to Mathias Bruen, New York, June 10, 1801, Hewitt Letters.

68. James Beekman Account Book of Personal Affairs, New York, 1761–1796, accounts with McEvers and Barclay, August 27, 1794, and Mr. Hoes, December 10, 1794, White-Beekman Papers.

69. Alexander H. Gilbert Account Book, Chester, Connecticut, 1831–1852, account with Thaddeus Beach, January 3, 1837, CHS. S. Durand Daybook, account with Charles P. Strong, June 6, 1824. Preston Ledger, 1795–1817, account with Jonathan Dickerman, January 24, 1807. John Doolittle Account Book, Wallingford, Connecticut, 1816–1837, account with Harmon Williams, March 19, 1830, DCM. Loomis Account Book, accounts with Lemuel Welch, November 4, 1801, and Ebenezer Wiman Jr., February 18, 1808.

70. Robert Cowan Bill to Aaron Wait, Salem, Massachusetts, November 30, 1802, Aaron Wait Papers, PEM. John Roulstone Bills to Caleb Davis, Esq., Boston, August 22, 1787, and January 1788, Davis Papers. William Bentley Ledger, Butternuts, New York, 1812–1815, account with Cornelius Jenny, July 28, 1812, DCM. Dominy Account Book and Daybook, accounts with Nathaniel Hunting, November 21, 1838, and Thomas Baker, October 2, 1817. William Kip Bills to Robert R. Livingston, Red Hook, New York, May 29 and November 7, 1833, Livingston Papers.

71. Slover and Taylor Bill to Nicholas Low, New York, April 10, 1805, Nicholas Low Papers, Rutgers University Library, New Brunswick, New Jersey. Knight Account Book, account with Zebulon Pease, March 10, 1801. Cole Account Book, account with Daniel Miles, August 1797. Jonathan Gavit Bill to Timothy Orne, Salem, Massachusetts, February 8, 1764, Timothy Orne Papers, PEM. William Capron Bill to Albert C. Greene, East Greenwich, Rhode Island, October 6, 1826, Greene Papers. Miles Benjamin Daybook and Ledger, Cooperstown, New York, 1821–1829, account with Jesse Graves, May 9, 1821, NYSHA. Cheney Ledger, 1799–1817, account with Elijah Wadsworth, January 25, 1800. J. Townsend Jr. Ledger, 1750–1778, account with Abraham Dennis, February 13, 1758. William Savery Bill to Joseph Pemberton, Philadelphia, June 15, 1774, Pemberton Papers. Boynton Ledger, 1817–1847, account with Jonathan H. Hubbard, March 1836. Jenkins Account Book, account with Capt. Phineas Pond, October 25, 1815. Preston Ledger, 1811–1842, account with Capt. Phineas Pond, October 25, 1815. Philemon Hinman Account Book, Plymouth, Connecticut, 1804–1817, account with Marcus Gaylor, August 21, 1812, CHS. Henry Mann Bill to Maj. Thomas Jones, Richmond, Virginia, March 8, 1790, Papers of the Jones Family of Northumberland County, Virginia, LC.

72. Moyers and Rich Account Book, account with Daniel Wiseley, August 13, 1834. Preston Ledger, 1795–1817, account with Jotham Tuttle, November 16, 1811. A. Taylor Account Book, account with Barnabas Adams, November 6, 1818. J. Townsend Jr. Ledger, 1750–1778, account with Matthew Cozzens, June 25, 1757. Richard Johns Bill to Deborah Morris, Philadelphia, September 27, 1767, Gratz Collection, HSP. Dominy Account Book and Daybook, account with Nathaniel Hunting, December 26, 1842.

73. Boynton Ledger, 1817–1847, account with Jonathan Chase, May 23, 1825. J. E. Townsend Ledger, 1794–1802, account with Capt. William Gardner, April 2, 1801. Evans Daybook, 1774–1781, account with [first name unknown] West, January 7, 1778. Benjamin Baker Account Book, Newport, Rhode Island, 1760–1792, account with Thomas Claggitt (clockmaker), April 2, 1774, NHS. Cheney Daybook, 1807–1813, account with Daniel Huntington, October 13, 1807. Houghton Ledger, account with George Sills, Esq., May 21, 1824. J. E. Townsend Daybook, 1778–1803, account with Simon Newton, February 6, 1801.

74. J. Avery Account Book, account with Thomas Stebbins, November 1834. Gilbert Account Book, account with Thaddeus Beach, January 3, 1837. Lyell Account Book, account with Thomas Post, June 1804. Jenkins Daybook, account with Capt. Isaac Downing, December 11, 1839.

75. Jonathan C. Loomis Account Book, Whately, Massachusetts, 1808–1822, account with Elihu Harvey, after June 11, 1813, DCM. Boynton Account Book, 1810–1817, account with Leonard Spaulding, August 2, 1813. Baker Account Book, account with Thomas Claggitt, early 1772. David Evans Daybook, Philadelphia, 1784–1806, account with John Davis (upholsterer), April 9, 1791, HSP.

76. J. E. Townsend Daybook, 1778–1803, account with Mr. Martinberry, July 19, 1783. Baker Account Book, account with Jacob Rodriguez Rivera, June 6, 1783. Nathaniel Appleton Bill to Moses Townsend, Salem, Massachusetts, May 20, 1836, Papers of Nathaniel Appleton, PEM. Jacob Brouwer Bill to Nicholas Low, New York, June 4, 1814, Low Papers (Rutgers). Cheney Ledger, 1799–1817, account with Elijah Wadsworth, January 25, 1800. J. R. Townsend Daybook, 1778–1803, account with Simon Newton, June 8, 1802. Danforth Ledger, account with Dr. Joseph Lee, January 16, 1797. Dominy Account and Daybook, account with Thomas Baker, December 9, 1825.

77. Evans Daybook, 1774–1781, account with Owen Biddle, February 9, 1776. Advertisements of John Elliott Jr., *Pennsylvania Journal* (Philadelphia), July 14, 1784, and James Reynolds, *Pennsylvania Gazette* (Philadelphia), May 12, 1784, both as quoted in *The Arts and Crafts in Philadelphia, Maryland, and South Carolina, 1721–1785*, compiled by Alfred Coxe Prime (Philadelphia: Walpole Society, 1929), p. 197. Samuel Powel III Ledger, Philadelphia, 1760–1774, account with James Reynolds, ca. early 1770s, Library Company of Philadelphia.

78. John Spurlock Bill to Maj. Thomas Jones, prob. Northumberland County, Virginia, October 1, 1791, Jones Family Papers. Dominy Account Book and Daybook, account with Eli Parsons, June 7, 1815. Danforth Ledger, account with Jabez Bowen, August 17, 1801. Daniel Trotter Bill to Stephen Girard, Philadelphia, June 11, 1793, Girard Papers. J. Townsend Jr. Ledger, 1750–1778, account with Philip Wanton, March 28, 1752. Jonathan Gillett Account Book, Canaan, Connecticut, 1782–1789, account with Ashbell Lane, April 2, 1785, DCM. Jonathan Kettell Account Book, Newburyport, Massachusetts, 1781–1794, account with Angier March, October 6, 1797, PEM.

79. Houghton Ledger, account with Robert Henry, July 19, 1817. John Elliott Sr. Bill to Hollingsworth and Rudolph, Philadelphia, April 6, 1768, Harrold C. Gillingham Collection, HSP. Robbins Account Book, account with Thomas C. Perkins, April 10, 1834.

80. Abraham S. Egerton Bill to Nicholas Low, New York, March 10, 1824, Low Collection. John Elliott Sr. Bill to Gen. John Cadwalader, Philadelphia, July 8, 1772, Cadwalader Papers, Gen. John Cadwalader.

81. John Penn Receipt Book, Philadelphia, 1774–1849, account with James Reynolds, December 9, 1771, Physick Papers, LC. John Elliott Jr. Bill to Hannah Morris, Philadelphia, July 3, 1779, Gillingham Collection. Charles Del Vecchio Bill to James L. Brinckerhoff, New York, October 7, 1816, Papers of Robert Troup, NYPL. Sheraton, *Cabinet Dictionary*, 2: 271. Cumberland and Beazor Bill to Nicholas Low, New York, November 17, 1796, Low Collection.

82. E. H. Holmes Ledger, 1825–1830, account with Henry D. Braddock Jr., November 8, 1826. Holcomb Account Book, account with Eliphalet Fuller, March 1811. Charles N. Robinson Bills to Charles Wistar, Philadelphia, June 18 and 28, 1830, Charles Wistar Papers, DCM. Bills of P. Vannuck, October 7, 1809, and Barnard Cermenati, April 19, 1810, to Joshua Ward, Salem, Massachusetts, Ward Family Manuscripts, PEM. Cumberland and Beazor Bill to Nicholas Low, New York, November 17, 1796, Low Collection.

83. William Sherman Bill to Stephen Girard, Philadelphia, December 2, 1824, Girard Papers. Daniel and Samuel Proud Daybook and Ledger, Providence, Rhode Island, 1810–1834, account with Philip Lewis, July 11, 1828, RIHS. J. E. Townsend Ledger, 1778–1794, account with Henry Barber, January 11, 1793. C. C. Robinson Daybook, account with Hugh Mc[illegible], June 22, 1821. Boynton Ledger, 1817–1847, account with Joseph Flood, June 1, 1825. Moyers and Rich Account Book, credit listing for E. M. D. Reed, July 12, 1837. Knight Account Book, account with Nehemiah Prudden, April 7, 1803. Grinnell and Taylor Bills to Rev. Enos Hitchcock, Providence, Rhode Island, May 9 and December 3, 1789, as published in Joseph K. Ott, "Still More Notes on Rhode Island Cabinetmakers and Allied Craftsmen," *Rhode Island History* 28, no. 4 (November 1969): 113.

84. Charles Del Vecchio Bill to Robert L. Livingston, New York, June 13, 1815, Livingston Papers. Charles N. Robinson Bill to John Cadwalader, Esq., Philadelphia, June 1, 1836, Cadwalader Papers, Judge John Cadwalader. David Kennedy Bill to John Francis, Philadelphia, February 20, 1821, Cadwalader Papers, Gen. Thomas Cadwalader. S. Powel III Ledger, accounts with James Reynolds, ca. early 1770s, and Robert Kennedy, April 1770. James Hamil-

ton Daybook, Philadelphia, 1768–1782, account with Robert Kennedy, June 1768, James Hamilton Papers, HSP. Edmund Physick Receipt Book, Philadelphia, 1766–1780, account with Robert Kennedy, April 1768, Physick Papers. Robert Kennedy Bill to William Barrell, Philadelphia, before 1772, Collins Papers.

85. Helen Comstock, "Venetian Blinds in the Eighteenth Century," in *The Antiques Book*, edited by Alice Winchester (New York: Bonanza Books, 1950), pp. 261–65. Carl Dreppard, *First Reader for Antique Collectors* (Garden City, N.Y.: Doubleday, 1946), p. 120. John A. H. Sweeney, *Winterthur Illustrated* (Wilmington, Del.: Winterthur Museum, 1963), p. 121.

86. William Savery Bill to Joseph Pemberton, Philadelphia, February 2, 1775, Pemberton Papers; David Evans Daybook, Philadelphia, 1796–1812, account with Ann Head, April 12, 1796, HSP. Advertisement of C. Alder, *Federal Gazette* (Philadelphia), July 14, 1797, as quoted in Prime, comp., *Arts and Crafts in Philadelphia, Maryland, and South Carolina, 1786–1800*, p. 215. Lyell Account Book, account with Jane Micheau, June 25, 1808. Scadin Daybook, 1829–1831, account with Henry Scott, May 13, 1830. E. H. Holmes Ledger, 1825–1830, accounts with widow Patty Hayden, September 29 and October 3, 1827.

87. Jacob Sass Bill to Peter Trezevant, Charleston, South Carolina, November 20, 1806, as published in Rauschenberg and Bivins, *Furniture of Charleston*, 3: 1208. Timothy M. and John Minott Bill to David S. Greenough, Boston, August 19, 1796, Greenough Papers. George Landon Daybook and Ledger, Erie, Pennsylvania, 1813–1832, account with Thomas H. Sill, February 23, 1818, DCM. Boynton Ledger, 1811–1817, account with Stephen Child, June 15, 1811. Charles N. Robinson Bill to James J. Skerrett, Philadelphia, November 2, 1825, Loudon Papers.

88. Richard Johns Bill to Deborah Morris, Philadelphia, July 8, 1767, Gratz Collection. Michael Allison Bill to Gerald Beekman, New York, April 3, 1828, White-Beekman Papers. Grinnell and Taylor Bill to Rev. Enos Hitchcock, Providence, Rhode Island, July 20, 1789, as published in Ott, "Still More Notes," p. 113. Jacob Brouwer Bill to Nicholas Low, New York, June 1, 1797, Low Collection.

89. A. Taylor Account Book, account with Oliver Ives, January 14, 1819. J. Durand Account Book, account with Joshua Cove, December 3, 1761. Houghton Ledger, account with widow Abigail Wheeler, March 1826. J. Townsend Jr. Ledger, 1750–1778, account with Jacob Rodriguez Rivera, March 15, 1757. H. Taylor Account Book, account with Thomas Beaumont, March 15, 1835.

90. Hawley Account Book, account with Epenetus How, December 19, 1787. Daniel and Samuel Proud Ledger, Providence, Rhode Island, 1770–1825 (with William Proud until 1779), accounts with Charles Boller, April 11 and July 3, 1779, RIHS. William Lander Bill to Capt. Joseph Bowditch, Salem, Massachusetts, January 1739, Capt. Joseph Bowditch Manuscripts, PEM. R. Loomis Account Book, account with Dr. Amos Granger, October 1804. Boynton Ledger, 1817–1847, account with Henry Roby, September 15, 1827. Lewis Chandler Account Book, Bernardston, Massachusetts, 1814–1826, account with Aaron Grover, 1822, DCM. Ross Account Book, account with Asa Baker, February 1, 1802. Louise Conway Belden, *The Festive Tradition* (New York: W. W. Norton for the Winterthur Museum, 1983), pp. 173–74.

91. H. Taylor Account Book, account with Margaret Pearce, July 20, 1836.

92. Hawley Account Book, account with Moses Ingersoll, August 15, 1793. Douglas Account Book, account with Benjamin Beckwith, November 30, 1825. Preston Ledger, 1795–1817, account with Cornelius Cook, April 21, 1803. Danforth Ledger, account with Andrew Dexter, December 3, 1794. J. E. Townsend Daybook, 1778–1803, account with Philip Morse, September 22, 1781. R. Loomis Account Book, account with Deborah Harmon, June 1820. Aaron Ogden Account Book, Newark, New Jersey, 1804–1823, account with John Mitchell, April 30, 1817, private collection (microfilm DCM). Jesse Tuttle Daybook, North Haven, Connecticut, 1815–1826, account with Peter Eastman, Esq., June 1, 1816, CHS. Wilder Daybook and Ledger, account with Aaron Davis, June 22, 1837. Ellinger Account Book, account with John Bixler, October 5, 1833. Landon Daybook and Ledger, account with Adam Lowry, August 11, 1817.

93. Sheraton, *Dictionary*, 2: 320. Nehemiah Munroe Bill to Maj. William Erving, Roxbury, Massachusetts, August 18, 1788, Greenough Papers. Robert Borland Bill to Richard Blow, Portsmouth, Virginia, January 10, 1791, Blow Papers. J. Townsend Jr. Daybook, 1762–1778, account with Nathaniel Stone, May 25, 1772. Boynton Ledger, 1810–1817, account with John Simonds, March 11, 1816.

94. J. E. Townsend Daybook, 1803–1828, account with Harvey Sessions, December 5, 1821. Isaac Nichols Bill to Gen. Henry Knox, New York, April 13, 1790, Knox Papers.

95. Loomis Account Book, account with Benajah Owen, April 1811. James Gere Ledger, Groton, Connecticut, 1809–1839, credit listing for Allyn Chapman, July 3, 1814, CSL. Houghton

Ledger, 1816–1827, account with widow Abigail Wheeler, July 14, 1824. Holcomb Account Book, account with Joshua Weaver, July 1821. J. E. Townsend Daybook, 1778–1803, account with Mrs. Sarah Ingraham, March 20, 1798.

96. Jesse Tuttle Account Book, North Haven, Connecticut, 1792–1813, account with Jonathan Tuttle, June 13, 1808, CHS. Nathan Lucas Ledger, Kingston, Massachusetts, 1800–1853, account with Jedidiah Holmes, July 13, 1824, DCM. George Claypoole Bill to Samuel Meredith, Philadelphia, July 5, 1782, Clymer-Meredith-Read Papers. Filer Account Book, account with Benjamin Wright, October 10, 1809. Cheney Daybook, 1802–1807, account with Oliver Wolcott, December 3, 1802. J. E. Townsend Daybook, 1778–1803, account with Jeremiah Clark, April 28, 1792. *Prices of Cabinet and Chair Work* (1772), p. 33.

97. Dominy Account Book and Daybook, account with Sarah Gardiner, September 3, 1818. Danforth Ledger, account with Amos Throop, February 13, 1798. J. E. Townsend Daybook, 1778–1803, accounts with George Clark, August 21, 1798, and Joseph Smith, June 17, 1780.

98. Danforth Ledger, account with Jabez Bowen, August 4, 1806. J. E. Townsend Ledger, 1778–1794, account with John Franklin, June 24, 1785. Abraham Overholt Account Book, Plumstead Township, Bucks County, Pennsylvania, 1790–1833, account with Karla Zelner, February 5, 1798, as published in Keyser et al., *Accounts of Two Pennsylvania German Furniture Makers,* p. 10. Ellinger Account Book, account with Jacob Early, October 1, 1833.

99. Barnes Account Book, account with Samuel Eells (Ellis?), April 16, 1822. D. and S. Proud Ledger, 1770–1825, account with Benjamin Bourne, January 2, 1795. Baker Account Book, account with Samuel Mosers, September 1770.

100. J. E. Townsend Daybook, 1778–1803, account with Mary Collins, September 22, 1795. Danforth Ledger, accounts with Jabez Bowen, November 13, 1804; William Billings, August 18, 1791; and Gershom Jones, September 3, 1795.

101. Joshua Delaplaine Account Book, New York, 1720s–1770s, account with Dr. Brownjohn, 1741, N-YHS. Robert Borland Bill to Richard Blow, Portsmouth, Virginia, April 29, 1791, Blow Papers. J. Townsend Jr. Daybook, 1762–1778, accounts with Job Howland, May 14, 1769, and William Townsend, November 22, 1765.

102. Daniel Trotter Bill to Stephen Girard, Philadelphia, February 17, 1790, Girard Papers. Samuel Matthews Bill to Charles Norris, Philadelphia, 1761, Norris Family Accounts, HSP. Samuel Cheever Bill to John Derby, Salem, Massachusetts, November 19, 1804, Derby Papers, PEM. Henry Mann Bill to Maj. Thomas Jones, Richmond, Virginia, January 6, 1790, Jones Family Papers.

103. J. Durand Account Book, account with Samuel Sanford, September 23, 1762. Jacob Falconer Bill to John Cadwalader, probably Kent County, Maryland, October 6, 1778, Cadwalader Collection, Gen. John Cadwalader. Landon Daybook and Ledger, account with George W. Gallagher, November 4, 1829.

104. D. and S. Proud Ledger, 1770–1825, account with Grindale Reynolds, January 25, 1791, and Ledger, 1810–1834, account with Galend Richmond, January 2, 1819. J. E. Townsend Ledger, 1778–1794, accounts with Henry Barber, September 8, 1791, and Daniel Antony, January 22, 1790. J. Townsend Jr. Daybook, 1762–1778, account with B. Nichols, May 14, 1766. Ross Account Book, account with Aaron Smith, January 27, 1792. Tobey Daybook, account with John Blackwell, February 14, 1785. Lindsey Ledger, account with Christopher Bubier, December 16, 1745.

105. James Gillingham Bill to William Barrell, Philadelphia, October 7, 1766, Collins Papers. J. E. Townsend Daybook, 1778–1803, account with William Roberson, September 6, 1779. Hawley Account Book, account with Ebenezer Olmstead, January 21, 1787. Nathaniel Heath Account Book, Warren and Barrington, Rhode Island, 1767–1791, account with Thomas Allen, 1775, RIHS. Judkins and Senter Bill to Jacob Wendell, Portsmouth, New Hampshire, April 14, 1814, Wendell Papers, BL. Shaw and Chisholm Bill to James Brice, Esq., Annapolis, Maryland, April 26, 1775, Brice-Jennings Papers, Maryland Historical Society, Baltimore. Douglas Account Book, account with Arnold Crane, March 13, 1813. Ross Account Book, accounts with Aaron Smith, December 2, 1786, and April 29, 1785. Preston Ledger, 1811–1842, account with Samuel Cook, September 3, 1814.

106. Elisha Adams Bill to David S. Greenough, Boston, June 1810, Greenough Papers. J. E. Townsend Daybook, 1778–1803, account with Capt. John Oldfield, December 30, 1784. Cheney Ledger, 1799–1817, account with Tapping Reeve, August 1799. Bills to Gen. John Cadwalader, Philadelphia, from Thomas Affleck, May 10, 1784, and January 14, 1771, and Robert Jewell, December 4, 1775, Cadwalader Papers, Gen. John Cadwalader. *Prices of Cabinet and Chair Work* (1772), p. 22. Robert Borland Bill to Richard Blow, Portsmouth, Virginia, ca. 1789,

and George Seddon and Son Invoice of Shipped Furniture, London, England, August 15, 1785, Blow Papers.

107. Nina Fletcher Little, *Country Arts in Early American Homes* (New York: E. P. Dutton, 1975), pp. 178–91.

108. Elisha Adams Bill to David S. Greenough, Boston, April 1811, Greenough Papers. Little, *Country Arts,* p. 189.

109. Benjamin Bardine Bill to William Arnold, East Greenwich, Rhode Island, October 10, 1792, Greene Collection. Filer Account Book, account with James Lynch, February 22, 1807. Barnes Account Book, account with Dr. Charles Dyer, May 21, 1823. Boynton Ledger, 1810–1817, accounts with Frederick Pettes, February 8, 1813, and Alden Spooner, August 9, 1813, and Boynton Ledger, 1817–1847, account with Mrs. Sarah Townsend, August 29, 1817. Holcomb Account Book, accounts with Capt. Dan Smith, February 17, 1821, and V. P. Van Rensselaer, June 2, 1822.

110. Cheney Ledger, 1799–1817, account with Caleb Bacon, September 25, 1799. Evans Daybook, 1774–1781, account with Benjamin Rittenhouse, March 29, 1776. J. E. Townsend Ledger, 1778–1794, account with John Bass, January 13, 1783. Landon Daybook and Ledger, account with John C. Wallace, May 20, 1823. Merrifield Account Book, account with H. B. Haswell, January 22, 1841.

111. Jacob Hinsdale Ledger, Harwinton, Connecticut, 1723–1774, account with Robert Webster, April 1731, SL. Wilder Daybook and Ledger, account with Nathan P. Cummings, April 15, 1843. Jonathan Dart Account Book, New London, Connecticut, 1793–1800, account with George Daniels, March 1, 1800, CHS. Robert Crage Ledger, Leicester, Massachusetts, 1757–1781, accounts with Matthew Scott, July 1763, and Samuel Richardson, August 1769, OSV. Lucas Ledger, account with Pelham Brewster, June 30, 1823.

112. Overholt Account Book, accounts with Philip Kraut, January 24, 1811, and David Hoch, February 15, 1828, as published in Keyser et al., *Accounts of Two Pennsylvania German Furniture Makers,* pp. 14, 19. Samuel Fithian Ware Account Book, Lower Township, Cape May County, New Jersey, 1826–1849, account with Dr. R. Wales, October 18, 1828, DCM.

113. Boynton Ledger, 1810–1817, account with Samuel Sprague, October 28, 1813. Preston Ledger, 1811–1842, account with Samuel Johnson, November 16, 1815. Carr Account Book, account with Timothy Chase, March 5, 1802. John Paine Account Book, Southold, Long Island, New York, 1761–1815, account with Ezra L'hommedieu, May 1786, Institute for Colonial Studies, State University of New York at Stony Brook (loan). Crage Ledger, account with Matthew Scott, March 1763. J. E. Townsend Ledger, 1778–1794, accounts with William Potter, July 5, 1787, and Daniel Antony, March 26, 1791. Dominy Account Book and Daybook, accounts with Isaac Barnes, February 21, 1818, Ebenezer Philips, April 2, 1816, and Elisha Miller, November 28, 1817.

114. Crage Ledger, accounts with Samuel Richardson, August 1769, and John Brown, August 10, 1769.

115. Douglas Account Book, account with Allyn Wilcox, October 27, 1811. Paine Account Book, accounts with William Hubbard, February 17, 1808, and Thomas Torey, October 29, 1810. Overholt Account Book, account with Henrich Meyer, October 5, 1792, as published in Keyser et al., *Accounts of Two Pennsylvania German Furniture Makers,* p. 7.

116. Dominy Account Book and Daybook, accounts with Eli Parsons, March 4, 1815, Elisha Miller, April 3, 1818, and Isaac Hedges, August 28, 1817. A. Low Account Book, account with Joseph Oatton, July 6, 1798. Overholt Account Book, accounts with Henrich Meyer, October 15, 1792, and Johannes Meyer, June 10, 1791, as published in Keyser et al., *Accounts of Two Pennsylvania German Furniture Makers,* pp. 4, 7. J. E. Townsend Ledger, 1778–1794, account with William Potter, December 29, 1786.

117. Philip Deland Account Book, West Brookfield, Massachusetts, 1812–1846, account with Horace F. Rich, May 16, 1839, OSV. Preston Ledger, 1795–1817, account with Cornelius Cook, February 7, 1803. Thomas Pratt Account Book, Malden, Massachusetts, 1730–1768, account with Capt. Samuel Wait, ca. 1735, DCM. Tiffany Account Book, accounts with Capt. Samuel Trapp, May 1757, and Lt. Gershom Breed, May 4, 1757. Gifford and Scotland Bill to Walter Livingston, New York, March 13, 1792, Livingston Papers.

118. Davison Ledger, account with Daniel Clark, August 7, 1795. Danforth Ledger, account with Andrew Dexter, July 19, 1790. J. E. Townsend Daybook, 1778–1803, account with George Clark, July 19, 1799.

119. S. Durand Account Book, account with Sarah Newton, June 24, 1818. Joseph Stone Bill to Capt. William Arnold, East Greenwich, Rhode Island, July 17, 1790, Greene Collection.

Overholt Account Book, accounts with David Hoch, February 4, 1826, and Samuel Frey, August 25, 1827, as published in Keyser et al., *Accounts of Two Pennsylvania German Furniture Makers,* p. 19. Dominy Account Book and Daybook, account with Eli Parsons, May 29, 1818. J. E. Townsend Ledger, 1778–1794, account with William Carcell, June 25, 1788.

120. Tiffany Account Book, accounts with John Elderkin, September 11, 1755, and January 5, 1756. Joseph Griswold Daybook, Buckland, Massachusetts, 1816–1843, account with Joseph Spaulding, October 1821, private collection (microfilm DCM). Houghton Ledger, 1816–1827, account with widow Abigail Wheeler, October 1822. Lyell Account Book, account with Obediah Bowne, April 11, 1806.

121. J. E. Townsend Daybook, 1778–1803, account with Morey Biglay, June 29, 1799. Jules D. Prown, *John Singleton Copley* (Meriden, Conn.: Meriden Gravure, 1965), pp. 74, 77. Lyell Account Book, accounts with David A. Cumming, February 14, 1805, and John B. Graves, July 8, 1807.

122. Samuel Matthews Bill to Charles Norris, Philadelphia, 1761, Norris Family Accounts. Symonds Account Book, account with Benjamin Magry, March 12, 1752. J. Townsend Jr. Ledger, 1750–1778, account with Col. Joseph Wanton, May 26, 1770.

123. J. Durand Account Book, account with John Marshall, October 19, 1767. Hawley Account Book, account with Ezra Meed, July 23, 1784. Tobey Daybook, accounts with Capt. Obed Nye, October 1, 1797, and Jirah Swift, April 15, 1775. J. E. Townsend Daybook, 1778–1803, account with William Douglass, December 2, 1799, and Ledger, 1778–1794, account with Joseph Beeby, October 5, 1779. Richard Booker Bill to St. George Tucker, Williamsburg, Virginia, July 22, 1791, Tucker-Coleman Collection.

124. Cheney Ledger, 1799–1817, account with Tapping Reeve, February 1, 1800. Boynton Ledger, 1810–1817, accounts with Leonard Cummings, May 31, 1816, and Thomas Leverett and Son, March 20, 1817, and Ledger, 1817–1847, account with Jonathan H. Hubbard, June 22, 1837. Nina Fletcher Little, *Neat and Tidy* (New York: E. P. Dutton, 1980), pp. 97–109.

125. Danforth Ledger, account with Andrew Dexter, July 26, 1797. Rookesby Roberts Bill to St. George Tucker, Williamsburg, Virginia, January 29, 1795, Tucker-Coleman Collection. Barnes Account Book, accounts with Samuel Williams, August 17, 1821, and Mr. G. Burrows, June 24, 1823. Boynton Ledger, 1811–1817, account with Thomas Leverett and Son, March 20, 1817. Mark Pitman Bill to Charles Moses Endicott, Salem, Massachusetts, July 9, 1839, Charles Moses Endicott Papers, PEM. J. E. Townsend Daybook, 1778–1803, account with Simon Newton, February 1, 1800. Kettell Account Book, account with Thomas Pearson, ca. January 1793.

126. Danforth Ledger, account with Benjamin Gladding, September 3, 1799. William Savery Bill to Joseph Pemberton, Philadelphia, July 12, 1775, Pemberton Papers. J. E. Townsend Daybook, 1803–1828, account with Samuel Tygatt, September 29, 1804. Benjamin Ellery Bill to Estate of Eliakim Prindel, Gloucester, Massachusetts, September 1815, Rogers Papers. Nicholas Silberg Bill to William Wragg, Esq., Charleston, South Carolina, August–November 1799, as quoted in Rauschenberg and Bivins, *Furniture of Charleston,* 3: 1217. Evans Daybook, 1796–1812, account with William Guier, December 31, 1801. Hodghton and Company Bill to Samuel Larned, Lima, Peru, September 27, 1832, Greene Collection.

127. Alexander Edward Bill to Grant Webster, Boston, April 12, 1785, Greenough Papers. Preston Ledger, 1811–1842, account with Capt. Phineas Pond, July 20, 1813. James Poupard Bill to Gen. John Cadwalader, Philadelphia, December 14, 1773, Cadwalader Collection, Gen. John Cadwalader. William Jenkins Bill to Joshua Ward, Salem, Massachusetts, August 28, 1792, Joshua Ward Papers, PEM. Lindsey Ledger, account with Jacob Fowle, July 27, 1762. J. Townsend Jr. Ledger, 1750–1778, account with William Roberson, January 6, 1758, and Daybook, 1762–1778, account with Stephen Wanton, September 27, 1762. James Linacre Bill to John Sanders, Albany, New York, February 9, 1795, Sanders Papers, N-YHS. Richard Johns Bill to Deborah Morris, Philadelphia, September 27, 1767, Gratz Collection. William Savery Bill to Joseph Pemberton, Philadelphia, October 23, 1775, Pemberton Papers. Daniel Trotter Bill to Stephen Girard, Philadelphia, October 8, 1782, Girard Papers.

128. J. E. Townsend Daybook, 1778–1803, accounts with Dr. Jonathan Easton, February 3 and May 12, 1798, and Doctor Turner, July 30, 1800. Ebenezer Smith Jr. Bills to Robert Rantoul, Beverly, Massachusetts, February 22, 1806, October 1, 1796, and February 4, 1797, Rantoul Papers.

129. Little, *Neat and Tidy,* pp. 31–39. Parkhurst Account Book, account with Job Pearce, June 29, 1824. Lyell Account Book, account with John Lang, February 1804. G. and D. Cleveland Bill to Mrs. Jones, Providence, Rhode Island, March 15, 1838, Greene Collection. Preston

Ledger, 1795–1817, account with widow of Timothy Carrington, May 18, 1807. J. E. Townsend Daybook, 1778–1803, account with Peter Philips, November 1, 1794. Knight Account Book, account with Samuel Reynolds, August 30, 1797.

130. Cheney Daybook, 1807–1813, account with Col. Benjamin Tallmadge, May 24, 1811. T. A. Guttwaldt Bill to Nicholas Low, New York, February 14, 182[?], Low Collection. Duncan Phyfe Bill to James L. Brinckerhoff, New York, May 6, 1816, Troup Papers. Pennell Beale Bill to Gen. Henry Knox, Philadelphia, September 24, 1791, Knox Papers. Loud and Brothers Bills to James J. Skerrett, Philadelphia, April 28, 1832, and November 9, 1833, Loudoun Papers.

131. Robbins Account Book, account with William James Hamisly, April 5, 1834. Barnes Account Book, account with Mrs. Esther Williams, June 20, 1824. Lyell Account Book, account with James B. Graves, November 4, 1809. Cheney Daybook, 1807–1813, account with Col. Benjamin Tallmadge, May 24, 1811. Duncan Phyfe Bills to James L. Brinckerhoff, New York, May 6 and 11, 1816, Troup Papers. Loud and Brothers Bills to James J. Skerrett, Philadelphia, April 28, 1832, and November 9, 1833, Loudoun Papers.

132. John Green Account Book, Southampton, Long Island, New York, 1790–1803, account with Ebenezer Bourne, October 13, 1791, DCM. Boynton Ledger, 1810–1817, accounts with Curtis and Coolidge, October 26, 1813, and Sewell Cutting, June 15, 1814. Kettell Account Book, account with Joshua Greenleaf, March 1794. J. E. Townsend Daybook, 1778–1803, accounts with Richard Clark, December 28, 1795, and Lewis Builod, February 23, 1801. E. H. Holmes Daybook, 1825–1830, account with Robert F. Denison, February 6, 1827. Short Account Book, account with Amos Kimball, April 15, 1816.

133. Advertisement of Isaac Greenwood, *Boston Gazette* (Massachusetts), June 20, 1763, and advertisement for house furnishings, *Boston Gazette,* January 26, 1761, both as quoted in *The Arts and Crafts in New England, 1704–1775,* compiled by George Francis Dow (Topsfield, Mass.: Wayside Press, 1927), pp. 287, 170. Advertisement for lost umbrella, *New-York Journal or the General Advertiser,* June 30, 1774, as quoted in *The Arts and Crafts in New York, 1726–1776,* compiled by Rita S. Gottesman (1938; reprint, New York: Da Capo Press, 1970), p. 334. J. E. Townsend Daybook, 1778–1803, account with Mr. Smith, August 16, 1799. Landon Account Book, account with P. S. V. Hammot, September 11, 1817. Preston Ledger, 1795–1817, account with Capt. Phineas Pond, August 11, 1810. Dominy Account Book and Daybook, account with Isaac Barnes, September 1817. Samuel Matthews Bill to Charles Norris, Philadelphia, August 1766, Norris Family Accounts. Samuel Benge Bill to Stephen Girard, Philadelphia, 1790s, Girard Papers. Samuel Benge Bill to Gen. Henry Knox, Philadelphia, June 3, 1793, Knox Papers.

134. William Savery Bill to Joseph Pemberton, Philadelphia, January 1, 1774, Pemberton Papers. Samuel Matthews Bill to Charles Norris, Philadelphia, September 1763, Norris Family Accounts. Philip Warren Bill to Gen. Thomas Cadwalader, Philadelphia, November 11, 1823, Cadwalader Papers, Gen Thomas Cadwalader.

135. J. Townsend Jr. Ledger, 1750–1778, account with Jacob Rodriguez Rivera, March 16, 1757. Lyell Account Book, account with Richard J. Tucker, October 27, 1808. J. E. Townsend Daybook, 1803–1828, account with Joseph Ailsworth, December 27, 1823.

136. J. E. Townsend Daybook, 1778–1803, accounts with William Douglass, July 27 and August 18, 1797. Advertisement of John Ernst Juncken, *New-York Gazette or the Weekly Post-Boy,* January 1, 1759, as quoted in Gottesman, comp., *Arts and Crafts in New York, 1726–1776,* p. 254. J. E. Townsend Daybook, 1778–1803, account with Martha Smith, October 5, 1802; J. Townsend Jr. Daybook, 1762–1768, account with John Warren, June 29, 1765. Merrifield Account Book, account with Mr. Kelso, April 30, 1836. C. C. Robinson Daybook, account with John White, February 22, 1816. Jane Carson, *Colonial Virginians at Play* (Williamsburg, Va.: Colonial Williamsburg, 1965), pp. 100–101. Elisabeth Donaghy Garrett, *At Home: The American Family, 1750–1870* (New York: Harry N. Abrams, 1990), pp. 73, 92, 106. Daniel Trotter Bills to John Girard, Philadelphia, February 15, 1788, Girard Papers.

Book Reviews

Frances Gruber Safford. *American Furniture in the Metropolitan Museum of Art.* Vol. 1. *Early Colonial Period: The Seventeenth-Century and William and Mary Styles.* New York: Metropolitan Museum of Art; New Haven: Yale University Press, 2007. xii + 451 pp.; 159 color illus., 117 bw illus., 45 line drawings, appendixes, concordance, bibliography, index. $90.00.

The seventeenth- and early-eighteenth-century American furniture at the Metropolitan Museum of Art has long been a subject of study for those interested in this period. Examples from the collection are included in all of the early major published works on the subject, among them Irving W. Lyon's *The Colonial Furniture of New England* (1891), Luke Vincent Lockwood's *Colonial Furniture in America* (1901), and Wallace Nutting's *Furniture of the Pilgrim Century* (1921) and *Furniture Treasury* (1928–33). Indeed, the collection continues to be cited in most modern works on the topic. Now Frances Gruber Safford's long-awaited *American Furniture in the Metropolitan Museum of Art*, vol. 1, *Early Colonial Period: The Seventeenth-Century and William and Mary Styles* has arrived, and it has proven to be worth the wait. In a quirk of publishing, this volume is number one in the series of catalogues documenting the Metropolitan's American collection, although its publication follows some fifteen years after the appearance of volume two. No matter. In one sense, we benefit from its being so long in the making: the production quality is excellent. Among other attributes, Safford's book has outstanding photography courtesy of Gavin Ashworth, well known to readers of *American Furniture*.

After first browsing random entries in the book, I took the time to go back and read the introductory material. The Notes on the Catalogue are just that. But there we learn that in this catalogue "right" means "proper left" and "left" means "proper right"—a useful bit of information for those keeping close track of the nuances of the objects.

The introduction is excellent. It gives a readable and informative synopsis of the history of the collection. The bulk of the collection is quite old, having been put together in the late nineteenth and early twentieth centuries. Safford details the forming of the American Wing at the Metropolitan and the arrangements to purchase the collection of Boston lawyer H. Eugene Bolles (1853–1910) in 1909. The Bolles collection accounts for half of the pieces in the catalogue. The next largest chunk is made up of the furniture donated by Natalie K. (Mrs. J. Insley) Blair, whose collection went to the museum in the 1940s and early 1950s.

Intertwined in the story of the collection's formation and how it went to the museum is the detailed description of factors accounting for the condition of many of the objects. "Original surface" need not apply. Like the Charles Hitchcock Tyler collection of early furniture at the Museum of Fine Arts, Boston, much of this collection has been reworked and refinished to a fare-thee-well. Hindsight being the best sight, modern collectors now eschew so much restoration, but it might very well be that these works would not have survived or been recovered but for the collectors in the period from the 1880s to the 1920s who pursued this furniture so diligently.

The concluding paragraph of the second section succinctly states the purpose of the book: "This volume is intended to provide a careful and detailed record of the physical and design aspects of the individual pieces included and of their history and to serve as a work of reference" (p. 10). The book achieves this goal nicely. Each entry has a photograph of the object, a textual entry, and then descriptions of its construction, condition, woods, dimensions, exhibition history, references, and provenance.

The catalogue is broken into three sections: Seating Furniture, Tables, and Case Furniture. Each of these sections is then further grouped into chapters, such as "Turned Chairs with a Spindle Back" or "Tables with a Stationary Top." Each of these chapters has its own introduction, usually about a page long. Any collection of furniture of this period leans heavily toward chests, the most common furniture form of the seventeenth century. This is reflected in the arrangement of the catalogue; the section "Chests and Chests with Drawers" has more than twenty entries, about half as many as all the types of chairs.

The text for each entry covers what is known about the object based on several factors. Usual sources for this information are its provenance and/or its recovery history, its history of publication, and knowledge of related objects. Also included are detailed descriptions of the objects' construction and condition. These two headings and Ashworth's photographs are often as good as seeing the object in person. There are times when Safford's descriptions need going over a bit to follow what is being presented. Each reader will sail along with some concepts and struggle with others. An example that stumped me for a bit was a folding table (cat. no. 68)—"The legs are splayed (about 7 degrees from the vertical) in two opposite directions"—until I read the following entry and learned that its similar legs were splayed "on all four sides" (cat. no. 69). These dense descriptions are the bane of this sort of catalogue. They are essential to the record of the object, but they can be difficult reading. Woodworkers will be especially pleased to see the degree of details Safford provides concerning stock dimensions, and even joinery details. What Safford calls the width of a tenon, I would call the thickness, but I could follow it once I caught on. For some reason, these details are given for some pieces in the catalogue, but not for others.

The collection contains numerous warhorses of seventeenth-century New England furniture; carved chests and boxes are represented by several examples of each, including two Hadley chests, two or three "sunflower" chests, and so forth. Similarly, there are single examples of some hallmark pieces;

a wainscot chair (cat. no. 18), a folding table (cat. no. 58), and a small cabinet (cat. no. 79) are some of the best examples from the period in any collection.

For example, the collection includes three chests attributed to the Searle-Dennis workshops in Ipswich, Massachusetts (cat. nos. 83–85). Reading the text for these entries results in a crash course in the published history of this well-trod group of objects, ranging from Irving P. Lyon in the 1930s to Robert Tarule in 1992 and most of the writers in between. Safford aptly describes some of the carving on the panels of cat. no. 84 as ill conceived and poorly executed, then suggests that perhaps a journeyman not trained in the shop might have been responsible for this poor workmanship. Safford notes that the arches cut by V-tool work on the panels of this chest are shaky at best, yet offers no rationale about why the outlines carved with the same tool on the upper rail are competent and precise. Perhaps her journeyman theory would explain it, he carving the panels and another craftsman carving the framing parts. Yet because we know next to nothing at all about how work in a seventeenth-century shop was administered, all we can do in that regard is speculate.

Naturally, Safford utilizes the research of many scholars in gathering much of this information. Certainly given the scope of the project, there would be no sense in undertaking new research that would effectively be re-creating the wheel for each entry. There are places where this approach might create a problem for some readers. Because so much of what we know about furniture of this period is conjectural, one author might accept some scholarship that others would challenge. This can make for lively debate eventually, but the forum for such discussion is lacking. This leads to my only complaint about the book, and it is really about the field of early furniture study in general.

There has been for many years a heavy emphasis on attribution, sometimes putting this speculation ahead of the object itself. This author has been party to this leaning and, having begun the long task of reforming, is in the midst of becoming a horrid boor with a soapbox. I can illustrate with a piece of my own scholarship, which was then taken by Safford and included in her book. A joint stool (cat. no. 21) was illustrated in an article I researched and wrote with John Alexander, published in the 1996 issue of this journal. We assigned the stool to a group of carved chests and boxes that we had good reason to believe was the work of William Savell of Braintree, Massachusetts, and his sons, John and William. We included the stool, even though it had no recorded history, nor any carved decoration to link it to the joined chests and carved boxes in the group. The main connection we made between the chests and the stool is a molding run along the upper rails of the stool. The molding has the same profile as one used on about half of the Savell chests. If I were to write that article today, I would certainly not include the stool as part of the group, but might only mention that the same molding appears on it and the chests.

Because we know nothing about how a joiner or carpenter acquired his molding plane irons, it is dicey at best to speculate about connections between otherwise dissimilar pieces based only on molding profiles. This mistake has since been repeated elsewhere, virtually verbatim. To take away the possible attribution of this stool in no way diminishes its positive characteristics. The stool is an excellent example of a form that was ubiquitous in seventeenth-century households and, for New England, is a rare survivor.

Related to this push for attribution is the desire to connect joiners in the New World with their English "origins" that will then help us fathom various "regional styles" transferred from Old England to New. Again, this is not a new phenomenon. But it is, in this writer's opinion, flawed in its basic principle. The search for a craftsman's English origins usually centers on finding his birthplace or, more specifically, place of baptism, the likely record to be found. Certainly most often the place of baptism in seventeenth-century England is either also the place of birth or quite near it, with some few exceptions.

But this tells us only where a craftsman was born, and his training in his trade did not begin at birth. What is really needed is the record of his apprenticeship, or his admission to a trade "company" (now termed "guild"). Studies of apprenticeship bindings show that young men traveled both small and great distances in search of an apprenticeship. As an example, between 1610 and 1620, the London Company of Turners bound 265 apprentices; only 8.3 percent of whom were London born. Studies of published apprenticeship registers also show that apprentices were not necessarily from the town in which they apprenticed.[1]

An example of how this approach is played out is seen in the entry for a carved box (cat. no. 70). The box has long been attributed to William Buell (1614–1681) based on a related example descended in his family. Buell is on record as being a carpenter-joiner in Windsor, Connecticut, arriving there by 1638. Safford writes that "Rosettes within a guilloche dominate the carving in the joinery tradition that is represented by these boxes and was presumably endemic to County Huntingdon, England, where Buell was born." The use of the word "presumably" is the caveat. There are several leaps of faith in this one sentence: one is that the birth record is correct for William Buell; and the other that he was trained where he was born. Once these things get in print it becomes difficult to offset them.[2]

There are several appendixes. The first discusses seven objects that for one reason or another, usually related to condition, are omitted from the catalogue proper. Yet these prove to be excellent study pieces, and their flaws and foibles are outlined in detail. Appendix 2 is the one that will get the most use from any reader; it is composed of 121 photographs, most in black-and-white, of construction details, decoration, hardware, and so on. Some of the pictures, chair finials for example, seem to be reproduced to scale, but I have yet to find verification of that in the text. Whether you start in the text or in the appendix, having these details here instead of in the text results in some flipping around while reading. Arguments can be made either way to have these illustrations with the text or here in the appendix. For comparing finials or baluster turning profiles, it is best to put them in the appendix, whereas for studying a given object in its details, it would be best to put these with the text. Thus, this falls under the "can't please all of the people all of the time" rule. Similarly, it would have been a great help to include in the text illustrations of related pieces from other collections referenced in the entries. This is done effectively in Benno M. Forman's *American Seating Furniture, 1630–1730: An Interpretive Catalogue* (New York: W. W. Norton, a Winterthur Book, 1988) and is quite helpful. With Safford's book, we either rely on memory of the related pieces or go off to the bookshelf to pull out numerous volumes. Next thing you know, you have fifteen books on the desk.

Appendix 3 is entitled "Explanatory Drawings." Some of these are excellent for some readers; for instance, woodworkers will be glad to have the full-scale moldings. The general reader will benefit from the diagrams of joints and wood conversion. The glossary of furniture terms is open for debate, except for the disclaimer at its heading, that these terms are not intended to represent an ideal or definitive terminology. The drawing of a turned chair has three names for the rear vertical member: "rear leg," "stile," and "rear post." The front post has a similar multiple personality. I see no need to give a single piece of wood two names. Yet, in the other extreme, some seventeenth-century documents would call the whole piece the "foot" of the chair. So you can't win.

In the end, this is a reference book and is not meant to be read straight through cover to cover. Few will do so. As noted earlier, the book sets out to establish a record of the collection at the Metropolitan, and in my eye it does this quite well. Even with my various negative comments, I am favorably impressed with this book. I know my copy will see a lot of use again and again. But there is one more reason to have this book. It might well be the last of its kind. As other museums put their catalogues on websites, published books of this ilk might go the way of all things. As I tried to think of books to compare this with, I came up with very few. Forman's *American Seating Furniture* also deals with one collection and covers the same time frame, but few institutions have enough material of this period to fill a book. That's the reason I usually read only the beginning of furniture books—the material I'm interested in is usually in the first third of the book. The Museum of Fine Arts, Boston, Wadsworth Atheneum, and Winterthur Museum could each probably come close to this scope. It seems now that most museums are working toward getting their collections online. While there is a lot to be said for the ease of updating an online catalogue, and the cost is much less than a physical book, I, for one, am still glad books exist and hope, perhaps in vain, that Safford's book will be joined by other similar books.

Peter Follansbee
Plimoth Plantation

1. Paul S. Seaver, *Wallington's World: A Puritan Artisan in Seventeenth-Century London* (Stanford, Calif.: Stanford University Press, 1985), p. 68. For English apprenticeships of the period, see Anne Daly, ed., *Kingston Upon Thames Register of Apprentices, 1563–1713* (Guildford, Eng.: Surrey Record Office, 1974); and Jill Barlow, ed., *A Calendar of the Registers of Apprentices of the City of Gloucester, 1595–1700* (Bristol, Eng.: Bristol and Gloucestershire Archaeological Society, 2001).

2. Buell's English origin is based on a suggestion in a flawed genealogy from the 1880s and has been picked up by several furniture scholars since then. The latest genealogical research has

shown that there is no connection between William Buell of Windsor, Connecticut, and William Beville of Chesterton, Huntingdon. In addition, somewhere Safford has adopted the irksome habit of making the English counties sound Irish, again, also seen recently in *American Furniture*. This is a minor point that will bother only fanatics.

Sarah D. Coffin, Gail S. Davidson, Ellen Lupton, and Penelope Hunter-Stiebel. *Rococo: The Continuing Curve, 1730–2008*. New York: Cooper-Hewitt Museum, National Design Museum, Smithsonian Institution, 2008. 265 pp.; numerous color and bw illus., bibliography, index. $45.00.

It is generally agreed that reviewers should assess publications on the basis of what they are rather than what they are not. They should attend to what a book does rather than what it does not do. They should answer the implicit question: What did this book set out to achieve and how well did it do it? These directives are all fair enough and easily understood in the abstract. But what if it is not clear what a publication is about or what it was intended to achieve? The reviewer's task becomes a bit more difficult. Which tack is fair and which is not? It is difficult to know how to proceed.

The present dilemma is prompted by *Rococo: The Continuing Curve*. The volume is visually splendid but intellectually unresolved. The exact goals of the publication are rarely stated explicitly and then only in the briefest of terms. In his foreword, museum director Paul Warwick Thompson speaks of a "rococo impulse" (p. 1). In her introductory essay, Penelope Hunter-Stiebel says that the words "sinuous, organic, sensuous" constitute "the mantra of this project" (p. 3). So which is it? Is this book an examination of some loosely defined but presumably recognizable rococo spirit, or is it a deep immersion in all things sinuous, organic, and sensuous produced across varied temporal, geographic, and cultural contexts? Are they the same? Are we to think that all impulses to curvilinearity after the eighteenth century bear some relation to the rococo, that they either derive from the original or are manifestations of similar values or traits? Is this impulse, if it exists, cultural or biological or both? These questions and many others that come to mind all too readily are occasionally raised in this volume but rarely if ever resolved or even explored at length. Instead, we find fourteen short essays of varied character and quality discussing a range of topics from the eighteenth century to the present. Looking at the total package, one could come to the justifiable conclusion that this volume actually consists of two related projects—the first dealing with the historical rococo and the second with sinuosity in design—the two butted together somewhat awkwardly. And this brings us back to the question of how to deal fairly and accurately with this publication, a decision requiring understanding what it is and was intended to be. As far as I can make out, the answer is: an elegant and very beautiful exhibition souvenir enriched with a sampler of pleasant essays for the curious.

And that rather lets the book off the hook. The ante is down and so are our expectations. But some expectations will be well met. It truly is a handsome volume, with copious photographs of very high quality. It includes plenty of the familiar but also a fair sprinkling of the unfamiliar. The layout, typeface, and all the other material aspects are of a high standard. But those are formal rather than content issues, and it is in content that readers of this journal will probably find the volume less rewarding.

The general argument sustaining this book seems to have three parts to it. First, that there was, in the eighteenth century, a style or manner of design that we now recognize and know as rococo. Second, in a subsequent era, the nineteenth century primarily, there occurred a rococo revival or neo-rococo, which replicated or paraphrased the original eighteenth-century material. Third, in still later eras—mostly the 1890s and after—many objects incorporated sinuous, organic, or sensuous features that might or might not have been inspired by or might or might not have borne any likeness to the original rococo. In short, first rococo, then rococo again, and finally more or less rococo.

It is hard to argue with any of this. It all seems to be true as far as it goes. It also seems to move from relative strength to relative weakness, or from the relatively finite and concrete to the vague and amorphous. This imbalance is reflected in the distribution of the essays. Two of the essays, in different ways and for different reasons, span more than one of the three eras. Of the remaining twelve, seven deal with the eighteenth century, three with the nineteenth century, one with art nouveau, and one with the twentieth century, an arrangement giving considerable asymmetry to the project. Furthermore, in these essays, two alternative formats or approaches seem to stand out. On the one hand are specialized, tightly focused discussions dealing with particular times or places. These are usually both readable and informative. On the other hand are catchall essays of sorts that attempt to craft narratives linking assemblages of loosely related objects of diverse origins. These objects were presumably selected for their exhibition value and are generally of significant aesthetic merit. But weaving a text connecting them in meaningful ways is not necessarily easy, and these narratives do not make for engaging reading. Perhaps conventional catalogue-style entries would have worked as well and spared authors the task of devising narratives.

Among the group of specialized studies devoted to the eighteenth century, Ulrich Leben's essay on the evolution of the German rococo stands out for its clarity of organization and expression and for its deft linking of the objects discussed to the political, economic, and cultural conditions of the many different political entities that only later became Germany. Leben's is a model survey essay—clear, sure, concise. The author is in full command of his story and has a firm grasp on the hierarchy of significance. A longer and more fully illustrated essay by him would have been welcome.

Much the same praise can be given to Reinier Baarsen's discussion of the rococo in Holland. Admittedly, Baarsen is at something of an aesthetic disadvantage, for the rococo's most stunning creations did not appear in the Low Countries. Yet, like Leben, he displays a solid understanding of the political, economic, and cultural conditions that both generated the objects he discusses and account for their distinctive properties. All this said, one wonders, Why a chapter on Holland, as fine as it is? Why not Portugal? Or

Russia? Or Estonia? The choice seems arbitrary. Other useful pieces in the eighteenth-century section deal with the career of Juste-Aurèle Meissonnier, here understood as the chief form-giver of the French rococo, and the distinctive manifestations of the rococo in the French city of Nancy.

The neo-rococo discussion is confined to essays on graphics, English and American silver, and American furniture. More about the last in a bit. The single chapter devoted to art nouveau recognizes that some aspects of that manner made explicit references to the rococo of the eighteenth century. Yet rather than systematically identifying and analyzing the rococo component of art nouveau, the essay wanders off into a vague history of the movement and shows little interest in close attention to the design of the objects illustrated. Finally, the last essay, on more or less rococo objects of the twentieth and twenty-first centuries, is profoundly unconvincing. Yes, no doubt about it, lots of curvy objects. Yes, the curve must continue. And yes, some very few of these objects (I counted six; others might argue for a couple more) actually do reference the eighteenth-century rococo, but most could have been created (and perhaps actually were) without the slightest awareness of that historical style. Interesting goods, beautifully photographed, but hardly demonstrating that the rococo lives on. Indeed, I would argue that they show just the opposite—that the rococo is dead, quite thoroughly dead.

Spanning three centuries, however, enables this volume to demonstrate three significant ways in which the art world of the eighteenth century differs from that of more recent eras. The first concerns the relation of artists to their patrons. The early chapters discuss the patrons of Meissonnier, the patronage of Louis XV, and the roles of patrons in Nancy, the Germanic countries, and the Netherlands. The final chapter, by contrast, is all about artists and designers. Patrons have become invisible, possibly extinct. Modern art discourse as represented here has come to see the art world through the eyes of artists and to adopt the ideology of autonomous creativity. Once upon a time artists glorified patrons, and patrons, in turn, enabled artists. Now, at least in theory, artists and designers create what they wish, and savvy patrons line up for an opportunity to own an example of the great man's or woman's work. Overstated, of course, for there are significant political and economic differences between the eighteenth century and today. Yet it is difficult not to be struck by the care with which authors of the early sections in this book weave the art they discuss into a larger cultural fabric and the way the designers mentioned in the final chapter seem to exist in independent worlds of their own devising. The early artists are deeply embedded in their worlds, the later float somewhere apart from or above it. That, at least, is the impression given here. And it is not totally inaccurate.

The second major point revolves around the idea of style as a communal cultural statement. Look carefully at the many examples of eighteenth-century rococo and note the repetition of key motifs. Study the copious graphics illustrated here and note how closely the designs of Meissonnier, Pierre Germain, Jacques de Lajoue, François Boucher, Alexis Peyrotte, Jean-François Cuvillies, and others resemble each other. Yes, with careful study it is possible to distinguish one from the other, but the differences are few while the similarities are many. The rococo was clearly a shared manner in the eighteenth century, a manner generated and disseminated by a substantial body of capable designers. Largely confined to the upper classes, it nonetheless spread across Europe and from there to parts of the world colonized by Europeans, where it was recognizable as an internationally understood cultural idiom.

Turn then to the last essay again and contemplate the objects assembled there. Yes, many of them do share design features of what might be called modern minimalist curvilinearity, but the resemblance they bear to each other is limited. Unlike the eighteenth-century designs, which seem to constitute a fairly tight and closely linked body of creativity, these later goods range freely within very broad parameters, with individuality and idiosyncrasy outweighing common design features. And thus the art world and its values change.

The third point concerns the importance that graphics once played in disseminating visual information. It is worth noting that every essay dealing with the eighteenth century illustrates designs, whether drawings or prints. Indeed, one of Gail S. Davidson's two essays explicitly treats rococo prints and drawings. The bulk of the piece offers a useful discussion of the role of prints in spreading design ideas in the eighteenth century, followed by comments on characteristic designs produced by major figures from Meissonnier, de Lajoue, and Nicolas Pineau onward. Even the small selection offered in this volume gives some indication of the exceptional design creativity of the key practitioners of the rococo manner. Rather underplayed, it seems to me, is the fact that the majority of the graphics included come from the Cooper-Hewitt's own collection and, more to the point, that the Cooper-Hewitt is one of the world's major repositories of eighteenth-century design prints and drawings.

Davidson notes that the Hewitt sisters, who founded the museum in 1897, thought that rococo and neoclassical objects "represented the greatest achievements in design history" (p. 43). That may or may not be a fashionable idea today, but it is very difficult not to be deeply impressed—and moved, if that is not putting it too strongly—by the creative energy expressed and preserved on these small pieces of paper. Some several hundreds of those now at the Cooper-Hewitt came early in the twentieth century through the purchase of all or portions of major European collections. One Jean-Léon Decloux, "a former painting contractor who specialized in ornamental gilded paneling" (p. 44), was one of many Europeans who recognized that well-heeled buyers, often foreign, valued earlier Continental arts and were willing to pay to own them. Decloux developed a strategy for acquiring collections and then selling them off, using the proceeds to repeat the process. He eventually became effectively the Hewitts' Paris agent, steering important prints, drawings, and objects in their direction. Although Davidson only briefly sketches out the history of the Hewitt-Decloux relationship, their man in Paris seems to have played a decisive role in shaping the collection.

This volume effectively demonstrates that students of European decorative arts of the eighteenth century are blessed with a glorious wealth of graphic material, most of it produced by a distinctive creative type who, with an eye on acquiring some combination of money and fame, specialized in generating and selling design ideas. We find this type of person emerging in Western Europe in the fifteenth century and proliferating throughout the sixteenth, seventeenth, and eighteenth centuries before going into decline around the middle years of the nineteenth century. These designers were so deeply embedded in the entire matrix of the decorative arts that it is possible to craft a reasonably accurate and balanced history of major media relying entirely on surviving graphic documents.

Nothing of the sort is remotely possible for America in the eighteenth century. The European designer needed very affluent patrons and a cadre of highly skilled artisans to operate effectively. Neither was abundant in the American colonies. Still, the rococo did appear in eighteenth-century America and occasionally made a pretty fine showing, despite the limitations of the region. American rococo appears occasionally in Sarah Coffin's whirlwind essay "The Dissemination of Style through Migrating Designers, Craftsmen, and Objects in the Eighteenth Century" (pp. 102–35). The objects, primarily gold, silver, and furniture, plus one Bonnin and Morris sweetmeat dish, make only cameo appearances, but they are well chosen and amply document the presence of the rococo in high-end colonial goods. The five pieces of furniture included are a mahogany pier table with marble top of Philadelphia origin (Metropolitan Museum of Art), a carved and gilded wall bracket by James Reynolds (Winterthur), a mahogany card table attributed to the workshop of Thomas Affleck (Philadelphia Museum of Art), an upholstered easy chair from Charleston (Winterthur), and a mahogany and cherry tea table attributed to Robert Walker of King George County, Virginia (MESDA). These, of course, represent just the tip of the American rococo iceberg, such as it is. Those interested in the rococo on this side of the Atlantic will already have the book by Morrison H. Heckscher and Leslie Green Bowman, *American Rococo, 1750–1775: Elegance and Ornament* (New York: Metropolitan Museum of Art; Los Angeles: Los Angeles County Museum of Art, 1992) on their bookshelves. The pages of this journal have also presented important studies of American rococo materials.

There is but one essay in the whole collection that deals entirely with American furniture: Jason T. Busch's discussion of rococo-revival furniture made in this country in the middle of the nineteenth century. This nicely illustrated piece relies on some of the usual suspects to tell its tale. These include furniture manufacturers or merchants Prudent Mallard, George Henkels, John Henry Belter, Alexander Roux, Charles H. White, architect Samuel Sloan, tastemaker Andrew Jackson Downing, and a number of others. Busch convincingly argues for the continuing authority of French design and its impact on American production, impact perpetuated by importation of examples of French furniture and French furniture publications. Among the latter he mentions works by Michel Jansen, Victor Quetin, and Désiré Guilmard. Guilmard's influential *Le garde-meuble, ancien et moderne,* gloriously illustrated with hand-colored and glazed lithographs, was published in serial form for many years starting about 1841 (the plates are not dated). One of the nice treats in Busch's essay is his persuasive demonstration that a very bizarre (or at least unconventional) upholstered seating piece at Melrose in Natchez, Mississippi, memorable to all who have ever seen it (or sat in it!), is actually based on plate 248 in the forty-fourth *livraison* of *Le garde-meuble*. There it is identified, appropriately enough, as "Causeuse. Fantaisie." Busch covers a lot of ground in a little space in this essay, and his coverage is necessarily thin. References in the text and the useful notes, however, provide helpful directions for those who might want a fuller picture of this particular cultural episode.

Busch's essay will be the most significant part of this volume for students of American furniture, provided, of course, that they are interested in the nineteenth century. Otherwise, there is very little here for the readers of this journal or for specialists of any sort or for those who believe themselves well informed about one rococo or another. But you never know when seeing things in a new context or juxtaposed in an unfamiliar way will lead to new perceptions. And there may be an item not seen before. However, the book will perhaps be most useful to a general audience, with little or no prior familiarity with the material. Elegantly packaged, beautifully illustrated, and furnished with "accessible essays," as the book's jacket puts it, *Rococo* just might open a few eyes to new visual delights and lure new readers to more advanced or specialized studies. In sum, as an exhibition souvenir it is impressive. And, in truth, it is rather more than just that.

Kenneth L. Ames
Bard Graduate Center

The Knight of Glin and James Peill. *Irish Furniture: Woodwork and Carving in Ireland from the Earliest Times to the Act of Union*. New Haven and London: Yale University Press for the Paul Mellon Centre for Studies in British Art, 2007. xi + 323 pp.; 400 color and 100 bw illus., catalogue, appendixes, bibliography, index. $125.00.

Scholars of Western furniture have long awaited the assessment of Irish furniture that the seasoned connoisseur the Knight of Glin and his coauthor aim to serve up in *Irish Furniture*. As the first and only book of its kind devoted to the subject of Irish furniture, this publication deserves to be included on the bookshelves of furniture scholars, especially those who focus on the study of American furniture. The impact of Irish émigrés on the stylistic development of American furniture made in early urban centers from Boston to Charleston, and especially evident in Philadelphia, has long been speculated on and supported with statistics about the sheer volume of Irish immigrant craftsmen and patrons who landed on our shores in the seventeenth, eighteenth, and early nineteenth centuries. The discussion and images of furniture and architectural woodwork presented in *Irish Furniture* further substantiate the profound effect the Irish had on America's vernacular furniture designs.

The five-page introduction, which inharmoniously moves from being written in the first-person singular (Knight of Glin) in the beginning to the first-person plural (both authors) at the end, provides a historiography of the literature on Irish furniture and an overview of the text. Like the mischaracterization of furniture from Connecticut or the South in American furniture analysis, the proportions, lines, and carved ornament of Irish furniture have been categorized as unsophisticated, mere bad interpretations of their more refined British cousins. Thus, standing just enough outside the canon, Irish furniture was deemed provincial. The authors discuss the oft-used term "Irish Chippendale," a derogatory descriptor applied to baroque and rococo Irish furniture of the mid-eighteenth century. Those authors who first embraced the term "Irish Chippendale" (specifically Constance Simon [1905], Owen Wheeler [1907], and Herbert Cescinsky [1910]) used it to describe furniture made contemporaneously with the Georgian masterpieces made in Great Britain: "Summarised, this Erse work shows good material and carcase construction, but poor outline and inferior, lifeless, carving."[1] Cescinsky's opinion of Irish furniture was equally inflammatory:

> the details and the workmanship of the carving indicate a degeneration, owing possibly to the fact that in the hands of provincial cabinet-makers and carvers the high traditions of their metropolitan fellow-workmen were either depraved or entirely absent. Work of this type suggests, above all, the result of a slavish copying of the same models over and over again, until all spontaneity is submerged in the dead level of commercial mediocrity.[2]

It is this prejudice against the merits of Irish furniture that the authors seek to end.

The introduction includes a disclaimer about the challenges inherent in the study of Irish furniture, namely the paucity of surviving accounts and bills to link much of the furniture that has a history in Ireland to its manufacture in Ireland. Part I of the book is an essay-style text with supporting photographs tracking the chronological history of Irish furniture making until 1800 (the year of Ireland's Act of Union), transcriptions of noteworthy bills and inventories, and commentary on Irish furniture. Part II is "a pictorial gazetteer of the many different types of furniture found in Ireland" (p. 5), a description that omits any definition of what makes a piece of furniture Irish. Appendix I is a detailed and useful encyclopedia of eighteenth-century furniture makers compiled by John Rogers, "gleaned from Irish (chiefly Dublin) newspapers" (p. 5). Appendix II is a transcription of a 1750 bill for furnishing a Dublin town house from Charles Coleman, a Dublin upholsterer, that was "discovered by chance by the Knight of Glin in the attic of Coolmore, the Newenham family seat in Co. Cork" (p. 5).

Part I, chapter 1, on furniture up to the Restoration of Charles II (1660), opens with references to such sophisticated works of art produced in medieval Ireland as the Book of Kells, a tour de force that begs the question of its furniture corollaries dating from the same period. Thus, like most histories, the assessment of the earliest periods and the roots of furniture making is based on fragmentary evidence—literally and figuratively. Domestic architecture and chimneypieces as well as church altars, stalls, screens, and reredoes offer the best evidence of the taste and style of late-fifteenth- and early-sixteenth-century Irish woodwork. Ownership of moveable and personal furniture, such as a trestle table or open armchair, was limited, and the objects do not survive in large numbers; those which do survive cannot be securely pinpointed to Irish manufacture. The much-celebrated Armada table (pp. 16–17) is the most glaring example of this difficulty.

As the Restoration period is considered in chapter 2, two oversights inhibit the reader's understanding of the subject: first, the lack of any images of the exteriors of the churches, castles, and houses that the furniture and woodwork inhabited; and second, a map of Ireland that shows the counties, castles, and major ports, cities, and towns frequently referenced. (Such maps can be accessed at www.lookaroundireland.com.) A map would also have been useful to trace the movements of various craftsmen and ethnic groups who settled in Ireland during the period of focus and who influenced the stylistic development of Irish furniture. Like similar waves of immigration and the movement of ethnic groups in America, particularly in the Southeast, the arrival and diaspora of these peoples profoundly influenced the aesthetics of Irish furniture. The trove of Ormonde inventories of Dunmore Castle, County Kilkenny (landlocked in southeast Ireland), and the detailed published studies of them by Jane Fenlon are referenced at length without any images.

Chapter 3 discusses carving in late-seventeenth- and early-eighteenth-century Ireland. Much of the talent was imported, and some of it exported (Lambert Emerson went to Philadelphia in 1731, for example, cited on p. 37). Organ cases, reredoes, pulpits, library stalls, chimneypieces, and staircases were great vehicles for the carver's art and receive worthy discussion. Another type of surface decoration found on a group of Irish furniture was marquetry, the discussion of which takes up a substantial eight pages at the end of the chapter on carving. A fascinating group of secretaire-cabinets embellished with marquetry inlay, an artisanal tradition likely brought to Ireland by émigrés, constitutes a distinctive form that appears to have manifested itself exclusively in Ireland. Glin and Peill do not delve into it, declaring only that "the retardataire use of marquetry on three of them [cabinets] clearly points to Irish manufacture" (p. 56). It seems the questions of who or what group of émigrés brought the furniture designs and art of marquetry to Ireland are open for further research.

Beginning in the second quarter of the eighteenth century, a flurry of architectural commissions spurred a flourishing of the arts in Dublin that lasted from, specifically, 1735 to 1752, a development addressed in chapter 4. Like the growing group of politically independent-minded Americans, Ireland was trying to encourage Irish manufacture of luxury goods to resist dependence on England's burgeoning manufactories. Unfortunately, protective guilds did not thrive and ceased to exist by the end of the eighteenth century (p. 63). Combined into the discussion of new Palladian architectural designs promoted by Edward Lovett Pearce, the William Kentian–inspired group of Irish lion's-mask tables is particularly interesting to scholars studying

Philadelphia furniture. The close relationship of this group of tables to the Philadelphia sideboard table attributed to carver Martin Jugiez is not referenced but, again, broadens the tale of that table and gives rise to further speculation about the origins of the elusive Jugiez.[3]

The relation between carvers John Houghton, who was active in Dublin in the 1740s and received numerous private and public commissions, and Thomas Johnson and then Hercules Courtenay of Philadelphia (p. 87) is particularly relevant to the reader interested in American furniture. Unfortunately, some of the images woven into the text to illustrate the work of Houghton and his contemporaries are only described and classified as "of incredible opulence and superb quality and must come from the best Dublin workshops." Perhaps a more focused connoisseurship study on documented works that allowed for analysis of construction, technique, condition, and history would have been helpful. When the authors declare that a carved bed is "Irish furniture at its best" (p. 88), the reader has not been presented with enough comparatives to know how they have arrived at that assessment.

Chapter 5, "Furniture of the Mid-Eighteenth Century," is where the most rewarding meat of the text lies. Furniture materials and idiosyncratic Irish characteristics such as distinctive forms, proportions, line, flat stretchers, arm shape, and carving designs are considered and illustrated, giving the reader a feel for Ireland's most prolific period of furniture patronage and manufacture. The profile of the legs on Irish dish-top squared tea tables (pp. 116–19), for example, has a particular poised stance, tall rails with carved overlay on the bulging lower part of the rails and pagoda-shaped lower edges, placing them into a distinct group. The overhangs are extremely shallow or exaggerated.

Cabinetmakers, carvers, upholsterers, and patrons who immigrated to colonial America had a profound influence on the character of American furniture. Owing to the good collegiality of American scholars, collectors, and museum curators who shared their collections and research files with them, the authors' understanding of the late Delaware antiques dealer David Stockwell is informed, revealing Stockwell as at once intuitive about the similarities and strong relationships between American and Irish idiosyncrasies and yet wrongly selling Irish furniture as American furniture. This discussion is helpful to furthering the study of Irish furniture and its influence on American furniture styles and traditions. The flattened stretcher is among the characteristics seen on American furniture that are credited with originating in Ireland. The mask-emblazoned cabriole knees of select Boston furniture offer another stimulating comparison. Ronald Hurst's measured work on the Irish influences on cabinetmaking in the Rappahannock River basin provides the best model for the study of Irish influences, showing how pockets of ethnic influence shaped the canon of a region.[4]

Other opportunities for tracking the Irish in America presented itself to me when reading this book. Upholsterer George Haughton advertised in Philadelphia in 1775 that he was lately from London, where he was "formerly a workman to Mr. Trotter in London." Trotter is referenced here on page 129 as London upholsterer to the Countess of Kildare in her 1759 refurnishing of Carton. As the authors point out, America and Ireland share the second row to the fashion capitals of the world—the highest fashions of Dublin and Philadelphia were once removed and filtered from those centers whether through artisans or patrons. For that reason, there is a strong kinship between American and Irish furniture, which would also suggest that the methodology that has been applied to American furniture studies be applied to Irish furniture studies. Second, the dominance of the late-eighteenth- and early-nineteenth-century Philadelphia cabinetmaking market by Irish-born cabinetmaker Joseph B. Barry (born in Dublin in 1758, died in Philadelphia in 1838) has always been credited to his training in Dublin and his intense desire to maintain his position as the importer of cutting-edge furniture fashion. Several elements of Irish furniture illustrated and described in the text merit a closer look at Barry's Irish roots and probable training in Dublin, which has never been substantiated (i.e., did he train in Dublin or London or precisely where?). For instance, the incorporation of Persians (also called "terms" or "mummy heads") and caryatids in Barry's furniture relates closely to Irish work and spans Barry's almost fifty-year American career. The ram termini of two chairs pictured on page 107 correspond to American furniture: the mask arm termini are similar to those on a sofa and set of chairs attributed to Barry, and the eagle's-neck arm termini closely resemble those on New York armchairs.[5] Paris-trained carver Charles Francis Le Grand worked in Dublin in the 1790s, and his experiences there impacted Le Grand's eventual Philadelphia work and the training of his three sons (pp. 179–81).

Frames are addressed in the text in a detailed way that American furniture scholars have rarely achieved. This strong analysis of the frame carver's work should be a rallying cry for American furniture scholars to remobilize and further collaborate with their paintings colleagues about the study of American frames.

The discussions of ornamental interior plasterwork (or stucco) in chapters 5 and 6 are integral to the art of carvers proficient in the florid rococo and the more restrained neoclassical styles. However, the fact that the carvers discussed at such length were responsible for carving the molds for the plaster workers, also discussed at length, is not mentioned, and therefore the connection between the two art forms is missed. Note 12 to the text on page 160 (see pp. 310–11) gives a detailed account of the export of the art of ornamental stucco to America through the emigration of Irish stucco workers (or *stuccodores*). Irish born and trained stucco workers John Rawlins (small dining room at Mount Vernon), Joseph Kennedy (mantelpieces at Mount Clare, Baltimore), and George Andrews (President's House, Monticello) all arrived in America from Ireland in the 1790s.

The chronological discussion ends with the Act of Union of 1800, and here begins the pictorial catalogue of Irish furniture. The introduction to this section gives a focused overview of attributes indigenous to Irish furniture. The subsequent sixty-four pages containing "tombstone" information, a minimal discussion of select works, and thumbnail-size images will long endure as usefully capturing the essence of Irish furniture.

Appendix I—the dictionary of eighteenth-century Irish furniture makers by John Rogers—is an immensely important piece of work. It is divided alphabetically into three sections: upholsterers and auctioneers; cabinetmakers, chairmakers, joiners, picture frame makers, and trunk makers; and carvers, turners, gilders, japanners, glass grinders, and looking glass sellers. The existence of women as artificers is noted in the text intermittently and their names are listed in the dictionary, but the subject is not addressed adequately. Some women were in partnership with their sons or carrying on their husbands' line of work, but others were seemingly independent, and their presence in these Irish arts in the eighteenth century is noteworthy.

Without setting a clear expectation and without defining what makes a piece of furniture Irish, *Irish Furniture* presents for the first time an Irish-centered monograph but fails to ask and answer lingering questions. When comparing Irish furniture to the English precedents and published designs on which the furniture was modeled, supporting photographs and images would have significantly strengthened the argument. The furniture of London maintains its position as the bar against which Irish furniture is judged. There are several areas where information is contradictory. The text is descriptive, but the material is not analyzed. Sometimes, more information would have been helpful, for instance, when color and dye are mentioned as important to the furniture and its value (pp. 16, 18, 19, 25, 96). Ideas mentioned in passing need to be synthesized: for instance, what was the lingering effect of the Continental artisans (Dutch, Italian, and French) who sought refuge in Ireland and brought their talents there? How did they synthesize in the shadow of London?

This first full-length monograph on Irish furniture will inform readers, educate them enough to move beyond any prejudices about Irish design, and certainly inspire further study of Irish furniture and the international cadre of craftsmen and -women who made it.

Alexandra Alevizatos Kirtley
Philadelphia Museum of Art

1. George Owen Wheeler, *Old English Furniture of the Seventeenth and Eighteenth Centuries: A Guide for the Collector* (New York: Charles Scribner's Sons, 1907), 1. See also Constance Simon, *English Furniture Designers of the Eighteenth Century* (London: A. H. Bullen, 1905).

2. Herbert Cescinsky, *English Furniture of the Eighteenth Century* (London: G. Routledge and Sons, 1910), 1.

3. See Luke Beckerdite and Alan Miller, "A Table's Tale: Craft, Art, and Opportunity in Eighteenth-Century Philadelphia," in *American Furniture 2004*, edited by Luke Beckerdite (Hanover, N.H.: University Press of New England for the Chipstone Foundation, 2004), pp. 2–45.

4. Ronald Hurst, "Irish Influences on Cabinetmaking in Virginia's Rappahannock River Basin," in *American Furniture 1997*, edited by Luke Beckerdite (Hanover, N.H.: University Press of New England for the Chipstone Foundation, 2004), pp. 170–95.

5. For the Barry chairs, see Beatrice B. Garvan, *Federal Philadelphia, 1785–1825: The Athens of the Western World* (Philadelphia: Philadelphia Museum of Art, 1987), 68.

Dean T. Lahikainen. *Samuel McIntire: Carving an American Style*. Salem: Peabody Essex Museum, 2007. 300 pp.; 458 color & bw illus., appendixes, bibliography, index. Distributed by University Press of New England, Hanover and London. $75.00.

At the back of this important book, published in conjunction with an exhibition of the same name mounted at the Peabody Essex Museum in the fall of 2007, is a bibliography compiled by Sarah N. Chasse that contains nearly one hundred titles on Samuel McIntire, famed architect and carver of Salem, Massachusetts. Thoroughly versed in the McIntire literature and sensitized to his legacy through his research for the restoration of the Gardner-Pingree House and—lucky man—by living with his family in McIntire's Peirce-Nichols House of 1782 for seventeen years, author and curator Dean Lahikainen recognized the need for a critical analysis of McIntire's carving career. In five chapters he admirably engages this task, first by demonstrating how our present-day view of McIntire and his work has been shaped by more than a century of interest in Salem's beautiful old houses, as well as by the avarice of museums and dealers who carried away from this historic seaport town pieces of the McIntire legacy to grace their period rooms and to satisfy a coterie of collectors hungry for this American original's distinctive, artistic work. This first chapter is followed by a compelling biography of McIntire emphasizing the role of Salem's elite society—his patrons—and McIntire's own library and art collection in the architect-carver's hard-won self-education. The final three chapters deal with the heart of the matter—the carving—and cover, in order, McIntire's distinctive style; the range and diversity of his carved ornaments; and his architectural and furniture carving in the coordinated schemes of interior decoration in four of his most important commissions for the Derby family, Jerathamiel Peirce, and John and Sarah Gardner.

It will please readers of *American Furniture* that Lahikainen gives McIntire's furniture carving equal billing with his renowned architectural carving: the fact that the front and back covers of the book are dominated by carved furniture details when other choices clearly were available shows that the author was intrigued with this aspect of McIntire's work. Dealing with McIntire's furniture carving is not without its complexities, however. In the author's words: "Tracing McIntire's career as a furniture carver has been one of the most contentious topics for previous scholars because of the scarcity and ambiguity of surviving documents" (p. 51). Attempting to skirt this problem, which plagues so many artisan studies, Lahikainen chose instead to present McIntire's carving from the perspective of style, describing its salient features, tracing its evolution, and measuring the degree of its originality. This approach has its rewards and offers the advantage of making the book accessible to a larger audience. But it may prove frustrating to those with a more intense interest in carved Salem furniture, for only selectively does the author provide the kind of detailed comparisons in closely aligned text and images that instruct the reader on what makes a McIntire attribution valid. Lahikainen's extensive experience certainly qualifies him as a McIntire expert, but his attributions to the master come fast and furious in chapters 3 and 4 as he marches through time and across motifs in explicating McIntire's style. A section in the book dedicated to issues of connoisseurship and attribution would have been a welcome addition.

Taken together, the first two chapters present a compelling story of how McIntire became famous in our time and what he was like as a man. Pathos is not something most decorative arts historians trade in, but Lahikainen manages to evoke a measure of sadness when McIntire's sterling character—the Reverend William Bentley and others commented after his death on his "fine person," "great self command," "unaffected native politeness," and "modest and sweet manners" (p. 23)—is compared with the greediness of the early-twentieth-century museum scouts, antiques dealers, and pickers who attempted to pry as much carved woodwork out of Salem's venerable old manses as possible, or with the querulous debate between Fiske Kimball and Mabel Munson Swan in the early 1930s, moderated by Homer Eaton Keyes, editor of *Antiques,* over whether McIntire actually made or carved furniture for the Derby family. The author brilliantly mined Kimball's correspondence in the archives of the Philadelphia Museum of Art to construct this tale.

Lahikainen expands our knowledge of McIntire's role in carving some of the Derby family furniture beyond that of Kimball and Swan in chapter 3 with his insightful discussion of the famous chest-on-chests at the Yale University Art Gallery and the Museum of Fine Arts, Boston. Two previously unpublished examples with a firm Derby provenance are brought to light to provide a convincing dating schema for the group and to make intriguing stylistic linkages with a Salem chest of drawers in a private collection (previously published in Morrison H. Heckscher and Leslie Green Bowman, *American Rococo, 1750–1775: Elegance and Ornament* [New York: Metropolitan Museum of Art; Los Angeles: Los Angeles County Museum of Art, 1992], p. 145), and another Salem chest-on-chest at the Museum of Fine Arts, Boston (acc. no. 50.2441). This discussion transitions seamlessly into another on early 1790s camelback sofas with serpentine mahogany top rails shaped by the carver in a manner very much like the C-scrolls on the bases of the chest-on-chests. Printed designs by Ince and Mayhew and Robert Adam are illustrated (p. 68) to make us consider the source of the sofas' shape in eighteenth-century rococo design despite their neoclassical thermed legs and delicately carved draperies suspended from bowknots in the crest.

The subsection on chair carving that follows (pp. 74–78) is less successful. It begins with the trenchant observations that the majority of mahogany chairs produced in Salem between 1794 and circa 1805 can be directly linked to patterns in Hepplewhite's *Cabinet-Maker and Upholsterer's Guide* (London, 1788, 1789, and 1794), and the fact that the Sanderson shop, which is documented as having employed McIntire's carving services for chairs on two different occasions (App. B, docs. 31 and 42), owned three copies of the *Guide.* Two paragraphs later, however, Lahikainen makes the broad assertion that "the carving on a majority of the authenticated 'Hepplewhite' chairs from Salem can be attributed to McIntire based on the consistency of the carving and the use of a well-defined ornamental vocabulary—waterleaves, feathers, wheat husks, and other details that McIntire used consistently during this period" (p. 75). One wishes that the author, to support this statement, had grouped together in *this* section compelling visual evidence to bolster his claim, as he did so successfully with the chest-on-chests. We are alerted at the start of the chapter that carvers E. Godfrey, Nathaniel Safford, Daniel Clarke, and Joseph Stokes were active in Salem during McIntire's career, but that "not a single example of their carved work is documented" (p. 45). This, of course, does not preclude any of them from having carved some of the "minority" of Salem "Hepplewhite" chairs. It would have been informative to see detailed photographs of the carved backs of some of these chairs in close proximity to the ones documented to McIntire or attributed to him even if the men who carved them cannot be precisely identified. In the next chapter Lahikainen presents a comparison between the carving on an exquisite documented Derby family chair with an oval back and Prince of Wales feathers with an example originally used in the architect's Gardner-Pingree House and one other undocumented chair that shares this carved feature (pp. 180–82). However, he never references these images in his discussion of McIntire's chair-carving style in the preceding chapter. The reader is left to stumble on it some hundred pages later.

The book is a rich visual feast with a remarkable 458 images. Among these are many very fine photographs by Dennis Helmar, who obviously worked closely with the author to capture McIntire's carving in precise detail. Deploying all these images across three chapters dealing with McIntire's carving was a considerable challenge. Chapter 4 is jam-packed with 238 of them. The length of this chapter and the density of images within it make it feel like the heart of the book. Lahikainen takes us on an exhilarating run through McIntire's favorite carved ornaments, which he divides into three broad categories—classical, pastoral, and patriotic—and many subcategories including the classical orders, baskets of fruit and flowers, and the American eagle, to name a few. His deep knowledge of art history propels the chapter along and leaves the reader with a clear sense of the origins and symbolic meaning of McIntire's classically derived ornaments from ancient times, through the Renaissance, and into the age of neoclassicism. Printed design sources from Vitruvius to Asher Benjamin are cleverly used as benchmarks to measure McIntire's level of sophistication and the quality of his work in the "international visual language" of the neoclassical style. It is particularly gratifying to find instructive pointers accompanied by detailed images scattered throughout this chapter that help in recognizing the hand of the master, like the way his acanthus leaves "flare out and have sharply pointed tips" with "smoothly cut lines that radiate out from the base" (p. 112).

The final chapter, "Patrons and the Coordinated Interior," for my money, is the best in the book. It is tightly focused, impeccably documented, and rich in images of McIntire's very best carved interior woodwork and furniture carving. In this most delightful chapter for furniture enthusiasts, the fixed and the movable in interior decoration are presented in as harmonious a fashion as McIntire and his sophisticated Salem clients could have conjured. Recent furniture historians have convincingly drawn parallels between furniture and fixed woodwork, not through documentation, but by making compelling arguments through visual comparisons. (Luke Beckerdite's work on carver Henry Hardcastle and Philipse Manor in Yonkers, New York [*American Furniture*, 1993], and Robert Trent, Alan Miller, Glenn Adamson, and Harry Mack Truax II's recent article on upriver Albany County *kasten* and the interior of the Glen-Sanders House in Schenectady, New York [*American Furniture*, 2004], are good examples.) McIntire's interiors and furniture in the Derby, Jerathamiel Peirce, and John and Sarah Gardner houses are the real deal. There is no supposition or theorizing involved. This final chapter truly justifies McIntire's reputation and renown as an American original. One can argue about the organization of the book and whether a critical analysis of McIntire's carving warranted a separate chapter dedicated to issues of connoisseurship and attribution. These small matters aside, this is a fine book and a remarkable effort on the part of the author. It deserves a careful reading and maybe even a second, if one wants to satisfy that particular craving. Its greatest strength lies in its revivifying McIntire and his extraordinary carving for a modern audience. Lahikainen did the field, his institution, and his city a remarkable service.

Peter Kenny
The Metropolitan Museum of Art

Richard Bebb. *Welsh Furniture, 1250–1950: A Cultural History of Craftsmanship and Design*. 2 vols. Kidwelly, Carmarthenshire, Wales: Saer Books, with the assistance of Amgueddfa Cymru—National Museum of Wales and the support of Llyfregkk Genedlaethol Cymry—National Library of Wales, 2007. Vol. 1, *Welsh Furniture, 1250–1700*. 365 pp.; 595+ color and bw illus., bibliography, index, glossary. Vol. 2, *Welsh Furniture, 1700–1950*. 441 pp.; 800+ color and bw illus., bibliography, index, glossary. £150.00.

While this astoundingly rich and somewhat confrontational publication has not received adequate attention in the United States, it ought to be high on any furniture scholar's list of desirable acquisitions. Not only is Welsh furniture of major importance to many American vernacular traditions, but the book itself is probably the single most important book about English furniture to appear since the late Christopher Gilbert's two-volume *The Life and Work of Thomas Chippendale* was published in 1978.

Richard Bebb is an antiques dealer and furniture historian in Kidwelly, Carmarthenshire, Wales, and has pursued the study of Welsh furniture for forty years. This two-volume, lavishly illustrated book reflects Bebb's desire not only to survey the material but to place the furniture in a cultural context. The study has the imprimatur of the National Museum of Wales in St. Fagan's, and it thus represents an official history of sorts.

Approaching Welsh furniture involves many of the same pitfalls found in histories of Scottish, Irish, and Cornish furniture. All these regions, once casually referred to by the English as the "Celtic fringe," are the focus of fierce ethnic and regional loyalties and equally strong animosity toward the dominant or ordinate culture centered in London and embodied in the local nobility and aristocracy. In this respect, the Welsh are in much the same position regarding the centralized state as are the Bretons in France. Both areas were peopled by a Gaelic-speaking "minority" that resisted the central authority after military conquest. Both areas were caricatured as backward and even barbaric by the central authority. Both areas enjoyed a curious and uneven renaissance as cultural entities during the twentieth century.

To this Celtic quandary may be added an underlying resentment that pervades the membership of the Regional Furniture Society in England, to the effect that English furniture history has been hijacked by elitist art historians who are interested only in metropolitan furniture and who misrepresent vernacular expressions as derivative and debased. Although Bebb is an urbane scholar, he continually sets up elitist straw men who are thought to embody this abusive stance. Indeed, one of the most alarming assertions in the book is that Benno M. Forman (1930–1982), the doyen of American vernacular furniture studies, was such an elitist, based on an isolated quotation from the first chapter of his posthumously published *American Seating Furniture, 1630–1730* (1988). Setting aside the questionable validity of this particular assertion, one senses that regional histories of furniture from Celtic areas of Great Britain and Ireland are a minefield of resentment against both elitist interpretations of style (as embodied, perhaps, by *Irish Furniture* published in 2007 by the Knight of Glin [a.k.a. Desmond FitzGerald] and James Peill and reviewed elsewhere in this issue) and more or less racist interpretations to the effect that almost everything made in Celtic areas reflects physical isolation, ignorance, poverty, and linguistic barriers.

Despite occasional outbursts of this sort of resentment, Bebb has established a detailed and sensitive treatment of the complexities in establishing a just appreciation of any given piece of Welsh furniture. Virtually the entire introduction (pp. 3–38) and chapter 1 (pp. 39–96) of the first volume are devoted to setting up valid frames of reference for Welsh furniture, and they constitute a model for any furniture scholar undertaking a regional study. Wales shares a long border with the English counties of Herefordshire, Shropshire, and Cheshire. It borders the Severn estuary that leads to the great West Country port of Bristol, and Wales has many rivers leading into the interior. Some areas had market towns and developed roads, and they functioned as part of the commercial life of the West Country. Remote mountain regions were accessible by horse but were perhaps too remote to have imported furniture from the town centers. Welsh influence often extended to the adjacent English counties, as well.

Still other factors include the evolving role of the gentry versus the farmers and artisans and the ambiguity of the Welsh-English language barrier. Bebb also cautions against too mechanical a model of regional styles, because furniture often was purchased from distant suppliers, or artisans moved from one location to another. Another important point is assessing what "metropolitan influence" meant in any given situation. Wales shared in international trade with many ports along the English Channel, and there is reason to think that some traditions were transmitted directly from the Continent, particularly from France and the Low Countries.

Bebb then rehearses the sorts of evidence used to establish regional traditions. These include makers' marks, owners' names or heraldry, documentation, fixed woodwork, architectural contexts, inventories, travelers' accounts, and the history of the woodworking professions. Many of these observations have been made by other authors, but Bebb displays a singularly acute use of them.

The survey in chapters 2 through 4 of the first volume, treating furniture made before 1700, perforce includes heterogenous material. Chapter 2 treats a great deal of ecclesiastical material, much of which previously was ascribed to unspecified foreign artisans. Save for the occasional dragon or other emblem, most of the carving differs little from contemporary French carving. One of Bebb's somewhat irrational claims surrounds the technique, style, and dating of the great three- and four-posted board-seated turned chairs for which Wales is famous. He seems determined to regard them as essentially a Welsh form, although the kinds of evidence he marshals to justify his claims are not convincing. Marginalia in medieval manuscripts demonstrate that such chairs were a pan-European tradition. The structural peculiarities associated with board seats trapped in grooves held in all four seat rails almost certainly evolved in the Low Countries, and similar chairs were made in England. What seems to have been peculiar about the Welsh chairs was their persistence well into the early eighteenth century, as well as extreme elaboration in format and decorative turnings. Why Bebb is compelled to push his arguments regarding the peculiarly Welsh character of these chairs is unclear, but he feels strongly enough about them to display personal rancor about those with differing opinions.

A series of monographs explicating famous groups of furniture associated with the Welsh gentry of the fifteenth and sixteenth centuries makes up chapter 3. Herein resides a difficult nexus of stylistic and iconographic problems. The Welsh gentry claimed descent from remote royal and noble houses, with suitable heraldic devices. They also employed Celtic bards to celebrate their lineage. At the same time, many of these figures were allied to the House of Tudor, which seized the English throne in 1485. Many of the Welsh gentry became English courtiers and served on diplomatic missions in France or elsewhere. The strong French influence already apparent in both English and Welsh furniture of this period was thereby reinforced. Bebb demonstrates that the mix of French carving and Welsh iconography seen in objects owned by Welsh grandees was not the result of foreign artisans, but represented the first Welsh style.

Chapter 4 closes the first volume and provides a bridge to the second volume. The late seventeenth century was the period during which the classic Welsh joined furniture forms were formulated, including the two-part cupboard *(Cwpwrdd deuddarn),* the three-part cupboard *(Cwpwrdd tridarn),* the dresser, the coffer, and the long-case clock. The divergence between noble and gentry patronage widened, but the yeoman class prospered enough to begin commissioning expensive case pieces. Once again, Bebb asserts that "hierarchal diffusion" is an inadequate explanation for the emergence of distinctively Welsh furniture forms, but many of the objects illustrated in this chapter are indistinguishable from furniture made in many regions of England under metropolitan influence.

The second volume (with chapter 5) begins with a discussion of the most metropolitan area of Wales along the Severn estuary. In this area, traditional configurations of case pieces and house plans persisted, save among the nobility and upper gentry. The typical interior coalesced into a two-room plan with lofts. The ground floor usually had a combined sitting room and kitchen *(Cegin)*, with case pieces and a settle forming partitions between the sitting room and a bedroom. Some bedrooms featured built-in box beds like the *lit clos* of Brittany. The principal case pieces remained much like their immediate late-seventeenth-century forebears but began to be made with characteristic tabled panels with shaped heads. Seating and tables tended to be much more like those of other regions in England.

A genre of inlaid furniture on the southern coast is of immediate interest to American scholars for two reasons. First, it provides a direct analogue and possible source for similar inlay in the Delaware River valley region. Second, some small coffers were mounted on stands with cabriole legs; this practice may reflect Dutch influence, and it is reminiscent of similar coffers from the Channel Islands, Bermuda, and the Connecticut coast.

As the eighteenth century progressed, some regional types began to influence each other, and certain furniture forms were hybridized. Some large coffers with drawers were provided with doors in the upper case and became short linen presses. The same process transformed some cupboards into linen presses. The three-part cupboard, which began as a cross between a cupboard and a dresser, completed an evolution into a dresser in many areas. At the same time, dressers became specific to local areas, with an important variant that had an open shelf or storage area in the lower case. Desks with drawers became more common and were associated with literacy and the Methodist religion. Another type associated with Methodism was the preaching chair used in Methodist chapels. Some of these may have been portable, because accounts of Methodist preaching in America during the Great Awakening mention preaching chairs, as well.

The impact of nineteenth-century revival styles and the slow industrialization of the furniture trade are analyzed in chapter 6. The genre of romantic views of Welsh interiors greatly augments written resources in this period. Metropolitan styles became much more influential, and the traditional joinery was largely displaced by dovetailed board construction. In progressive circles the successive historical styles were much in vogue, but in this respect the Welsh situation does not appear to have differed all that much from other regions of England.

Chapter 7 treats subsequent industrialism and the furniture trade in the late nineteenth and early twentieth century. Save for certain developments like bardic chairs associated with the revival of Gaelic poetry, these later objects are of limited interest and not notably different from developments elsewhere.

In the eighth and final chapter, Bebb recapitulates his arguments against what he terms the "orthodox" or elitist theory of stylistic diffusion. This chapter is largely redundant; the book might have been strengthened by reserving these theoretical arguments for the end, instead of confronting the reader with them at the beginning of the first volume. Ultimately, one comes away with the judgment that much of what Bebb is arguing for so vociferously already influences much of American vernacular furniture study. In some cases, one wonders why Bebb considers certain furniture forms or practices as especially Welsh, when they are also present in Scotland, Ireland, and Brittany.

Several telling criticisms can be made about the book as a whole. It does not present a comprehensive survey of regional types, although the text suggests a detailed knowledge of them that must be accepted on faith. This could have been addressed with CDs that explained regional data. Second, one would have appreciated a discussion of possible Welsh influence on America, particularly in the mid-Atlantic colonies, where large numbers of Welsh immigrants had such an impact.

Robert F. Trent
Wilmington, Delaware

Dena Goodman and Kathryn Norberg, eds. *Furnishing the Eighteenth Century: What Furniture Can Tell Us about the European and American Past.* New York: Routledge, Taylor and Francis Group, 2007. x + 245 pp.; numerous color and bw illus., index. $65.00.

In 2002 UCLA's Center for Seventeenth- and Eighteenth-Century Studies brought together scholars of American and Western European furniture to ponder the question that forms the subtitle of this book. A grant from the Chipstone Foundation helped to fund the cost of printing the color plates, and the J. Paul Getty Museum provided support for the conference. The scholars represented are not all furniture specialists; many study furniture and interior decoration as depicted in eighteenth-century literature or are historians who consider furniture and material culture key documents for the study of the past. The result is a volume that includes a broad range of approaches, from articles that concentrate on close physical examination of objects, such as Carolyn Sargentson's "Looking at Furniture Inside Out: Strategies of Secrecy and Security in Eighteenth-Century French Furniture," to those that depend almost entirely on documentation about furniture rather than the objects themselves, such as David Porter's "A Wanton Chase in a Foreign Place: Hogarth and the Gendering of Exoticism in the Eighteenth-Century Interior." Both approaches can be valuable, and the volume gives furniture scholars much to ponder. For the Americanist, intriguing issues arise from comparing the objects that we typically study with the information provided here about French furniture and interior decoration.

The book is broken into four parts: "Mapping Meaning Globally"; "Diffusing Furniture, Fashion, Taste"; "Making Meaning in the Domestic

Interior"; and "Forms, Function, Meanings." The three essays in the first section chronicle the use and popularity of exotic motifs, designs, and materials in England, France, and the French colony of Saint Dominique. Madeleine Dobie explores the possibility that the "attention to the Orient and under representation of the colonial world" in French furniture "are at least in a loose sense, structurally linked" (p. 13). She concedes that the number of objects made with colonial raw materials that employ imagery inspired by objects from China, Persia, Japan, and Turkey is small, and that the use of tropical American woods is just as often associated with pastoral imagery. Dobie asserts that "in the 18th century the incentive to overlook colonial conditions of production was strong, as it meant turning a blind eye to slavery along with the vicissitudes of plantation agriculture, notably lasting ecological evils such as soil erosion, drought, and flooding" (p. 32).

While Europeans were becoming critical of slavery by the middle of the eighteenth century, it is difficult to believe that they had a twentieth-century understanding of the relation between agricultural practices and the destruction of delicate tropical ecosystems. Dobie does not discuss the popular conception of the American colonies as idyllic societies existing in Jean-Jacques Rousseau's "state of nature," a phenomenon that should have led her to explain, rather than dismiss, the use of pastoral and natural imagery in eighteenth-century French furniture. Nonetheless, American readers will be interested in the provincial furniture, particularly from Rochelle, and the connection of the merchants in this region to West Indian trade.

"Mahogany as Status Symbol: Race and Luxury in Saint Dominique at the End of the 18th Century" by Chaela Pastore discusses how, until the late eighteenth century, most West Indian mahogany imported by French traders was immediately reexported to England. Eventually, craftsmen in the French coastal cities that were most directly involved in trade with the French West Indies began making mahogany furniture like that illustrated in Dobie's essay. Pastore documents the ownership of mahogany furniture in Saint Dominique by white inhabitants—artisans and shopkeepers as well as merchants and planters—through newspaper advertisements for the sale of furnishings owned by people preparing to return to France following the massive slave insurrection of 1791. Interestingly, in a discussion that in many ways mirrors Kathryn Norberg's article later in the volume, Pastore also finds widespread ownership of mahogany furniture among mixed-race women. She asserts that "luxury became cheap first because it was given over to the new rich, and second because it slowly became available to free men and women of color. But, most egregiously, luxury spun out of control when it became attached to slave ownership" (p. 45). Thus, slave ownership became part of the growing moral debate over luxury in France.

David Porter's "A Wanton Chase in a Foreign Place: Hogarth and the Gendering of Exoticism in the Eighteenth-Century Interior" also deals with connections between Chinese taste and excessive luxury. Porter begins with a discussion of William Hogarth's disparaging attitude toward Chinese style and Chinese goods in his *Analysis of Beauty* (1753) and demonstrates how Hogarth's works and contemporary popular literature equated the taste for Chinese exoticism with female vanity. He asserts that while Hogarth believed in the power of aesthetic experience "unconstrained by classicist pieties," he "rejected the Chinese taste as an alternative to classicism. . . . out of a sobering recognition that to grant the validity of the Chinese taste would be to legitimate a regime not only of female aesthetic self-determination, but also of the autonomy of female desire more generally conceived" (p. 59).

Section 2, "Diffusing Furniture, Fashion, Taste," focuses on the role of individuals in the dissemination of taste and includes essays on a Parisian upholsterer, provincial New England globemakers and cabinetmakers, and Parisian courtesans.

Natacha Coquery explores the business of Mathurin Law, an upholsterer who plied his trade on the rue Saint-Honoré in Paris, through the business records of the six years leading up to his bankruptcy in 1788. Coquery's findings will be familiar to readers conversant with works on American craftsmen, in that she shows that Law served a wide clientele, from artisans to aristocrats, and that a large portion of his business was devoted to repairs and maintenance. Her contribution here is in demonstrating that Law disseminated fashion not just through the sale of lavish furnishings and textiles but also by renting furniture in the latest style to those who wanted to remain at the height of fashion. By providing stylish goods in a wide price range, he helped to disseminate the latest design ideas to a broad audience.

David Jaffee explores the careers of provincial New England artisans, most born in rural areas, who learned their crafts in coastal urban centers and then returned to the backcountry. His work is largely based on previous research; his contribution here is in showing how these urban-trained "cultural entrepreneurs" recognized the market for refinement among the rising village gentry. These urban-trained artisans responded by providing furniture that combined knowledge of the latest styles with the aesthetic preferences of their clients. Producers and consumers thus participated in "processes of integration and creolization" (p. 92).

In "Goddesses of Taste: Courtesans and Their Furniture in Late-Eighteenth-Century Paris" Kathryn Norberg transports us to pre-Revolutionary Paris at a time when the homes of the celebrated courtesans of Paris were the subject of broad curiosity and auctions of their belongings were attended by thousands of people who paid to tour the courtesan's rooms in advance of a sale. Paris's courtesans were all performers, most in the opera, and as such their activities were well known to the general public through the popular press, and their lavish homes and apartments were chronicled in period engravings. It is difficult not to think of today's "MTV Cribs" as Norberg describes the critique of the excessive luxury of the courtesan's furnishings by one segment of society, concurrent with the prurient adoration of their belongings by other segments of society. In the final analysis, Norberg does not really assert that the courtesans were trendsetters but notes that "it is still a measure of the development of fashion and luxury that models of elegance were found even on the fringes of society, among the marginal and the unpedigreed" (p. 110).

Although the title of section 3 is "Making Meaning in the Domestic Interior," the real focus is on how style and goods unified the French elite and helped to create a French national identity. Using the logic of the essays earlier in the volume, this helped to focus the moral debate over luxury on the upper class and fueled the class conflict of the French Revolution.

Donna Bohann's essay, entitled "Color Schemes and Decorative Tastes in the Noble Houses of Old Regime Dauphine," begins with a description of the French style in the seventeenth century that was characterized by harmony and the extensive use of a single color or color scheme. Bohann finds that in the frontier province of Dauphine, noblemen followed the prevailing Parisian fashions. Dauphine was the scene of class conflict over taxation in the late seventeenth century that resulted in two classes of nobility. The old nobility remained exempt from taxation while those ennobled after 1602 were subject to taxation. As a result, Bohann suggests that "in Dauphine the world of goods might have been even more vital to the world of the nobility, as they struggled to define themselves in the eyes of their local community by other than traditional means" (p. 125). She concludes with the provocative suggestion that "perhaps the market was transforming Dauphinois elites into Frenchmen; perhaps the world of goods promoted a national identity" (p. 126).

This theme is echoed in "The Joy of Sets: The Uses of Seriality in the French Interior," in which Mimi Helman explores the vogue for matched sets of furniture in eighteenth-century France. The uniformity of these sets, and of French interior decoration in general, created a national style in which "spaces designed according to a shared decorative vocabulary . . . were legible and comfortable to negotiate" (p. 147). She brings four perspectives to bear on the question of why repetition was so pronounced in mid-eighteenth-century France and sharply contrasts preindustrial and postindustrial attitudes toward matched sets. While today we see sets as the product of mechanized production, in the eighteenth century the task of creating sameness presented the artisan with a technical challenge. Similitude was costly to create, because any mistake could ruin the set. She suggests that the uniformity of the French style created familiar formulas that solidified the bonds between participants engaged in common social rituals. Her treatment here shows how important it is in material culture studies to look beyond our postindustrial views and understand objects and their production within their original contexts.

Mary Salzman's "Decoration and Enlightened Spectatorship" focuses on the language of seduction as portrayed in two decorative paintings by Jean-François de Troy. Salzman explores the symbolism in the paintings that relates to proper social deportment and the rules of polite courtship in French society.

The essays in the fourth section, "Forms, Functions, Meanings," each focus on single furniture forms. Ann Smart Martin examines the tea table in colonial America, Dena Goodman takes a close look at the eighteenth-century French secretaire, and Carolyn Sargentson examines the elaborate locking mechanisms on Parisian case furniture, using as her primary objects a secretaire made circa 1785–1790 and a jewel casket of circa 1775. These essays explore issues of how furniture can help us to understand how people defined themselves through the objects that they owned and how the introduction of new furniture forms—or mechanisms to make them more private—can help us to understand the underlying needs of a particular society.

Martin calls the tea table "the most culturally charged" furniture form in the English colonies. The tea table, she asserts, is a form full of paradoxes. Sturdy, yet sometimes able to be folded, it "signified wealth and breeding if owned by the right people" (p. 169), but if the wrong sort gained possession of it, the indulgence in the luxuries surrounding tea drinking—the acquisition of costly porcelain and the neglect of duty and work in favor of the seductions of teatime—could lead to dissipation and ruin. A symbol of gentility, the tea table was also appropriated in the colonies for political action. It was the first feminized object in America; women presided over the presentation of tea and the parties that it occasioned. "Throughout England and the colonies, the table's meaning thus teeters depending on when and who and where" (p. 169). Martin's essay explores all of these themes and raises provocative questions about the origins and function of the tea table in colonial society.

Dena Goodman notes that "the creation of the secretaire signaled a new authorial need for a personal surface on which to write, as private persons shifted from dictating their letters to a confidential secretary to penning them themselves" (p. 183). Dictionaries of the eighteenth century, she notes, demonstrate a fundamental transformation of the word "secretaire" as a name for someone whose job it was to write letters to the name for a specific piece of furniture. The other type of eighteenth-century writing furniture, the bureau, was a working desk that was reserved exclusively for men, while the secretaire was a personal desk used by both men and women. The bureau was open and flat and could accommodate both the owner and his clerk, whereas the secretaire was an intimate object, large enough for only one person, with concealed writing surfaces, drawers, and other storage spaces hidden inside the desk that could be locked. Gradually, the secretaire, an object for the leisure writer, became associated with women. "As the bureau was the mark of a man who had moved up in the world, owning a secretaire showed that a woman was both literate and leisured enough to engage in correspondence." (p. 188). Goodman notes that the "secrecy of the secretaire was, at bottom, the secrecy of letter writing itself" (p. 194). The increase in the popularity of the secretaire was a sign of the desirability of privacy and the autonomy of the individual. The existence of locked drawers could unnerve a jealous husband, for instance, in a theme played out frequently in French literature.

The final essay in the volume and, to my mind, the best, is Carolyn Sargentson's "Looking at Furniture Inside Out: Strategies of Secrecy and Security in Eighteenth-Century French Furniture." Sargentson examines the tension inherent in the existence of locking furniture, largely by exploring in detail the ingenious and complex locking mechanisms found on a secretaire attributed to Guillaume Benneman of Paris and made circa 1785–1790 and a combined jewel casket, secretaire, and writing table made by Jean-Henri Riesener in Paris circa 1775. What I find most fascinating about this article is the close reading of the objects themselves, and how the questions Sargentson addresses are the questions that arise from her detailed examination of the furniture. Why did craftsmen expend so much energy, and patrons so much expense, on the creation of elaborate locking mechanisms—mechanisms that required an intimate knowledge of a specific piece of furniture and its hidden spaces? Sargentson discusses the dynamic and protective role of furniture in households "whose harmony appears to have been dependent on ideals of trust and confidentiality" between husband and wife, master and servant (p. 226). High-performance locks and mechanisms were "empowered actors in the drama and performance of safeguarding spaces and possessions . . . acting as guardians of protected spaces even when the house or key holder was absent" (p. 226). Sargentson notes that in some cases the release of these locks could produce so much force that persons unaware of their operation could be startled or even injured. Some pieces, once opened, could be closed only by their owners. The owner then could easily detect any violation of his or her secret space. She concludes that "[r]ather than these objects simply being part of a linear progression toward more specialized function in furniture, toward the design of smaller more mobile objects . . . and part of a development of writing furniture forms in general . . . they must also be read as having had the potential to be active players on the domestic stage" (pp. 232–33).

Here, in fact, is the conclusion of all the articles in this volume: furniture matters, because furniture helps us to order our lives. These thought-provoking essays will, one hopes, inspire more scholarship in this vein. The best works, those like Sargentson's, not only explore references in literature and painting to furniture as a social agent but involve detailed examination of the physical attributes and ingenious construction of eighteenth-century furniture forms. When these studies are the result of the work of scholars with a thorough knowledge of the objects, they can help us to ask questions—the questions that the objects themselves present—that will allow furniture to tell us even more about societies of the past.

Barbara McLean Ward
Moffatt-Ladd House and Garden
Tufts University

Compiled by
Gerald W. R. Ward

Recent Writing on American Furniture: A Bibliography

▼ THIS YEAR'S LIST includes works published in 2007 and roughly through September 2008. As always, a few earlier publications that had escaped notice are also included. The short title *American Furniture 2007* is used in citations for articles and reviews published in last year's edition of this journal, which is also cited in full under Luke Beckerdite's name,

Once again, many people have assisted in compiling this list. I am particularly grateful to Luke Beckerdite, Jonathan Fairbanks, Dennis Carr, Julie Muñiz, Nonie Gadsden, Kelly H. L'Ecuyer, Erin McCutcheon, Brett Angell, Michael K. Brown, Joseph Cunningham, Arthur Dion, Peter Follansbee, Josh Lane, Robert A. Leath, Johanna McBrien, Peter Spang, David Wood, Phil Zea, and Barbara McLean Ward, as well as to the scholars who have prepared reviews for this issue.

I would be glad to receive citations for titles that have been inadvertently omitted from this or previous lists. Information about new publications and review copies of significant works would also be much appreciated.

The Acme of Perfection Tea Table. New York: Sotheby's, January 19, 2008. 51 pp.; color and bw illus. (Re Philadelphia rococo-style tea table.)

Adamson, Glenn. "Craft and the Romance of the Studio." *American Art* 21, no. 1 (spring 2007): 14–19. 7 bw illus.

———. "Critic's Corner: Thinking through Craft." *American Craft* 67, no. 6 (December 2007–January 2008): 90–92. 5 color illus.

———. "Susan Working Works It Out." *Woodwork,* no. 112 (August 2008): 18–24. Color illus.

———. *Thinking through Craft.* Oxford and New York: Berg, 2007. x + 209 pp.; color and bw illus., index.

Alfody, Sandra. *Crafting Identity: The Development of Professional Fine Craft in Canada.* Montreal and Kingston, Ontario: McGill-Queen's University Press, 2005. viii + 300 pp.; bw illus., bibliography, index.

———, ed. *Neocraft: Modernity and Crafts.* Halifax: Press of the Nova Scotia College of Art and Design, 2008. 273 pp.; illus.

Allen, Thomas M. *A Republic in Time: Temporality and Social Imagination in Nineteenth-Century America.* Chapel Hill: University of North Carolina Press, 2008. xiii + 275 pp.; bw illus., bibliography, index.

[American Craft Council]. *Shaping the Future of Craft: 2006 National Leadership Conference.* New York: American Craft Council, 2007. 190 pp.; color illus., appendix.

American Period Furniture: Journal of the Society of American Period Furniture Makers 7 (2007): 1–80. Numerous color and bw illus. (See also individual articles cited elsewhere.)

Ames, Kenneth L. Review of Allison Boor et al., *Philadelphia Empire Furniture.* In *American Furniture 2007,* 255–61.

Apicella, Mary Ann. *Scottish Cabinetmakers in Federal New York.* N.p., 2007. 183 pp.; numerous color and bw illus., bibliography, index. Distributed by University Press of New England, Hanover and London.

Arnold, Mark. "Carving Lessons from Salem: The Work of Samuel McIntire." *Woodwork,* no. 111 (June 2008): 52–57. 16 color illus.

———. "Rediscovering the Christopher Collection." *American Period Furniture: Journal of the Society of American Period Furniture Makers* 7 (2007): 60–63. Color illus.

Attfield, Judy. *Bringing Modernity Home: Writings on Popular Design and Material Culture.* Manchester, Eng.: Manchester University Press, 2007. 256 pp.; 24 bw illus. (Re British design.)

Bailey, Chris. "Half a Century of Innovation and Trials: A Story of Silas B. Terry, Horologist." *NAWCC Bulletin* 50 (June 2008): 286–309. Color and bw illus.

Baker, Donna S., ed. *Atomic Dinettes: Mid-Century Kitchen Elegance.* Atglen, Pa.: Schiffer Books, 2005. 160 pp.; numerous color and bw illus., bibliography.

[Bayou Bend Collection]. "Gift of Rare Texas Furniture Boosts Bayou Bend Collection." *Antiques and the Arts Weekly,* May 30, 2008, 19. 2 bw illus.

Beach, Laura. "To Please Any Taste: Litchfield County Furniture and Furniture Makers, 1780–1830." *Antiques and the Arts Weekly,* June 20, 2008, 1, 40–41. 16 bw illus.

Bebb, Richard. *Welsh Furniture, 1250–1950: A Cultural History of Craftsmanship and Design.* 2 vols. Kidwelly, Wales: Saer Books, with the assistance of Amgueddfa Cymru—National Museum Wales and the support of Llyfrgekk Genedlaethol Cymru—National Library Wales, 2007. Vol. 1, *Welsh Furniture, 1250–1700.* 365 pp.; 595+ color and bw illus., bibliography, index, glossary. Vol. 2, *Welsh Furniture, 1700–1950.* 441 pp.; 800+ color and bw illus., bibliography, index, glossary.

Beckerdite, Luke, ed. *American Furniture 2007.* Milwaukee: Chipstone Foundation, 2007. vii + 292 pp.; numerous color and bw illus., bibliography, index. Distributed by Antique Collectors' Club.

Bell, Michael W., Betsy K. White, and Sumpter Priddy III. "'First Rate & Fashionable': The Furniture of John Erhart Rose." *Antiques* 173, no. 5 (May 2008): 102–11. 14 color and bw illus.

Binzen, Jonathan. "Tommy Simpson." In John Kelsey, ed., *Furniture Studio 5: The Meaning of Craft,* 110–21. Asheville, N.C.: Furniture Society, 2007. Color illus.

Blakesley, Rosalind P. *The Arts and Crafts Movement.* New York: Phaidon, 2007. 272 pp.; 250 color illus.

Bolgiano, Chris, and Glenn Novak, eds. *Mighty Giants: An American Chestnut Anthology.* Bennington, Vt.: American Chestnut Foundation and Images from the Past, 2007. x + 285 pp.; numerous color and bw illus., bibliography, index.

Bosley, Edward R., and Anne E. Mallek, eds. *A New and Native Beauty: The Art and Craft of Greene and Greene.* London and New York: Merrell in association with the Gamble House/USC, 2008. 272 pp.; numerous color and bw illus., bibliography, index. (Includes contributions by Margaretta M. Lovell, Edward S. Cooke Jr., Bruce Smith, and others.)

Bowett, Adam. Review of Frances Gruber Safford, *American Furniture in the Metropolitan Museum of Art.* Vol. 1, *Early Colonial Period: The Seventeenth-Century and William and Mary Styles.* In *Winterthur Portfolio* 42, nos. 2–3 (summer/autumn 2008): 183–84.

[Brandywine River Museum]. "Beyond Content: Wooden Boxes May 24 at Brandywine." *Antiques and the Arts Weekly,* May 16, 2008, 14. 2 bw illus.

Brocklebank, R. David, et al. *Made in Pennsylvania: A Folk Art Tradition.* Greensburg, Pa.: Westmoreland Museum of American Art, 2007. 80 pp.; color illus.

Brown, Michael K. "Important Group of Texas Furniture Given to Bayou Bend." *Intelligencer* (fall 2008): 2–5. 4 color illus.

Brown, Michael K., with an introduction by Jonathan Leo Fairbanks and contributions by Emily Ballew Neff. *America's Treasures at Bayou Bend: Celebrating Fifty Years.* London: Scala in association with the Museum of Fine Arts, Houston, 2007. xviii + 157 pp.; numerous color and bw illus., bibliography, index. Distributed by Antique Collectors' Club.

Brunk, Andrew. "Benjamin Randolph Revisited." In *American Furniture 2007,* 2–82. 61 color and bw illus., 4 appendixes.

Bruns, Craig. "Fore and Aft: Philadelphia Collects Maritime." *Antiques and Fine Art* 8, no. 4 (spring 2008): 158–63. Color illus.

Bryan, John M. "The John Hancock Desk: A Tale of Provenance." *Antiques* 174, no. 3 (September 2008): 50. 2 color illus. (Re desk, probably English, ca. 1760–1770, with John Hancock provenance.)

Burch, Abby. "Trust Research Grant: Joseph Murphy, Cabinetmaker." *Decorative Arts Trust* [Newsletter] 17, no. 3 (winter 2007–8): 5, 8. 2 bw illus.

Burks, Jean, ed. *Shaker Design: Out of This World.* New Haven: Yale University Press for the Bard Graduate Center for Studies in the Decorative Arts, Design, and Culture, New York, and the Shelburne Museum, Shelburne, Vermont, 2008. xxx + 245 pp.; numerous color illus., timeline, bibliography, index. (With contributions by Robert P. Emlen, Jean M. Humez, M. Stephen Miller, Sumpter Priddy, Kory Rogers, and Gerard C. Wertkin.)

Buskirk, Russell. "A California Collection." *Antiques and Fine Art* 8, no. 4 (spring 2008): 164–71. Color illus.

[Byers, John Eric]. *Squares and Rectangles: John Eric Byers, Gallery NAGA.* Boston: Gallery NAGA, 2008. Unpaged; color illus.

Callahan, W. Mickey. "North Bennet Street School Wins 2007 Cartouche Award." *American Period Furniture: Journal of the Society of American Period Furniture Makers* 7 (2007): 12–17. Color illus.

Carlisle, Nancy. "Sacred and Profane." *Historic New England* 9, no. 1 (summer 2008): 26. 1 color illus. (Re parlor organ, ca. 1875, by Prescott Organ Co., Concord, N.H.)

Carlson, Spike. *A Splintered History of Wood: Belt Sander Races, Blind Woodworkers, and Baseball Bats.* New York: HarperCollins, 2008. xv + 411 pp.; bw illus., list of resources, bibliography, index.

Carpenter, Ralph E. "A Reviviscent Newport Colonial: The Nichols-Wanton-Hunter House." *Antiques and Fine Art* 8, no. 4 (spring 2008): 182–87. 10 color illus.

[Castle, Wendell]. "New Work by Wendell Castle on View at Barry Friedman." *Antiques and the Arts Weekly,* May 23, 2008, 33. 1 bw illus.

Cerio, Gregory. "Showmanship and Fantasy: The Designs of James Mont." *Antiques* 174, no. 1 (July 2008): 76–81. 9 color illus.

———. "What Modern Was: Mid-Century Masters of Luxury." *Antiques* 173, no. 5 (May 2008): 112–19. 14 color illus.

Coffin, Sarah D., Gail S. Davidson, Ellen Lupton, and Penelope Hunter-Stiebel. *Rococo: The Continuing Curve, 1730–2008.* New York: Cooper-Hewitt Museum, National Design Museum, Smithsonian Institution, 2008. 265 pp.; numerous color and bw illus., bibliography, index.

[Colonial Williamsburg]. "Midwest Donor Presents Folk Art Gift to Colonial Williamsburg." *Antiques and the Arts Weekly,* June 27, 2008, 33. 3 bw illus. (Re collection of Juli Grainger.)

[Concord Museum]. "American Style: Russell Kettell's Pine Furniture." *Concord Museum Newsletter* (winter 2008): 1, 6. 3 bw illus.

[———]. "Discoveries: Timepiece of Daniel Munroe, Jr. (1775–1859)." *Antiques and Fine Art* 8, no. 3 (January–February 2008): 18. 2 color illus.

Cooke, Edward S., Jr. "Modern Craft and the American Experience." *American Art* 21, no. 1 (spring 2007): 2–9. 8 color and bw illus.

Cooke, Edward S., Jr., Ann Y. Smith, and Derin Bray. *To Please Any Taste: Litchfield County Furniture and Furniture Makers, 1780–1830.* Litchfield, Conn.: Litchfield Historical Society, 2008. 82 pp.; numerous color and bw illus.

Cooper, Dan. "Daniel Pabst's Furniture." *Style 1900* 20, no. 3 (fall 2007): 54–61. Color illus.

Cooper, Helen T., et al. *Life, Liberty, and the Pursuit of Happiness: American Art from the Yale University Art Gallery.* New Haven: Yale University Art Gallery in association with Yale University Press, 2008. xv + 368 pp.; numerous color and bw illus., index.

Cunningham, Joseph. *The Artistic Furniture of Charles Rohlfs.* New York: American Decorative Art 1900 Foundation; New Haven: Yale University Press, 2008. xxi + 282 pp.; 321 color and 16 bw illus., appendix, bibliography, index.

———. "Conversations in Western New York: Charles Rohlfs and Gustav Stickley." *Antiques* 173, no. 5 (May 2008): 120–29. 20 color and bw illus.

[Delaware Art Museum]. "Delaware Art Museum Presents Garry Knox Bennett, Chairmaker." *Antiques and the Arts Weekly,* June 27, 2008, 11. 2 bw illus.

DePillis, Mario S., and Christian

Goodwillie. *Gather up the Fragments: The Andrews Shaker Collection*. Hancock, Mass.: Hancock Shaker Village, 2008. vii + 392 pp.; numerous color and bw illus., catalogue, appendixes, index. Distributed by Yale University Press, New Haven.

Deutsch, Alexandra, and Bruce M. Schuettinger. "Conserving an Annapolis Masterwork One Step at a Time: The Story of a Tall Clock." *Antiques and Fine Art* 8, no. 2 (autumn/winter 2007): 222–27. 8 color illus.

Dixon, Jenny, et al. *Design: Isamu Noguchi and Isamu Kenmochi*. New York: Five Ties Publishing in association with the Isamu Noguchi Foundation and Garden Museum, 2007. 183 pp.; numerous color and bw illus., appendixes, index.

Douglas, Mary. "When Is a Teapot Not a Teapot?" *American Art* 21, no. 1 (spring 2007): 19–23. 4 color and bw illus.

Duncan, Alastair, et al. *High Style: Masterworks from the Bernard and Sylvia Ostry Collection in the Royal Ontario Museum*. Toronto: Royal Ontario Museum, 2005. 148 pp.; numerous color illus., bibliography, index, appendix.

Edwards, Clive. *Encyclopedia of Furnishing Textiles, Floorcoverings and Home Furnishing Practices, 1200–1950*. Aldershot, Eng., and Burlington, Vt.: Lund Humphries, 2007. vii + 255 pp.; numerous color and bw illus., bibliography.

Evans, Nancy Goyne. "The Written Evidence of Furniture Repairs and Alterations: How Original Is 'All Original'?" In *American Furniture 2007*, 191–249. 17 bw illus.

"Faculty Selects 2006." In John Kelsey, ed., *Furniture Studio 5: The Meaning of Craft,* 96–109. Asheville, N.C.: Furniture Society, 2007. Color illus.

Farago, Claire. Review of Joseph J. Rishel, Suzanne-Stratton-Pruitt, et al., *The Arts in Latin America, 1492–1820*. In *Winterthur Portfolio* 41, no. 4 (winter 2007): 305–10.

Filler, Martin. "Hope Springs Eternal Again." *Antiques* 174, no. 1 (July 2008): 64–67. 5 color illus.

———. "Miller's Tale: The Indianapolis Museum of Art Gets a Modern Design Collection." *Antiques* 174, no. 2 (August 2008): 68–71. 3 color illus.

———. "A Rare Kem Weber Chair Shows the European Side of Modernism." *Antiques* 173, no. 5 (May 2008): 90–93. 3 color and bw illus.

———. "The Real Menil." *Antiques* 174, no. 3 (September 2008): 78–85. 7 color and bw illus.

Fitzgerald, Oscar P. "Bespoke Interiors." In John Kelsey, ed., *Furniture Studio 5: The Meaning of Craft,* 81–95. Asheville, N.C.: Furniture Society, 2007. Color illus.

———. *Studio Furniture of the Renwick Gallery, Smithsonian American Art Museum*. Washington, D.C.: Smithsonian American Art Museum in association with Fox Chapel Publishing, East Petersburg, Pa., 2008. 224 pp.; numerous color illus., bibliography.

———. Review of Glenn Adamson with Gary Michael Dault, *Gord Peteran; Furniture Meets Its Maker*. In *Winterthur Portfolio* 42, nos. 2–3 (summer/autumn 2008): 195–96.

Flaherty, Duncan. *Remodeling the Nation: The Architecture of American Identity, 1776–1858*. Durham, N.H.: University of New Hampshire Press/University Press of New England, 2007. xi + 246 pp.; 15 bw illus., index.

Forsyth, Amy. "Martin Puryear: The Art of a Craftsman." *Woodwork*, no. 111 (June 2008): 64–69.

Fort, Megan Holloway. "Current and Coming: Historic Deerfield." *Antiques* 173, no. 5 (May 2008): 24–26. 2 color illus. (Re "Into the Woods: Crafting Early American Furniture" exhibition on view through 2012.)

Freinkel, Susan. *American Chestnut: The Life, Death, and Rebirth of a Perfect Tree*. Berkeley: University of California Press, 2007. xi + 284 pp.; map, index.

[Frid, Tage]. *Tage Frid: Woodworking Profile*. Newtown, Conn.: Taunton Press, 2006. DVD.

"Gallery." *Woodwork*, no. 108 (December 2007): 42–50. Color illus.

"Gallery." *Woodwork*, no. 109 (February 2008): 42–48. Color illus.

"Gallery." *Woodwork*, no. 110 (April 2008): 40–47. Color illus.

"Gallery." *Woodwork*, no. 111 (June 2008): 39–46. Color illus.

"Gallery." *Woodwork*, no. 112 (August 2008): 40–46. Color illus.

Garrett, Elizabeth Donaghy. "Living with Antiques: A Lakeside Retreat." *Antiques* 173, no. 1 (January 2008): 172–83. 23 color illus.

Garrison, Ritchie. Review of Harvey Green, *Wood: Craft, Culture, History*. In *Winterthur Portfolio* 42, no. 1 (spring 2008): 84–86.

Gómez-Ibáñez, Miguel, and Oscar Fitzgerald. "At the Crossroads." In John Kelsey, ed., *Furniture Studio 5: The Meaning of Craft,* 48–57. Asheville, N.C.: Furniture Society, 2007. Color illus.

Gontar, Cybèle T., and Jack D. Holden. "The Butterfly Man of New Orleans: A Rare Group of Creole-Style Armoires Identified." *Antiques* 173, no. 5 (May 2008): 136–45. 13 color illus.

Goodman, Dena, and Kathryn Norberg, eds. *Furnishing the Eighteenth Century: What Furniture Can Tell Us about the European and American Past*. New York: Routledge, Taylor and Francis Group, 2007. x + 245 pp.; numerous color and bw illus., index.

Gordon, Glenn. "Functional Sculpture: An Eclectic Show of Furniture from the Upper Midwest." *Woodwork*, no. 112 (August 2008): 59–65. Color illus.

Gordon, John Stuart. Review of

Christopher Long, *Paul T. Frankl and Modern American Design*. In *Studies in the Decorative Arts* 15, no. 2 (spring/summer 2008): 127–29.

Green, Nancy E. "Living with Antiques: Stephen Gray's Collection of Arts and Crafts Furnishings." *Antiques* 174, no. 3 (September 2008): 104–13. 15 color illus,

Grieve, Victoria M. "'Work That Satisfies the Creative Instinct': Eleanor Roosevelt and the Arts and Crafts." *Winterthur Portfolio* 42, nos. 2–3 (summer/autumn 2008): 159–82. 18 color and bw illus.

Griffin, William, Florence Griffin, et al., with foreword by Deanne D. Levison. *Neat Pieces: The Plain-Style Furniture of Nineteenth-Century Georgia*. 1983. Reprint. Athens: University of Georgia Press, 2006. 236 pp.; color and bw illus. (New edition of classic work by Harvey P. Green.)

Griffith, Robert. "Craft and the Designer." In John Kelsey, ed., *Furniture Studio 5: The Meaning of Craft*, 58–65. Asheville, N.C.: Furniture Society, 2007. Color illus.

Gura, Judith. *Sourcebook of Scandinavian Furniture: Designs for the 21st Century*. New York: W. W. Norton, 2007. 304 pp.; 500 color illus., 2 appendixes, bibliography, index.

Gustafson, Eleanor H., ed. "Collectors' Notes: The Kelloggs and Clocks in Connecticut." *Antiques* 172, no. 5 (November 2007): 56–58. 2 color illus. (Reporting research by Nancy Finlay.)

Hampton, Monica, and Lily Kane, eds. *Shaping the Future of Craft: 2006 National Leadership Conference, Houston, Texas, October 19–21, 2006*. New York: American Craft Council, 2007. 190 pp.; numerous color and bw illus., appendix, CD.

Hargreaves, Gayle. "Classical Revival: Classical Furniture Graces a Greek Revival Home." *Antiques and Fine Art* 8, no. 2 (autumn/winter 2007): 176–88. Color and bw illus.

Harvard, Ralph. "A Baroque Virginia Treasure House: Landon Carter's Sabine Hall." *Antiques* 173, no. 4 (April 2008): 104–15. 18 color illus.

———. "Lifestyle: A Virginia Country Estate." *Antiques and Fine Art* 8, no. 6 (summer/autumn 2008): 140–51. Color illus.

Headley, Jeff. "Handmade." *American Period Furniture: Journal of the Society of American Period Furniture Makers* 7 (2007): 18–21. Color illus.

Herman, Todd, and Brian Lang. "Carolina Collects." *Antiques and Fine Art* 8, no. 6 (summer/autumn 2008): 152–58. Color illus.

Herrmann, Ruth. "A Tallcase Clock at the Harry S. Truman National Historic Home." *NAWCC Bulletin* 50, no. 4 (August 2008): 399–400. 3 bw illus.

"Highlights: The Fix on Colonial Philadelphia Furniture." *Antiques and Fine Art* 8, no. 6 (summer/autumn 2008): 42. 1 color illus. (Re exhibition at Philadelphia Museum of Art.)

[Historic Deerfield]. "Into the Woods: Crafting Early American Furniture Opens May 3 Historic Deerfield." *Antiques and the Arts Weekly,* May 2, 2008, 56. 3 bw illus.

Holden, Jack D. "Echoes of an Island Past: Flush-Panel Armoires in Saint-Domingue and Louisiana." *Southern Quarterly* 44, no. 3 (spring 2007): 118–26. Illus.

Hummel, Charles F. Review of Philip D. Zimmerman, *Delaware Clocks*. In *Winterthur Portfolio* 41, no. 4 (winter 2007): 316–18.

[Johnson Collection]. *Property from the Collection of Mr. and Mrs. George Fenimore Johnson*. New York: Sotheby's, January 19, 2008. 147 pp.; color and bw illus.

Journal of Modern Craft 1, no. 1 (March 2008): 1–172. Numerous bw illus. (First issue of new journal, edited by Glenn Adamson, Tanya Harrod, and Edward S. Cooke Jr.)

Katra, Joseph R., Jr. *Clockmakers and Clockmaking in Maine: 1770–1900*. Columbia, Pa.: National Association of Watch and Clock Collectors, 2008. 154 pp.; illus.

Kelsey, John, ed. *Furniture Studio 5: The Meaning of Craft*. Asheville, N.C. Furniture Society, 2007. 128 pp; numerous color illus., index.

Kirwin, Liza. "Primary Sources for the Study of Studio Craft." *American Art* 21, no. 1 (spring 2007): 23–27. 5 color and bw illus.

Koomler, Sharon Duane. "An Eye toward Perfection: John S. Williams, Sr., and the Shaker Museum and Library, Old Chatham and New Lebanon, New York." [*Catalogue of the*] *54th Annual Winter Antiques Show*, 114–19. New York, 2008. Color and bw illus.

———. "Seeking Perfection: The Shakers' Material World." *Antiques and Fine Art* 8, no. 3 (January–February 2008): 268–75. Color illus.

Kopf, Silas. "Italian Intarsia and Figurative Work." *Woodwork,* no. 110 (April 2008): 48–54. 12 color illus. (An excerpt from the same author's *A Marquetry Odyssey*. See also pp. 52–53, re bevel cutting.)

———. *A Marquetry Odyssey: Historical Objects and Personal Work*. Montpelier, Vt.: Image and Word, 2008. 232 pp.; illus.

Kraak, Deborah E. "Early Protective Covers for Upholstered Furniture: Fit, Fabrics, and Applicability to Today's Interiors." *Antiques and Fine Art* 8, no. 3 (January–February 2008): 254–59. 8 color illus.

Kriesman, Lawrence, and Glenn Mason. *The Arts and Crafts Movement in the Pacific Northwest*. Portland, Ore.: Timber Press, 2007. 398 pp.; numerous color and bw illus., bibliography, index.

Krzyzanowski, Michael. *Laverne Furniture, Textiles, and Wallcoverings*. Atglen, Pa.: Schiffer Publishing, 2007. 192 pp.; color illus.

LaFond, Edward F., Jr., and J. Carter Harris. *Pennsylvania Shelf and Bracket Clocks: 1750–1850*. Columbia, Pa.: National Association of Watch and Clock Collectors, 2008. 134 pp.; illus.

Lahikainen, Dean T. "A McIntire Restoration: The East Parlor in the Peirce-Nichols House, Salem, Massachusetts." *Antiques* 172, no. 6 (December 2007): 82–91. 19 color and bw illus.

———. *Samuel McIntire: Carving an American Style*. Salem, Mass.: Peabody Essex Museum, 2007. 300 pp.; 458 color & bw illus., appendixes, bibliography, index. Distributed by University Press of New England, Hanover and London.

———. "Samuel McIntire: Carving an American Style." *Antiques and Fine Art* 8, no. 2 (autumn/winter 2007): 200–208. 12 color illus.

———. "Samuel McIntire: Carving an American Style." *American Art Review* 19, no. 5 (September–October 2007): 98–101. 14 color illus.

Landrey, Gregory J. "Two Gaming Tables: A Comparison." *Antiques and Fine Art* 8, no. 6 (summer/autumn 2008): 172–79. 9 color illus.

Lasser, Ethan. "Reading Japanned Furniture." In *American Furniture 2007*, 168–90. 19 color and bw illus.

Lavine, John. "Donald Fortescue: Maker and Teacher." *Woodwork*, no. 111 (June 2008): 18–25. Color illus.

———. "Inspired by China." In John Kelsey, ed., *Furniture Studio 5: The Meaning of Craft*, 66–80. Asheville, N.C.: Furniture Society, 2007. Color illus.

Leath, Robert A. "Servitude and Splendor: The Craftsmen and the Carved Furniture of the Rappahannock River Valley, 1740–1780." *Antiques* 173, no. 5 (May 2008): 94–101. 11 color illus.

Loftheim, Kaare. "The German Factor." *American Period Furniture: Journal of the Society of American Period Furniture Makers* 7 (2007): 36–41. 6 color illus.

Long, Christopher. "Paul T. Frankl's Skyscraper Furniture." *Antiques* 173, no. 1 (January 2008): 162–71. 14 color illus.

Loomes, Brian. *Watchmakers and Clockmakers of the World: Complete Twenty-first Century Edition*. London: NAG Press, 2006. 888 pp.; illus. (Revised edition of work published by G. H. Baillie in 1929.)

Luhrs, Kathleen. "Museum Accessions." *Antiques* 173, no. 2 (February 2008): 36. 2 color illus. (Re oak library table of 1901 designed by Charles Rohlfs and acquired by the Huntington Library.)

———. "Museum Accessions." *Antiques* 174, no. 3 (September 2008): 32, 34. 3 color illus. (Re Texas furniture acquired by the Bayou Bend Collection.)

Lutz, Terry. "Reflections on the Role of Decorative Arts in the Production of American Furniture." *American Period Furniture: Journal of the Society of American Period Furniture Makers* 7 (2007): 22–31. Color illus.

MacAdam, Barbara J. *American Art at Dartmouth: Highlights from the Hood Museum of Art*. Hanover, N.H.: Hood Museum of Art, Dartmouth College; Hanover, N.H.: University Press of New England, 2007. ix + 244 pp.; 220 + color and bw illus., bibliography, index.

Mack, Daniel. *The Adirondack Chair: A Celebration of a Summer Classic*. New York: HNA Books, 2008. 128 pp.; illus.

[Maloof, Sam]. *Sam Maloof: Woodworking Profile*. Newtown, Conn.: Taunton Press, 2006. DVD.

Mansfield, Howard. "Frank Lloyd Wright's Zimmerman House." *Antiques* 174, no. 2 (August 2008): 72–77. 9 color illus.

Marx, Ina Brosseau, and Allen Marx. *Furniture Restoration*. New York: Watson-Guptill, 2007. 272 pp.; numerous color illus., list of resources, bibliography, index.

Mascolo, Frances McQueeney-Jones. "American Style: Russell Kettell's Pine Furniture." *Antiques and the Arts Weekly*, March 28, 2008, 1, 40–41. 8 bw illus.

———. "'Gather Up the Fragments': The Andrews Shaker Collection at Hancock Shaker Village." *Antiques and the Arts Weekly*, July 26, 2008, 1, 44–46. 19 bw illus.

———. "Samuel McIntire: Carving an American Style." *Antiques and the Arts Weekly*, October 19, 2007, 1, 40–41. bw illus.

Matthews, Lydia. "Homespun Ideas." In John Kelsey, ed., *Furniture Studio 5: The Meaning of Craft*, 20–29. Asheville, N.C.: Furniture Society, 2007. Color illus.

Mauritz, Larry. "The Sunflower Chests of Hartford and Wethersfield, Connecticut." *American Period Furniture: Journal of the Society of American Period Furniture Makers* 7 (2007): 42–51. Color illus.

Merrill, Todd. *Bruce Mont: The King Cole Penthouse*. New York: Todd Merrill and Associates, 2008. 112 pp.; illus.

Metcalf, Bruce. "News Flash." In John Kelsey, ed., *Furniture Studio 5: The Meaning of Craft*, 336. Asheville, N.C.: Furniture Society, 2007. Color illus.

Meyer, Jonathan. *Great Exhibitions: London, New York, Paris, Philadelphia, 1851–1900*. Woodbridge, Eng.: Antique Collectors' Club, 2006. 336 pp.; color and bw illus., bibliography, index.

Mijuskovic, Ben. "The Collector's Find: The Lost Shakespeare." *Maine Antique Digest* 36, no. 10 (October 2008): 40B–41B. 5 bw illus.

Miller, Angela, Janet C. Berlo, Bryan J. Wolf, and Jennifer L. Roberts. *American Encounters: Art, History, and Cultural Identity*. Upper

Saddle River, N.J.: Pearson Prentice Hall, 2008. xvii + 686 pp.; numerous color and bw illus., bibliography, index.

Miller, M. Stephen. *From Shaker Lands and Shaker Hands: A Survey of the Industries.* Hanover, N.H.: University Press of New England, 2007. xv + 190 pp.; numerous color illus., bibliography, index.

Montgomery, Gladys. "Connecticut Pastoral." *Antiques and Fine Art* 8, no. 3 (January–February 2008): 222–35. Color illus.

Moss, Peter, ed. *Asian Furniture: A Directory and Sourcebook.* London: Thames and Hudson, 2007. 308 pp.; 451 color illus., index. Distributed by W. W. Norton, New York.

Muñiz, Julie M. "A Personal Touch: Furniture from the Wornick Collection." *Antiques and Fine Art* 8, no. 2 (autumn/winter 2007): 218–21. 6 color illus.

Murphy, Kevin D. "Early Folk Art Collecting in Maine: Its Contributions to Modernism." *Antiques* 174, no. 1 (July 2008): 82–89. 11 color illus.

———, ed. *Folk Art in Maine: Uncommon Treasures, 1750–1925.* Camden, Me.: Down East Books, 2008. 143 pp.; color and bw illus., bibliography, index.

Newell, Aimee E. "Celebrating 275 Years of Brotherhood: The Grand Lodge of Masons in Massachusetts." *Antiques* 173, no. 4 (April 2008): 84–91. 11 color illus.

Newell, Laurie Britton. *Out of the Ordinary: Extraordinary Craft.* London: V&A Publications, 2007. 143 pp.; 70 color and 12 bw illus.

Nutt, Craig. *500 Chairs.* New York: Lark Books, 2008. 408 pp.; color illus.

O'Neill, Stephen C. "Pilgrim Hall Museum's Collection: A Case Study." *Pilgrim Society News* (winter/spring 2008): 13–15. 4 bw illus. (Re Boston caned chair, ca. 1715–1725.)

Palmer, Arlene M. "Douglas Volk and the Arts and Crafts in Maine." *Antiques* 173, no. 4 (April 2008): 116–23. 18 color illus.

Pearce, Clark, Catherine Ebert, and Alexandra Alevizatos Kirtley. "From Apprentice to Master: The Life and Career of Philadelphia Cabinetmaker George G. Wright." In *American Furniture 2007*, 110–31. 33 color and bw illus.

Peeters, Natasja, ed. *Invisible Hands? The Role and Status of the Painter's Journeyman in the Low Countries, c. 1450–c. 1650.* Louvain: Peeters, 2007. xxv + 174 pp.; bw illus., tables, graphs, bibliography, index.

[Philadelphia Museum of Art]. "New Exhibition Brings 1772 Philadelphia Furniture Price Book to Full Disclosure." *Antiques and the Arts Weekly*, July 11, 2008, 4. 3 bw illus.

Philbrick, Richard W. "Simon Willard's Astronomical Shelf Timekeeper." *NAWCC Bulletin* 50, no. 2 (April 2008): 131–46. 10 bw illus., table, graphs.

Phillips, Rebecca. "MESDA's Barber Family Desk and Bookcase." *Antiques and Fine Art* 8, no. 4 (spring 2008): 218–19. 1 color illus.

Pierce, Kerry. "Mark Soukop: The Authentic Eye." *Woodwork*, no. 108 (December 2007): 18–25. Color illus.

———. "Shaker Storage Furniture." *Woodwork*, no. 112 (August 2008): 80. 1 color illus.

[Powell, Phillip Lloyd]. "Phillip Lloyd Powell (1918–2008)." *Modernism* 11, no. 2 (summer 2008): 26. 1 color and 1 bw illus. (Re obituary of studio furniture maker.)

Prouty, F. Shirley. *Master Carver from Germany's Passion Play Village to America's Finest Sanctuaries: Johannes Kirchmayer, 1860–1930.* Portsmouth, N.H.: Peter E. Randall, 2007. xii + 124 pp.; numerous color and bw illus., appendixes, bibliography, index.

Quimby, Ian M. G. *American Family Treasures: Decorative Arts from the D. J. and Alice Shumway Nadeau Collection.* Lexington, Mass.: National Heritage Museum, 2005. ix + 194 pp.; numerous color and bw illus., bibliography, index.

Raizman, David, and Carma R. Gorham, eds. *Objects, Audiences, and Literature: Alternative Narratives in the History of Design.* Newcastle, Eng.: Cambridge Scholars Publishing, 2007. 184 pp.; 62 bw illus., index.

Retford, Kate. *The Art of Domestic Life: Family Portraiture in Eighteenth-Century England.* New Haven: Yale University Press, 2006. ix + 294 pp.; numerous color and bw illus., bibliography, index.

[Ribic-Kingsley Collection]. *The Drs. John R. Ribic and Carla M. Kingsley Shaker Collection.* Portsmouth, N.H.: Northeast Auctions, August 2, 2008. 123 pp.; numerous color illus.

Riegler, Shax. "Windows on the Past: Watercolors of Long-Vanished Houses and Gardens." *Antiques* 174, no. 2 (August 2008): 60–67. 12 color illus.

[Riordan Collection]. *The Collection of Marguerite and Arthur Riordan, Stonington, Connecticut.* New York: Christie's, January 18, 2008. 163 pp.; numerous color illus., index.

Risatti, Howard. "Craft and Design: What's the Distinction?" *American Craft* 68, no. 1 (February–March 2008): 116–19. 6 color illus.

———. *A Theory of Craft: Function and Aesthetic Expression.* Chapel Hill: University of North Carolina Press, 2007. xvi + 327 pp.; illus. bibliography, index.

Robertson, Cheryl, with contributions by Terrence Marvel and a new essay by John C. Eastberg. *The Domestic Scene (1897–1927): George M. Niedecken, Interior Architect.* 2nd rev. and enl. ed. Milwaukee: Milwaukee Art Museum, 2008. 120 pp.; numerous color and bw illus., chronology, bibliography, checklist, index. Distributed by University of Wisconsin Press, Madison.

Romeu, Gabriel, ed. "The

Indianapolis Manifestoes." In John Kelsey, ed., *Furniture Studio 5: The Meaning of Craft,* 8–19. Asheville, N.C.: Furniture Society, 2007. Color illus.

Ryerson, Mitch. "An American Benchmaker in Paris: Vive la Différence!" In John Kelsey, ed., *Furniture Studio 5: The Meaning of Craft,* 122–27. Asheville, N.C.: Furniture Society, 2007. Color illus.

Sack, Albert. "An Americana Odyssey." *Antiques* 174, no. 3 (September 2008): 114–17. 5 color and bw illus.

———. *Fine Points of Furniture: Early American*. 1950. 2nd rev. ed. Atglen, Pa.: Schiffer Publishing, 2007. 304 pp.; 708 bw illus.

———. "On Collecting: Regional Identification of American Queen Anne Flat-Top High Chests." *Antiques and Fine Art* 8, no. 6 (summer/autumn 2008): 189–91. Color and bw illus.

Safford, Frances Gruber. *American Furniture in the Metropolitan Museum of Art*. Vol. 1, *Early Colonial Period: The Seventeenth Century and William and Mary Styles*. New York: Metropolitan Museum of Art in association with Yale University Press, 2007. xii + 451 pp.; 158 color and 170 bw illus., appendixes, concordance, bibliography, index.

———. "Early Colonial Furniture at the Metropolitan Museum of Art." *Antiques and Fine Art* 8, no. 3 (January–February 2008): 248–53. 8 color illus.

Schinto, Joanne. "Samuel McIntire: Carving an American Style." *Maine Antique Digest* 35, no. 12 (December 2007): 18C–19C. bw illus.

[Schnall Collection]. *The Schnall Collection of American Furniture and Folk Art*. Portsmouth, N.H.: Northeast Auctions, August 2, 2008. 151 pp.; numerous color illus.

[Schoedinger Collection]. *Property from the Collection of George and Lesley Schoedinger*. New York: Christie's, January 18, 2008. 87 pp.; numerous color and bw illus.

Sennett, Richard. *The Craftsman*. New Haven: Yale University Press, 2008. ix + 326 pp.; index.

Sfirri, Mark. "Anatomy of a Masterpiece: The 1931 Corner Desk by Wharton Esherick." *Woodwork,* no. 112 (August 2008): 52–56. Color and bw illus.

———. "The Hammer-Handled Chairs: Found Object Art by Wharton Esherick." *Woodwork,* no. 110 (April 2008): 60–62. Color illus.

———. "Hogbin Reflecting." *Woodwork,* no. 109 (February 2008): 18–27. Color illus.

[Shaker Museum and Library]. *An Eye toward Perfection: The Shaker Museum and Library: The Loan Exhibition at the 54th Winter Antiques Show, January 18–27, 2008*. N.p., 2008. 23 pp.; color illus.

Sharpe, Shannon. "A Tale of Two Houses." *American Craft* 67, no. 6 (December 2007–January 2008): 70–79. Color illus.

Shove, Elizabeth, Matthew Watson, Martin Hand, and Jack Ingram. *The Design of Everyday Life*. New York: Berg, 2007. vi + 174 pp.; illus., bibliography, index.

"Sideboard Goes to Governor's Mansion." *Maine Antique Digest* 35, no. 12 (December 2007): 8A. 2 bw illus. (Re sideboard, ca. 1795, with a history in Wiscasset, acquired by Maine State Museum.)

Smith, Anita M. *Woodstock: History and Hearsay*. 1959. 2nd ed. Woodstock, N.Y.: Woodstock Arts, 2006. 336 pp.; numerous color and bw illus., bibliography, index.

Smith, Ann Y. "Litchfield County Cross-braced Furniture." *Antiques* 173, no. 5 (May 2008): 130–35. 9 color illus.

Snyder, Alan. "Two Rare Federal Tripod Fire Screens." *Maine Antique Digest* 36, no. 9 (September 2008): 23C. 7 bw illus.

Solis-Cohen, Lita. Review of Luke Beckerdite, ed., *American Furniture 2007*. In *Maine Antique Digest* 36, no. 7 (July 2008): 8D–10D. 1 bw illus.

Somerson, Rosanne. "Show Us Your Drawers." In John Kelsey, ed., *Furniture Studio 5: The Meaning of Craft,* 37–47. Asheville, N.C.: Furniture Society, 2007. Color illus.

[Speed Art Museum]. *The Speed Art Museum: Highlights from the Collection*. London: Merrell for the Speed Art Museum, 2007. 240 pp.; illus., glossary, index.

Sperling, David A. "Making a Case for a Transitional Case: One Man's Opinion." *NAWCC Bulletin* 50, no. 4 (August 2008): 461–64. 13 bw illus., bibliography.

Stender, Thomas, ed. *The Penland Book of Woodworking*. Asheville, N.C.: Lark Books, 2006. 224 pp.; numerous color illus., index. (Re studio furniture.)

Stensrud, Rockwell. *Newport: A Lively Experiment, 1639–1969*. Newport, R.I.: Redwood Library and Athenaeum, 2007. xvii + 510 pp.; illus., maps, bibliography, index.

"Stickley's 'Enlightened Home' at Fenimore Art Museum." *Antiques and the Arts Weekly,* May 9, 2008, 4. 1 bw illus.

Storb, Christopher. "Conservation of a Fabled Masterpiece: The Fox and Grapes High Chest at the Philadelphia Museum of Art." *Antiques and Fine Art* 8, no. 4 (spring 2008): 142–49. Color and bw illus.

Swan, Christopher. "Going Green in the Eighteenth Century: Understanding Original Windsor Furniture Color." *Antiques and Fine Art* 8, no. 3 (January–February 2008): 300–301. 4 color illus.

Sweet, Fay. *Vintage Furniture: Collecting and Living with Modern Design Classics*. Woodbridge, Eng.: Antique Collectors' Club, 2007. 224 pp.; numerous color and bw illus., directory, index.

Taylor, Ruth S. "Connected to the Past: Objects from the Collections of the Newport Historical

Society." *Antiques and Fine Art* 8, no. 6 (summer/autumn 2008): 180–85. Color illus.

Taylor, Snowden. "The Clocks and Movements of C. Jerome & Co., Richmond, Virginia." *NAWCC Bulletin* 50, no. 4 (August 2008): 402–17. Color and bw illus.

Tillou, Jeffrey. *Jeffrey Tillou Antiques*. Litchfield, Conn.: Jeffrey Tillou Antiques, 2008. 79 pp.; numerous color illus.

Trent, Robert F., and John D. Alexander. "American Board-Seated Turned Chairs, 1640–1740." In *American Furniture 2007*, 83–109. 43 color and bw illus, line drawings.

Tucker, Kevin W. Review of Martin Eidelberg et al., *The Eames Lounge Chair: An Icon of Modern Design*. In *American Furniture 2007*, 261–65.

Van Dyk, Stephen. "Focus On: A Unique Kimbel & Cabus Furniture Album." *Nineteenth Century* 28, no. 1 (spring 2008): 30–33. 5 bw illus., bibliography.

Veiteberg, Jorunn. *Craft in Transition*. Translated by Douglas Ferguson. Bergen, Norway: Bergen National Academy of the Arts, 2005. 110 pp.; 52 color and bw illus., bibliography.

Ward, Gerald W. R., comp. "Recent Writing on American Furniture: A Bibliography." In *American Furniture 2007*, 271–80.

Waterhouse, George. "Clocks of the State of Georgia Governor's Mansion." *NAWCC Bulletin* 50 (June 2008): 259–66. bw illus.

Watkin, David, and Philip Hewat-Jaboor, eds. *Thomas Hope, Regency Designer*. New Haven: Yale University Press for the Bard Graduate Center for Studies in the Decorative Arts, Design, and Culture, New York, 2008. xxiv + 527 pp.; numerous color and bw illus., catalogue, appendix, bibliography, index.

Wheary, Dale Cyrus. "Vanity of Vanities: A Tiffany and Company Rediscovery." *Antiques* 173, no. 4 (April 2008): 102–3. 2 color illus.

Wilkins, Robert W. "The Shaker Aesthetic Reconsidered." *Antiques* 173, no. 1 (January 2008): 194–201. 12 color illus.

Wilson, Kristina. Review of Christopher Long, *Paul T. Frankl and Modern American Design*. In *American Furniture 2007*, 251–55.

Wood, David F. Review of Philip D. Zimmerman, *Delaware Clocks*. In *American Furniture 2007*, 265–69.

Woodward, Ian. *Understanding Material Culture*. Los Angeles: Sage Publications, 2007. vii + 191 pp.; bibliography, index.

[Woolley Collection]. *The Mark Woolley Collection of Vintage Radios*. New York: Bonhams, December 19, 2007. 83 pp.; numerous color illus,

Yale University Art Gallery. *Collecting for a New Century: Celebrating the 175th Anniversary of the Yale University Art Gallery and the Centennial of Paul Mellon's Birth*. New Haven: Yale University Art Gallery, 2007. 422 pp.; numerous color illus., catalogue, index.

Zea, Philip. "A Presidential Case." *New England Antiques Journal* 27, no. 2 (August 2008): 35–37. 3 color illus. (Re Seymour sideboard.)

Zimiles, Murray, et al. *Gilded Lions and Jeweled Horses: The Synagogue to the Carousel*. Hanover, N.H.: University Press of New Hampshire in association with American Folk Art Museum, New York, 2007. xviii + 171 pp.; numerous color and bw illus., bibliography, index.

Zimmerman, Philip D. "Early American Furniture Makers' Marks." *American Furniture 2007*, 132–67. 55 color and bw illus.

Index

Abberley and Hartley (New York City), 158
The Academy (Sweerts), 35(fig.)
Acanthus pilasters, 123
Account books, Nathaniel Gould, 1(&fig. 1), 3–13(&figs. 8, 9, 12)
Ackermann, Rudolph, 102(&fig. 17), 105(fig.)
Adam, Robert, 96, 99, 226
Adams, Elisha, 162, 181, 183
Adamson, Glenn, 228
Affleck, Thomas, 182, 218
African American artisan, shaved chair of, 53–54(&fig. 33)
Ailsworth, Joseph, 193
Alder, C., 173
Alexander, Jennie, 57n1
Alexander, John, 211
Alexander, John D., Jr., 57n1; armchair, 38(&fig.), 40(fig.); side chairs, 41(fig.), 42(figs.), 43(fig.), 56(fig.)
Alexander, Richard, 163
Allen, Edwards, 10
Allison, Michael, 173; clothespress, 159(fig.); pier table, 91(fig. 3)
Amboma, pier table, 103(fig. 18)
American black walnut, dresser, 157(fig. 13)
American furniture: influence of French design on, 218; influence of Irish émigrés on, 219, 222–23; rococo-revival, 218–19
American Furniture in the Metropolitan Museum of Art. Vol. 2. *Late Colonial Period* Heckscher), 13
American Furniture in the Metropolitan Museum of Art. Vol. 1. *Early Colonial Period* (Safford), 209–14
American Rococo, 1750–1775 (Heckscher & Bowman), 218, 226
American Seating Furniture, 1630–1730 (Forman), 213, 229
Americans in mahogany trade, 70–73
Ames, Kenneth L., 214–19
Analysis of Beauty (Hogarth), 233
Andrews, George, 223
Annin, William B., 77(fig. 13), 80(fig.)
The Annunciation Triptych, 28(fig.)
Antiques, 226
Appleton, John, 7–8(&fig. 9)
Appleton, Nathaniel, 167
Appleton, William, secretary-and-bookcase, 140(fig.)
Apprenticeships, 212

Archer, Samuel, Jr., 1, 24n1
Argand lamp, 105
Armada table, 221
Armchairs, 45(fig. 21); based on European art and New England armchairs, 38–41(&figs.); birch, 51(fig.); maple, 36(fig. 11), 37(fig.), 46(fig. 24), 47(fig.), 48(fig.), 52(fig.); oak, 40(fig.), 44(fig.), 45(fig. 22)
Arms: blade, 46(&fig. 23); scroll, 44(&fig.), 48(&fig.)
Arnold, Joseph, 64–65
Arnold, William, 186
Artists, patrons and, 216
Ash: armchairs, 36(fig. 11), 37(fig.), 44(fig.), 46(fig. 24), 48(fig.); flax wheel, 183(fig.); high chest of drawers, 148(fig.); rot and, 49; side chairs, 53(fig.), 55(fig. 35)
Ashton, Isaac, 163
Ashworth, Gavin, 209
Atmore, Rachel, 133
Atsey chayim, 84
Austin, Josiah, 65
Austin, Perez, 139, 155
Avery, Jeduthern, 132, 146, 149–50, 166
Avery, Oliver, 133, 135, 146
Aymar, John Q., 95(fig.)

Baarsen, Reinier, 215
Bachman, Jacob, 156, 158
Backgammon board repair, 193
Backstool, 29(figs.)
Baize, replacing, 134
Baker, Benjamin, 166, 167
Baker, Thomas, 167
Bakongo culture, 83
Baldwin, Isaac, 138
Ball, John T., 154
Baltimore: oak armchairs, 38(fig.), 40(fig.); oak side chairs, 41(fig.), 42(figs.), 43(fig.), 56(fig.)
Bancroft, James, 135
Bandbox, 189
Bardine, Benjamin, 183
Bark seat, 50
Barnes, Elijah, 189
Barnes, Elizur: andiron board repair, 183; bookcase refinishing, 143; bottle drainer repair, 178; chest of drawer repair, 150, 154, 155; desk repairs, 137, 139, 143; musical stool, 191; sideboard repair, 161, 162, 163

Barrell, William, 143, 171, 181
Barry, Joseph B., 223
Barry and Krickbaum (Philadelphia), 130*n*39, 162; pier table, 122(&fig.)
Bartlet, Nicholas, 8, 25*n*11
Bartlett, William, 133
Bass, John, 183
Bassett, Nathaniel, 156–57
Bast (bass) seat, 50
Bastian, Friedrich, 142, 147, 154, 158
Batchelder, Josiah, 8, 25*n*11
Bayntun, Andrew, 77(fig. 13), 80(fig.)
Bay Settlement, 62
Beale, Pennell, 143, 154, 162
Beautiful Homes: or, Hints in House Furnishings, 126
Bebb, Richard, 228–32
Beckerdite, Luke, 228
Beech, pier table, 97(fig.)
Beekman, James, 138, 164
Beesley, William G., 143, 158
Belize, mahogany trade and, 62(&fig.), 71, 73–79(&fig. 10)
Bellangé, Pierre-Antoine, 129*n*35
Belter, John Henry, 218; étagère, 124(fig.)
Bement, Mary, 150
Bench, slaughterer's, 30(fig.)
Benge, Samuel, 193
Benjamin, Asher, 227
Benjamin, Miles, 165
Benneman, Guillaume, 236
Bentley, William, 164, 226
Berks County (Pennsylvania), cupboard, 156(fig.)
Bernard, Nicholas, 99(fig. 12)
Beville, William, 214*n*2
Biddle, Nicholas, 122
Biddle, Owen, 167
Bigley, John, 132
Billings, William, 179
Birch, 49; armchair, 51(fig.), 52; for bureaus, 153, 199*n*47; side chair, 53(fig.)
Birch veneer, bureau, 152(fig.)
Birdcages, repairs to, 194
Birth of the Virgin Mary (von Kulmbach), 34(fig. 9)
Blackwell, John, 181
Blade arms, 46(&fig. 23)
Blair, Natalie K. (Mrs. J. Insley), 209
Blind tenons, 33, 35(fig.)
Blow, Richard, 142, 154, 180, 182
Board seats, 51(fig.)
Bohann, Donna, 235

Bolles, H. Eugene, 209
Bolts, on cupboards, 156
Bombé chests, 24–25*n*10
Bombé desk-and-bookcase, 18, 19(fig.)
Bombé shaping, 7–8, 22
Bond, Matthew, 75
Bonnet box, 189
Bookcases, repair of, 138, 142–43
Booker, Richard, 189
Book of Kells, 220
Boom chain, 76, 78(&fig. 15)
Borland, Robert, 176–77, 180, 182
Boston: bureau, 152(fig.); desk, 14(fig. 19); *The Dinner Party,* 114(fig.); furniture construction details, 17; high chest of drawers, 148(fig.); looking glass, 167(fig.); mahogany trade and, 67; tape loom, 188(fig.); *The Tea Party,* 111(fig.), 112(fig.); teapot, 179(fig.); warming pan, 180(fig.)
Boston Gazette, 63
Bottle case, 189
Bottle chests, 130*n*40
Bottle drainer, 178
Boucher, François, 216
Bouvier, Michael, 141
Bowditch, Ebenezer, 157
Bowditch, Joseph, 175
Bowen, Jabez, 168, 179
Bowl: painting wooden, 177; pearlware, 83(fig.)
Bowling pins, 193
Bowman, Leslie Green, 218, 226
Box beds, 231
Boxes: carved, 212; repairs to, 188–91
Boynton, Thomas: bookcase repairs, 143; box repairs, 189; bread tray ornamentation, 175; bureau repair, 154, 155; clock repair, 165, 166; cornice repair, 173; desk repairs, 135, 137, 138, 142; fireboard repair, 183; hardware polishing, 154; musical instrument repairs, 192; picture frame repair, 170; spinning wheel repair, 185; tea waiter, 177
Braintree (Massachusetts), armchair, 44(fig.)
Braziletto, 86*n*28
Bread tray, 175
Bread trough: repair of, 174; walnut, 174(fig.)
Brettstuhl, 27, 29(figs.), 30
Brewster, John, Jr., 136(fig.)
Bridle joints, 42, 43(fig.)

Brinckerhoff, James L., 169, 191
British Honduras, 62
Bronson, Arthur, 160
Bronze powder stenciling, 89, 115
Brouwer, Jacob, 135, 161, 163, 167, 173
Bruen, Matthias, 160, 163
Bubier, Christopher, 181
Buckland, William, 99; pier table, 97(fig.); sideboard table, 98(fig.)
Buell, William, 212, 214*n*2
Buffet, 155
Bull, Henry, 145
Bunnel, John, 163
Bureaus, 199*n*45; columned, 151–52; defined, 150–51; desks and, 131–32; mahogany, 7(fig.), 151(fig.), 152(fig.); repairs to, 150–55; wood choices for, 153, 199*n*47
Bureau table, 7, 24*n*9
Burling, Samuel, 65
Burling, William S., 65
Burnsville (North Carolina), 55(&fig. 35)
Burrel, James, Jr., 162
Busch, Jason T., 218, 219
Butter molds, 178
Butternut, for bureaus, 153, 199*n*47
Butt hinges, 134

C. W. Wirth and Brothers, ice skates, 193(fig.)
Cabinet Dictionary (Sheraton), 131–32, 169, 171
The Cabinet-Maker and Upholsterer's Drawing-Book (Sheraton), 100(fig.), 101(fig.), 142
Cabinet-Maker and Upholsterer's Guide (Hepplewhite): chair patterns, 226; chest of drawers design, 146(fig.), 149(fig.); on secretary-and-bookcase, 140, 141; sideboard design, 161(fig.)
Cabinet-Maker's London Book of Prices (Sheraton), 142
Cabot, Andrew, 6(fig.), 7(fig.), 20(fig.), 22, 25*n*17
Cabot, Anna (Orne), 18, 20(fig.)
Cabot, Catherine, 6(fig.)
Cabot, Elizabeth (Higginson), 21(fig.), 22, 25*n*17
Cabot, Francis, 21(&fig.), 25*n*17
Cabot, Francis, Jr., 22, 25*n*17
Cabot, George, 10, 21(fig.), 22, 25*n*17
Cabot, Henry, 25*n*17
Cabot, John, 18, 20(fig.)

Cabot, John (III), 18, 20(fig.)
Cabot, Joseph, 8, 10, 18, 20(fig.), 21, 25n17
Cabot, Lydia (Dodge), 6(fig.), 25n17
Cabot, Nancy, 25n17
Cabot, Samuel, 18, 20(fig.)
Cabot family: desk-and-bookcases, 19–23(&figs. 30 & 31), 25n17; genealogy, 18, 19–20(fig.)
Cadwalader, John, 162, 168–69, 171, 180, 182, 190
Cadwalader, Thomas, 134, 193
Cahoon, William, 72
Cahoone, John, 64–65
Caledonia, 81–82(&figs.)
Camelback sofas, 226
Camman, Charles R., 137
Campin, Robert, 28(fig.)
Canada, shaved chairs in, 50–53(&figs. 29 & 31)
Candle box, 188
Candle molds, 178
Capron, William, 165
Caqueteuse joined armchairs, 44
Card, James, 72–73(&fig.)
Card, Jonathan, 72–73
Card, Sarah, 73
Card tables, pier tables *vs.*, 100
Carr, Moody, 158, 185
Carved box, 212
Caryatids, 223
Case of drawers. See Chest of drawers
Cases, repairs to, 188–91
Casters, 127n7; bureau, 154; sideboard, 162
Cavetto molding, 89, 118
Cedar, desks, 11(fig. 14)
Center for Seventeenth- and Eighteenth-Century Studies (UCLA), 232
Cermenati, Barnard, 169
Cescinsky, Herbert, 220
Chafing dishes, 181
Chair carving, 226–27
Chairs. See also Armchairs; Side chairs: *Brettstuhl*, 27, 29(figs.), 30; Nathaniel Gould, 5; settin', 31, 55(fig. 34), 58n8, 60n23; shaved. See Shaved post-and-rung chairs
Chamfers, 34(fig. 9)
Champlin, Christopher, 139, 149
Chandler, Lewis, Jr., 175
Channel Islands merchants, 72
Charlestown (Massachusetts), Nathaniel Gould in, 3

Charlotte, 71, 86n18
Chasse, Sarah N., 225
Checkers, 193
Cheever, Samuel, 180
Cheney, Silas E.: bonnet box repair, 189; bookcase repair, 143; bureau repair, 155; chest of drawers repair, 147, 148; chest repair, 149, 150; clock case assembly, 167; clock case repair, 165, 166; clotheshorse repair, 177; desk repair, 138, 141, 142; fire screen repair, 181–82; hand bellow repair, 183; piano repair, 191; repairs by, 135
Cherry: for bureaus, 153, 199n47; desks, 11(fig. 14); pier table, 97(fig.); tall clock case, 165(fig.); tape loom, 188(fig.); venetian blinds, 172(fig.)
Chest of drawers: designs for, 146(fig.); high, 148(fig.); mahogany, 6(fig.), 7; repair of, 146–55
Chest-on-chests, 226; design for, 149(fig.); mahogany, 9(fig.), 64(fig.); repair of, 149
Chests: alterations of, 149–50; bombé, 7–8, 24–25n10; in Metropolitan Museum of Art, 210–11; oak, 63(fig.); pine, 144(fig.); repair of, 143–46, 188–91
Chever, James, 65, 68
Chimney board, 182–83
Chimney glass, 168
Chinese exoticism, 233–34
Chipman, John, 15
Chippendale, Thomas, 99, 132, 228
Chipstone Foundation, 232
Choate House (Ipswich Harbor), 36(fig. 11)
Churn, repairs to, 176
Claggett, Thomas, 166
Clammons, John, 24n4
Clapier, Louis, 102
Clarke, Daniel, 227
Claw-and-ball feet, 17(&fig. 25)
Claypoole, George, 145, 160, 177
Clock cases: repair of, 164–67; tall, 165(fig.)
Clock hinges, 18(fig. 28)
Clock reel, 186
Closet, 155
Clotheshorse, 177
Clothespress, 159(fig.)
Coates, Samuel, 147
The Cobbler (Velner), 34(fig. 8)

Cock beading, 153, 199n46
Cockburn, Robert, 139
Coffeepot handles, repair/replacement of, 180
Coffee mill, repairs to, 178
Coffers, 231
Coffin, Sarah D., 214, 218
Cogswell, John, 2(fig.), 3
Cole, Solomon, 144, 164–65
Coleman, Charles, 220
Collection de meubles et objets de goût (de La Mésangère), 102(fig. 16), 104(fig.)
Collins, John, 142, 162
Collins, Mary, 179
Collins, Stephen, 158
Colonial Furniture in America (Lockwood), 209
The Colonial Furniture of New England (Lyon), 209
Coloring, 135, 146
Columned bureaus, 151–52, 199n45
Commode, 150
Company of the Eleutherian Adventurers, 86n28
Conger, John, gingerbread mold, 175(fig. 22)
Connelly, Henry, 138
Console tables, 97, 101, 125
Cook, Samuel, 181
Cooper-Hewitt rococo collection, 217
Copley, John Singleton, 188
Coquery, Natacha, 234
Corner cupboard, 157(fig. 12), 158
Cornice, 173
Courtenay, Hercules, 222
Courtesans, furnishings of Parisian, 234
Cowan, Robert, 164, 183
Coxon, Captain, 74–75
Cozzens, Matthew, 165
Crage, Robert, 184, 185
Craig, Charles, 69
Crane, Arnold, 181
Crapo, Philip, 138
Crosby, Daniel, 134
Crossbanding, 153, 199n46
Cruger, Henry, 72
C-shape handle, 179(&fig.)
Cuban mahogany, 61
Cullity, Brian, 46
Cumberland and Beazor (New York City), 169
Cummings, Nathan P., 184
Cupboards: closed rectangular,

156(fig.); corner, 157(fig. 12), 158; open rectangular, 157(fig. 13); repair of, 155–60; Welsh, 230, 231
Cupboard turn, 156
Currier, True, 154
Curtin, Ted, 49
Cutting and Trucking Mahogany in Honduras (Day and Son), 77(fig. 12)
Cuvillies, Jean-François, 216
Cwpwrdd deuddarn, 230
Cwpwrdd tridarn, 230
Cyma curves, 17, 18(fig. 28)

Dallas, Alexander J., 121
Dallas, Mathilda, 121
Dane, Nathan, 1
Danforth, Job: box repair, 189; chest of drawer repair, 147, 150; church repair, 176; coffee mill repair, 178; desk repair, 133, 134, 137–38; looking glass repair, 168; moving clock, 167; sideboard repair, 161–62; swift repair, 186; teapot handle repair, 179
Daniels, George, 184
Dart, Jonathan, 184
Dashwood, Charles, 79(fig.)
Dauphine (France), 235
Davidson, Gail S., 214, 217
Davis, Caleb, 164
Davison, Samuel, 147, 186
Daybooks, Nathaniel Gould, 1, 2(fig.), 3–13(& figs. 3–5, 7, 11, 14)
Deblois, George, 10
Decloux, Jean-Léon, 217
Deland, Philip, 186
Deleplaine, Joshua, 179
Delgado, Joseph, 74
Del Vecchio, Charles, 169, 170
Derby, John, 180, 183
Derby, Richard, 16(&fig. 24), 25n13
Derby family furniture, 225, 226, 228
Designs: chest-on-chest of drawers, 149(fig.); chests of drawers, 146(fig.); drapery, 104(fig.); pier table, 99–100(&fig. 14), 101(fig.); sideboard, 161(fig.); window treatment, 104(fig.), 105(fig.), 125(fig.)
Designs of Furniture (Wm. Smee and Sons), 92(fig.)
Desk-and-bookcases, 132; bombé, 18, 19(fig.); in Cabot family, 19–23 (&figs. 30, 31), 25n17; mahogany, 12(fig.), 13–16(&fig. 16); Nathaniel Gould, 5, 8–10; repair of, 139–40

Desk fall, repair of/replacement, 132–33, 134
Desk feet, repair of, 134
Desk-on-frame, 134
Desks: Henry Rust, 14(fig. 19), 15(figs.); mahogany, 66(fig.); Methodism and, 231; Nathaniel Gould, 5, 10, 11(fig. 14), 13(fig. 17), 14(fig. 18); repairs and alterations, 131–42
Devereaux, John, 134, 142
The Dinner Party (Sargent), 110, 113, 114(fig.)
Dipper handles, 180–81
Director (Chippendale), 99
Dobie, Madeleine, 233
Doerflinger, Thomas, 115
Dolphin supports, 123
Dominy, Nathaniel, IV, 165(fig.)
Dominy, Nathaniel, V: bureau repair, 154; chest alteration, 150; clock case, 164, 165(fig.); clockcase assembly, 167; coffee mill repair, 178; looking glass repair, 168; quill wheel repair, 186–87; spinning wheel repair, 185; umbrella repair, 192
Doolittle, John, 164
Doolittle, Nathaniel, 117
Double bass repairs, 191–92
Double parlors, pier tables and, 104
Dough tray, 174
Douglas, Samuel, 132, 145, 149, 156, 176, 181, 185
Douglas, William, 193–94
Douglass, Peter, 161
Dovetailing, 15, 16(figs. 22, 23), 17(&fig. 26), 22(&fig. 35)
Downing, Andrew Jackson, 218
Downing, Daniel, 139
Downing, Isaac, 166
Drapery design, 104(fig.)
Drawer repair, 133, 147, 154
Drawing Book (Sheraton), 102
Dressers, 155, 157(fig. 13), 158, 201n56, 201n57, 231
Dressing bureau, 152, 199n45
Drinker, Henry, 70
Dunmore Castle (Ireland), 221
Durand, John, 146, 174, 180, 188
Durand, Samuel, 145, 164, 186
Dutch: armchair in Dutch tradition, 45(fig. 22), 46; rococo furniture, 215
Duties, on mahogany, 68–69
Dyer, Charles, 183

Early, Jacob, 178
Earthfast dwelling, reproduction, 26(fig.)
East Hampton (New York), tall clock case, 165(fig.)
Easton, Jonathan, 190
East Room (White House), pier tables in, 117, 119–20(&fig. 29), 129n35, 129n36
Ebony, secretary-and-bookcase, 140(fig.)
Edouart, Augustine, 106(fig.)
Edward, Alexander, 190
Edwards, Alexander, 133, 134
Edwards, Dick, 86n17
Edwards, Quam, 86n17
Egerton, Abraham S., 138, 155, 168
Eichholtz, Jacob, 117–119(&fig. 28), 127n3, 129n32
Elderkin, John, 187
Ellery, Benjamin, 154, 189
Ellinger, John, 139, 176, 178
Elliott, John, Jr., 167, 169
Elliott, John, Sr., 168–69
Embry, Mary, 145
Emerson, Lambert, 221
Emerson, Peter, 156, 158
Empire pier table, 96
Enfilade, 104
Erving, William, 176
Escutcheons, 133
Étagère, 124(fig.), 125
European shaved post-and-rung chairs, 32–38(&figs. 6–10)
Evans, David, 133–34, 166, 167, 173, 183, 190
Exoticism, 233–34

Falconer, Jacob, 180
Fallboard, 22(fig. 32), 23
Fall-front desk, 134
Family in Silhouette (Edouart), 106(fig.)
The Family of John Q. Aymar (Twibill), 95(fig.)
"Fastening," 167
Feet: claw-and-ball, 17(&fig. 25); clock case, 166; French bracket, 146(fig.), 154; lion's paw, 89, 102, 118, 123; pier table, 127n2. *See also* lion's paw; stake, 29(fig. 4), 30
Felling Mahogany (McGahey), 76(fig.)
Fenlon, Jane, 221
Field crafts, 31

Filer, Phillip, 143, 177, 183
Fireboard: repairs to, 182–83; white pine, 182(fig.)
Fire fender repair, 183
Fire screen repair, 181–82
Fisher, Sidney George, 115
"Fitting up," 132
Fitzgerald, Desmond (Knight of Glin), 219–24, 229
"Fix," 144, 164
Flags (rush), 50
Flax (little) wheel: ash, 183(fig.); repairs to, 183–85
Follansbee, Peter, 38, 49, 209–14; side chair, 50(fig.)
Foot brackets and drops, 22(&fig. 34)
Foot stove repair, 183
Forman, Benno M., 213, 229
Foster, Caleb, 24n7
Foster, Charles Chauncey, 6(fig.)
Fotterall, Stephen E., 110
Fowler, Lemuel, 156
Frames: Irish, 223; looking glass, 168; picture, 170–71
France, protection for artisans, 58n6
Francis, James, 150
Francis, John, 171
Francis, Mrs. John, 163
Freedom, 86n17
French bracket feet, 146(fig.), 154
French-Canadian shaved chairs, 53
French rococo, 216; influence on American design, 218
Front parlors, pier tables and, 110
Fruitwood, teapot handle, 179(fig.)
Furnishing the Eighteenth Century: What Furniture Can Tell Us about the European and American Past (Goodman & Norberg), 232–37
Furniture carving, Samuel McIntire, 225–28
Furniture of the Pilgrim Century (Nutting), 209
Furniture repairs and alterations: bookcases, 142–43; boxes, cases, chests, and trunks, 188–91; chests, 143–46; chests of drawers, 146–55; clock cases, 164–67; cornice, 173; cupboards, 155–60; desks, 131–42; gunstocks, 181; handles, 178–81; hearth equipment, 181–83; household objects, 170–73; kitchen and laundry equipment, 174–78; looking glasses, 167–69; musical instruments, 191–92; personal items, 191–94; picture frames, 170–71; sideboards, 160–64; textile equipment, 183–88; umbrellas, 192–93; window blinds, 171–73
Furniture sets, matched, 235
Furniture Treasury (Nutting), 209

G. and D. Cleveland (Providence), 191
Gadrooned moldings, 123
Gale, Matthias, 81–82(&figs.)
Le garde-meuble ancien et moderne (Guilmard), 218–19
Garde-meuble system, 58n6
Gardiner, Sarah, 178
Gardner, Francis, 10
Gardner, John, 225, 228
Gardner, Sarah, 225, 228
Gardner, William, 166
Gardner-Pingree House (Salem, Massachusetts), 227
Garrett, Elisabeth, 112
Gas lighting, demise of pier table and, 125
Gavit, Jonathan, 165
General Green, 190
George Seddon and Son (London), 182
Gere, James, 133, 153, 155, 177
Germain, Pierre, 216
Germanic influence, on shaved chair, 53, 54(fig. 32)
German rococo, 215
Germany, ice skates, 193(fig.)
Gifford and Scotland (New York City), 162, 186
Gilbert, Alexander H., 164, 166
Gilbert, Christopher, 228
Gilding, 115, 170–71; oil, 89
Gillett, Jonathan, 168
Gillingham, James, 181
Gingerbread mold, 175(fig. 22); repair to, 175–76
Girandole, 169
Girard, John, 194
Girard, Stephen, furniture repairs for, 133, 138, 141, 160, 168, 170, 180, 193, 194
Gladding, Benjamin, 189
Glass knobs, 141, 153, 199n46
Glen-Sanders House (Schenectady, New York), 228
Globes in stands, 193
Glue blocks, 15
Goddard, John, 84

Goddard, Townsend, 139, 149
Godey's Magazine and Lady's Book, 125(fig.)
Godfrey, E., 227
Goodhue, Benjamin, 10
Gooding, Timothy, Jr., 3
Goodman, Dena, 232, 235, 236
Gostelowe, Jonathan, bureau, 150–51(&fig.)
Gould, Elizabeth (French), 3
Gould, James, 3
Gould, Nathaniel: account book, 1(&fig.), 3–13(&figs. 8, 9, 12); biography, 3; chairs, 5; chest of drawers, 6(fig.); chest-on-chest, 9(fig.); day-books, 1, 2(fig.), 3–13(&figs. 3–5, 7, 11, 14); desk-and-bookcases, 5, 8–10, 12(fig.), 13–16(&fig. 16), 18, 19(fig.); desks, 5, 10, 11(fig. 14), 13(fig. 17), 14(fig. 18); furniture construction details, 15–17, 22, 25n14; furniture forms, 5; furniture prices, 8; identifying work of, 13–23; invoice, 16(fig. 24); stands, 13; tables, 5–7
Gould, Nathaniel (Sr.), 3, 24n3
Gould, Rebecca (Wood), 3
Graff, David, 156
Grafton, Joseph, 8, 25n11
Grand United Order of Moses, 54
Grant, Scotland, 86n17
Graphics, conveying visual information, 217
Gray, William, 5
Great wheel, 183; repairs to, 185
Green, John, 192
Green, Nathanael, 190
Greene, Albert C., 139
Greene, Isaac, 138
Greene, Richard W., 154, 160
Greenough, David S., 162, 181, 183
Greenwood, Isaac, 192
Green woodworking, 31, 58n7
Grinnell and Taylor (Providence), 170, 173
Griswold, George, 150
Griswold, Joseph, 187
Gronning, Erik, 59n15
Ground rent system, in Philadelphia, 109, 110
Guide (Hepplewhite), 151
Guier, William, 190
Guild system, 30–31
Guilmard, Désiré, 218–19
Gunstocks, repair of, 181

Hadley chests, 210
Hamilton, James, 171
Hand bellows, repairs to, 183
Handles, repair/replacement of, 178–81
Hand reel, 186
Hardcastle, Henry, 228
Hardware: bureau, 154; chest, 145; chest of drawers, 147–48; desk, 133; secretary-and-bookcases, 141–42; sideboard, 162
Harriot, 67
Harvard College Endowment Fund, 86n28
Harvey, Elihu, 166
Haswell, H. B., 183
Hat stand, 173
Haughton, George, 222
Haven, Abner, 149, 155
Haven, David, 146, 159
Hawley, Elisha, 144, 149, 157, 175, 176, 181, 188
Hayden, Polly, 173
Healy, Hezekiah, 138
Hearth equipment, repair of, 181–83
Heath, Nathaniel, 181
Heckscher, Morrison, 13, 16, 218, 226
Helman, Mimi, 235
Helmar, Dennis, 227
Hemming, Billy, 86n17
Henkels, George, 218
Hepplewhite, George, 99–100, 132, 140, 226; chests of drawers designs, 146(fig.); double chest of drawers design, 149(fig.); sideboard design, 161(fig.)
The Hermitage (Tennessee), 122(&fig.), 130n39
Hero, 69
Hesser, Christian, 193(fig.)
Hewitt, John, 160, 163
Hewitt sisters, 217
Hickory, 49
High chests: alteration of, 150; maple, 148(fig.)
Hill, J., 145
Hinges, 17, 18(fig. 28)
Hinman, Philemon, 165
Hinsdale, Jacob, 184
Hitchcock, Enos, 170
Hoadley, R. Bruce, 56
Hoch, David, 184
Hockaday, John, 135, 147, 160
Hodghton and Son (Lima), 190
Hodgson, James, 69

Hogarth, William, 233
Holbein, Hans (the Elder), 33(fig.)
Holcomb, Allen, 139, 141, 149, 169, 183
Hollingsworth and Rudolph (Philadelphia), 168
Holly, secretary-and-bookcase, 140(fig.)
Holmes, Elisha Harlow: bureau repair, 154; desk repair, 134, 135, 138, 141; double bass repair, 192; looking glass repair, 169; venetian blinds, 173
Holmes, Nathaniel, 143
Homewood (Pittsburgh), 122, 130n39
Honduran mahogany, 61, 65–66
Honduras, 62, 65, 77(figs.)
Hopkins, John G., 142, 154
Horry, Robert, 86n17
Hotel industry, pier tables and, 126(&fig.)
Houghton, John, 222
Houghton, Luke: bowl painting, 177; bread trough repair, 174; clock case repair, 166; cupboard turn, 156; desk repair, 133; drawer repair, 147; looking glass repair, 168; quilting frame repair, 187
Household objects, repair of, 170–73
The House Servant's Directory, 105
Hubon, Henry, 162
Hunneman, Samuel H., warming pan, 180(fig.)
Hunneman, William C., Jr., warming pan, 180(fig.)
Hunneman, William C., warming pan, 180(fig.)
Hunter-Stiebel, Penelope, 214
Hunting, Nathaniel, 165
Huntington, Daniel, 166
Huntington, Felix, 142, 160
Huntington, Joshua, 142, 160
Hurd, Jacob, teapot, 179(fig.)
Hurst, Ronald, 222
Hutchinson, Israel Pemberton, 115

Ice skates, 193(fig.); repair of, 193
Imlay, John, 172
Ince, William, 132, 226
Ink box, 189
Inlaid furniture, Welsh, 231
Ipswich (Massachusetts): armchair, 36(fig. 11); Searle-Dennis workshops, 211
Irish Chippendale, 220

Irish Furniture: Woodwork and Carving in Ireland from the Earliest Times to the Act of Union (Knight of Glin & Peill), 219–24, 229
Irish influence, on shaved chairs, 51(fig.), 52, 53
Irish stucco workers, 223
Ironing board repair, 178
Isle of Jersey, 68
Italian renaissance shaved chairs, 32(fig.), 33

J. Paul Getty Museum, 232
Jackson, Andrew, 119–20, 122, 127n3, 129n35, 130n39
Jaffee, David, 234
Jamaican mahogany, 61, 65–66, 68
James Buchanan Foundation for the Preservation of Wheatland, 129n32
James Prince and Son, William Henry (Brewster), 136(fig.)
Jansen, Michel, 218
Jefferson, Thomas, 73
Jenkins, Paul, 135, 138, 142, 154, 162, 165, 166
Jenkins, William, 190
Jenny, 68
Jenny, Cornelius, 164
Jewel casket, 236, 237
Jewell, Robert, 182
Johns, Richard, 165, 173, 190
Johnson, Thomas, 222
Joined chairs, shaved chairs evoking, 43–48(&figs.)
Joiners, connecting with "origins," 212
Joints, stresses on, 49
Joint stool, 211–12
Jones, Asa, 147, 149
Jones, Basil, 71
Jones, Gershom, 133, 179
Jones, Ned, 86n17
Jones, Thomas, 165, 167
Joseph B. Barry & Sons (Philadelphia), pier tables, 102, 103(figs.)
Joseph Meeks and Sons, 152
Judkins and Senter (Portsmouth), 181
Jugiez, Martin, 99(fig. 12), 222

Kasten, 228
Katey, 68
Keels (Newfoundland), armchair, 51(fig.)
Kennedy, David, 171
Kennedy, Joseph, 223

Kennedy, Robert, 143, 171; trade card, 171(fig.)
Kenny, Peter, 59n15, 225–28
Kettell, Jonathan, 168, 189, 192
Keyes, Homer Eaton, 226
Kimball, Fiske, 226
King, William, desk, 66(fig.)
Kingston (New York), armchair, 45(fig. 22)
Kink teapot handle, 179
Kip, William, 164
Kirtley, Alexandra Alevizatos, 219–24
Kitchen equipment, repair of, 174–78
Kneeding [sic] trough, 174
Kneeland, Seth R., 138
Knife case, 162–63
Knight, Stephanus, 138, 145, 164, 170, 191
Knight of Glin, 219–24, 229
Knowlton, Nathaniel, 153, 154
Knox, Henry, 143, 163, 177, 191, 193
Krause, Nathaniel, 42, 43(fig.)
Kraut, Philiph, 184
Krimmel, John Lewis, 187(fig.)

Ladies cabinet, 142
Lahikainen, Dean T., 65, 225–28
Lajoue, Jacques de, 216, 217
Lamb, David, 81(fig.)
Lamb, Joe, 86n17
La Mésangère, Pierre de, 102(fig. 16), 104(fig.)
Lander, William, 5, 175
Landon, George, 173, 176, 180, 183, 192
Land-ownership, wealth and status and, 109–10
Lang, William, 25n17
Lannuier, Charles-Honoré, 100
Lanny, David F., 163
Larned, Samuel, 190
Laundry equipment, repair of, 174–78
Law, Mathurin, 234
Layback, 36, 37, 38, 40–41
Leach, Nathaniel, 11(fig. 14)
Leben, Ulrich, 215
Lee, Chapman, 132, 157, 159
Lee, Jeremiah, 8–10(&figs. 11, 12), 11(fig. 13), 24n9, 25n11
Lee, Joseph, 10(fig. 12), 24n9
Le Grand, Charles Francis, 223
Leman, Henry Eichholtz, 129n32
Lemon squeezer, 178(fig.)
Leslie, Eliza, 128n13
Lewis, Eliza, 129n34

Lewis, John F., 129n34
Lewis, John Frederick, 119
Lewis, Mrs. John Frederick, 118–19(&fig. 28)
L'hommedieu, Ezra, 185
The Life and Work of Thomas Chippendale (Gilbert), 228
Light, sociability and, 112–13
Linacre, James, 190
Lincoln, Levi, 120
Lindsey, Joseph, 147, 181, 190
Linen presses, 231
Linville, Abigail, 60n22
Lion's-mask tables, 221–22
Lion's-paw feet, 89, 102, 118, 123
Liquor cases, 189
Little wheel, repairs to, 183–85
Livingston, Robert L., 170
Livingston, Robert R., 164
Livingston, Walter, 162, 186
Livre de miroirs, tables et gueridons (le Pautre), 96(fig.)
Locking furniture, 236–37
Locks: desk-and-bookcase, 18(fig. 27); installation of bookcases, 143; installation of chests, 144, 145; installation of desk, 133–34; trunk, 191
Lockwood, Luke Vincent, 209
London Company of Turners, 212
Long, Joe, 86n17
Looking glasses: mahogany, 167(fig.); pier tables and, 89, 96–97; repairing, 167–69
Loomis, Jonathan C., 166
Loomis, Reuben, 147, 164, 175, 176, 177
Loomis, Timothy, 145
Lopez, Aaron, 70–71(&fig.), 83–84, 86n18
Lord Nelson, 86n17
Loud & Brothers (Philadelphia), 191; piano, 116(fig.)
Louis XIV, 96
Louis XV, 216
Low, Alexander, 147, 149, 150, 156, 185
Low, Nicholas, furniture repairs for, 138, 154, 155, 161, 163, 164, 167, 168, 169, 191
Lowater, Stephan, 25n13
Lucas, Nathan, 177, 184
Lunt, Skipper, 155–56
Lupton, Ellen, 214
Lyell, Fenwick: backgammon board repair, 193; bookcase repair, 142, 143; clock case repair, 166; desk repair, 132, 134, 137, 142; piano repair, 191; quilting frame repair, 188; sideboard repair, 161, 162, 163; tambour frame repair, 188; trunk repair, 191; venetian blind repair, 173
Lyon, Irving P., 31–32, 33(fig.), 36(&fig. 11), 45–46(&fig. 21), 59n12, 211
Lyon, Irving W., 209

Madison, James, 129n35
Mahogany: bombé desk-and-bookcase, 19(fig.); bureaus, 7(fig.), 151(fig.); for bureaus, 153, 199n47; chest, 63(fig.); chest of drawers, 6(fig.); chest-on-chest, 9(fig.), 64(fig.); clothespress, 159(fig.); desk-and-bookcase, 12(fig.); desks, 14(fig. 19), 66(fig.); drawer dividers and fallboard supports, 17–18; gingerbread mold, 175(fig. 22); looking glass, 167(fig.); piano, 116(fig.); pier tables, 88(fig.), 90(fig.), 93(fig.), 94(fig.), 99(figs.), 103(figs.), 118(fig.), 120(fig.), 121(fig.), 122(fig.), 123(fig.); quality available to cabinetmakers, 6(fig.); secretary-and-bookcase, 140(fig.); squared log, 69(fig.), 78(fig. 16), 85n11; as status symbol, 233; tall clock case, 165(fig.); tea chest, 191(fig.); for wardrobes, 159–60
Mahogany trade, 61–87; Americans in, 70–73; archaeology of wood-cutting camps, 79–84; in Belize, 74–79; harvesting trees, 75–79(&figs.); history of, 61–65; slavery and, 61, 70, 72, 75–79, 80, 83; transshipment and regional variation, 65–70
Mahogany veneer: bureau, 152(fig.); clothespress, 159(fig.); pier table, 118; secretary-and-bookcase, 140(fig.); tea chest, 191(fig.)
Mallard, Prudent, 218
Mann, Henry, 165, 180
Manner of Trucking Mahogany in Honduras (Annin & Smith), 77(fig. 13)
Maple: armchairs, 36(fig. 11), 37(fig.), 46(fig. 24), 47(fig.), 48(fig.), 52(fig.); for bureaus, 153, 199n47; chest, 63(fig.); cupboard, 156(fig.); desk interior, 131(fig.); flax wheel, 183(fig.); high chest of drawers,

148(fig.); rot and, 49; side chairs, 50(fig.), 54(fig. 33); slaughterer's bench, 30(fig.)
A Map of that part of Yucatan...for the cutting of Logwood (Lamb), 81(fig.)
Marblehead (Massachusetts), furniture construction details, 16
Marble tops, on pier tables, 104–5
Marsh, Charles, 142
Marshall, John, 135, 150
Martin, Ann Smart, 235, 236
The Martyrdom of Saint Paul (Hans Holbein the Elder), 33(fig.)
Mason, Thomas, 10
Massachusetts: desk interior, 131(fig.); fire board, 182(fig.); mahogany entering ports in, 67–68
Massachusetts Historical Society, 1
Matthews, Samuel, 180, 188, 193
Mayhew, John, 132, 226
McConachy, Robert, 161, 163
McDonald, Elizabeth de Hart Bleecker, 162
McEvers and Barclay (New York City), 164
McGahey, J., 76(fig.)
McIntire, Samuel, 225–28
Medicine chest repair, 190
Meissonnier, Juste-Aurèle, 216, 217
"Mend," 132, 144, 164
Merchant's House and Yard for Siding the Mahogany Trees before Putting them on Board Ship for England (Dashwood), 79(fig.)
Meredith, Samuel, 145, 160, 161, 177
Merode Altarpiece, 27, 28(fig.)
Merrifield, George, 147, 148, 162, 183, 194
MESDA (Museum of Early Southern Decorative Arts), 218
Metcalf, Levi, 155, 159
Methodism, Welsh furniture and, 231
Metropolitan Museum of Art, 218; American furniture in, 209–14
Meyer, Heinrich, 185
Micheau, Jane, 173
Middleton, Septima Sexta, 122
Middleton-Rutledge, Henry, 122–23
Middleton-Rutledge House, 130n41
Mifflin, Mr. and Mrs. Thomas, 188
Miller, Alan, 228
Miller, James R., 141
Miller, Jeremiah, 150
Minott, John, 173

Minott, Timothy, 173
Mirrored plate glass, pier tables and, 101–2
"Mode of Travelling of the Woodcutters in . . . Honduras" (Annin & Smith), 80(fig.)
Modern minimalist curvilinearity, 217
Moisture content, for seating, 56
Molding profiles, attibution and, 211–12
Monkton, 72
Montague (New Jersey), armchair, 48(fig.)
Moore, Oliver, 149, 150, 154, 158
Moricet, J. A., 160
Morris, Deborah, 165, 173
Morris, Hannah, 169
Morris, John, 86n17
Mortises: cylindrical, 28(fig.); locating, 39(&fig.)
Mosers, Samuel, 178
Moses Hall shaved chairs, 53–54(&fig. 33), 60n22
Mosquito Shore, 65
Mount, Joel, 142
Mount Airy (Virginia), 97
Mount Lebanon (New York), pail, 177(fig.)
Moyers, Thomas J., 134, 141
Moyers and Rich (Wytheville, Virginia), 153, 154, 156, 165, 170
Mrs. John Frederick Lewis (Eichholtz), 119(fig.)
Mudget, John, 158–59
Mummy heads, 223
Munroe, Nehemiah, 176
Museum of Early Southern Decorative Arts (MESDA), 218
Museum of Fine Arts (Boston), 210, 213, 226
Musical instruments, repairs to, 191–92
Music case repair, 190

Napoleon, 96
Nassau County (New York), chest, 144(fig.)
Nathan Dane Papers, 1
Nathaniel Tracy House (Newburyport, Massachusetts), 11(fig. 13)
Nearpass, Jacobus, 47–48
Needham, Thomas, 162
Neo-rococo, 215, 216
Newdigate, John, 71

New England artisans, provincial, 234
New England cognates of European shaved post-and-rung chairs, 36–38(&figs. 11, 12)
Newfoundland, 68
New Hampshire, desk interior, 131(fig.)
Newport (Rhode Island), mahogany trade and, 70, 71, 72, 73, 75, 84
New Providence, 67, 85n10
New River, 78(fig. 14), 80–81, 82, 83
Newton, Sarah, 186
New York City: clothespress, 159(fig.); étagère, 124(fig.); gingerbread mold, 175(fig. 22); mahogany trade and, 68, 70, 73, 75; pier tables, 89, 91(figs.), 125, 126n1; tea chest, 191(fig.)
Nichols, Isaac, 177
Nichols, Walter, 138, 143, 160–61
Niddy noddy, 186
Norberg, Kathryn, 232, 233, 234
Norris, Charles, 180, 188, 193
Norris, Mary, 144
North Carolina, side chair, 55(fig. 35)
Nova Scotia, side chair, 53(fig.)
Nutting, Wallace, 209

Oak. *See also* Red oak; White oak: armchairs, 37(fig.), 38(fig.), 40(fig.), 45(fig. 22), 46, 47(fig.); board backstool, 29(figs.); chest, 63(fig.); flax wheel, 183(fig.); side chairs, 50(fig.), 55(fig. 35)
O'Brien, Robert Francis, 81(fig.), 82–83(&fig. 21)
Office of Humphrey Hathaway, at the Head of Rotch's Wharf (Russell), 137(fig.)
Oficina Arcularia (van de Passe), 92(fig.)
Ogden, Aaron, 176
Oil lighting, marble tops and, 105
Oldfield, John, 181
Old North Church (Boston), 75
Omni William Penn Hotel, pier table, 126(fig.)
One-slat armchair design, 41–43(&figs.)
Ornamental Designs (Smith), 92(fig.)
Ornamental plasterwork, 223
Ornaments, carved, 227
Orne, Rebecca, 8
Orne, Timothy, 165

Overholt, Abraham, 178, 184, 185, 186
Oxford English Dictionary, 132, 143, 150, 190

Pail: repair of, 177; white pine, 177(fig.)
Paine, John, 185
Paine, Robert Treat, II, 18, 20(fig.)
Paine, Ruth (Cabot), 18, 20(fig.)
Painting, 135; bookcases, 143; chest of drawers, 148–49; chests, 144, 145; cupboards, 157–58; dressers, 158–59; household containers, 177
Parisian case furniture, 235–36
Parker, Philemon, 5(fig.4), 10, 11(fig. 14)
Parkhurst, Moses, 148, 156, 191
Parlor: furnishings in upscale Philadelphia, 110; pier tables in, 99, 104, 110–13; window treatment design, 125(fig.)
Parrot cages, 194
Pastore, Chaela, 233
Patrons: artists and, 216; McIntire and, 225
Pautre, Jean le, 96(fig.)
Peabody Essex Museum, 63, 225
Pealing [sic] machine, 178
Pearce, Edward Lovett, 221
Pearlware bowl, 83(fig.)
Peckham, Jonathan, 139
Peddle, Walter, 51
Pediment, 22(fig. 33); repair of, 168
Peel, repair of, 174–75
Peill, James, 219–24, 229
Peirce, Jerathamiel, 225, 228
Pemberton, Joseph, 160, 165, 172, 189, 193
Penn, John, 169, 171
Pennsylvania: board backstool, 29(figs.); bread trough, 174(fig.); corner cupboard, 157(fig. 12); dresser, 157(fig. 13); pipe box, 189(fig.)
Pennsylvania Germans, dressers and, 158
Perkins, James, 147
Persians, 223
Pettes, Frederick, 137
Peyrotte, Alexis, 216
Philadelphia: bureau, 151(fig.); comparative wealth of pier table owners in, 108(table 4); flax wheel, 183(fig.); Irish influence on furniture in, 222, 223; parlor furnishings in, 110; percentage of population owning pier tables, 107–8(&table 2); piano, 116(fig.); pier table construction, 126n1; pier tables, 99(&figs.), 103–4(figs.), 118(fig.), 120–23(figs.); *The Quilting Frolic,* 187(fig.); social competition and pier tables in, 117–26; social standing and pier tables in, 105–17; tape loom, 188(fig.); trade card, 171(fig.); venetian blinds, 172(fig.)
The Philadelphia Cabinet and Chair Makers' Union Book of Prices, 93
Philadelphia Museum of Art, 218, 226
Philipse Manor (Yonkers, New York), 228
Phyfe, Duncan, 191
Physick, Edmund, 171
Pianos: mahogany, 116(fig.); ownership of, 107(table 2), 116–17; repairs to, 191
Pickman, Clark Gayton, 4(&fig.), 24n7
Picture frame, repair of, 170–71
Pier glass, 168
Pier tables: average value by year (1830–1850), 108(table 3); cherry, 97(fig.); cultures of sociability and, 104–17; demise of popularity of, 125–26; in East Room, 119–20, 129n35, 129n36; empire, 96; genealogy of form, 96–102; mahogany, 88(fig.), 90(fig.), 93(fig.), 94(fig.), 99(figs.), 103(figs.), 118(fig.), 120(fig.), 121(fig.), 122(fig.), 123(fig.); New York City, 91(figs.), 125; owner occupations, 109(table); parlors and, 110–13; percent ownership by year (1830–1850), 107(&table 2); Philadelphia, 88–94(&figs. 1, 2, 6, 7), 99(&figs.), 103–4(figs.); social competition and, 117–26
Pigeonhole valences, 17
Pigget, William, 133
Pine: armchairs, 51(fig.), 52(fig.); board backstool, 29(figs.); bureaus, 151(fig.), 152(fig.); for bureaus, 153, 199n47; chest, 144(fig.); corner cupboard, 157(fig. 12); cupboard, 156(fig.); desk, 66(fig.); venetian blinds, 172(fig.); watch case, 190(fig.)
Pineau, Nicolas, 217
Pinwheel rosettes, 22
Pipe boxes: repair of, 188–89; walnut, 189(fig.)
Pistol repairs, 181
Pitman, Mark, 189
Pittsburgh (Pennsylvania): Omni William Penn Hotel lobby, 126 (fig.); pier table, 121–22(&fig. 30)
Planing, 135; of chest of drawers, 148
Plate glass, pier tables and, 101–2, 126
Pleasants family, 129n38
Plimoth Plantation (Massachusetts): replica shaved chairs, 49–50(&figs.); reproduction furniture, 26(fig.), 27
Plymouth (Massachusetts): maple armchair, 37(fig.); side chair, 50(fig.)
Polishing: bookcases, 143; chest, 149; sideboard, 162
Pond, Phineas, 190
Population of urban places, 107(table 1)
Portable desk, repair of, 135, 137
Porter, David, 232, 233
Post-and-slab chairs, 27
Pottage, Robert, 54(fig. 33), 60n22
Poupard, James, 190
Powel, John Hare, 127n8
Powel, Samuel, II, 167
Powel, Samuel, III, 171
Pratt, Thomas, 186
Preaching chair, 231
Preparing the Eggs of Silkworms (van der Straat), 32(fig.)
Press, 155
Preston, Titus: chest repair, 145, 147; churn repair, 176; clock case repair, 164, 165; clock reel repair, 186; gunstock repair, 181; spinning wheel repair, 185; tea chest repair, 190; trunk repair, 191; umbrella repair, 192
Price books, pier tables and, 93
Prices of Cabinet and Chair Work, 137
Prince, James and William Henry, 136(fig.)
Prince, Orlean, 157
Pritchard, David, 143, 160
Proctor, James R., 155
Proctor, Leonard R., 155
Prospect doors, 17, 18(fig. 28)
Prospect-front bureau, 199n45
Proud, Daniel, 170, 175, 178, 181
Proud, Samuel, 170, 175, 178, 181
Proud, William, 147
Public auctions, furniture, 123–24

Quadrant box, 189
Quervelle, Anthony G., 94(fig.), 119, 120(fig.); pier table, 129n35
Quetin, Victor, 218
Quill wheel, repair of, 186–87
Quilting frames, repair of, 187–88
The Quilting Frolic (Krimmel), 187(fig.)

Ranck, Peter, 145, 155
Rantoul, Robert, 135, 190
Rappahannock River basin, Irish influence on furniture of, 222
Rawlins, John, 223
Rawson, S. and J., 160
Rawson, William, 153
Raymond, William, 135
Red cedar, chest, 63(fig.)
Red oak: rot and, 49; side chairs, 41(fig.), 42(figs.), 43(fig.), 56(fig.)
Reed, E. M. D., 170
Reed and Hollis (Salem, Massachusetts), 134, 142
Reeve, Tapping, 150, 182, 189
Regilding, 169, 170–71
Regional Furniture Society (England), 229
"Repair," 132, 144, 164
Repository of Arts (Ackermann), 102(&fig. 17), 105(fig.)
Resurfacing. *See also* Painting; Polishing; Varnish: on chest of drawers, 148–49
Revolutionary War, mahogany trade and, 65
Reynolds, Enos, 157
Reynolds, James, 167, 169, 171, 218
Rich, Fleming K., 134, 141
Richmond County (Virginia): pier table, 97(fig.); sideboard table, 98(fig.)
Riesener, Jean-Henri, 237
Rittenhouse, Benjamin, 183
Rivera, Jacob Rodriguez, 167, 174, 193
Roach, William, 73
Robbins, Philemon, 161, 162, 168, 191
Roberson, William, 181
Roberts, Rookesby, 189
Robinson, Charles C., 158, 170, 194
Robinson, Charles N., 169, 170–71, 173
Robinson House (Wilmington, Delaware), 54(fig. 32)
Rochester (Massachusetts), armchair, 37–38(&fig. 12)

Rococo: The Continuing Curve, 1730–2008 (Coffin et al.), 214–19
Rococo-revival furniture, 218–19
Rogers, Asa, 155
Rogers, John, 220, 224
Roorbach, Sophia, 158
Ropes, Nathaniel, 63–64(&fig. 3)
Ropes Family Collection (Peabody Essex Museum), 63
Rosewood: étagère, 124(fig.); pier tables, 91(figs.), 123(fig.)
Ross, Daniel, 139, 148, 175, 181
Rotary churn, 176
Rough surfaces, workmanship and, 30
Roulstone, John, 164
Rousseau, Jean-Jacques, 233
Routh, Richard, 10
Roux, Alexander, 218
Ruggles, Levi, bureau, 152(fig.)
Rung, replacing, 49(&fig.)
Rural field crafts, 31
Rush (flags), 50
Russell, Edward S., 137(fig.)
Russell, Porter, 162
Rust, Henry, 13, 25n13; desk, 14(fig. 19), 15(figs.)

Safford, Frances Gruber, 209–14
Safford, Nathaniel, 227
Safford, Thomas, 139
Sager, John, 132, 158
Saint Dominique, 233
Salem (Massachusetts). *See also* Gould, Nathaniel: bombé desk-and-bookcase, 19(fig.); cabinetmaker mahogany cartel, 65; chest, 63(fig.); chest of drawers, 6(fig.); chest-on-chests, 9(fig.), 64(fig.); desk-and-bookcases, 12(fig.), 13(fig. 16); desks, 13(fig. 17), 66(fig.); furniture construction details, 15–17; mahogany plank, 61; mahogany trade and, 67; secretary-and-bookcase, 140(fig.)
Salzman, Mary, 235
Samuel McIntire: Carving an American Style (Lahikainen), 225–28
Sanderson, Elijah, 154
Sandwich (Massachusetts), shaved armchairs in, 46–47(&figs. 24, 25)
Santo Domingan mahogany, 61
Sargent, Henry, 110, 111(fig.), 114(fig.)
Sargentson, Carolyn, 232, 235, 236–37
Sass, Jacob, 147, 162, 173

Sassafras, side chair, 54(fig. 32)
Satinwood, pier table, 103(fig. 18)
Satinwood veneer, clothespress, 159(fig.)
Savage, Elias, 155
Savell, John, 211
Savell, William, 211
Savery, William, 160, 165, 172–73, 189, 190, 193
Scadin, Robert C., 138, 162, 173
Scalloped edges, 51(&fig.), 60n19
Schryer, George, 109
Scolley and White (Newtown, Connecticut), 155
Scorching/charring, of chair, 49–50(&fig. 28)
Scraping, 134, 135
Scroll-and-paw supports, 93, 121
Scroll arms, 44(&fig.), 48(&fig.)
Searle-Dennis workshops (Ipswich, Massachusetts), 211
Sears, William Bernard, 99; pier table, 97(fig.); sideboard table, 98(fig.)
Seat height, 43
Secondary woods, 17
Secretaires, 235, 236–37
Secretary, 138
Secretary-and-bookcase, 140–42(&fig.)
Seddon, George, 182
Senate House (Kingston, New York), 45(fig. 22)
Senter, Isaac, 138, 161
Settin' chair, 31, 55(fig. 34), 58n8, 60n23
Settle, 27, 28(fig.)
Sgabello, 29(fig. 3), 30
Sharpe, Bartholomew, 74
Shaved post-and-rung chairs, 26–60; based on European art and New England armchairs, 38–41(&figs.); early European, and New England cognates, 32–38(&figs.); maple, 36–37(&fig. 11); in North America, 50–54(&figs.); Plimoth Plantation replica chairs, 26(fig.), 49–50(&figs.); shaved chairs with parts and construction evoking joined chairs, 43–48(&figs.); study side chairs based on European precedents, 41–43(&figs.); survival rate of, 31–32; twentieth-century, 55–56(&figs. 35, 36)
Shaw and Chisholm (Annapolis), 181

Sheraton, Thomas, 131, 142, 169, 171; pier table designs, 99–100(&fig. 14), 101–2, 101(fig.); on tea trays, 176
Sherman, William, 170
Shipley, George, 68
Short, George, 154, 192
Sibley, Solomon, 154
Sideboard cloth, 162
Sideboards: design for, 161(fig.); repair of, 160–64
Sideboard tables, 97, 98(fig.)
Side chairs: birch, 53(fig.); maple, 50(fig.), 54(fig. 33); oak, 41(fig.), 42(figs.), 43(fig.), 55(fig. 35); sassafras, 54(fig. 32); shaved, based on European precedents, 41–43(&figs.); shaved, survival of, 32; white oak, 56(fig.)
Silberg, Nicholas, 189
Simon, Constance, 220
Sisson, Gilbert, 135
Skerrett, James J., 160, 173, 191
Slab/board seats, 29(fig. 4)
Slab tables, 97
Slant-front desk, 131–32(&fig.)
Slats: in bridle joints, 42, 43(fig.); one-slat armchair, 41–43(&figs.)
Slaughterer's bench, 30(fig.)
Slavery: mahogany trade and, 61, 70, 72, 75–79, 80, 83; turning blind eye to, 233
Slead, Edward, 139, 149
Sleeper, Henry Davis, 36(fig. 11), 37
Sloan, Samuel, 218
Slover and Taylor (New York City), 164
Smart, Doctor B., 142
Smith, Aaron, 181
Smith, Ebenezer, Jr., 190
Smith, George, 92(fig.)
Smith, George G., 77(fig. 13), 80(fig.)
Smith, Howard, 143
Smith, Joseph L., 141
Smither, James, 171(fig.)
Smithsonian Institution, 193(fig.)
Social standing, pier tables and, 104
Society of Journeymen Cabinetmakers, 101
Sofas: camelback, 226; ownership of, 107(&table 2)
Southwick, Joseph, 7, 8(fig. 8)
Spanish colonial shaved chairs, 50
Spanish mahogany, 65
Sparrow, 67
Spaulding, Leonard, 166

Speedwell, 67
Spinning wheels, 183(fig.); repairs to, 183–87
Spoke shave, 39
Spoon bit, 28(fig.)
Spurlock, John, 167
"Square-Post Slat-Back Chairs," 31–32, 33(fig.), 45(fig. 21)
Squash squeezers, 178(&fig.)
Squirrel cage, 194
S-shape handle, 179
Staining, 135; bureau, 155
Stake-and-slab chairs, 27
Stake feet, 29(fig. 4), 30
Stands, 13
Stenciling, 89, 115
Stockwell, David, 222
Stoddard, Isaac, 145
Stokes, Joseph, 227
Stone, Joseph, 186
Stone tops, 125, 128n13
Stool, joint, 211–12
Stringing, 153, 199n46
Stucco, Irish, 223
Style as communal cultural statement, 216–17
Sugar box, 188
Sunflower chests, 210
Surface treatments for desks, 134–35. See also Painting; Polishing; Varnish
Swan, Mabel Munson, 226
Sweerts, Michael, 35(fig.)
Sweet, Stephen, 139
Swietenia, 65
Swietenia macrophylla, 85n7
Swietenia mahogani, 85n7
Swift, repairs to, 186
Symonds, Benjamin, 5
Symonds, Joseph, 149, 188
Symonds shop, chest, 63(fig.)

Tables: Armada, 221; card, 100; console, 97, 101, 125; lion's-mask, 221–22; Nathaniel Gould, 5–7; pier. See Pier tables; sideboard, 97, 98(fig.); slab, 97; tea, 13, 107(table 2), 222, 235, 236
Tall chests, 149
Tallmadge, Benjamin, 191
Tambour frame, 188
Tape loom: cherry, 188(fig.); repair to, 188
Tarule, Robert, 49(&fig.), 211
Tayloe, John, II, 97

Taylor, Abner, 138, 146, 156, 165, 174
Taylor, Alexander, 154
Taylor, Dorothy, 73
Taylor, Hiram, 134, 174, 176
Taylor, Robert, 158
Taylor, Zachary, 121
Tea chests: mahogany, 191(fig.); repair of, 190
The Tea Party (Sargent), 110, 111(fig.), 112–13(&fig.)
Teapot, silver with fruitwood, 179(fig.)
Teapot handles, repair/replacement of, 178–80
Tea tables, 13, 222, 235, 236; ownership of, 107(table 2)
Tea trays, repairs to, 176–77
Tenons: blind, 33, 35(fig.); through-, 33, 35(fig.), 39, 41–43, 46, 49
Terms, 223
Textile equipment, repairs to, 183–88
Thaw, Benjamin, 143
Thompson, Paul Warwick, 214
Thompson, William, 43
Thornton, Peter, 59n10
Through-tenons, 33, 35(fig.), 39, 41–43, 46, 49
Tiffany, Isaiah, 133, 186, 187
Tobey, Lemuel, 149, 181, 188–89
Topsfield (Massachusetts), armchair, 52(fig.)
Torah, 84, 87n37
Torah rollers, 84
Touro Synagogue (Newport, Rhode Island), 84
Towel roll, 178
Townsend, Edmund, 72
Townsend, Job, Jr.: birdcage repair, 194; bowling pin alteration, 193; bread trough repair, 174; clock case repair, 165, 166; desk repairs, 133, 134; drawer repair, 147; looking glass repair, 168; punch ladle handle, 181; tea chest repair, 190; teapot handle repair, 180; tea tray repair, 177; wig box repairs, 188
Townsend, Job E.: birdcage repair, 194; bottle case repair, 189; box repair, 189; bureau repair, 154; chest alteration by, 150; chest of drawers repair, 147; chest repair, 144–45; chest repairs, 149; churn repair, 176; clock case assembly, 167; clock case repair, 166; coffee mill repair, 178; cupboard repair,

157, 158; desk-and-bookcase repair, 139; desk repair, 132–33, 134, 138; desk surface treatments, 135; dipper handle repair, 181; double bass repair, 192; fire screen repair, 181; gunstock repair, 181; hand bellow repair, 183; ice skate repair, 193; ironing board repair, 177–78; medicine chest repair, 190; picture frame repair, 170; pipe box repair, 188–89; quill wheel repair, 187; spinning wheel repair, 185; squirrel cage, 194; swift repair, 186; tape loom repair, 188; teapot handle replacement, 179; tray repair, 177; trunk repair, 191; umbrella repair, 192; wash tubs, 177
Tracy, Mary (Lee), 9–10(&fig. 12), 11(fig. 13)
Tracy, Nathaniel, 9–10, 11(fig. 13)
Trade card, 171(fig.)
Trade disputes, 17th-century London, 30, 57n5
Trades, distinction between, 30–31
Transshipments, of mahogany, 65–70
Trays: bread, 175; repairs to, 175; tea, 176–77; voider, 177; wooden, 175(fig. 21)
Trent, Robert F., 60n22, 228–32; armchair, 38(&fig.)
Trezevant, Peter, 162, 173
Trimmings. See Hardware
Trotter, Daniel: bookcase repair, 143; chest of drawers repair, 147; clothespress repair, 160; coffeepot repair, 180; desk repair, 133; looking glass repair, 168; parrot stand, 194; tea chest repair, 190
Troy, Jean-François de, 235
Truax, Harry Mack, II, 228
Trunks, repairs to, 188–91, 190–91
Tuck, Sewell, 133
Tucker, Elisha, looking glass, 167(fig.)
Tucker, Richard J., 193
Tucker, St. George, 133, 160, 189
Tucker, William, 72
Tufft, Thomas, 144
Tulip poplar, pier tables, 88(fig.), 91(fig. 3), 93(fig.), 94(fig.), 103(fig. 18), 118(fig.), 120(fig.), 121(fig.), 123(fig.)
Turners Company of London, 57n3, 58n7
Tuttle, Jesse, 176, 177
Tuttle, Jotham, 165

Twibill, George W., 95(fig.)
Tyler, Charles Hitchcock, 210
Tyson, Jonathan, flax wheel, 183(fig.)

Umbrellas, 192(fig.); repairs to, 192–93
United States, rococo in 18th century, 218
Upright churn, 176

van de Passe, Crispijn, 92(fig.)
van der Straat, Jan, 32(fig.)
Vannuck, P., 169
Varnish, 135; on bookcases, 143; on boxes, 189; on bureau, 155; on chest, 149; on chest of drawers, 148; on clock case, 166; on looking glasses, 169; on piano, 191; for secretary-and-bookcase form, 141; on sideboard, 162
Velner, Paul, 34(fig. 8)
Venable, Charles, 13, 14–16
Veneers, on pier tables, 115, 123. See also individual veneers
Venetian blinds: cherry, 172(fig.); repair of, 171–73
Vert antique, 123
Very, Jonathon, 5(fig. 5), 24n7
Violin repairs, 191–92
Virgilina (Virginia), shaved chair, 54(fig. 33)
Vitruvius, 227
Voider, 177
von Kulmbach, Hans, 34(fig. 9)
Vose, Isaac, 142

Wadsworth, Elijah, 165, 167
Wadsworth Atheneum, 213
Wait, Aaron, 164
Walker, Robert, 218
Waln, Robert, 113, 115, 128n27
Walnut: bread trough, 174(fig.); in exchange for furniture, 64; pier table, 99(fig. 13); pipe box, 189(fig.); sideboard table, 98(fig.)
Wanton, John, 134
Wanton, Joseph, 188
Ward, Barbara McLean, 232–37
Ward, Joshua, 169
Ward, Miles, 133, 157, 158
Ward, Samuel, 161
Wardrobe, 155; repair of, 159–60
Ware, Samuel Fithian, 184
Warming pan, 180(&fig.)
Warner, Oliver Ring, 72

Warren, Philip, 134, 193
Washing machine, 177
Washtubs, 177
Watch case: pine, 190(fig.); repair of, 190
Waters, Joseph G., 138
Watkins, James Y., 175(fig. 22)
Watson, Abraham, 15, 64; chest-on-chest, 64(fig.)
Wayland armchair, 44–45(&fig. 21)
Wealth, of pier table owners, 108(table 4)
Weatherly, Daniel, 145
Weaver, Thomas, 147
Webb, William, IV, 138
Webster, Grant, 190
Webster, John, 171–72
Webster, Peletiah, 8, 25n11
Webster, Robert, 184
Welsh Furniture, 1250–1950 (Bebb), 228–32
Wentworth, Mark Hunking, 8, 24n10
West, Thomas, 24n6
Whatnot, 125
Wheeler, Abigail, 174
Wheeler, Owen, 220
White, Charles H., 160, 218
White House, East Room pier tables, 117, 119–20(&fig. 29), 129n35, 129n36
White oak: rot and, 49; side chairs, 41(fig.), 42(figs.), 56(fig.)
White pine: bombé desk-and-bookcase, 19(fig.); chest of drawers, 6(fig.); chest-on-chests, 9(fig.), 64(fig.); clothespress, 159(fig.); desk, 14(fig. 19); desk-and-bookcase, 12(fig.); desk interior, 131(fig.); fireboard, 182(fig.); high chest of drawers, 148(fig.); looking glass, 167(fig.); pail, 177(fig.); pier tables, 88(fig.), 91(fig. 4), 103(fig. 18), 121(fig.); secretary-and-bookcase, 140(fig.); tall clock case, 165(fig.); tea chest, 191(fig.)
Whitewood. See Yellow poplar
Wig boxes, 188
Wilder, Josiah P., 135, 176, 184
Wilkins, William, 121
Williams, Mrs. Esther, 161
William Smee and Sons, 92(fig.)
Willington, Nehemiah, 58n7
Wilmington (Delaware), shaved chair, 53, 54(fig. 32)
Window blinds, repair of, 171–73

Window treatment designs, 104(fig.), 105(fig.), 125(fig.)
Windsors, 52, 60n20
Wine cistern, 173
Wine cooler, 173
Wing, Walter, 139
Winterthur Museum, 213, 218
Wiseley, Daniel, 165
Wistar, Charles, 169
Wolferspergen, John, 139
Women: low-seated shaved chairs and, 33; shaved side chairs and, 41
Wood: donations of, 75, 86n28; secondary, 17
Wood, Thomas, 3, 24n4
Wood choices: for bureaus, 153, 199n47; for desks, 132
Woodcutting camps, 79–84 (&figs.)
Woodenware containers, 177
Woodwork, carved, 227–28
Wool (great) wheel, 183; repairs to, 185
Wragg, William, 189
Wright, George, 102
Writing compartment, 18(fig. 28)
Writing desks, 137–38(&fig.)
Writing table, 138

"X" mark, 83

Yale University Art Gallery, 226
Yellow pine, pier table, 99(fig. 13)
Yellow poplar: bureau, 151(fig.); for bureaus, 153; clothespress, 159(fig.); corner cupboard, 157(fig. 12); cupboard, 156(fig.); dresser, 157(fig. 13); high chest of drawers, 148(fig.); tea chest, 191(fig.)

Zelner, Karla, 178